KU-611-531

PIMLICO

812

CUTTINGS

Christopher Lloyd, the youngest of six children, was born at Great Dixter. Educated at Rugby and Cambridge, he served in the army during the war before taking a BSc in horticulture at Wye College, where he also worked as a lecturer. In 1954, he returned to Great Dixter to set up a nursery specialising in unusual plants. He published numerous influential books including *The Mixed Border*, *Clematis*, *The Well-Tempered Garden*, *Foliage Plants* and *Meadows*, as well as *Succession Planting for Adventurous Gardeners*, a collaboration with his head gardener, Fergus Garrett.

Christopher Lloyd first learnt about gardening from his formidable mother, known at Great Dixter as 'The Management'. He constantly reshaped and replanted the garden, for, as he said, 'We don't want to be wishy-washy or to sit on the fence'.

He was awarded a honorary doctorate from the Open University and an OBE for his services to horticulture, but it was the Royal Horticultural Society's Victoria Medal of Honour (VMH) which gave him the greatest satisfaction.

Beth Chatto has won ten consecutive gold medals at the Chelsea Flower Show. In 1960, she began the Beth Chatto Gardens, which she created from rough farmland in Essex. She collaborated with Christopher Lloyd in publishing their letters in book form (*Dear Friend and Gardener*, 1998).

Stephen Anderton is – at the request of Christopher Lloyd himself – writing the official biography with the support of the Trustees of Great Dixter. Previously National Gardens Manager for English Heritage, Stephen Anderton is a freelance garden journalist, author and lecturer. He writes a weekly column for *The Times*.

By the same author

The Mixed Border
Clematis
The Well-Tempered Garden
Foliage Plants
Meadows
Gardener Cook
Exotic Planting for Adventurous Gardeners
Colour for Adventurous Gardeners
Succession Planting for Adventurous Gardeners
(with Fergus Garrett)
Dear Friend and Gardener (with Beth Chatto)
Garden Flowers from Seed (with Graham Rice)

CUTTINGS

A year in the garden with Christopher Lloyd

———

CHRISTOPHER LLOYD

Selected by
RUTH PETRIE

Preface by
BETH CHATTO

Introduction by
STEPHEN ANDERTON

Photographs by
JONATHAN BUCKLEY

Published in association with the *Guardian*

PIMLICO

Published by Pimlico 2008

2 4 6 8 10 9 7 5 3 1

Copyright this edition © Christopher Lloyd 2007
Introduction copyright © Beth Chatto 2007
Preface copyright © Stephen Anderton 2007
Photographs copyright © Jonathan Buckley 2007

Christopher Lloyd has asserted his right under the Copyright, Designs
and Patents Act 1988 to be identified as the author of this work

This book is sold subject to the condition that it shall not, by way of trade or
otherwise, be lent, resold, hired out, or otherwise circulated without the
publisher's prior consent in any form of binding or cover other than that
in which it is published and without a similar condition, including
this condition, being imposed on the subsequent purchaser.

First published in Great Britain in 2007 by Chatto & Windus

Pimlico
Random House, 20 Vauxhall Bridge Road,
London SW1V 2SA

In association with Guardian Books, an imprint of Guardian Newspapers Ltd

theguardian

www.rbooks.co.uk

Addresses for companies within The Random House Group Limited can be found at:
www.randomhouse.co.uk/offices.htm

The Random House Group Limited Reg. No. 954009

A CIP catalogue record for this book
is available from the British Library

ISBN 9781845951078

Royalties paid to the Trustees of Great Dixter

The Random House Group Limited supports The Forest Stewardship
Council (FSC), the leading international forest certification organisation. All our
titles that are printed on Greenpeace approved FSC certified paper carry the FSC logo.
Our paper procurement policy can be found at www.rbooks.co.uk/environment

Mixed Sources
Product group from well-managed
forests and other controlled sources
www.fsc.org Cert no. TT-COC-2139
© 1996 Forest Stewardship Council

Printed and bound in Great Britain by
Clays Ltd, St Ives plc

Contents

Contents

Contents

List of Illustrations

1. Christopher Lloyd with head gardener, Fergus Garrett, standing under Malus floribunda

2. Looking towards the house from the Lower Moat: Anemone nemorosa, Primula vulgaris and Ranuncula auricomus growing wild

3. Spring in the High Garden: Tulipa 'Queen of Sheba' and Tulipa 'Golden Memory'

4. Christopher Lloyd chopping herbs in the kitchen at Dixter

5. Euphorbia amygdaloides var. robbiae

6. Dahlia 'Wittemans Superba'

7. In the vegetable garden: Christopher Lloyd holding his dog, Canna, and leaning against the compost heap up which he has grown gourds

8. The Exotic Garden: Dahlia 'Moonfire', Canna 'Wyoming', Musa basjoo and Verbena bonariensis

9. Pears 'Doyenne du Comice'

10. The Long Border in autumn

11. Storm clouds brewing over the Peacock Garden. Iris are growing between the rows of the aster hedges

12. Frost in the Peacock Garden, with topiary and aster hedges (Aster lateriflorus 'Horizontalis')

All photographs © Jonathan Buckley

Preface

by Beth Chatto

One of my young students once commented how strange it was that Christopher Lloyd and I were such friends since we were so different. I replied that perhaps our friendship had lasted *because* of our differences: we were not standing in each other's light.

Perhaps the most obvious difference lay in our style of gardening. From a child Christo was influenced by growing up in a medieval manor house where the garden had been laid out by Sir Edwin Lutyens and Christopher's father, who had framed the view overlooking acres of East Sussex farmland with clipped yew hedges, archways and strange topiary birds. Christopher's unique contribution during his lifetime lay in constantly changing the characters that performed in this dramatic setting, with shrubs, bulbs and herbaceous plants, delighting or shocking visitors with outrageous colour schemes.

My garden began with several acres of wilderness situated at the back of my husband's fruit farm. Here in 1960 we built a modern, split-level house. In 1996, after forty years of fruit growing, my husband, Andrew, retired to spend the rest of his life studying the natural homes of garden plants, while I wanted to use his research in transforming problem areas into advantages. These problem places included sun-baked gravel, dry shade beneath several ancient oaks and a spring-fed hollow.

Before reading The Well-Tempered Garden I did not know Christopher Lloyd, not having contributed to the journals for which he wrote. But, immediately, I was captivated by his very personal style of writing, often nodding and saying to myself, yes, that's so, chuckling at his witty asides; then, next moment, I would be knocked off my perch by having some long-held traditional practice dismissed in a highly opinionated manner. Far from tossing the book aside, I read on into the night. However, there was a particular bone of contention: Christopher gave bergenias short shrift, while I cannot garden without them. These large, handsome clusters of smooth, simple leaves, suffused with shades of wine-red in winter, act for me as a focal point, a full stop at the end of a busy sentence. I wrote to the great man. He wrote back, 'Come to lunch.' I did.

Over the years, we discovered how much we enjoyed together. Dixter was a meeting place for people of all ages, young in heart and mind, an oasis from the outside world where friendships were made and retained. After he died, family and friends organised a wonderful party to celebrate Christo's eighty-fifth birthday. More than two hundred people were there to represent his zest for living and his need to share his loves with like-minded friends.

Until the last few years of his life, Christo could often be found in his kitchen, once he had taken an early-morning walk round the garden to find inspiration for an article, and then typed it in his deceptively conversational style on his laptop. Seasons were observed, as they would have been in his mother's day. I recall the familiar scent of bubbling marmalade, helping to fish the smooth stones out of damson jam, sieving blackberries, using up green tomatoes to make sweet chutney. Although a most generous host, Christo retained the wartime memory of waste-not, while his kitchen garden introduced urban friends to the luxury of fresh-picked artichokes, asparagus and unusual salads. I loved to slip into the kitchen, knowing where to find the old-fashioned utensils used by his mother, still in use. On either side of the long wooden table we each had our task. One day I was asked to make pastry for a flan case. I was presented with a sealed tin of white flour, the last one, Christo informed me, from the cellars where it had been stored during the last war. Startled to say the least, I decided this was not the moment to remonstrate since I was also presented with butter, ground almonds and egg yolks. There were enough nutrients there to make up for anything missing in the flour. No one came to any harm.

One wintry weekend we sat by the vast log fire in the parlour with the late Giles Gordon, a good friend and our literary agent. He suggested that Christo and I exchange letters concerning life and gardening. I was intrigued by a fresh approach to writing on subjects which sometimes became repetitive. So *Dear Friend and Gardener* began, bumpily to start with. One of Christopher's early letters berated me for making my new Gravel Garden without first putting in irrigation: I was in fact trying out an experiment to see what could survive our typical Essex droughts. Bah! I thought, throwing the letter down and storming off to the Wood Garden to cool down; but suddenly I laughed out there among my plants, provoked – as no doubt he had intended – to get going and make my reply.

Dear Christo, how we miss you. Your cherubic face, sharply quizzical glance beneath bushy eyebrows, your distinctive voice which still echoes through my head whenever I open any of your books. The flame from the log fires may have died down, but the sparks you ignited in us will spread far and wide, long down the ages.

Beth Chatto
November 2006

Introduction

by Stephen Anderton

If ever a gardener's journalism was worth publishing in permanent, book form it is Christopher Lloyd's. When he died in 2006 at the age of eighty-four he was Britain's best-known and most respected gardener. Armchair gardeners and television addicts today might know the names of gardeners whose profiles are currently high, but in fifty years, a hundred years, it will be Christopher Lloyd who will be remembered and to whose writings working gardeners will refer again and again. They will discover a man who took huge pleasure in satisfying a public hungry for knowledge, and who wrote with the voice of authority and genuine experience. This collection of his pieces for the *Guardian*, written between 1989 and 2006, demonstrates exactly what Christopher Lloyd did so well.

The British, more than any nation on earth, have had a continuing love affair with gardens and the business of gardening; no fling, this. For the British, it is not enough to put in a few bedding plants and sit under dusty street trees. They want to know about the small spring bulbs you can grow in grass, about big summer borders full of perennials, about flowering trees and shrubs, and wild ponds and lily ponds, woodland gardens and gravel gardens – everything. And Christopher Lloyd wrote about everything. Admittedly he wrote from the base of his own rather grand domestic garden at Great Dixter, but he wrote about the plants themselves in such particular detail that it did not matter where they were growing; it was how to keep them happy that counted, and *that* could be done in a garden as large or small as you liked. It was doing interesting things with interesting plants that mattered to him.

One of the things in which he was not interested was labour-saving gardening: in his opinion, it led to boring results. Rather, he enjoyed gardening with his foot to the floor, gardening which raced along through the seasons, producing all the colour and excitement it could. If this meant experimenting with plants so much the better, and he was able to pass on this sense of urgency and fun in his writing. So what, if a reader did not want to garden at the full Lloydian pace! Christo documented and explained his methods, and every individual gardener could (and still can) take from his writings whatever he wanted – a planting combination here, a way of pruning or propagation there.

Lloyd was no designer and he never professed to be, but Dixter was a bold canvas upon which he was thrilled and grateful to work. As a skilled plantsman, he could make the detail of a garden soar; and as a colourist, he was without equal. All the practical side of gardening was there in his writing, the *how* of gardening. He knew the difficulties of keeping a garden going, as plants with different life-spans flourished and declined, so he had plenty to say on pruning and keeping the peace between plants, whether they were rampant shrubs or cosy perennials. Propagation was one of his greatest satisfactions.

The late-twentieth-century passion for ecologically sustainable gardening did little to stir Christopher Lloyd, mostly because he had been doing something like it all his life. Certainly he used chemicals from time to time, but he had been practising what we would call wild gardening and meadow gardening since the 1920s and regarded them as just another part of gardening. He was always as interested in the life cycles of moths and butterflies and songbirds and the night sky as he was in the latest hormone rooting powder or new variety of Cosmos.

It was that eye for detail and for timing which made Lloyd stand so far above most other gardening writers. 'Spring' was never a precise enough time for him to recommend, say, taking cuttings of Achillea; he could tell his reader the exact month and why, just as he could explain how long it takes for a cyclamen's seed to ripen or at which time of day *Impatiens tinctoria* will release most perfume. All this from spending time looking in detail, hard and long, at his garden.

Patience was never Christopher Lloyd's strong point. To the general public visiting Dixter, this apparently wise and genial old man was sometimes a wasp in sheep's clothing (friends might call him a sheep in wasp's clothing). Yet he loved the notion of the amateur gardener, someone who enjoyed being down on his or her knees, observing and working closely with plants; and so, when it came to writing for a general audience of amateur gardeners (home gardeners, as the

Americans would say), he showed unusual patience. He would spend paragraphs explaining how to undertake a particular way of planting or pruning, never wasting words on the obvious points but always answering those less obvious questions which anyone undertaking the job would be bound to ask; the watch points, the FAQs. Lloyd had been a lecturer in horticulture at Wye College in Kent in the early post-war years and it pleased him a great deal, then, to find that he was good at something other than gardening – at teaching. It is a pleasure which comes through clearly in his writing, as does his other professed love, the English language.

Lloyd's journalism, like his books, was full of wit and charm. He had a way of combining a rather precise, sometimes archaic prose with romping colloquialism, a combination which makes for very lively reading. One minute he would be using words such as 'sere' or 'costive' and the next he would be calling himself a 'fig pig' and wondering if the damp English air gives *Viburnum carlesii* asthma. Gertrude Jekyll was a garden writer whom he hugely admired and there is a sense, on occasion, that he is taking a lead from her sober Edwardian style. At other moments, you can hear the lighter pace of Vita Sackville-West's writing. But the true Lloyd is never far away, getting down to the nitty-gritty of his subject in an easy, lean, conversational prose and spiking it up with his own brand of wit. Try finding humour in Gertrude and Vita!

Lloyd could be very funny in his writing, to the point sometimes of making you laugh out loud. A cruel humour, some would say, but if you look closely you see that the joke was most often upon himself, like someone playing the bluff Brigadier. It amused him, it was a game, to expound his pet hates or to be flabbergasted by people's naivety or laziness. And there was also a touch of surrealism in his humour which was put to good effect when extolling or decrying the character of a plant.

Above all, his writing was direct. It addressed the reader personally and individually, sometimes in encouragement, sometimes in warning and sometimes in amused conspiracy. It is as if he was there in your garden telling you what might work, what you should try or what a stupid mistake you made. One of the pleasures of reading Lloyd is that gradually you get to know and predict the man's attitudes to gardening and gardens, although curiously, for someone who seems to speak so directly and honestly, little is given away about the man himself.

It goes without saying that anything written by Christopher Lloyd was based around his garden at Great Dixter. Even when he was spurred on to write about things he had seen in other gardens and other countries, he always turned the spotlight of the experience back on his beloved Dixter. Dixter was something joyful to him but from which he could never break away. In a sense it worked in his readers' favour; Dixter is a well-visited garden – many of the pilgrims being the type of keen gardeners who were his readers – and, once Dixter had been seen, it was easy for a reader to picture the reality of Lloyd's thoughts.

Undoubtedly Lloyd loved the place, and why not. He was actually born there in 1921, the youngest of six children. His father, Nathaniel Lloyd, who was a successful printer in London, had bought Dixter in 1910 and employed the fashionable architect Edwin Lutyens to renovate and extend it. Lutyens also laid out most of the garden, but it was Nathaniel Lloyd himself who designed the Sunk Garden with its octagonal pool where Christopher worked in his seventies, laptop on knee. Nathaniel also planted the yew hedges and set down his experiences and wisdom in *Garden Craftsmanship in Yew and Box*.

Even as an infant, Lloyd was learning gardening with his mother, also a passionate gardener, and he was introduced to Gertrude Jekyll herself who 'blessed him and hoped he would grow up to be a very great gardener'. Well she might have done, for even at the age of nine Lloyd was instructing his mother in letters from prep school on how to plant the garden, and reeling off the Latin names.

After school at Rugby he read Modern Languages at King's College, Cambridge, but before he could graduate he was called up into the army. He was not a good soldier but confessed to 'doing as he was told'; for him there had always been much more appeal in gardening, botany, embroidery (which his mother had earnestly taught all her children) or playing the piano or the oboe. Some describe him as wholly incompetent as a soldier (he was not the square-bashing type and was famous among his friends for getting on the wrong side of his sergeant major by collecting wild flowers in a fire bucket). However, he certainly did not hate his army years, and at least they got him to India and the Middle East where he could see new plants.

After the war he took a BSc in decorative horticulture at London University's Wye College, graduating in 1949 and staying on as an assistant lecturer until 1954 when he fell out with the management (it was 'incompetent'); as ever Lloyd was right and others were wrong. Fed up and cross, he moved home to Great Dixter and set up his nursery specialising in clematis and unusual plants. From the early 1950s he and his mother began to open the house to the public, and so it continued until Lloyd's death. The dark Jacobean furniture and Lloyd's pale new designer pieces polished like glass, the distressed soft furnishings and smell of dogs and wood smoke, sent out clear signs of a thoroughly lived-in house. Visitors from Britain and abroad looked adoringly upon the great man's desk and pondered upon his life and thoughts, as if the house were Chartwell and Lloyd the Churchill of gardening.

His books began to flow in the 1950s, *The Mixed Border* in 1957 followed by *Clematis* in 1965 and *The Well-Tempered Garden* in 1970. Many of his first books have remained in print over several decades and are still read worldwide.

Lloyd was an admirer of everything hard-working, and this ethic allowed him to admire new trends in gardening as well as the old. He launched a trend himself with his book *Foliage Plants* (1973) and in the 1990s, when he was in his late seventies, he was leading fashion by the nose towards the use of dramatic or subtropical plants in his exotic garden at Dixter (his book on the subject, *Exotic Planting for Adventurous Gardeners*, was part-finished at his death and has been completed by his head gardener, Fergus Garrett, and others). Lloyd and his mother had been experimenting with flowering meadows and American 'prairie gardening' long before the current fashion for planting massed perennials and grasses in the German/Dutch manner; his book *Meadows*, of 2004, is so far the best on the subject. Even in the 1970s ornamental grasses had already been very much part of his planting vocabulary.

He refused to revise his books for reprinting, because he wanted always to write about new preoccupations and not look back, although he would occasionally revise a book by working on it with someone else who shared his interest. But he loathed being typecast by the commissioning editors of papers and magazines, who regularly asked him to theorise on subjects such as colour association or foliage which he had long since covered to his own satisfaction. Even so, *Colour for Adventurous Gardeners* appeared in 2001 as a summary of his thoughts on a subject which, he admitted, would never close.

In his later years he began to write books in collaboration with other people: *Garden Flowers from Seed* with Graham Rice (1991), *Dear Friend and Gardener*, a charming exchange of letters with Beth Chatto (1998). *Succession Planting for Adventurous Gardeners* (2005) explored the way he and Fergus Garrett produced the year-round flow of colour at Dixter, by setting one layer of planting upon another to flower in sequence or by replacing a bedding scheme mid-season. The theme was not new to him – it was central to his way of gardening and he had been doing it for years at Dixter – but with Garrett he was able to practise it with superb results, and it appeared in his journalism with constant enthusiasm.

Cooking was a passion for Lloyd and after his mother's death he filled Great Dixter with weekend guests for much of the year, cooking expertly for great numbers. It was not at all unusual for him to meet a couple of visitors in the garden, take to them, and invite them in to lunch, even if he already had half a dozen people staying for the weekend. His book *Gardener Cook* was published in 1998.

Books were only part of Lloyd's great output as a writer; for much of his career he had at least a couple of gardening columns running in newspapers and magazines, sometimes abroad. His famous weekly column for *Country Life*, 'In My Garden', began in 1963 and was the magazine's first gardening column. At his interview for the job the editor, John Adams, showed him a worthy article on machinery and mowing and asked Lloyd if he could turn out a piece like that. 'No. I'm afraid I couldn't,' replied Lloyd firmly. He got the job and wrote weekly about his garden until 2005, even writing from his hospital bed in 1998 after a triple bypass operation.

In 1979 he was given the Royal Horticultural Society's highest award, the Victoria Medal of Honour, making him very much part of the gardening establishment. It was testament indeed to Lloyd's standing in the gardening world in Britain and abroad, because for forty years he had mercilessly criticised the Society for its unimaginative, institutional gardening. Of the Society as a whole, however, he was a great admirer, and pleased to sit on its floral and trials committees.

His taste in garden styles, as in most things, was remarkably catholic. What he truly abhorred was lazy or unadventurous gardening. His mother Daisy, who lived with him at Great Dixter until her death in 1972, was a formidable woman and known among his friends as 'The Management'. She drummed into her children the rule that they should never, ever be idle, and Lloyd heeded it. He rose with the dawn, after sleeping with windows and curtains wide open, then worked, wrote, cooked and socialised until bedtime. He could easily write a first article before breakfast. He refused ever to have a television – 'I never watch television, unless I am on it!' – but was a passionate follower of opera and a familiar face at Glyndebourne where for a time he advised on the garden.

Throughout his life Lloyd had surrounded himself with young people and young ideas, and he was always extraordinarily generous to students and young people wanting to learn. Friends and contemporaries who complained that their old friends were dying off got short shrift from him: 'Find yourself young ones, I tell them.' He loved Americans for their fresh, uninhibited attitudes. At the age of sixty-eight he found huge pleasure and inspiration in a world tour, accompanied by his friend, the gardener and nursery woman Beth Chatto, lecturing at conferences in Canada and Australia. He was awarded an honorary doctorate from the Open University in 1996 and the OBE in 2000.

With so much time committed to writing, Lloyd had constant need of a head gardener with whom he could develop the Dixter garden. His way of working was to discuss the garden at length, walking it from end to end, looking critically at what was happening, and chewing the fat about how to improve things (this vigorous, unforgiving approach could be unnerving when practised for the first time on other people's gardens). Sometimes Lloyd found himself a head gardener who was game for this sport, and the Dixter garden would go through a period of great success. At other times, it could look weedy, and people said so, especially in comparison with the ever-immaculate Sissinghurst, just a few miles away, once the home of Vita Sackville-West and today run with formidable polish by the National Trust.

Lloyd finally found his ideal head gardener in a young half-Turkish gardener, Fergus Garrett, a horticulture graduate from Wye College, whose positive manner and openness to new ideas matched Lloyd's own. With Garrett, he could genuinely collaborate on the garden, sharing its planning in great detail and even sharing travel to see other gardens at home or abroad for inspiration. It was an ideal partnership and Dixter has never been more admired than under their joint care during the last ten years of Lloyd's life. In those years, so many of the ideas and preoccupations which had for decades appeared in Lloyd's writing came brilliantly to life – the big borders, the meadows, the bedding-out, the succession planting.

Dixter became known as the most imaginative flower garden in Britain. To his amusement Lloyd was sought out by television producers, and wheeled on as the flambuoyant voice of authority; in his loud shirts and polychrome cardigans, he loved to play the naughty *deus ex machina*, both genial and critical. Provocation to him was a game, even when the subject upon which he was being provocative was important to him.

He knew perfectly well that people found him outspoken, but he would rather be regarded as rude than uninteresting. It was another of his games, to see how far he could go. People who stood up for themselves, intellectually, he liked; people who caved in, or took umbrage, he ignored. On occasion his bluntness got the better of him. On a lecture tour of America he was billeted with a woman who ran one of the horticultural societies he was to address and who was anxious to touch the hem of her gardening guru. Lloyd found the husband dull and a bore, and wrote words to that effect in his diary. While Lloyd was out visiting gardens in the morning, his hostess took the opportunity to sneak a look at his diary and, when he came back, his cases were on the doorstep. Similarly, at Dixter generations of his faithful dachshunds – Canna, Dahlia, Yucca, Tulipa and the rest – always roamed the garden and even if Lloyd caught one of 'his babies' with a visiting infant halfway down its throat, he would always protest that the child was at fault; this led to some tense moments.

Lloyd was never so happy as when he was planning the practical details of next season's planting or tomorrow's lunch. Until his last few years he refused to dwell on what should happen to the garden after his death (like the rest of his family, he despised sentimentality), this despite knowing that Dixter was a place of pilgrimage for gardeners from all over the world. He clung to the view that he had done his best by it, and that his energies should always go into developing Great Dixter *for the present* and doing what he himself was good at – gardening. The last thing he wanted was to see it 'fall into the hands' of the National Trust or English Heritage, whose institutional management he regarded as fossilising. Nevertheless, shortly before his death, conscience or peer pressure wore him down, and the Great Dixter Charitable Trust was set up. He found comfort in the idea that his beloved Dixter – the *Lloyds'* beloved Dixter – would stay together and remain a canvas upon which other gardeners could paint. On 27 January 2006, he died a gardener's death – as a result of complications from an operation on his knees. There was to be no funeral, no sentiment, no time wasted. But there *was* a big party in the Great Hall at Dixter. And if a memorial is needed, it's there, polished and crisp as marble, in his writing.

Stephen Anderton
December 2006

GREAT DIXTER
October 1999

The Garden at Great Dixter

My mother was a tremendous reader of the classics, and reading aloud was an experience I was brought up with: first she to me, later I to her. When away at boarding school, it was insisted that each of us wrote home weekly; and she did quite as much or more by us. I was also lucky, between the ages of 10 and 13, to have an excellent English teacher, Morgan Shelby, who gave me a thorough grounding in grammar (sadly lacking in most teaching) and in the writing of essays. Reading and writing became second nature.

I am one of those once common, now rare, people who still, near the end of a long life (78 years, to date),* lives in the house where he was born. My parents bought Dixter (as it was then called, and as I always think of it) in 1910 – they later added the 'Great' to distinguish it more certainly from neighbouring Little Dixter, which they also bought. My father then engaged Edwin Lutyens to make the restorations and additions, and to design the garden.

Dixter, a manor house, is a large, timber-framed building, built around 1460 and situated in the high weald. The weald of Kent and Sussex lies between the chalk of the North and South Downs, in south-east England, and the high weald is the centre part of this area. Luckily for us, Dixter was sited on a south-west-facing slope, 55m above sea level (the sea being some 10 miles distant), and although not very high, it is near the top of its hill and commands all-round views (once you have stepped outside the garden) in every direction except east. The land slopes down to the Rother valley; the River Rother, which here forms the boundary between Sussex and Kent (we being in Sussex), was tidal as I first remember it. The valley, as is the way of valleys, attracts frost and fog. It is marvellous to be perched above all that. On the other hand, we are, or were, exposed to wind from most directions. Wind is a great enemy to gardening, and we have blithely planted out our views with trees and hedges so that wind damage has been considerably mitigated.

*Christopher Lloyd wrote this piece in 1999.

The whole of the weald (German: *Wald*, a wood, has the same stem) was once covered by oak forest (it is still well wooded and, in spring, the woods are crammed with primroses, anemones and bluebells). There is little suitable building stone just where we are, so nearly all the houses were built of oak, infilled with lath and plaster. Those of any size belonging to our period were hall houses. Our great hall is a large room made for communal living, open from floor to roof and from outside wall to outside wall. The large oak beam tying these walls is 10m long. But when, in Tudor times, fashion changed to smaller rooms and greater privacy, our hall, with all others like it, was filled in with extra floors and numerous partitions. Other rooms in the house were similarly treated.

Lutyens restored the building to the status quo ante as far as was reasonable for a more modern style of living, and without resorting to too much guesswork where the evidence was no longer extant. This lost the building much floor space, so two principal additions were made. Another, smaller, hall house (dated circa 1500) was to be destroyed by its owner at Benenden, nine miles distant. My father bought it for £75; its beams were all numbered, it was taken down, moved to Dixter and re-erected. The other new, built-on wing was entirely of Lutyens's design, but working in the vernacular so as to marry discreetly with the original.

There was virtually no garden at Dixter in 1910. The property had in any case been on the agent's books for 10 years – as an agricultural property with farmhouse attached – and was occupied only by a summer tenant. There were two mixed orchards – the trees planted along ridges show that the land had been ploughed in medieval times – and a few odd trees besides. A bay laurel, a wild pear and a fig survive. But there were farm buildings – a barn (possibly as old as Dixter itself) and oast house alongside (dating from around 1890), a thatched (now shingled) stable unit, and cow houses, locally known as hovels.

Lutyens designed the garden walls and how the hedges should run. My father had a great interest in topiary and oversaw the planting, training and care of the yew and box hedges, and of the many topiary pieces. He wrote and illustrated a book, *Garden Craftsmanship in Yew and Box*, based on his experiences, mainly at Dixter. This has lately been republished, with additional photographs. The book was first published in 1923, but remains a useful guide. In later editions of *The English Flower Garden*, William Robinson, who loathed topiary, made a snide reference to its use in Northiam (our village), for it was also notable at Brickwall, a house at the other end of the village.

My father was originally a colour printer, and founded his business, Nathaniel Lloyd & Co., in Blackfriars, central London. He gave this up on coming to live at Dixter (he was 44 in 1910) and trained himself to be an architect (in a small way) and, more importantly, an architectural historian, and also a photographer of buildings. Two of his major works are still in print. Apart from the topiary, my father's main contribution to the gardens was the Sunk Garden, made in 1923. It has an octagonal pool surrounded by flagstone paving; then dry walling up to grass slopes (beasts to mow), and so to the garden's main level – the framework being barns on two sides, a Lutyens wall on the third and a yew hedge on the fourth.

With his architect's eye for strong design, my father originally planted the four corners of the quadrangular Barn Garden with *Yucca gloriosa*. The corner bed surrounding each yucca was planted with bearded irises. The theme was of spear and sword leaves. My mother, who was my great gardening influence and inspiration, was a plants-woman. She did not love the yuccas because of the danger to her children (six of us) and to everyone else from those sharp points. After my father died in 1933, the yuccas went. She replaced them with four *Malus sargentii*, having fallen for them at a Chelsea Flower Show. This is seldom a sound basis for an important choice. The shrubs grew large; they had no particular shape, their fruits were minute, and so they gave only a week of pleasure in the year and made no kind of unifying impact in their important positions.

She didn't like me for replacing them, in 1950, with *Osmanthus delavayi* (from Marchant's, in Dorset), but she did come to like the replacements very much. Apart from their April flowering, they are comely evergreen shrubs (clipped annually) with neat little leaves, but I have to admit that, year-round, *Yucca gloriosa*, properly looked after with its dead leaves pulled off, would look better. I would not reinstate the irises; the bearded kinds look sordid for too much of the year, and there is no way to disguise them, as their rhizomes require a summer baking. My mother doted on irises and used to accept gifts of bearded varieties which, when in bloom, swept her off her feet. This made me cross, and I made her grow them in spare corners where they did not interfere with the garden proper. (Your own children can become

5

dictators, when power comes their way.) When you have two strong-willed people working in the same garden (my mother died in 1972, and was active until the last 10 days of her 91 years) there are sure to be many clashes, and there were. But, as we loved each other, our shared pleasures in the garden were by far the strongest element in this partnership.

Gertrude Jekyll had no involvement in the planting of the garden at Dixter, though my parents visited her at Munstead Wood on at least two occasions, and I – as a small boy, very much impressed – was there on one of them. Miss Jekyll blessed me and hoped I would grow up to be a great gardener. The original planting of our borders was in fact planned by Sir George Thorold, a member of the old Lincolnshire family. Clearly, he was under the Jekyll influence – witness large corner-blocks of *Bergenia* (at that time *Megasea*) *cordifolia*. However, my mother's gardening bible was *The English Flower Garden*, and never mind what Robinson thought about topiary. Our battered, back-broken edition, with 'N. Lloyd' inscribed on the first page in my father's hand, was published in 1906, and it is larded with bookmarks.

Mother's taste for wild gardening in rough grass was probably derived from Robinson, and also the manner of planting he recommended. Our orchard, adjoining the Long Border, was planted with such daffodils and narcissi as were fashionable at that time. Robinson wrote proudly of his own plantings that they throve, and that 'the flowers are large and handsome, and in most cases have not diminished in size'. By modern standards, the flowers were of modest proportions, and so they are at Dixter in the orchard. What is so pleasing here is that perhaps only one-third of the area is planted up with daffodils. The rest is left as fine turf, wherein earlier-flowering snowdrops and crocuses also find a place. There is no feeling of overcrowding or showing off.

The area around the Horse Pond, including the pond itself, was originally iron-ore workings. The excavations terminated at a steep bank, on which my brother Oliver planted birch and aspen saplings collected from one of our woods in the 30s. Between this and the approach drive, called the forstal, are a few 60-year-old oaks which were seedlings self-sown at a time when, following my father's death, this area was neglected and filled with brambles, broom and rabbits. We cleaned it up and I have planted rhododendrons (they are none too happy), as well as smaller things that enjoy some shade.

The Horse Pond is so called because the farm horses used to be led into it to drink and wallow at the end of their working day. It is a water garden now, and the grassy banks overlooking it are a particularly pleasant place of relaxation where I and my less formal friends (the majority) like to bring our coffee after lunch. There are a few relic heathers, *Calluna vulgaris*, here, improbably reaching out over the pond. My father planted two large patches of them and of gorse, which he called whins from habit. His mother was a Scot and he was brought up in Scotland.

My own interest in gardening goes back as far as I can remember, and it was encouraged by both my parents. In 1947, after demobilisation, I studied horticulture at Wye College, in Kent. I spent the next four years teaching there. Wye is only 25 miles from Dixter, so I was able to spend one or two days a week in my garden, while leaving my mother a list of instructions for the days I was away. In the meantime, my brother Quentin looked after the estate. He died in 1995, and I now have a business manager. In 1954, I returned home for good and started a nursery devoted to the kinds of plants, many of them unusual, that I like to grow.

An all-important improvement in the fortunes of Dixter came about when Fergus Garrett became head gardener. Before he arrived, many areas in our labour-intensive garden were semi-neglected. I could see what needed doing to them and did what I could myself, but there was insufficient dynamism – or staff – to do the job thoroughly. I first met Fergus in 1988 when, aged 22, he was one of a party of visiting students from Wye College. We soon became firm friends. I rather belatedly had the bright idea of asking him to be my head gardener. He started in 1993. As staunch a member of my staff as Fergus is Perry Rodriguez, who started at Dixter a couple of months before Fergus. If anything goes wrong, indoors or out, Perry is the man to turn to. The growing of vegetables was assigned to him. There are three other permanent members of staff, and we have quite a few extras, from time to time – volunteers, mainly. We are a remarkably happy team.

I am not tempted to make any changes to the garden's overall design; the original bones were so sound and satisfying. If I have done what I can for Dixter in my lifetime, that is enough for me. I only want to concern myself about the future; to the extent of making it easier for my niece, Olivia, who will inherit, to take over. Since she lives abroad, it seems unlikely that she will want, or be able, to live at Dixter. She must make provisions for it as she sees fit.

What the public appreciate about Dixter most, perhaps, is that it is a home, not an institution. I am asked if I don't rattle about on my own, here. Not in the least. I fill the house perfectly, changing the rooms I occupy according to the season. And I am visited by plenty of friends and relations, for whom I enjoy cooking.

Christopher Lloyd
16 October 1999

JANUARY

New Year's Resolutions

With a fresh year in front of us, what should we plan to do that we haven't done in the past? A sensible notebook is essential. I keep two of them going concurrently. One is for ongoing notes with names of plants seen or acquired, injunctions to remind me of what wants doing and for notes on relevant things seen in other gardens. This I carry with me, so it must be a sensible size to fit into a pocket or handbag, but not so small as to be niggling, with minimal room on a page. The notebook's cover must be weatherproof.

The other notebook is for when I'm away from home for two or more days. It spends most of its time at my bedside and is a diary of events which I write up in bed, early the following morning, while all is still fresh in my mind. In future years, it is an invaluable source of reference – people's names and addresses, when I was with them, and much else. It is a true diary but I keep it only when I'm away.

Next resolution: use your eyes, both in other people's gardens and in your own. Make yourself more observant. You miss so much that you shouldn't. So much around you is interesting and deserves a mental image. Note it down there and then, and make a good description that will mean something to you when you next look it up. If you can, reread your entry the next day. That helps to fix the image.

Use a camera by all means, but don't lean on it too heavily. Time and again I see visitors to my own garden photographing everything madly, but they may go away without having absorbed any feeling for the garden. They may not even remember where their photos were taken, until they look up a reference. I have noticed people in a frenzy but only half alive, and often trying to fit in far too many garden visits in one day or on one holiday. Quite understandable, of course.

When you visit a garden for the first time, start by giving yourself an impression of it overall, leaving the detail till later. What is its structure and does that serve its purpose? Then look at the plants. How well does the garden enhance them? Or is it just a one and one and one garden – the plants grown well, perhaps, but with no reference to the general setting?

Every garden reflects the individuality of its owner. Gardens are a great giveaway; that in itself makes them fascinating. The more you observe and take in, one way or another, the more intensely you are living and the younger you will keep in mind, if not in body. Have a good year.

The Winter Garden

The garden seemed to be aware of the New Year, with many flowers coming on in a rush. Half a dozen different kinds of *Crocus chrysanthus* put in an appearance in the sodden meadow turf. Of snowdrops, the tall *Galanthus antarctica* 'Atkinsii' is always precocious. It is marvellously prolific and, although it doesn't set seed, it clumps up generously, so you can spread it around as soon as flowering is done (the best time).

I have planted that among clumps of *Helleborus orientalis* subsp. *abchasicus* Early Purple Group, which is always out by Christmas and has a long season. The snowdrop helps to highlight its rather dark colouring. *H. foetidus*, our native stinking hellebore, is never slow to follow. Its pale green inflorescence is set off by a frame of its handsome, dark green, fingered foliage. That is evergreen and semi-shrubby, but I find that young plants are the best-looking and have no qualms about getting rid of three-year-olds, as there are always plenty of self-sown replacements. They tuck themselves into the bottom of deciduous shrubs, where you might not think of planting anything.

Rhododendron dauricum 'Midwinter' is spangled over with rich, purple blossom at the tips of leafless twigs. That is ideal for bringing into the house as, of course, is Chinese witch hazel, *Hamamelis mollis*, which grows with and above it. I brought pieces of that indoors ten days before Christmas, and they were flowering comfortably by Christmas Day and in full blossom in the garden by New Year. Such a good scent. So, too, has *Lonicera* x *purpusii*. That makes a large, unruly, deciduous shrub, and I prune old branches regularly. It had a scattering of blossom in the old year, then a mighty tide of it in the new.

Sarcococca were early and equally heavy-scented on the air. I have several of these. *S. ruscifolia* (1.5m) makes the best shrub, possibly because I have given it shade. Its dark red berries from last year's blossom are quite an asset. *S. confusa* (1m) is the most prolific in flower and fruit, the latter black. Old branches need to be sorted out. Being in a rather sunny position, some of its foliage is on the yellow side, but all sarcococcas are excellent in limey soil. Flowers are small and white – hardly a display, but nice to see, and their scent is overpowering, and often too much for those of a weak and nervous constitution.

Wintersweet, *Chimonanthus praecox* (3m), has a spicy aroma. It is worth seeking the less dingy var. *luteus*: it is a decent shade of yellow. Provide as hot a site as you can, but don't try it north of the Trent.

The lesser periwinkle, *Vinca minor*, flowers at the ends of last year's foliage strands in a rather desultory manner until spring, when it comes through in earnest on short shoots from ground level. There are a number of colour variants and a few doubles. I am also fond of *V. difformis*, which starts flowering abundantly in September, becomes rather wan and hesitant in winter, and then has another huge surge of blossom in May. It is pale mauve at its best, but almost white when feeling the cold.

The behaviour of *Coronilla valentina* (30cm) depends on the condition of your shrub and the mildness of the winter. If, respectively, they are soft and cold, it will probably get frosted and set back rather than killed. But if its old wood is firm and there are long, frost-free spells, it can flower abundantly at any time between autumn and spring, with circlets of bright yellow, pea flowers, richly scented in mild weather (a rather heavy, foody sort of smell).

Daphne odora is showing no colour at all as yet, but it won't be long. *Clematis cirrhosa* var. *balearica* is coming into full flower, and will continue until April. Its pale green bells (speckled inside) are highlighted by dark green foliage. Its leafing habits are peculiar: although officially evergreen, it loses all its old foliage in autumn and then immediately puts out a new crop. Some strains of *C. cirrhosa* flower in autumn and early winter. The popular 'Freckles' is at it for six months, with extra-large flowers and its chocolate spotting extra-heavy. But its foliage is coarse, whereas in var. *balearica* it is a great asset.

I have never made a success of winter aconites, *Eranthis hyemalis*, though I am still trying. Why can't I have a huge, yellow carpet of them like some of my friends do, with no apparent effort? The brilliant magenta *Cyclamen coum* is another failure – it is a small thing, and I fear that it gets swamped in my garden. That should be flowering now.

The pomponette, quilled daisies, *Bellis perennis*, which we have grown as an under-storey for tulips, are already in flower. As are the pansies, which I wish would stop reminding me that I have a large slug population. Slugs eat the primroses, too, but less aggressively. Those are great self-sowers, and will flower in every mild spell. They seem to suit the season better than pansies, which look as though their alarm clocks have gone off prematurely.

Conifers

From where I sit at breakfast, I have a good view of *Abies spectabilis* var. *brevifolia*, a stately conifer that I planted perhaps 50 years ago. Its branches are weighed down with snow, but it is well constructed to take the load with equanimity. It shows up well, now that the oaks behind it are naked.

I love coniferous trees. Even if your garden hasn't room for one, keep your eyes open for those in other people's gardens. The cones of abies, the silver firs, stand upright on their branches, in contrast to the spruces, on which they are pendulous. The best-known species of *Abies* is *koreana*, which has many variants, the most convenient of which, for the small garden, grows 1.8m high. I don't want everything to be on a miniature scale, myself, and I am proud of my tall plant – tall by some standards, anyway, though in the east Himalayas, it can grow to 46m.

My *Abies koreana* cones regularly, but near the top of the tree, so you get a crick in your neck trying to get a view of them. When I first saw this species, it was in my friend Alan Roger's garden at Dundonnell, in Wester Ross. His cook asked if we had seen the tree 'with the navy cones' – navy blue, that is. They certainly are a remarkable colour, quite intense.

Of course, I wanted one like it and ordered a plant. Its cones turned out to be quite an ordinary colour, but, with familiarity, I have come to like it.

The thuggish habits of the Leyland cypress – of which the earliest specimens grew at Bedgebury National Pinetum, near Tunbridge Wells – have undeservedly earned coniferous trees a bad name. Bedgebury has a wonderful range. There are so many good ones that take you by surprise. Even the familiar monkey puzzle has its charms. Some make me drool at the mouth, but are infuriatingly difficult to find.

There was one, at Bedgebury, whose grace I particularly noted in August 1965, until a storm blew it down. It was *Picea omorika* 'Pendula', a variant of the Serbian spruce. The branches were indeed pendulous, and they had a twist on them which revealed the silvery channels on their undersides.

Once you see the charms of conifers – the trees, that is – you'll be hooked. Never mind those stupid Leylands: there are so many better things and you should grab at them. My love of them dates back to the 1950s, as a student. Their fascination can never lose its hold of you.

Planning for Late Summer

Every gardener's New Year starts with a euphoric gush of hope. This year will be different, we assure ourselves. Maybe it will, but it would be no bad thing to have a definite plan in mind. The one I would suggest is that your garden should not go to pieces after the end of July.

Holidays may in part be to blame for this common condition, but it is far more a question of the owner unnecessarily giving up. If you can keep your garden looking exciting right to the end of October, you will be able to enjoy it during some of the most relaxing weather of the year. How often does one not shudder in the April garden and long to get back to the warmth of indoors? That is not so at the other end of the season. But if wreckage is all that you see around you, the urge to cut everything down, or back, will be irresistible – and so unnecessary.

Structural plants are most important to think about; later, you can infill with colourful annuals, bedding plants, dahlias and the like. My yuccas, which look like vegetable explosions, were much enlivened this year by a couple of plants of *Petunia* 'Purple Wave', when some strands managed to climb into their crowns.

At the back of my main bedding-out area, a couple of important shrubs hold things together: the light, airy, green-and-white-variegated dogwood, *Cornus alba* 'Elegantissima' (admirable in winter for its carmine stems), and an evergreen, shrubby umbellifer, *Bupleurum fruticosum*, which carries domes of pale green flowers for several months. White Japanese anemones weave among these, and they all make a pleasing background for whichever annuals I choose to grow in front – sometimes the rich red *Amaranthus* 'Red Fox' and the small but persistently flowering *Zinnia* 'Chippendale'.

Cornus controversa 'Variegata' and *C. alternifolia* 'Argentea' are other green-and-white-variegated dogwoods, but with a permanent structure in horizontal layers. They go well with colourful hydrangeas and with the tall, glaucous-leaved giant reed, *Arundo donax*. But a hydrangea that you grow much more for the scalloped outline of its bold oak leaves is *Hydrangea quercifolia*. I prune that back quite hard each spring, so as to obtain the largest leaves, and these colour bronze in autumn, lasting for many weeks in this condition.

The cardoon, *Cynara cardunculus*, contributes in different ways for most of the year. Its large, jagged leaves are the main attraction up to midsummer. Then the flower heads take over, bursting into large blue thistle-heads in August. I like to see them then, behind the summer-flowering tamarisk, *Tamarix ramosissima*, which makes a haze of pink blossom in August. You can control its size by a hard cut-back each winter and it lends itself to having a permanent planting of tulips beneath it. When the cardoon heads ripen, they retain their interesting shapes and I do not cut them down till spring.

You don't want to think about plants in categories that are to be kept apart; they all help one another. There is an excellent flowering grass, *Stipa calamagrostis*, which is green and fluffy in July but gradually dries to pale fawn and retains its shape right through to now. It is about a metre tall, and keeps itself upright best in an open situation. I like it with the pink-and-grey-green-variegated *Fuchsia magellanica* 'Versicolor', which keeps to the same height as the grass if cut to the ground each winter. Punch is given to this scene by the purple-leaved form of annual orach, *Atriplex hortensis*, which self-sows abundantly. You merely need to weed out most of the seedlings each spring.

Hardy fuchsias are a great standby in autumn. Being tolerant of shade, they go well with ferns: for instance, partner the purple and red 'Tom

Thumb' with the bright green young fronds of the cut-leaved polypody, *Polypodium* 'Cornubiense'.

The horizontal umbels of *Sedum* 'Herbstfreude' give a feeling of strength right from midsummer, when they are rather like the green heads of calabrese; through their flowering time, when they gradually deepen from dusky pink to deep red, and on to winter, when they are brown but retain their shape. They look nice in September and October, with the deep blue plumbago flowers of *Ceratostigma willmottianum*, which is technically a shrub, though it often gets cut to the ground in winter, never attaining a height of much more than a metre.

Some of the salvias are at their best in autumn, notably the sky-blue, 2m-high *Salvia uliginosa*, which contrasts so well with the firmer outlines of pink or yellow dahlias of medium size. Another excellent salvia for the late-summer and autumn garden is the 1.5m – sometimes taller and always very upright – *S. guaranitica* 'Blue Enigma', which is a true, deep blue. That looks well with yellow sunflowers, such as the perennial, 1.5m-high *Helianthus* 'Capenoch Star', which has enlarged central florets in its disc (what is known as anemone-centred).

Deep blue monkshoods, cultivars of *Aconitum carmichaelii*, are strong features in the autumn garden, notably 'Kelmscott' and 'Barker's Variety'. I mean to grow these with *Senecio tanguticus* (now tiresomely renamed *Sinacalia tangutica*), which reaches up to 2m in damp soil and is quite a coloniser. Its pyramidal heads of spidery yellow flowers change in October to fluffy grey as they ripen, and are excellent for cutting and arranging with chrysanthemums and autumn berries – if you catch them just before the fluff disintegrates and makes a somewhat unpopular mess indoors.

Winter Scent

Winter honeysuckles are quite unlike those that flower in summer, the only similarity being their powerful fragrance. Currently holding the stage in my garden is *Lonicera* x *purpusii*, a hybrid and an improvement on two similar species, *L. fragrantissima* and *L. standishii*. 'Winter Beauty' is considered the best cultivar, and is the one given an Award of Garden Merit by the Royal Horticultural Society. *L. x purpusii* makes a large, bushy shrub, 2m high and more across. It is deciduous, which is just as well, because its oval leaves have nothing to recommend them. As the shrub is rather ugly I conceal it, but then suddenly, in January or February, there comes a great gust of its airborne fragrance. The white, or off-white, flowers occur the length of each young shoot, generally in pairs. You can pick them for the house, but they quickly drop. It is, in any case, a scent better enjoyed at a distance. If you want to prune it, wait until it has flowered.

Wintersweet, *Chimonanthus praecox*, with its spicy scent, bears similarities. The bulky shrub, with coarse, deciduous leaves, comes into its own only after these are shed in early December and a host of knob-like flower buds is revealed. You can pick a spray to bring indoors, but keep it cool, otherwise the scent quickly dissipates. I have grown it from seed, but six or more years will pass before the first bloom is vouchsafed. Seedlings are variable. Our original plant set a few seed pods, which ripened in August and germinated quickly. We were lucky as the resultant seedling turned out to be better than its parent. However, it is safest to buy a vegetatively propagated plant of known credentials that will start flowering forthwith.

The flowers of wintersweet are naturally in two shades: dusky yellow on the outer petals, maroon on the inner ring. *C. praecox* var. *luteus*, however, is clear yellow all through. It's a bit later flowering than the type-plant, and won't be out for Christmas. A sunny, sheltered spot is needed for flowering to be free; not necessarily against a warm wall, though that does help. If you are north of the Midlands, success is rather unlikely. It is a more interesting shrub than the lonicera, but more unpredictable.

Witch Hazels

The most stalwart of all winter-flowering shrubs must be the Chinese witch hazels, *Hamamelis mollis*. They, including the flowers themselves, are amazingly hardy. The yellow petals are like ribbons and have a curl

on them. They are fragrant, with rather a spicy smell. The variety
'Pallida' is a paler yellow and its petals are longer. If I could have only
one, this would be my choice.

These shrubs prefer acid or neutral soil, though they will put up with
some lime. Hamamelis are said to like potash, so no doubt they do – but
in moderation. Ash from Dixter's fires was so generously and
persistently dumped on one of mine that it was killed. The rounded,
rather mundane leaves change to yellow in autumn before falling.
Naked branches suit this shrub. It is excellent to pick and bring into a
cool room.

H. mollis is nearly always grafted on to the American species *H.
virginiana*, which is a vigorous, autumn-flowering shrub, not really worth
growing for itself. It will sometimes sucker and these may take over if
you don't remove them as they appear.

If you can be bothered, and for the sake of a bit of fun, you can layer
a few of the lowest branches to make your own non-suckering plants,
feeding on their own roots. Without breaking it, make a sharp kink in
the branch to be layered and peg it firmly so it is absolutely rigid in the
ground. The wood, being tough, will take two years to make roots. After
it has rooted, sever the shoot from the parent, close to where it enters
the ground, and leave it undisturbed for long enough to be sure it really
can be treated as a separate plant. You probably won't want to be
bothered with all this, but it's fun experimenting.

There are other witch hazels to be considered, notably *H. japonica*
and its hybrids with *H. mollis*, called *H. x intermedia*. In many of them
there are rich autumn tints before leaf fall. One of the best, from
Belgium, is named 'Jelena', after a great gardener, Jelena de Belder. It is
good in flower – yellow with hints of orange – and the leaves have
excellent autumn tints with orange and red.

One, raised by Hilliers and called 'Sandra', has particularly vivid
flaming autumn colour. The flowers are yellow in the usual late-winter
period and, when all is said, it is for the midwinter-to-March period and
their flowering that we most value Hamamelis.

Winter Stems and Bark

Trees and shrubs that have colourful stems or bark cheer us through the winter. The low sunlight (on the scarce occasions when it puts in an appearance) is particularly flattering on vertical features; which it strikes with the full effectiveness of a right angle.

The shrubs' young wood made during the previous summer is nearly always the brightest. To encourage plenty of this, we cut them back hard at frequent intervals. But if we're too enthusiastic, the shrubs will eventually become weakened or diseased and will need replacing. Pruning should be at two- or three-year intervals.

The red-stemmed dogwood, *Cornus alba*, is invaluable in boggy places and I like to interplant it with spring-flowering snowflakes, *Leucojum aestivum*, which will survive happily even when submerged in shallow water.

The brightest, carmine-stemmed cornus variety, 'Sibirica', is a weak grower and won't thrive in dense turf. I grow the white-variegated 'Elegantissima', which is charming among white Japanese anemones. Its stems, in winter, may not be among the brightest, but they are cheerful enough. It gets hard pruned in March. 'Spaethii' is a yellow-variegated version.

As a contrast to their winter stems, these dogwoods are often interplanted with the equally bog-tolerant *Cornus sericea* 'Flaviramea', which has lime-green stems.

Betula jacquemontii is the birch most famous for its white bark, but we should not despise *B. pendula* because it is a native. The down-drooping of its branch tips makes it one of the most graceful of all trees, but it is fairly short-lived. Some my brother planted in the 30s are going down like ninepins. I am replacing them with another native, the Scots pine, *Pinus sylvestris*. Although not specially interesting when young, this species develops great character of form in old age and the trunk takes on a rosy red glow which looks wonderful in winter, especially when it's wet.

My clay soil suits the majority of maples none too well and it was only after 15 years and a move that my *Acer palmatum* 'Senkaki' decided to enjoy life. It is nice when a shrub or tree has more than one seasonal virtue. 'Senkaki''s young shoots are a vivid shade of pink in winter, but its palmate foliage is neat and charming and takes on a soft yellow glow before shedding.

The bright-red-stemmed A. *pensylvanicum* 'Erythrocladum' died on me within a year. This has to be a grafted plant (there is no other satisfactory way to propagate it) and, for its health and vigour, it should be grafted on to a seedling of its own species.

Acer griseum, the paper-bark maple, makes a delightful small tree with neat, small leaves. Its smooth, warm, brown bark is constantly peeling, and your instinct to help it shed by giving it a good rub each time you pass, is entirely correct. Unrubbed trees never look so good. Same story with *Prunus serrula*, a cherry which we grow for the smooth brown skin under its horizontally peeling bark.

I should love to be able to grow the madrone, *Arbutus menziesii*, from the Pacific north-west of America. Its trunks are as smooth as human limbs. I have seen healthy specimens as far north as Inverness but it can be the devil to establish, and I have made three unsuccessful attempts.

I wish rhododendrons liked me better. My *Rhododendron thomsonii* is a mess. *R. smithii* died after four years and I have little doubt that *R. barbatum*, a close relation, would do the same. But if rhodos succeed in your garden, you should certainly grow these species, which develop the most beautiful pink and red, smooth-barked stems. They also have blood-red flower trusses and pretty leaves.

If you live in the south-west or in Ireland, then the Chilean myrtle, *Luma apiculata* (*Myrtus luma*), is for you. Not only is it generous with several flushes of white blossom, but it also develops glowing cinnamon-coloured trunks.

Of the roses, my pick is *Rosa virginiana*, which makes a suckering thicket and has carmine young stems, so I prune out all its second-year wood, down to ground level, at this time of year. The prolonged display of autumn tints on its foliage is also remarkable.

The brambles are close relations and several species have a waxy white coating on their young stems, at their palest in winter. By far the best is *Rubus thibetanus*. It suckers mildly and grows only 1.2m tall. Its grey-green, cut leaves are an asset in summer. But don't forget to cut the whole colony down to ground level by the end of March.

FEBRUARY

Combining Colour

I am associated with bright, harsh colours because I do not mind using them when the situation suggests they are needed. But I have no special preference for their brightness per se. All colours are essential, bright or soft. It is their quality that varies and requires assessment. If they were all bright, we'd get indigestion. The point is, are they good of their kind?

Pink is a difficult colour when there is too much blue in it. Sidalceas are a classic example. Watch out if the word rose appears in the name, such as 'Rose Queen' or 'Rosy Gem': chances are there will be a villainous element of blue included in its make-up. The one (as far as I know the only one) to go for is 'Elsie Heugh', which is pink with no element of blue to speak of.

Another good pink is the charmingly shaped dahlia, 'Pearl of Heemstede'. I grow this with *Salvia involucrata* 'Bethellii' and light purple *Verbena bonariensis*. Still with pink, *Canna* 'Erebus' is a winner. It has narrow, upright leaves that are glaucous. The flowers are prolific and a pleasing shade of salmon. My last pink plug shall be the fragrant, double pink tulip, 'Angélique'. The doubling is quite loose and relaxed.

I've had success combining two whites flushed with lilac – *Dahlia* 'Porcelain' and *Solanum jasminoides*. The dahlia (1.8m) is a relaxed water-lily type and with its uncrowded petals the solanum is one you seldom see – not the familiar 'Album', but larger flowered and more glamorous. We saw it in Brittany and pounced. We put the two in our Old Rose Garden, the solanum trained up a sweet-chestnut pole, the dahlia in front of it; the two flower shapes complementing each other. The solanum twined into the dahlia, which was not premeditated but made a pleasing combination.

Soft yellow is always in demand as an antidote to bright yellows. One of the prettiest is *Dahlia* 'Clair de Lune' (1.8m). *Coreopsis verticillata* 'Moonbeam', meanwhile, is weak, and I'd go for the typical bright yellow variety of this – a lot more effective and it will compete on equal terms with other bright colours, such as the red *Crocosmia* 'Lucifer' or the metallic blue of *Eryngium* x *oliverianum*. Meanwhile, the pale yellow form of *Anthemis tinctoria* – we call this 'Wargrave Variety' but there is confusion, as 'E. C. Buxton' is very similar – goes well with the rich blue of *Campanula lactiflora* 'Prichard's Variety'.

Pears: Fruit and Tree

In writing about pears, I am torn between the fruit and the tree. An old pear tree, whether or not it fruits, is venerable and can achieve a great age, with thick stems and rough, scaly bark. It is easy to admire the trees without caring whether or not they fruit. They just are splendid to look at, especially, but not only, when in flower, and that is enough.

I have a particular affection for *Pyrus amygdaliformis*, which has no culinary pretensions, but 'Cherry' Collingwood Ingram had a specimen of it in his garden in Benenden, Kent, which was noted in 1972 as being 12.5m high. I knew this tree and saw it after a storm had broken it. However, I had meantime taken a fruit, out of which I raised two seedlings. These have now grown into decent trees themselves, quite distinct in habit, but sturdy, with good trunks, which I had to train myself, as their natural inclination was to make bushes. Since there is no fruit to write of, you might feel dismissive, but a good-looking tree is not to be sniffed at.

My father was passionate about dessert pears, in particular 'Doyenné du Comice', which is still the quality dessert pear that has never been excelled. Our climate is not ideal for growing this wonderful fruit to perfection – the French will always beat us there – but with help from a good year and the advantages of a sheltered garden over more exposed conditions, we can do pretty well. At least one pollinator is needed for it to fruit.

One of our dessert pears is 'Olivier de Serres', a smallish, rounded, January-ripening variety. It's rather gritty, which is a cardinal fault in any pear intended for dessert: a dessert pear must be 'fondant'; it must melt in the mouth. How nice it would be to have someone to peel it for you. It is a messy job.

I think my father's passion for pears was very much of his period. In some ways we do them better now. As has long been understood, they need to be stored before being ready to consume, but we now understand that, if stored in lettuce bags which are made from perforated polythene, they will be greatly improved.

Storage may be for the period shortly before ripening, or it may be for weeks. It has the great advantage that ripening is uneven and thus conveniently spreads the consumption of the pears. There isn't that hectic rush that I remember, when all the pears ripen simultaneously.

Ordering Seed

Ordering seeds is a complex affair, because the kinds you want may be scattered through half a dozen catalogues. This is the main reason I am always late in placing my orders.

That said, it is more likely that seeds will be sown too early than too late. Sown now, seedlings may be kept hanging around for more than three months before conditions become right and the positions ready for planting them out.

Among the slow developers that do benefit from early sowing are the bedding verbenas. I had a great combination last year by intermingling *Verbena rigida* (syn. *V. venosa*) and *Salvia coccinea* 'Lady in Red'. The verbena is generally slow and uneven to germinate, so it is as well to order more seed than you would normally think necessary. The flower heads are a very bright shade of purple.

The salvia makes a much prettier, more elegant plant than the strains of commoner *S. splendens*, but seedlings 'damp off' and flop readily. I should delay sowing till April and protect the seedlings with a fungicide spray, applied once a week.

Coleus hybrids will benefit from the same treatment, but sow them early in March. These are normally regarded as foliage pot plants, their leaves beautifully patterned in different colours. But they can be effectively bedded out and will revel in a warm summer.

We grew 'Wizard Mixed', 'Volcano Hybrids' and 'Dragon Sunset' last year, and 'Wizard Golden' and 'Wizard Scarlet'. They were all exciting, but we sowed them rather too late. This year, we plan to have them in front of 1m-tall *Zinnia* 'Giant Dahlia Flowered Mixed'. Early May is soon enough to sow them (to follow tulips underplanted with Bellis). The seeds germinate within four days and, if not inhibited by cold nights, grow quickly thereafter. If they do fall victim to the cold, they will turn yellow and look miserable. Hence the late sowing.

For the same reason, we sow dahlias for bedding late. If ready to plant out in mid-June, they'll be unlikely to encounter cold nights. A late-April sowing will be early enough. Mixed seed strains tend to look patchy, the colours and heights being so varied. I have gone off those with purple leaves, which can look rather funereal, and 'Figaro' types are too small and dumpy – they run out of steam unless extremely heavily fed.

We have enjoyed the mixture 'Collarette Dandy', and saved the tubers to do another year or more. Most dahlias raised from seed make lovely fat tubers, which can be easily stored in boxes of old potting soil, kept frost-free and slightly moist. Collarettes have a ruff of half-sized petals, often of a different colour, inside the outer row of normal rays.

The trial of nicotiana at the Royal Horticultural Society's Wisley gardens last year was wiped out by downy mildew, which has become prevalent in the past two or three years. If it has so far missed you out, play on your luck and pretend it doesn't exist. If it has hit you, a regular spray programme must be adopted, as it will be at Wisley, in a repeat trial. It is at least now known that no nicotianas are resistant to the disease, where the fungus is present. I shall give up growing them for a while.

If rust disease attacks antirrhinums in your district, I should avoid them, too. None is resistant, as was amply demonstrated in another Wisley trial. These trials deliberately set out to test disease resistance, which makes them far more useful than if all precautions were taken from the start. Understandably, most amateur gardeners do not want to be bothered with spraying their annuals.

A pretty combination is to be had with *Rudbeckia* 'Green Eyes' (syn. 'Irish Eyes') and *Ageratum* 'Blue Horizon', the former up to 1m, the latter to about 0.7m. The rudbeckia is pure, clear yellow, the ageratum lavender-mauve, making an excellent show – without dead-heading – over a long period.

I do recommend avoiding very dwarf ageratums, whose initial explosion of blossom on a cauliflower-like plant is quickly past, the whole of the centre of each plant turning irremediably brown.

All begonias benefit from early sowing – now, that is – if you can give them the heat they need: not much less than 20°C for germination and 16°C for growing on, gradually hardening them off for planting out in June. If you haven't the heat for the initial stages, sow the tuberous kinds in a cold-frame in June. The heat of the sun will keep them happy. By the autumn, you'll have tubers which are easily overwintered, dormant, under a frost-free greenhouse bench. In the following year, they can be started into growth quite late (in moist peat) but will be ready in time to give a splendid summer display. Likewise, in years to come.

The February Workload

At Dixter, there is a lot of detailed work to be done on our borders now. This is because we like to encourage self-sowers – or volunteers, to use the American term. If you don't want these, then you can simply apply an overall mulch, with bark, mushroom compost or green waste (sterilised, from the council).

Self-sowers, encouraged in moderation, give a relaxed feel to a garden and sometimes have brilliant ideas of their own. The organic material that we add has to be sterile – that is, weed-free in the first place, with no bits of couch grass lurking, nor weed seeds – and your home-made garden compost would need to be of the highest standard. It is worked into the soil so as not to form a barrier. This is not so simple a task.

First, we mark plants with short pieces of bamboo cane before cutting them down, so that we know where they are before they are cut flush with the ground, leaving no snags to jab one when working nearby. Bulbs, which we plant in abundance among the perennials, are visible by now and so can be avoided.

We never recklessly throw a whole barrowload of compost on to the border and then start forking it in; we would lose track of where the plants are. Instead, we shovel and lay down pockets of compost in between the plants, spreading it out either by hand or with a narrow border fork, tickling it in as we go. We use a special three-pronged, long-handled fork for this, which saves on backache and works easily in between plants because it's not too wide. These can be found in good garden centres (we stock them at the nursery at Dixter); if unavailable, a narrow border fork will do.

Working off planks or wood boards resting on the soil spreads our weight as we move about. The plank is carefully placed in a gap around which we will tackle the next area.

If we have noted, during the growing season, that something wants splitting and replanting, we do it on a piecemeal basis, rejuvenating just that plant or group. Taking a good look at the excavated soil often reveals that something needs adding to it. Now is the opportunity to get organic matter deep into the ground. Furthermore, if your soil is heavy and draining badly, a dressing of coarse horticultural grit will last indefinitely.

Organic material needs to be chosen carefully. Moss peat looks good when wet, but is generally useless as a soil conditioner, lacking the necessary fibrous texture. It needs to be nutritious and with 'body', but also sterile. A suitable range is available from garden centres. There's no such thing as a quiet life if you want the best.

Early Bulbs

February is a most encouraging month. The days are lengthening by leaps and bounds and the garden is visibly coming to life. Small bulbs are a major theme. Have we enough of them?

The garden is doubtless full of bare spaces, but they need assessing. First big question: what happens in those spaces during the summer? Shall I be wanting to dig in them, thereby disturbing my bulbs, when they should be allowed tranquillity and the chance to colonise where they are? Are they going to be visually in the way? Daffodils with large leaves become a menace once they have flowered, and will remain an eyesore until June. But the little ones, close to a species such as *Narcissus cyclamineus* or *N. bulbocodium* or even our own native Lent lily, *N. pseudonarcissus*, are no problem. Their leaves are small and narrow enough to be quickly absorbed.

But what about those perennials I do not want to disturb for many years at a stretch – eryngiums, for instance, and Japanese anemones?

They cry out for inter- or over-planting. I like lightweight narcissi – those that are classified as triandrus hybrids, for example – among my clumps of day lilies (hemerocallis). As the perennials grow up, their own strap leaves totally mask the bulbs.

Deciduous shrubs have bare ground around them that is full of light, until their own foliage unfolds. To give the bulbs a little headroom, I may cut some of the lowest branches of *Weigela florida* 'Florida Variegata', for instance, away. That leaves room for sweet-scented violets, *Viola odorata*, for the hardy *Cyclamen neapolitanum*, whose marbled foliage makes such fine patterns from autumn to spring, and for primroses. I especially enjoy pale yellow primroses with the dwarf yellow trumpet daffodil, 'Tete-a-Tete'. This is a chunky little number with no pedigree to flaunt, but so cheerful and willing and a great multiplier. It is early, too; the first blooms should be out by now.

Beneath rooty trees is a difficult place to colonise. Plants that will tolerate all that dry shade in the summer tend not to be really worth growing, anyway. And they would be a lot happier in the open. But early bulbs, out and growing while there is still moisture and light about, are ideal, especially if you spread an organic mulch over the surface in the autumn – leaf mould, well-rotted bark or mushroom compost (if its alkaline nature won't upset anything).

Crocus tommasinianus, slender and mauve, opening to the sun all this month, is an ideal coloniser as it is such a good self-sower. I consistently fail with winter aconites, *Eranthis hyemalis*, but many gardeners find them as easy as falling off a log and they make ideal partners under a tree (a beech tree, even) for the crocus. They are also good among hostas. These self-sowers are especially rewarding, as they'll put themselves where you could never plant – right into the crown of a late-developing hosta, such as *H*. *sieboldiana* var. *elegans*, for example.

I am grateful to the many cranesbills, the hardy geraniums, that have a rambling habit but die back to a central crown in the autumn, leaving a lot of vacant space around them. In one of these I have a prosperous colony of the February-flowering *Iris reticulata*. The flowers of that are deep purple, and I thought they'd benefit from being enlivened with a paler, simultaneously flowering, bulb mixed in. So with them I have planted the little snowdrop 'Tiny'. It is a miniature form of the common *Galanthus nivalis*. I didn't want anything as muscular or competitive as *G*. *antarctica* 'Atkinsii' (of which I have a great deal). That would, anyway, have been flowering too early; it is one of the earliest. I have a great drift of it in a damp border that in summer is devoted to rodgersias, *Euphorbia palustris* and the herbaceous *Aralia cachemirica*.

I am thinking of places for snowdrops all the time. Among the crowns of deciduous ferns is one of the best spots. Any of the male ferns, dryopteris, are good, and even the evergreen shield ferns, polystichum. They do not greatly object to having their fronds cut away in the new year, just as the snowdrops are pushing through. We also plant snowdrops among hydrangeas and among the stems of the suckering shrub, *Clerodendrum bungei*, which flowers in late summer and autumn but is utterly stark in winter and spring. Another suckering shrub that is a good host for early bulbs is the tree poppy, *Romneya coulteri*, if you can grow it. I don't know why I am having so much difficulty. When it takes off, it can become quite aggressive, but you can treat it like a herbaceous perennial and cut it right to the ground in winter, leaving the field clear for all sorts of bulbs.

Early bulbs with small leaves are great among roses, if you are not neurotic about treating these as a monoculture. The scilla-like, blue-and-white *Chionodoxa luciliae*, a self-sower, entirely filled a bed of Hybrid Tea roses in the garden of friends. They rated it a weed, and it kept coming back; personally, I don't mind that sort of weed at all. Dutch crocuses, at their best next month, love it under and among roses. True, their foliage is a bit of a mess later on, but then the roses are not yet worth looking at themselves. By the time they are, the crocuses will have gone.

The First Snowdrops

February is the month of the snowdrop, though in Scotland it is perhaps more usually March. Quite when this flower will be out is always uncertain. More and more gardens and woodlands are opening to the public at what they hope will be the best time of year, but anything can happen, including vile conditions on the day.

However, galanthophiles, as they like to call themselves – lovers of galanthus (snowdrop) – are tough, and they are prepared to spend a few hours of acute discomfort examining minute differences between cultivars. Twenty to 30 new ones appear each year, nearly all arising from chance seedlings. They will flatter the owner by being named after themselves or their spouse, their home or village, or some reference point that means a lot to them but nothing to the rest of us. It's all a little too easy, or so it seems to me.

'I think I like my snowdrops straight,' garden designer John Codrington once said to me, and one can see his point. They love our climate and in many areas (especially in Scotland) they have become densely naturalised over large acres of woodland. Deer, rabbits and other pests don't touch them; squirrels merely move them around, thereby increasing their territory. Despite its success here as a species, the snowdrop is probably not a true native. (Its ability to establish itself, however, has prompted much debate on the subject.)

The emergence of these flowers is the first wholehearted evidence that winter is on its way out. That said, a few species flower in autumn or early winter, and there is nothing in the way of a cheat about this. It just comes naturally to them. Others flower so late that they may easily run into April. So, one way or another, they give us a good spread and plenty of opportunities on a garden scale to grow them in combination with a number of other early flowers. Or they can bloom with summer-performing perennials, always provided you do not have to replant or in other ways disturb the area too often. Some disturbance every five years or so may actually be beneficial, because some snowdrops, grown in cultivated ground, increase at such a rate that their bulbs diminish in size, push each other out of the ground and eventually kill themselves. The good news is that, when naturalised in turf, the snowdrop's overcrowding problem (if it can be called one) is less obvious.

The early-flowering *Galanthus antarctica* 'Atkinsii', which is tall, with long, teardrop-shaped flowers, never sets seed but is immensely prolific, so that you can build up stock at great speed. Of course, it is easy to understand how people get hooked. You see a different one that appeals to you and, naturally, you want it. But that is different from being bitten by the snowdrop bug and avidly collecting. I might have 20 identifiable kinds, but a genuine nutter might have upwards of 300 and still be far from sated.

The collecting instinct is so natural to many of us (better snowdrops than stamps, I should say) that it would be pointless to be sniffy about it, but galanthophiles can easily become galanthobores. There is a kind of vanity involved. If you can make yourself an expert in your subject, however narrow it may be, you have a vantage point. And if it really means so much to you, chances are that you are, overall, a bit of a bore.

None of which should in any way tarnish the delights provided by snowdrops. They do command pretty colossal prices – £20 for one bulb seems quite a lot to pay. Two enthusiasts, interviewed for an article in the Royal Horticultural Society journal, *The Garden*, are reported to have said that neither of them 'uses any commercial methods of propagation to increase their snowdrop stock. They prefer to rely on nature.' That, surely, is sheer snobbery, suggesting that there is, by definition, something a bit underhand about commerce and that its methods are of necessity not nice.

Had these same enthusiasts been trained to be handy with a knife and to practise the basically quite simple techniques for increasing stock more quickly than Dame Nature manages, they would be singing a different tune. The practice of scooping out a bulb's base-plate and then giving it warm, moist conditions, so that it fairly quickly starts to make little bulbils around the rim of the cut, is very old (particularly on hyacinths) and the more rapid increase of valuable stock that it enables is of great benefit to us all. Ignorance has a lot to answer for. It is often inevitable, but nothing to take pride in.

Another point to make about the spate of newly named snowdrops is that, while they may be curious, they are often downright ugly – far from an improvement.

Nothing will turn me off growing snowdrops. I want more and more of them, and am constantly cudgelling my brains to think of new places where they will be both happy and appropriate. If we want to divide or move them around, there is no better moment than immediately after they have flowered.

Pruning Clematis and Roses

I was writing recently about pruning, cutting back and generally keeping shrubs under control. There are principles that apply to all shrubs and, to show this, it might be helpful to compare clematis and roses.

The earliest clematis to flower do so from the axils of the young shoots they made the previous year. Such are *Clematis armandii*, *C. macropetala*, *C. alpina* and *C. montana*. After that, they have more or less finished until the next year. By the autumn, you may be thinking they are in a pretty lumpy mess and be tempted to have a good old tidy-up (autumn being the time many gardeners get the urge). But this would be a mistake, because the prominent growth that you are likely to be removing is just what would be flowering for you the next spring, if you left it alone, that is.

However, you clearly can't leave the plant to become even bulkier and full of birds' nests and other debris. The time to do your pruning is immediately after flowering, which will be around the end of May, when you can remove as much of the flowered wood as you like. During the rest of the growing season, your clematis will have the time to make lots of new shoots on which to flower the next year, and we must hope you will not be tempted to give it a second pruning come autumn.

It is much the same with the early-flowering rose. If they have a great burst of blossom in late May or early June, they'll have no great urge to do much again. So sort through your bushes thoroughly at the end of June, and remove those multiple-branching aggregates that are unlikely to have much of a future, while leaving any young shoots that are sprouting (these will, in any case, be mostly lower down and inside the bush). This thinning out, combined with feeding, will reduce the overall circumference of the bush, but it will also rejuvenate it.

It is a great advantage to do some of this sorting out every year, so you are not presented with problems of a shrub that has been left unpruned for several years in succession. If the rose is a good fruiter, such as the

35

sweet briar, *Rosa eglanteria*, you should delay pruning until its hips have been flaunting their scarlet swags for long enough, then remove all these fruited branches – a horrible job, I might say – and leave all the unflowered, unfruited, young shoots (it is easy to see which these are) to do their stuff the next year.

Roses such as the Gallicas ('Tuscany Superb') and Albas (Celestial – syn. R. 'Céleste') are much better for thinning out after flowering. Unpruned, once-flowering roses certainly make swags of attractive blossom, but they have a tendency to flop all over the place, lolling on top of the bare hedges that you intended to frame them – all of which I find most irritating.

All Hybrid Tea and Floribunda types come into this category, giving considerable choice of pruning severity according to how bulky a bush is required. The snag is that they do make rather lumpy bushes with aggregates of blossom in blobs, which is not an elegant arrangement. Rugosas arrange their affairs better, and you often have the choice between allowing them to flower and fruit without any mid-season pruning, or following the flowering with the pruning, so that fruits are sacrificed but a good second crop of blossom is obtained. Notable in this category are the single-flowered Alba, 'Scabrosa' (magenta) and 'Frau Dagmar Hastrup' (pink).

Hybrid Musk roses, especially in the south, where two crops can be fully developed, are excellent repeat-flowerers if the first crop is dead-headed. Clematis are not so obliging in this way, although a clematis such as 'Bill MacKenzie' follows its first crop of yellow lanterns with more and yet more blossom, while the first flush runs to seed in a most attractive manner.

The whole subject gives great scope for variable pruning and, hence, different results, though this is to turn the subject into more of a science than a rule-of-thumb procedure.

Repeat-flowering roses can be pruned early or late, according to when you want them to flower. In some old-fashioned establishments, they may not be pruned until early May, with the consequence of flowering in August, but not really that much again thereafter.

Some clematis will produce their longest, sometimes double blooms on short shoots from axils of the previous year's young growth. But if they are hard-pruned the previous winter, they will behave like summer flowerers, producing all their flowers from young wood, and quite generously at that. So if you see the blue 'Lasurstern' or white, small 'Marie Boisselot' doing their stuff in August, you know this is what has happened.

However, hard pruning cannot be guaranteed to work with all varieties, of which some, if hard-pruned at the wrong time, will refuse to flower. I have also noticed that 'Ernest Markham', in the north, where it gets less sun, may flower on the old wood in June, but fail to put on a second (which should be its main) crop later on.

Some clematis, especially of the montana group, will take several years of non-pruning to settle down and flower freely. Some of the most vigorous roses likewise. The double, yellow Banksian rose has tremendous vigour, but may spend several years simply having its young shoots tied in before they start flowering. Don't prune them prematurely – I know of more than one case in Scotland where this rose took all of nine years before reaching a flowering state. Differences of this kind depend entirely on ripening conditions; if the ambient air is warm, direct sunshine may not be needed to promote flowering.

Clematis cirrhosa is quite often recommended for a sheltered north wall in the south and will go on to flower well there – especially in a city such as London. In Edinburgh, it will grow well facing north or south, but you will be lucky to get flowers from it.

Apparent contradictions of this kind apply to many shrubs and, unfortunately, no one will be able to offer you firm, accurate predictions. But I think the principal message should be to give every plant its chance, but not for too long – and never (unless, of course, you are ill) to let the garden get on top of you. You might have to 'rationalise' it (that horrible word for cutting corners, though 'streamlining' is much worse) or even move somewhere less exacting.

Consistently Good Performers

Some plants do a tremendous amount for you in the course of a year. Not all year long, perhaps, but some can stretch that far. Personal preference has to come into it. My head gardener Fergus and I think the world of *Olearia solandrii*, but it is rare for any visitor to notice it. Perhaps it is one of those plants that gradually insinuates itself into your consciousness if you spend enough time with it.

It is a shrub which grows up to 2.5m high in a sheltered situation but is also capable of taking a battering from the wind on sea coasts. Its growth is fine and twiggy and rather upright. The stems are fawn-coloured, as are the undersides of the tiny, evergreen leaves, so the whole shrub glows. As you pass it, thinking of something totally different (that is essential), it stops you in your tracks – it is the arch-waylayer – with a wafted scent of heliotrope. That's all, but isn't it enough? Well, in August, you suddenly become aware of a smother of tiny white blossom. You can't say it makes a show, but it is nice to see and the heliotrope scent has been turned up several notches.

Having rather greater impact (though impact is hardly what you grow it for) is *Bupleurum fruticosum*, one of the few woody members of the parsley tribe. Evergreen, it has a satisfying appearance even as I write. But as summer progresses, it gradually expands into a dome of domes – a multitude of parsley flower heads in lime green. It makes a satisfying mixer among summer flowers such as annuals, Japanese anemones, or bedding dahlias.

Melianthus major is looking awful right now; I shall cut it to the ground at the end of March. But from May to December, it becomes increasingly beautiful and dominant – the best foliage plant in the garden. If you garden near the sea, it may bring its old growth through the winter. But even so, you should cut it right down in spring. As a shrub, it becomes a scrawny object. The large, bluish leaves are pinnate, with deeply jagged margins. It is a wonderful plant to see in low sunlight, when it is casting shadows on itself. It is also a great mixer, with dahlias and cannas and all sorts of late summer and autumn flowers. Protect its crown with a deep litter of fern fronds in the winter, and it will be perfectly hardy once established.

Rodgersias are comparable with hostas in as much as they like the same conditions and are stalwart summer foliage plants. Their advantage over hostas is that their rough-textured, deeply veined leaves do not attract slugs and snails. *Rodgersia pinnata* 'Maurice Mason' is a sturdy plant, 1.2m high at flowering, and it flowers freely, with panicles of pink blossom in June. These gradually deepen, till they are rich, tawny red by autumn, but they keep their shape throughout. The young foliage is suffused with purple. This is a much stronger growing plant than the well-known clone, 'Superba'. You can interplant with snowdrops or other small, early-flowering bulbs to fill the winter gap.

If I bring in *Verbena bonariensis*, it is because many gardeners are still unaware of it. A short life but a merry one, is its motto. Probably at its most prolific in its second year from seed, this verbena flowers from late June into late autumn. If it looks a bit over the top by late August, you can cut the whole 2m plant back to less than half a metre, and off it will go again, rejuvenated. *V. bonariensis* has masses of stiff, green stems – more important to it than leaves. Every branch is terminated by a head of tiny, light purple flowers. Butterflies relish them. There is a long succession of flowers and, the fabric of the plant being pretty stemmy, it doesn't block the view even when it is sited at a border's margin. It is a great mixer with more heavyweight summer flowers. Usually, it self-sows abundantly, but if your climate does not allow it to ripen seed, cuttings of soft young shoots root with ease.

Many ornamental grasses give long-term value. I can single out *Hakonechloa macra* 'Aureola'. Dwarf and deciduous, it appears in April with spears of vivid yellow and green. This variegation continues with little abatement of intensity throughout the summer. The haze of tiny flowers in October comes as a bonus. The whole colony turns to warm rufous shades and only collapses into sodden exhaustion at the end of the year.

Some ferns are at their best in winter, but even if they have lost their foliage, it should not be assumed that they are without interest. Take the common male fern. Its fronds shrivelled around Christmas and we were in a hurry to cut them back for use as protection for plants of doubtful hardiness – such as *Melianthus major*. What's left is a series of thick, writhing, sometimes interlocking rhizomes (you can plant between them with winter aconites, snowdrops and the like), each of them terminated by the growing point of next season's fronds, seen now as a circle of scaly, brown bumps. 'What are you up to, down there?' you ask of them, because they have a curiously animal-like quality.

This is further accentuated in spring, when the fronds begin to expand, rising snakily. Shield ferns, Polystichum, are good this way, too, as are Hart's tongues. Best is the greatest of all male ferns, *Dryopteris wallichiana*, whose young growth is covered with dark, almost black scales. Some people feel uncomfortable because of the animal resemblance, but that's silly. The plant is both fascinating and beautiful.

How to Space Plants

When planting out perennials, biennials or annuals, their best spacing needs quite a bit of thought, because it can vary a good deal. Tall, imposing plants that appear as sentinels need to be far apart. Such would be the biennial 2.5m *Verbascum olympicum*, which I like to scatter through a border at different levels. Hollyhocks can be clustered around a front porch to give a cottagey effect, but it is also nice, in the paving cracks through which they happily grow, to have thinly spaced outliers.

The biennial, 1.3m *Salvia sclarea* var. *sclarea* will make an imposing statement at the top of a retaining wall, but I also have groups of it in my borders. They are interplanted with the earlier flowering *Allium hollandicum* 'Purple Sensation'. That takes up little lateral space, so the spacing of the salvias themselves is about 0.6m. In her recent, most helpful book called *Plant Partners*, however, Anna Pavord suggests sowing annual Californian poppies, *Eschscholzia californica*, between the salvias, these growing a mere 25cm high, but with a spreading habit.

First establish the salvias; then cultivate a fine tilth between them for the direct sowing of the poppies (which are typically orange, though there are more subtle shades. The salvias make an overall pinkish-mauve impression). As there is a great disparity of heights, and the poppies enjoy light and sunshine, I would leave 1.3m between salvia plants.

When planting a border with perennials, there is no need to be rigid about the shape or spacing of the groups. Plants can be fairly dense at a group's centre, but it is very effective to allow outliers to appear among groups of other species. These should be widely spaced. You may deliberately leave gaps in your plantings, which can later be occupied by something completely different. It might be a self-sowing (or planted) annual, such as the purple-leaved variety of the 2m orach, *Atriplex hortensis*. Once you have that in a border, it can be guaranteed to reappear annually.

It is normal to leave a wider space between adjacent groups of perennials than between the individual plants within a group. But this space will look uncomfortable if retained throughout the summer. Plant growth needs to interlock in the growing season to produce an integrated tapestry.

The annuals that you plant out will generally deserve wider spacing than you are accustomed to giving them. This means using fewer plants, but they will make prosperous, bushy individuals and will flower for much longer than plants that have become spindly through overcrowding.

I think a mixed border without annuals is soulless, but there is a danger of their getting squeezed out if the shrubs are too numerous. You need to visualise the size that shrubs will attain within a few years, and to be quite sparing in their use. They are good for structure, but if overdone they are liable to become dull dogs for much of the year.

Wisteria

A problem affecting many gardeners is the failure of their wisteria to flower. *Wisteria sinensis* was introduced from China in 1816 and it seems probable that it has been propagated from the original clones, vegetatively, ever since. This was usually done by layering, but it can also be done by cuttings. A reputable nursery will sell you a plant from the original clones – May-flowering, deliciously scented and often carrying a light second crop of blossom in August.

However, it is much easier for the nursery to get seed-raised stock. This may take many years to reach sufficient maturity to flower and, when it eventually does, the flowers may be of disappointing quality.

Another common reason for not flowering is that birds, usually sparrows, eat all the flower buds just as they are swelling in early spring. I get this trouble on mine from time to time, but find that it can be prevented by stretching strands of black cotton over the wisteria – not a thick network, but enough to worry the birds. If your wisteria does carry the second August crop, but nothing in spring, this is the likely reason.

W. *sinensis* is my favourite because, although its racemes are not the longest, they have by far the best fragrance. However, the long racemes of *W. floribunda* 'Multijuga' are particularly effective, visually, in certain positions – such as hanging over the sides of a bridge or from the top of a pergola. This species normally takes a few years to settle down to flowering. If you grow it against a house, you must prune to allow it to bulk a little forwards from the house face, so that its tresses hang free.

Now is a good time to be pruning. If supported in its early years, a wisteria can be trained as a free-standing shrub, 2m or so high, by continually reducing shoots to short spurs.

Such is the vigour of wisterias that they will often, from low down, make tremendously long, unbranched shoots all in one season. Unless you need one or more of these for extending the plant's range, they should be removed entirely at the base. Wispy shoots that are made in summer can be shortened back throughout the growing season if they are in the way, but otherwise you can leave all pruning till the plant is dormant, which is often not until December.

If you want an extra plant, you can yourself layer one of these long shoots. In fact, you can layer it into soft ground, at a number of points, so that it becomes a sort of snake, dipping into and then up again from the soil. Layer it now, if necessary pegging where it goes underground, so that it remains steady and secure.

When to Cut Back

Do you cut back your borders in the autumn, or do you leave it until later on, perhaps as late as spring? What is right for one garden or, indeed, for one plant, may not be right for another.

Mark and Amanda Buchele, only a few miles into Kent from where I live, run one of the best plant centres in the south of England (Merriments of Hurst Green, since you asked). Separate from it, but still an integral part of the enterprise, they have made a large garden in which they explore a whole range of ideas and experiments with plants. It is open to the public through the summer, for an entrance fee. But at the close of the season, the two women looking after it like to weigh in, cut everything down and do most of the necessary work that will last till the garden reopens in spring.

That works perfectly for them. I don't suppose that Mark and Mandy themselves have cause to visit the garden during the off-season, apart from making plans. With my garden, and possibly with yours, the situation is quite different. It surrounds the house. By whichever door you leave the house, you are right in the garden. Even in winter, I go right round it with the dogs, almost every day, and therefore I am acutely aware of how it is looking.

So, I do not want all its furnishings, apart from shrubs, to disappear in autumn. If some of them are still looking beautiful, even though dying or dead, I like to leave them. Ornamental grasses are a notable example. Most miscanthus continue to look good till the turn of the year. At the New Year, they shed their old leaves, leaving just stems and seed heads. The leaves make a colossal mess. More than that, however, I find that the gales, to which we have been subjected even more than usual, strip the seed heads too, or make them look shabby. So as his rounds take him near to them, Fergus cuts them down, and when I say down I mean right down – not an inch of stem remaining. We hate to see a forest of cut-off stalks; to us they are an eyesore. They just get in the way.

But there are other grasses which we leave because they continue to be an asset right up to March. *Calamagrostis* x *acutiflora* 'Karl Foerster', with its pale, vertical rods, is notable among these. It retains a ghostly presence.

I grow quantities of border phloxes, mostly cultivars of *Phlox paniculata*, because they make a huge display in July–August and they love our heavy soil. Their dying stems are not particularly beautiful but, till the end of the year, they are not an eyesore either. One of our chief reasons for leaving them is that they take months to die completely. Withdrawal of all their sap is only complete at the end of December. By then, the stems are paper-light and break off cleanly, right at the base (lower than you could reach with secateurs) simply by being given a sideways kick (very satisfying to do, and quick). These leave the field clear for snowdrops and tulips growing among them.

Red hot pokers, or other kniphofias, are evergreen but with masses of lanky leaves. We shorten these by about half. If the colonies need replanting – and they do flower less freely when congested – we shall tackle that job in late March or April. Kniphofias are not 100 per cent hardy and should not be disturbed until then. They can do with a further cleaning up at that time, by peeling away tired, old outer leaves.

Snails love to doss down among kniphofia shoots, and you can have quite a field day collecting and disposing of them.

I love the skeletons of old cardoon flower heads, but even they may break up after months of being battered and there is already strong new basal foliage prominent by the end of January. We shall take the hint and remove their old stakes and ties and cut down the stems. My cardoons have never needed replanting in 50 years.

Some plants continue to look so good right up to mid-spring that it is a wrench to say goodbye to their old growth even then. The thistly, autumn-flowering *Serratula seoanei* is a prime example. When its dead flower heads are completely sere and dry, as they will be in the face of chill March winds, they open out into pale brown rosettes which look like a kind of second flowering. The dead heads of sedums are another classic example of skeletons that will remain admirable till the very last moment.

Once you have cut down a plant, it is difficult to imagine just what was, and is, growing where or how tall and how bulky it was. This will make life more difficult if you subsequently need to do some replanting. Fergus tends to define the outline of groups by laying canes horizontally at the margins of where they were. He then knows how near to them he can go with adjacent plantings. The canes are removed when all plantings have been completed. Alternatively, leave just one short length of old stem on the outside of each clump. These are removed when they have served their purpose. Sometimes, though, we like an overlapping of two different kinds at the margins or to allow a planting to wander from its epicentre into neighbouring groups.

Ferns

Ferns give wings to a garden, as someone once said. I wish I'd thought of it: their fronds often look as though they're taking off. Most of them will be stirring next month, so now is a good time to do any messing around with them. You might want to increase some, while others might grow more strongly if their sites were cultivated deeply by replacing unpleasant subsoil with nice, juicy organic stuff.

There is also the question of where and how to grow them. Don't make a fernery or a bed devoted entirely to ferns, not because they look bad, but because that's the sort of mindless, pigeon-holing exercise we see too much of in the gardening world already. Far better to integrate your ferns with other plants that enjoy the same conditions. Then they'll help to set one another off.

Ferns like the damp and they like enough shade to stop them from scorching. I find they go admirably with fuchsias and with the variegated-leaved arum that we know as *Arum italicum* 'Marmoratum'. For foliage, this arum is at its best in winter and spring, so I team it up with forms of evergreen polypody, Polypodium, such as 'Cornubiense', which has freshly coloured, parsley-like leaves, and 'Bifidocristatum', which branches into antlers at the tips of each frond. In August, the arum, its leaves having died away for the summer, presents us with a crop of brilliant red berries. Subject to blackbirds looking the other way, these are a great bonus.

The maidenhair ferns are generally thought of as conservatory pot plants, but some are remarkably hardy. *Adiantum venustum* makes a little carpet of its delicate fronds, which are almost evergreen but which change to warm brown tones if the weather turns cold. It gets on the move early next month. Only 15cm or so high, you could plant it beneath a deciduous shrub such as a hydrangea, but be sure to prune away the hydrangea's lowest branches first and retain it as an overhead sunshade. *A. pedatum* (30cm) has fascinatingly shaped fronds distributed as spokes about an arc. It looks frail, but is actually tough, even without shade, though it is happier with that and moisture.

Another slow-motion coloniser is the tatting fern, *Athyrium filix-femina* 'Frizelliae' (20cm), whose crinkly greenery is strung out in blobs along each frond – prettier than I've made it sound, perhaps. I've grown that in a bit of paving on the north-west side of a building. Ferns stand out as features in this way. Another, derived from the same lady fern, is *A. f-f.* 'Minutissimum' (10cm), a bipinnate, mini-replica of the wild species. Small though it is, it stands out remarkably on the corner of a ledge, for instance.

An airy, feathery delight of more normal height for the lady fern is *A. f-f.* 'Plumosum Axminster' (50cm). It makes an excellent contrast to a more solid foliage feature, such as the rounded, light-reflecting leaves of the clump-forming *Asarum europaeum* (10cm), planted in front.

Deciduous ferns such as this needn't just leave you with bare ground between autumn and spring, as they offer a perfect opportunity for colonising snowdrops, winter aconites or scillas.

The proudest and most striking of all deciduous ferns – and definitely one to grow by your front porch, if that faces north – is *Dryopteris wallichiana* (1m). Its uncurling fronds are covered with dark brown scales, and these remain a feature as the pale, yellow-green leaflets expand, the whole eventually forming an open, funnel-like vortex of fronds arranged in a circle. You don't want this circle to be interrupted by competitive, adjoining circles. If there are any of these when you buy your plant, detach them immediately and treat them as separate plants, which in fact they are. For this species is raised from spores and the sporelings are pricked out in small clumps, which are hard to separate at this early stage. So you are probably getting several plants for the price of one.

The shuttlecock fern, *Matteuccia struthiopteris* (1m), arranges its fronds in a similar way, encouraging you to peer down the centre of each funnel. Its spring colouring is an incredibly bright, fresh shade of green, but its growth is totally different. It spreads by producing runners just beneath the soil surface, and quickly makes a colony if the ground is nice and damp. But it doesn't altogether relish the dry air that we get in the south in summer (you may not have noticed it), and is apt to scorch mid-season. It is happiest in Devon, Wales and anywhere in Scotland, even on the east side, where the rainfall is low, but the air is still humid.

Another runner with a particular freshness is the sensitive fern, *Onoclea sensibilis* (0.5m), with rather short, broad, once-pinnate fronds. I have it in dense turf, near the side of our natural pond, where it copes. It would luxuriate more, however, with less competition: in open woodland, for example, it combines happily with bluebells and takes over from them as they wither.

And last, the oak fern, *Gymnocarpium dryopteris* (20cm): a deciduous native of acid soils in the north, this fern's leaflets are divided more like a maiden-hair's, above dark stems. Not only is this outstandingly fresh in spring, but it continues through the summer to make new fronds of equal freshness. Give it plenty of top-dressing with well-rotted compost and it will fill in along a shady hedge bottom, where there is a lawn or paving in front. It makes a colony rather than a specimen.

Garden Worries

Some people are worriers. Their brows become permanently furrowed from an early age. They get stomach ulcers, lose sleep, suffer from eye strain and take to wearing spectacles. They either put on weight or can't put on weight; they're a wreck.

Gardening is supposed to be a therapy for these people, but instead it arouses as many anxieties as elsewhere in their lives. So here are a few suggestions on what *not* to worry about.

Bearing in mind that where there's life there's trouble, don't get upset over garden deaths. Nothing is irredeemable; all you need to do is to throw away the relevant label and try quickly to forget. Some deaths will probably show up at the end of this winter. Don't take them as a personal insult (many do). Don't flail around in a grand tragedy act: 'I loved it, I watered it, I talked to it . . .' Most of the plants which die suddenly are short-lived anyway, but also fast-growing. In no time, a replacement will fill the gap.

Bare areas under trees are not cases of indecent exposure; green mosses will appear throughout winter and spring, and you can always add winter aconites and self-sowing crocuses. Then the tree will leaf out and the ground will become dark and dry. Let it stay that way until the next winter. Don't bother asking what will grow in dry shade; some things will, but they'll often look scraggy and resentful. Take the situation in a dignified way – and cut the tree down if it's a sycamore.

There is no need to feel hurt when trees shed their leaves in autumn; they're not doing it to annoy you. And there's no need to rush out every day to clear them away. Leaves can look rather nice on the ground for a while, and a time will come when the wind blows them into heaps, making them easier to gather. Evergreens are not the answer. Instead of one period of leaf-fall, they shed all year round, but with a special concentration in May.

It is far better to get it over in one dose.

What about moss in lawns? I'm always being asked how I tackle mine, usually with the obvious insinuation that I don't. And I don't. I love the

47

mosses' brilliant green, and look forward to its company for the next two or three months. They make a deep, plushy pile, like a carpet, that it is a joy to sink into.

Why worry so much about daisies? They make a wonderful display each spring, changing at different times of the day; pink when closed, morning, evening and in rain; white when they open to warmth and sunshine.

And there's no need to get cross when plants bulge out from their border sites and obligingly break the monotony of a lawn's hard edge. You want your garden to look relaxed, and the plants to enjoy themselves. At the end of the season, you will shear things back and there'll be a bare patch to record the invasion. But nature, as we are always being told, abhors a vacuum, even if it is only annual meadow grass that takes over until the same plant advances again in the next growing season.

Gardeners horrified by deaths are often no happier when a plant grows faster and larger than expected. 'What am I to do about it? Nobody told me,' they gasp, as though trifids were advancing. Well, the worst course of action is to cut the offender hard back so that it looks awful and cannot perform in the manner intended – it can't flower, fruit or luxuriate. Far better to choose one of two more sensible courses of action. The first is to get rid of the plant; the second is to move its threatened neighbours out of its way and let it show what it's capable of. Sometimes plants supply you with good ideas, and it is worth taking them on board gratefully.

'Nothing will grow there; but nothing. I have spent the earth on all those plants, but look how miserable they are,' is another worrier's complaint. You may be certain there's a simple remedy. Most often, the ground is starved. I have no compunction about telling this sort of gardener what brutes they are, and that there should be a society for the prevention of cruelty to plants. Because, all along, they've imagined themselves the most solicitous of owners. The other probable cause is bad drainage. Tree roots could be the culprits, but then we're back with the dignity of bare earth.

There's algae in your pond. I'm sorry about that, but it always happens with new ponds, and especially in early summer when there's so much light on the water and the water-lily pads haven't yet cut it down sufficiently. Once your pond fauna and flora have reached a balance, the trouble, if it occurs at all, will be over by the end of June. Don't use copper sulphate – it will do the trick momentarily, but the required balance will never be achieved if you destroy the possibility of it in that way.

You will be more relaxed for realising that there's no need to make a fuss about creepy-crawlies. It is quite undignified to be seen flailing around when a wasp approaches your sweet drink, or to react absurdly when an earwig drops out of the lovely old-fashioned rose that you were sniffing. I admit that snails are more satisfying to crush underfoot than slugs, but you can even learn to handle slugs – if you make up your mind to do it. It is surprising how we can train ourselves, if we want to.

March

An Early Spring

An early spring is always tremendously encouraging, and never mind what follows in the way of April frosts, or what have you. The great thing in life is to fling yourself into wholehearted enjoyment of the present, whenever there's something to be enjoyed.

Our pond is rather thick with de-hibernated newts; less than three weeks earlier, Fergus had uncovered a cluster of three, stiff and torpid, beneath a paving slab. Ladybirds and butterflies are more active in the garden.

Interesting to see the colour contrasts between tortoiseshell butter-flies and various crocuses. They also like the snowdrops, while a somewhat battered peacock was taking nectar from the heavily scented, yellow pea flowers of *Coronilla valentina*. It is always worth hanging on to a few old wallflower plants, because they will often be flowering by mid-February and their scent is powerful. I picked some yellow-headed ones and gave them pink *Erica carnea* 'King George' for company, which worked surprisingly well.

Clematis cirrhosa var. *balearica*, with its greenish-white bells speckled brownish-red, is flowering as never before and, although planted on the north side of a wall, it has grown up and over the top and the display is all on the south side.

Daphne bholua, with clusters of pale pink blossom and a scent that carries 50 metres, is a highlight of the early weeks of the year. It grows strongly and is of somewhat upright habit. It is most safely planted with some protection; though the huge colony from wild-collected seed at Wakehurst Place, mid-Sussex, is in open woodland.

This daphne species is most often evergreen or semi-evergreen, 'Jacqueline Postill' being a well-known clone of the latter type. The 'Darjeeling' form is more reliably evergreen, and a friend, who was recently admiring a specimen, particularly liked the rosette formation of its leaves as a setting for the flower clusters.

However, I do rather like daphnes that flower along naked branches, and such is *D. b.* var. *glacialis* 'Gurkha', which grows in my neighbour's garden. As a young plant, it seemed less free than 'Jacqueline Postill', but it flowers abundantly now. March is a time to be thinning and mulching bamboos and also to be thinking of which varieties to plant. Many are looking their worst at winter's end, bruised and battered by winter gales, but some survive with remarkable freshness, and I would put the forms of *Phyllostachys nigra* at the top of my list. In most soils, these grow to a height of 4m or 5m and, although they make colonies in time, they do not (in our climate) spread very fast, laterally. *P. aurea* is another winner, as are the forms of *P. bambusoides*.

Bamboos last for many years, and I think it is worth going to a specialist, in such cases, even if you have to pay a bit more.

When bamboos reach the age at which they flower (usually after many years), the colony is generally ruined, and I think it best to make up your mind at once to get rid of and replace it. But you might choose to wait and see, as I did with the graceful *Himalayacalamus* (Arundinaria) *falconeri*. It flowered two years ago, and is now dead as a dodo, but I have a nice batch of self-sown seedlings, so I can rid myself of the old carcass with an easy mind.

The thinning of old bamboo colonies is not nearly as widely practised as it deserves to be, and it is certainly energetic work. You need to get busy with a thin-bladed saw and cut each cane (choosing the oldest and weakest) at ground level so that no stumps are left to make the job more difficult next time. When the job is done, you will be able to see right through your colonies again and they will look remarkably rejuvenated.

In the case of some of the low-growing kinds, such as *Pleioblastus viridistriatus* or *P. variegatus* (*Arundinaria variegata*), I cut the whole colony to the ground every spring and the resulting growth is far fresher and more brilliant, growing 1m tall in the course of a season.

We have been spreading our snowdrops around, thinning old, dense clumps, even before they have finished flowering. The plump and pleasing *Galanthus* 'S. Arnott' is one of the best for making up quickly, so that you have material for splitting. Snowdrops look splendid among the dark, marbled leaves of *Cyclamen hederifolium*. Nice, too, beneath the naked branches of deciduous magnolias and anywhere in thinnish turf under oaks, limes and other trees.

We also plant them among infrequently divided clumps of rodgersias, hostas, *Aralia cachemirica*, *Euphorbia palustris* and other such moisture-loving perennials.

Lathyrus vernus is coming into flower as I write, with its dense, 20cm clumps of purple pea flowers. Theirs is such a bright shade that they could have been dipped in an aniline dye. They flower for quite a while, and I like them near to a pale yellow hyacinth such as 'City of Haarlem'.

Any shrub elders that you grow for foliage effect should be hard-pruned now, if you've not already done so. Such is *Sambucus racemosa* 'Plumosa Aurea' and the boldly variegated *S. nigra* 'Marginata', which is yellow at first, becoming white. But if you are after flowers, as with *S. n.* f. *laciniata*, the cut leaves being a bonus, leave the young branches full length and merely thin out those that have already flowered last year.

The Importance of Feeding

All plants need feeding, as we do. There are three primary ways to feed a plant. You can water food in with a foliar feed (through the leaves) or into the soil with a liquid feed. Alternatively, food can be put on to the ground as a feeding mulch, then tickled into the soil surface. Thirdly, you can dig fertiliser into the structure of the soil, before you plant.

The principal ingredients that plants need are nitrogen, phosphates and potash – always abbreviated to NPK. Nitrogen prompts lush growth, phosphates are specific for root action, and potash encourages ripening. All feeds contain these three elements in varying proportions.

Feed, or fertiliser, is organic (natural matter) or inorganic (from a chemical factory). Both can be purchased in bags from garden centres, but the inorganic version will come as pellets or powder. It is clean to use and easily applied, and the amount of N, P or K can be deliberately selected. However, it has no soil-conditioning properties.

Organic fertiliser is imprecise in its content. It can be full of weed seeds – as when farmyard manure has been lying around and nettles have seeded into it – as well as awkward to store, due to its bulk. And it must be well rotted if applied to growing plants, or it burns them. But its advantage is that it conditions as well as feeds the soil, increasing water-holding capacity and opening up its structure. It also acts as a buffer

55

against climatic extremes, such as drought, and against excess soil acidity or alkalinity.

To get organic fertiliser deep into your soil where the roots will benefit from it most, dig it in prior to planting. If you need to feed established plants, lay it on the soil surface and allow the worms and the rain to filter it down. Try to tickle the fertiliser in between plants with the fork tips, just before the plant comes out of dormancy (in early spring, for example). Around shrubs, roots may prevent digging in (with magnolias, damage to fleshy roots kills the plant). In this case, just spread the compost evenly over the surface, avoiding contact with the stem, which might cause neck-rot.

To reach a good balance, try to feed organically and inorganically around the same time (though you can do this separately). This is because organic fertiliser is slow acting, taking a while to filter down, whereas chemical (inorganic) feed will do its job rapidly and happily from the surface. If you top up with inorganics, in spring, for example, it gives awakening plants a fast-acting boost.

To apply inorganic fertiliser, make sure you follow the instructions. If applying in powder or pellet form, do so in windless weather (keep your hand low and don't let fertiliser get on to leaves, or it will burn them). Don't exceed the recommended dose. Water, if necessary, after application.

Liquid foliar feeds can be sprayed on to a plant's leaves. Other liquid feeds, whether organic or inorganic, can be watered on to the ground around the plant. The simplest way to do this is from a long-spouted watering can with a rose fixed on it.

Crocuses

I don't know whether snowdrops are actually more popular than crocuses, but they are certainly more adept at hitting the headlines. There are galanthus openings and meetings of a kind that is unheard of for crocuses. The reason for this is almost certainly that crocuses are moody; snowdrops are not. If the weather is not right for them, crocuses simply remain shut – and a closed crocus is no more enlivening than a closed golf umbrella, however bright that may be when fully expanded. However, when crocuses do open it means that the sun is shining and we ourselves can experience the same happiness, and the feeling that spring is finally with us.

We feel expansive about crocuses. That is what I love about them, together with their great range of colours and markings, and the differences between the inside and outside of the flower. When seen together, the presentation is ideal. The gardening writer Ernest Bowles described them as his first garden love, and admitted that his raptures may appear the vapourings of a lovesick monomaniac (he was not far wrong).

No bulb could be easier to grow, always provided you are not plagued by mice or voles. On my heavy soil, in which they find it hard to work, there is no problem. The corms (the globular stem base) multiply at a great rate, and many of them self-sow. By now, we are probably in the full tide of the Dutch hybrids, the largest kinds, which are purple, mauve, white or stripy. They are not refined, but they make a tremendous and gladdening show – and they self-sow like mad.

When planting in turf, use a long-shafted bulb planter, if you possibly can, and take out individual plugs at irregular intervals, so that the planting looks relaxed and natural. Taking short cuts, there is a fashion for cutting a turf on three sides, turning it back as a flap and crowding corms in the rectangle underneath, then replacing the flap. This looks terrible; if you can persuade yourself otherwise, you can believe anything.

Planting in turf is the ideal, as long as it isn't in self-conscious circles around a tree, as the mower will then reluctantly have to leave that area uncut for a few weeks to allow the crocus 'grass' to finish its cycle, which won't be until as late as May. Planting in a meadow area among daffodils is also a good idea, because the crocuses flower before the daffodils are tall enough to spoil their display. I planted a few hundred *Crocus tommasinianus* 'Whitewell Purple' in our old orchard three years ago, and where there was originally one corm, there were up to eight or nine blooms this year. They are of a far richer colour than the plain species, too. 'Whitewell Purple' is, in fact, one of the most enthusiastic self-sowers, and it was already at its best last month.

The Dutch yellow crocus is one of the most popular. It is an early flowerer, and Fergus likes it so well that he has marked some of the largest clumps with a view to dividing and spreading them around later this month. The point about this crocus is that it is sterile, and so cannot self-sow; one has to help it. This is the one that sparrows love to tear to shreds. Equally early and even more beautiful in its way is the species from which it derives, C. *flavus* subsp. *flavus* (also C. *aureus*). It is smaller-flowered but of a richer shade of orange, and is a great self-seeder, though less widely offered. It combines and contrasts well with C. *tommasinianus*. These crocuses are good in borders, too, provided you don't get impatient with their lanky foliage after flowering. This foliage is narrow, and I don't find it unduly irritating for a few weeks. If you are not neurotic about their manurial regime, you can liven up your rose beds with crocuses in early spring. There won't be a trace of them left by the time the roses are ready to perform.

Among the jolliest and most varied of the species is C. *chrysanthus*. It is naturally yellow, but varies tremendously thanks to selection. My favourite is 'Snow Bunting', which is creamy white with some dark stripes on the outside. It is deliciously scented and also one of the earliest. Unfortunately, a different cultivar is often sold under its name; whiter, but late-flowering and with no scent. So I was glad, at the February RHS show in Westminster, to see 'Snow Bunting' correctly named and identified. This species is so amazingly fertile that, after a few years of growing one next to another, you will find that they have given birth to some really exciting variants, with subtle combinations of mauve and yellow. It is difficult not to feel proud of one's offspring.

At this time of the year, the easiest autumn-flowering species to colonise – C. *speciosus* and C. *nudiflorus* in my case – are making carpets of their 'grass'. They have no leaves when flowering, but become green in late winter. And they have this colonising, carpeting habit. Spring flowerers will not thrive among them. If you want to increase the range of your autumn flowerers, lift them in the next few weeks, while you can still see where they are. In a meadow setting, this is particularly easy while the turf is still short and tight.

The regime to follow in such cases is to give the grass its first and main cut in July or August, after its contents have scattered their seed; then to await the flowering of colchicums and autumn crocuses, complete by the end of October; after which the turf can be cut again, tight as you can get it, so as to set off the short-stemmed snowdrops and crocuses to best effect.

Pruning: When and Why

Rather than do a job by rote, it helps to know why you are doing it. That's how it is with pruning.

Many forsythias are hacked or trimmed – the result is the same – back in autumn. With every branch that is removed go a hundred flower buds, thus drastically reducing the next spring's display. It's the same with that rampant *Clematis montana* growing over your porch. No doubt it requires reducing but, if you do it in autumn, you're a self-inflicting wounder.

If you tell me that you couldn't bear that dropsical lump a moment longer, that's fair enough. But many people fail to appreciate the price they're paying. If, every time they made a snip, a quiet voice interposed through their Walkman, 'that's another 33 flowers you won't be seeing next May', it might give them pause. Unfortunately plants can't speak and only the mandrake can shriek.

One of the best ways to prune a forsythia is by bringing branches of its buds into the house to force gently. Failing that, wait until it has flowered in the garden and then cut it back or, alternatively, thin it out, removing the oldest branches. By this method you are allowing it the whole of the summer's growing season to make new wood on which to flower in the following spring.

Your *Clematis montana* will flower in May, your C. *armandii* in April. As soon as the blossom has shattered, get at them with shears and secateurs. Don't worry that they're already putting on strong young growth and that you're removing that too. This is inevitable but of no consequence as they've plenty of time in which to make a lot more.

Perhaps you have the bridal veil, *Spiraea arguta*, or the closely related S. *thunbergii*, which flowers even earlier. Old and unpruned, they're a horrible mess. If that's what's happened to yours, cut it to the ground after flowering. The plant will be rejuvenated.

If you have more space and want a larger shrub, shorten back after flowering rather than cutting right back. You can do that once in a while, if total rejuvenation seems desirable. To a large extent, you tailor your pruning to the circumstances that prevail.

Many people grumble about the size of their hydrangea and maybe they did plant a variety that was unnecessarily vigorous for its position. But instead of allowing the plant to build on its original foundations year after year, so that they're eventually forced to cut it hard back, thereby losing most of its blossom, they can reduce its circumference by an annual thinning out of old branches, which also has the beneficial effect of rejuvenating the entire shrub. This should be done now, before the shrub has burst into new leaf. Cut out all those twiggy, pale brown old branches and leave the straight, unbranched, dark brown young shoots full length.

Finally, feed the shrub with a good surface mulch or dressing. There's no satisfaction in pruning (let alone owning) a starved plant that would sooner be dead than ailing.

Exochorda x *macrantha*, 'The Bride', has a dense, spreading habit with branches that constantly arch downwards. It will be a revelation, shortly, and makes a lovely background for late tulips. However, in course of time, it does build to a considerable height, even to 1.8m. I hadn't appreciated this point when I planted mine next to a path. But, without loss of blossom I keep mine to a reasonable height by pruning its flowered branches hard back every other year.

Spring flowering barberries such as *Berberis darwinii*, B. x *stenophylla* and B. *linearifolia* are well known for their good temper under correct pruning treatment. Delay this operation until they have flowered and you can be as severe as you please. That and its production of graceful, arching stems are what make B. *stenophylla*, with its wands of crocus yellow blossom, such good material for a flowering hedge.

Spring-flowering ceanothus require a different schedule from the summer- and autumn-flowerers. Those of spring can be pruned (though, if space allows, this is not essential) immediately after flowering but should not be cut back into old wood. Take them no further than where they started last year's growth. Those that flower on their young wood in summer and autumn can now be pruned (as you do the butterfly bush, *Buddleja davidii*) as hard back as you like. 'Gloire de Versailles' and 'Topaze' are typical examples of the deciduous kinds, while 'A. T. Johnson' and 'Autumnal Blue' are more or less evergreen.

All the winter-flowering mahonia should be pruned now and a

spring-flowerer such as M. *aquifolium* or 'Undulata', as soon as flowering is past. You can cut all those terminal leaf rosettes back into old, bare wood without detriment to next season's flowering. You only have to look around you to see what stemmy, upswept scrags mahonias become if left unpruned, which is their all too normal fate.

Sowing Annuals

There is always so much to be said about what seeds one might plan to sow this year that it is difficult to know where to start. I went back to calendula, the pot marigold, last year and did not regret it. Although it is a hardy annual, we sowed seeds in March under glass and brought the plants on quickly in individual pots so that they were ready to follow spring bedding by mid-May.

I like bright orange, fully double marigolds, myself, and the Extra Selected strain of 'Radio' served us well. That combines and contrasts nicely with love-in-a-mist. Instead of using the familiar blue 'Miss Jekyll' strain of *Nigella damascena*, we went for the purplish N. *hispanica*, which has striking flowers over quite a long June period. We raised this the same way as the calendula.

This kind of bedding gives you a few weeks but then needs a follow-on. One suggestion I would make is the bedding collarette dahlia 'Dandy', which is single but with an inner circle of half petals, often in a different colour. This is an intriguing arrangement. If you sowed the dahlia under cold glass in the first week of May and grew the seedlings on in one-litre pots, by the first week in July they'd have made nice bushy plants that are almost ready to flower. A late sowing of a cold-sensitive subject such as this gets over the danger of it being set back by cold nights in its early stages of development. Naturally, you'll want them to be well hardened off by planting-out time.

An annual that responds well to a late-ish sowing is the spider flower, *Cleome pungens*. When bruised, the plant has a strong, mustard-oil smell and, be warned, is attractive to the caterpillars of the cabbage white butterfly. But, if well grown, single plants have almost the habit of a sturdy shrub, with a central leader to 1.5m. The palmate leaves are handsome and the dense flower heads continue to perform without need of dead-heading for three months. They do tend to wilt somewhat in strong sunshine, so a half-shaded position is ideal. There are separate colour strains available in white, pink or rosy purple, or a mixture of the three, which are all compatible colours. But I often want to combine the white one with orange tithonias. A mixture that included pink would not be suitable.

The one thing this annual insists on is to be grown well and without a check. A late-April sowing will be early enough. Get the seedlings into individual pots and, if they need to be kept waiting, pot them on so that they never starve. Each plant should have the support of a single, strong cane with just one tie to its main stem.

An annual planting that I have made twice now, and mean to repeat again this year, is a pretty even mixture, 0.3m tall, of *Helenium amarum* and *Gaillardia* 'Red Plume'. You rarely see the helenium, which has very bright green, linear foliage (each plant is the better for a little brushwood support) and a long succession of small, yellow, typical helenium daisies. The gaillardia, basically another daisy, is fully double and a rich shade of deep, brownish red. August to October is their season.

The everlasting *Helichrysum* 'Dargan Hill Monarch' is a small shrub (0.5m) that can be grown from seed or cuttings. There is a long succession of its papery yellow daisies held above rather greyish-green foliage. It has a season lasting till the first frosts.

There are three annual climbers that make wonderful fillers to clamber over other plants. The black-eyed Susan, *Thunbergia alata*, comes in three separate colours or a mixture of the three. Always, unless you have a prejudice against the colour, go for the orange strain, which is its natural colour and the most effective. The flower is rounded, spreading out from a tube, and has a black centre. *Ipomoea lobata* has short chains of tubular flowers whose colouring changes as the flowers age, from white, through yellow to orange. It is an unusual-looking climber. I have seen it making a column up peasticks, but I like it over *Cotoneaster horizontalis*, or over a rose or the dying stems of alstroemerias or delphiniums. It has many uses.

And *Rhodochiton atrosanguineus* makes long trails of dangling purple blossom with a seemingly unending season. The persistent calyx is like a lampshade. You get the longest flowering season from this if you sow it in September, pot the seedlings individually and overwinter them under just-frost-free glass, planting out in May. You will still get decent results by sowing now.

Another annual, or short-lived perennial, whose seeds it might be best to keep by for an August sowing so as to get strong, bushy plants to bed out the following spring, is the sweet scabious, *Scabiosa atropurpurea* (1m). I like this in its deep maroon 'Ace of Spades' strain, in which the pincushion of white stamens shows up in delightful contrast – a good cut flower for late summer.

Splitting and Replanting

The time to do a job is when you are in the mood to do it. The calendar is of less importance. If you wait till the 'right time', the chances are that you'll be thinking of other matters when that time arrives.

That said, your choice of the moment will make a difference to a plant's performance in the short term. For instance, when moving it or, even more radical, splitting and replanting it. Plants with a good network of fibrous roots can often be moved successfully at any season, by lifting them with a fat ball of soil and straight away transferring them to ready-made holes. But those with sparse or fleshy roots will not be so obliging.

Such perennials would be oriental poppies, lupins, anchusas, bearded irises, or peonies. In March they are already strongly active, both shoots and roots, and they will all be set to flower within a couple of months. Flowering will be badly affected if the plants are disturbed now. Even so, it may still be worth doing. Look beyond this year.

Your irises may have become so congested that they would produce little blossom anyway. If you replant the strongest pieces now, they'll get over their sulks within two or three months and be making wonderful fans of foliage by July, to the extent that they'll be all set to lay down flower bud initials before autumn's arrival and will put on an excellent performance next year.

For most plants whose flowering season is late summer to autumn, this is positively the best time to split and replant. *Schizostylis coccinea* (known in the days before political correctness as kaffir lilies) flower more freely and boldly if frequently replanted, but to perform well they do need plenty of moisture. In the south-east it is abnormally dry; you'll need not only to water in whatever you're moving – that's routine – but to soak from time to time during droughty summer conditions.

Michaelmas daisies benefit enormously from being replanted, even on an annual basis, and allowing one crown at each station in a group. Their moisture demands are not great, though mildew will be a problem on *Aster novi-belgii* varieties in a dry season. My advice would be to concentrate on other kinds of michaelmas.

Kniphofias, the genus of red hot (white hot, yellow hot) pokers, can now be lifted and split with impunity, shortening their lanky foliage to a convenient length as you do it. The June-flowering kinds will suffer in performance as a result, but not those that flower from August to October.

Disturb and replant your crocosmias if you wish but remember that their young shoots are extremely brittle. However careful you are, a large proportion will snap off. They'll be replaced, but flowering will be reduced. Crocosmias make chains of corms, one for each year. Only the terminal corm will be active until you split them up. You can then make a new plant from each dormant corm. On being treated as a separate unit, it will become a revitalised plant. They are very generous.

Ornamental grasses love to be split and replanted now. The glaucous-leaved *Helictotrichon* (*Avena*) *sempervirens* makes a porcupine hummock which looks extremely dowdy at this time of year, being interleaved with so much dead foliage. Put on your gloves and run your fingers repeatedly through its hair, and enormous quantities of dead leaves will come out. That may be all the attention that's required. If you can leave the clump undisturbed, it will rise to 1m and flower gracefully in late May. If it still looks bad after treatment, rather than cut the foliage hard back all over – which seldom gives good results in this case or with *Stipa gigantea* – lift the whole lot, split it, and replant a split. That'll give you a rejuvenated plant, with the brightest blue foliage later in the summer.

Stipa gigantea is one of the most beautiful of all flowering grasses from June to late summer. From a clumpy plant it rises to 1.8m with a gauze of diaphanous oat heads, rosy at first, then bleaching. Its foliage is unexciting at best, but you must never shear it back, as you can pampas and many other grasses. Tease out the dead stuff and only replant when the clump goes dead in the middle. If replanting is called for, now is the moment, but there'll be no flowering this year.

In my colony of *Molinia caerulea* 'Variegata', a clumpy grass with green and cream striped leaves and a haze of 60cm flower heads in autumn, rivers of mauve *Crocus tommasinianus* have seeded themselves into the channels between clumps. Expanded to the sun, they make a joyful display at the turn of this month and last.

This is a simple way to make better use of garden space and enjoy more than one season of interest. Start a few crocus corms, preferably choosing those that self-sow, among perennials that seldom need disturbing and which are relatively dormant until later spring. The subsequently dying crocus foliage will scarcely be noticed (especially if you look the other way) as the host's own young foliage takes over.

Snowdrops are my other great ally in this respect. I lift some clumps after flowering and spread them into any bare space that I do not expect to disturb for a while. With hostas and rodgersias, euphorbias and colchicums, for instance, and among clump-forming ferns.

The Perfect Tulip: Queen of Sheba

If I could have only one spring flower, it would be the tulip; if I could have only one type of tulip, it would be the lily-flowered, because of its elegance; and if I could choose but one of those, it would be 'Queen of Sheba'.

Its shape is beyond reproach, and seems to improve even when approaching dissolution. The warm, browny-orange colouring develops first on a still partially closed bloom, but already you can see that the petal margins are a lighter shade, close to yellow. The stem is on the slender side, so the flower is apt to arch over a little in one direction or another. As it matures, the flower becomes more relaxed and readier to open in sunshine. Soon, it is wide open, almost flat, and revealing its extraordinary interior. Around the centre is a design in murky, even lurid shades of green. The bloom is positively flaunting. You think it must imminently collapse, but it holds on beyond all expectations. What an achievement!

No other tulip comes anywhere near to this, although 'Queen of Sheba' comprises many features characteristic of the flower. It combines wonderfully with 'Fire King' wallflowers or, for a little more contrast, with pale yellow wallflowers. You can either distribute its bulbs among them or mass them in a block behind. If there is a dark background for much of the day, say in a north-west-facing border, so much the livelier.

Don't fuss it up by providing a background of mixed colours, such as mixed polyanthus or mixed wallflowers, because the tulip will fail to be highlighted in such a context. Simple theming will have greatest impact.

Euphorbias tune in especially well with many orange or red tulips. You can stick with lily-flowered types, whatever colour you prefer between them, they cover the whole range of the tulip's possible colourings. The softer, lighter orange of 'Ballerina' is another favourite, while 'Dyanito' is as unadulterated a shade of scarlet as you will find. Both are excellent with the shrubby *Euphorbia* x *martini*, for instance, or with *E. polychroma* and *E. polychroma* 'Major'. 'Queen of Sheba' would go well with them, too. Flowers in combination are generally more satisfying than when alone.

My one criticism of 'Queen of Sheba' in my garden is that, over the years, its bulbs decrease in size and numbers, and so need replenishing. There is nothing unusual about that, but on my rather heavy soil, tulips of many kinds actually increase if left undisturbed. But then, disturbance is often inevitable if spring bedding needs to give way to summer's.

Spiky Plants

It is essential to have spiky plants in any British garden, where most of the vegetation is soft-looking. They give an immediate lift (much like the first glass of champagne on a Sunday morning). The eye homes in on them, and only then seeks out the supporting cast. When I begin to think about them individually, they all seem to have one fault or another, but then that's no worse than with people.

One of the trickiest of these faults is hardiness. But this is a good time of the year to be writing about less hardy plants. We can worry about how to carry them over once we have enjoyed them through the summer. Grasses obviously qualify as spiky plants, but many of them have too narrow a leaf to look truly noble. Exceptionally, *Setaria palmifolia* has quite a broad leaf with handsome parallel ridges along its entire length. By the end of the season it will have made a large clump and you'll be tremendously proud of it, but it is tender and must be potted up and overwintered under frost-free glass – well worth the trouble, I assure you. It will grow about 0.5m tall, but more than double that height if it decides to flower in the autumn.

Of course, there are many other grasses. *Stipa gigantea* is one of the best, flowering at 2.5m in June and remaining presentable for at least three months if not exposed to fierce winds. But here, it is the flowering stalks rather than the spiky leaves that hold our attention. The leaves themselves are pretty mundane.

I am a great protagonist of blue lyme grass, *Leymus arenarius* (0.7m), which is tough as they come and very blue on its young foliage in early summer; either harmonise it with blue flowers (siting it at the border's front) or contrast it with red. I find that one clump is generally enough and it is the devil of a spreader, like a nightmare version of couch. Every spring, you need to dig it out and trace all runners that have strayed a metre or more; then replant the core material, cutting it back so that all its foliage is young and fresh. Fergus does this willingly, but not everyone would.

The desert-loving agaves from North America have a wonderful presence, the best known being *Agave americana*, which is glaucous, and, even more popular, 'Variegata', which has a broad yellow stripe either side of its long, fleshy leaves. These leaves, arranged in a loose rosette, take on seductive curves, and they are intriguingly marked with the shadow, so to speak, of the neighbouring leaf, left on it when the two were tightly furled together.

These agaves are hardy only in our coastal resorts, but it is well worth growing a few of them in pots and plunging these in key positions for the summer, as Beth Chatto does in her gravel garden, where the flattened domes of *Sedum* 'Herbstfreude' make a telling background.

Another way to use an agave is in a cluster of pots arranged for summer display on your patio or outside your entrance porch. Other plants around it can then be as soft as you like, but the agave will hold everything together.

Yuccas, also from North America, are as spiky as they come. Boldest, stiffest and as hardy as any is *Yucca gloriosa*. This makes a large globe of rather dangerously spiky leaves, and when a rosette is large enough it will flower dramatically, at 2m, with a huge candelabrum of waxy, cream-coloured bells. They may be borne any time from July to October. This yucca is so domineering that some people resent its overbearing presence, but it certainly makes its mark. It needs looking after; feed it well if you want flowers, and do not allow too many competing foliar crowns. It is also important, for the sake of smartness, to pull off old, dead foliage. The variegated form is a lot less solemn; also less vast.

Furcraea longaeva bears a strong resemblance to a yucca, but has a notably blue bloom on its leaves which are neither stiff nor sharply pointed. But it is not hardy and must be transferred in and out of doors as and when the weather demands.

Given milder winters, many phormiums have proved hardy. This is the New Zealand flax. *Phormium tenax* and its many named cultivars will make huge clumps, 2m or more high, which are, I have to say, rather awkward to manage. A clump can outgrow its allotted space and need reducing, but this is easier said than done. Even if you don't kill yourself lifting a colony and dividing it, the phormium itself will take a dim view of the proceedings and sulk for a long while afterwards. Still, you can't be ruled by your plants for ever.

P. cookianum is hardier and has flexible, not stiff, foliage. I am fond of *P. c.* 'Tricolor', which has green, purple and cream striping. It also flowers regularly, which is quite an event, although unconventional. On a low scale, *Sisyrinchium striatum* (0.5m), with spiky, iris-like leaves, makes a pretty plant in youth and has pale yellow flowers in early summer, but plants age badly, their leaves turning black. The variegated 'Aunt May' is a charmer in youth, but must be frequently renewed.

Irises themselves, especially the bearded kinds, are notably spiky, but generally become an eyesore once they have flowered. They do in my garden, anyway, whatever your claims (which I don't have to believe). If you repeatedly replant *Iris pallida* 'Argentea Variegata' (white variegated) and 'Variegata' (yellow variegated) in spring, forgetting about their flowers, they will remain smart foliage plants right through summer and autumn.

Soil Sickness

When a plant dies, or goes gaga, and needs replacing, we tend to put another of the same in its place. We cannot think, or don't want the bother of thinking, where we should like it better, or of anything we'd prefer instead.

Most of the time, this laissez-faire attitude works perfectly well. In fact, there are cases where it would be unwise to change the site: with border phloxes, for example, or oriental poppies. I'd like a change, you think.

But these plants come from bits of root that are left behind, and they'll always have the last laugh – if you thought you were replacing a pink phlox with a red one, say, you might well find you had both together.

But there are other cases when the ground mysteriously gets sick when replanted with the same species. Rose sickness is the best-known example. A rose may remain healthy for many years, but if you change your mind and want another in its place, the replacement is likely to be inhibited. It may, to an extent, recover from this initial setback, but it will never be as strong as if initially planted on ground where it was not preceded by another rose. In severe cases, it may even pine and die.

So, we are told to replace the soil in which the original rose grew with fresh soil from another part of the garden, or imported from elsewhere. Which is a crashing bore. But, in institutional gardens especially, where there is and has always been a rose garden or bed, its necessary presence is assumed. I inherited a rose garden, designed by Lutyens, and endured it for 75 years, but then rebelled. That garden has completely changed its character and I am a happier man. Its soil is the same as always, but now it grows plants other than roses to perfection.

Other plants are liable to replant troubles too. Liliums, most definitely: if you have a healthy colony of madonna lilies, *Lilium candidum*, for example, leave it undisturbed as long as it is productive. Encourage it with dressings of organic mulch, by all means (but not too thickly, as the bulbs like to be near the surface), but don't replant the bulbs unless you intend moving them to another site.

Primulas, including primroses and polyanthus, suffer from soil sickness. If you always do your spring bedding with polyanthus in the same bed, don't be surprised if half of them are dead by the spring after your autumn planting. But how many years must one wait before it's safe to plant them again in that position, without changing the soil? An obvious question, maybe, but one to which I have no certain reply; six or seven years, perhaps.

In an orchard, don't replant a pear with a pear, an apple with an apple, a plum with a plum or a cherry with a cherry. You might get away with it, but there is a risk of at least partial failure.

Another risk, when an old tree is being followed by a young one, is that the old tree might have been killed by a parasitic fungus, notably honey fungus, and that any residues left behind on old roots will move on to the young tree and kill that too – not at once, perhaps, but as soon as its initial growth slows down.

You can see when a tree has been parasitised by a fungus from the clusters of toadstools produced, often at the base of its trunk, but sometimes some way up it or from roots some distance from the trunk. When we want rid of such a tree at Great Dixter, we trace and remove as many roots as possible, and then let the ground rest for a couple of years. Often, a cluster of toadstools will appear within its previous orbit, so we mark the spot and then dig it, invariably finding a piece of old root that we had missed before. After three years or so, we find it is safe to plant again.

In general, then, if a plant grows healthily, it will keep ahead of serious parasitisation by soil-borne fungi. But when its growth slows, it becomes increasingly vulnerable. Yew, however, seems immune. I have lost trees growing in the middle of yew hedging, but the yew itself has never been infected.

Roses are at risk from honey fungus, as are *Euphorbia characias* subsp. *wulfenii* and irises, but it is easy – albeit wrongly – to blame deaths on a well-known cause.

I wish I could still grow monardas. I once had a fine colony of 'Cambridge Scarlet', sited where I needed its colour. By giving it top dressings of old potting compost in spring, it enjoyed good health for years. But now, I can't grow it there. Yes, I know about powdery mildew on monardas and I am prepared to protect against that. It has made no difference.

Bamboo

Even the smallest garden has room for a bamboo. It is a feature of powerful character and might often be considered instead of a tree. It makes a good lawn specimen; if its suckers show a tendency to wander, they are easily dealt with by the mower (provided your holidays are not too prolonged). Its appearance is enhanced if you have paving or a wall against which bamboo shadows can be cast. On a larger scale, I recommend planting a bamboo – as complete contrast to the huge leaves of *Gunnera manicata* – by a pond.

Don't just buy any coarse or too-easily propagated old thing from the nearest shop. It really is worth going to a specialist, even if you do have to pay a bit more. A further reason for this is that so much bamboo stock is misnamed. Some of us like to know what we're buying.

One thing often forgotten about a bamboo is that if you want it as a specimen, rather than as a screen, it will handsomely repay annual, or at least biennial, pruning. Cut out tired or weakened canes so that you can remove all accumulated debris and see right through the colony to the other side and beyond. Use a saw, and cut as low as you possibly can. This makes the job easier to repeat when it next comes round.

Bamboos have terrible names, and they are constantly changing. This has to be accepted. By and large, the genus Phyllostachys has changed less than most, and it is one of the best. Most evergreens, including bamboos, look pretty battered by the time they have come through the winter, but my phyllostachys are as fresh as ever. Best, and so graceful against a background of clipped yew, is P. *nigra*, in which the canes become black as they age, and that is a smart feature. Mine was an unnamed clone from another garden. It is as well to take advice on this question, as some forms of the species never turn black at all, or take a long time about it.

Then there is P. *aurea*, which isn't actually golden, but does make a luminous impression. Most of these bamboos will reach a height of 4m or 5m when settled in. Feed (with organic mulches) and water them generously. P. *bambusoides* includes a famous cultivar, 'Castilloni', in which the canes are a light shade of beige, but the flat side of each internode – this being a diagnostic feature of Phyllostachys – is green.

One thing about bamboos that makes people nervous is a tendency in some of them to spread at the edges – to be invasive. In our climate, with our relatively cool summers, the phyllostachys are pretty well behaved. 'Castilloni' does spread a little more than some, but friends will be glad to take pieces of it away for their own gardens. The time to move bamboos around, or to split them, should you want to, is in spring or summer, when they are active.

Some bamboos have very flexible canes, which is graceful, as in *Himalayacalamus falconeri*, especially when laden with raindrops, catching the light, but it can be space-consuming and administer an unwanted shower to passers-by.

By contrast, a very upright, even stiff, bamboo that keeps itself to itself and can do its duty for a fastigiate specimen, is *Semiarundinaria fastuosa*.

Its foliage is luxuriant. If you are including a bamboo in a mixed border planting, as a contrast in foliage and form, be sure that it is of a reasonably upright habit, otherwise it will overlay its neighbours.

The bamboo section at Kew Gardens is seldom visited as it is not too easily found, but one of its crowning glories is *Thamnocalamus crassinodus* 'Kew Beauty'. This is fantastically graceful, with narrow, elegant leaves, yet reasonably upright. However, its performance with me has been a bit disappointing, though it is growing well. I must move a piece to a slightly shaded position. In full sun, its foliage is apt to roll inwards at the margins – a habit of thin-leaved bamboos when they are over-exposed to sunshine.

A most extraordinary bamboo that I have grown for years on my front lawn (replacing a very boring ball-and-saucer topiary yew) is the Chilean *Chusquea culeou*. Perhaps it should be seen before deciding whether it is for you. Also, since it has frequently been raised from seed (when this is obtainable from Chile), it is very variable. Of stiff habit, the thick canes have internodes (solid, not hollow) every few inches, with a dense growth of foliage from each. This creates a giant 'bottlebrush' effect.

I must have had mine for 20 years or more, and we are taking the plunge of replanting a piece of it this spring, first excavating its site, removing the clay to a considerable depth (I fear I did not do this in the first instance) and replacing it with really good topsoil.

A piece that I gave to Beth Chatto has done so much better than mine, so I know we can do better. Mine is only 3m tall; hers, a lot more and it can be more still. Do keep control by removing old wood, so that it remains a see-through bamboo.

There are also two extremely charming, edge-of-border bamboos, both variegated, that I treat like grasses, cutting them to the ground each spring. Their young foliage is then of the freshest, and they grow no more than a metre high by the end of the season.

Pleioblastus (*Arundinaria*) *viridistriatus* is yellow and green, and quite dazzling in the early part of the season.

Choosing a Tree

Many gardeners will wish to plant trees this spring, as a result of the casualties of a stormy winter. Try and be a little original. After all, you can admire a double pink cherry in practically every roadside garden, during the few days when they're worth admiring; then you can turn your back on them and look at the more interesting trees you have planted yourself.

Evergreens to block out the neighbours are often a popular thought. *Ilex* x *altaclerensis* 'Belgica Aurea' is smart, of a good conical habit (leave it clothed with branches to the ground) and with long, elegant leaves margined in pale yellow. There are few prickles, and this is a welcome attribute for those of us who scrabble about among dead leaves with ungloved hands.

I.a. 'Golden King' also has a bold marginal variegation on a shorter leaf. I have enjoyed mine for more than 30 years and it is my handsomest border feature in the winter garden.

A bay tree, *Laurus nobilis*, will bulk up a good specimen in the course of time. Don't try to keep it to a single stem. The flowers smell delicious in spring and the leaves will be a valued component in your bouquet garni. The yellow-leaved form, 'Aurea', is excellent given a dark background.

The strawberry tree, *Arbutus unedo*, makes a good specimen in the south. Don't bother to shape this. It develops its own personality without assistance and the rufous colouring of its bark will slowly assert itself. The clusters of cream-coloured flowers appear in late autumn and are popular with Red Admiral butterflies. You can't count on getting strawberry-like fruits; they are pretty but taste of nothing.

If autumn colour appeals to you, remember that it doesn't last for long (any more than cherry blossom), so the tree's appearance at other seasons is of greater importance. With its constantly peeling cinnamon-coloured bark, so that each time you pass you can rub it to expose a smooth, fresh surface, *Acer griseum*, the paperbark maple, makes a delightful specimen. Even better in a group, if you can spare the space.

The sweet gum, *Liquidambar styraciflua*, has a maple-like leaf, though unrelated. It generally forms a tall but fairly narrow tree. To be sure of autumn colour, buy a named clone such as 'Lane Roberts' or 'Worplesdon'.

In wet (but not stagnant) soils, nyssas and the swamp cypress are a good bet. *Nyssa sylvatica* and *N. sinensis* both make small, shapely trees with branches that sweep to the ground.

Taxodium distichum, the swamp cypress, is a deciduous conifer that always changes to a warm foxy red in autumn. It does not demand a wet soil, so long as it doesn't dry out. It is slower growing than the comparable dawn redwood, *Metasequoia glyptostroboides*, but I much prefer its greater refinement.

Anyone who has admired the golden-rain-tree, *Koelreuteria paniculata*, growing in the Chelsea Physic Garden, might wonder why it is not more frequently seen. I was allowed to take cuttings of young shoots on that specimen's trunk and they rooted easily, but it is more often raised from seed.

Laburnums also carry the name of golden rain. Perhaps gardeners need no encouragement to plant them but they can't be too numerous for me. I would plead, however, that the clone called 'Vossii', which has the longest tresses, is not necessarily the best to plant. To dangle from an arbour or tunnel, yes, but as a free-standing specimen its habit develops less personality than does the Scotch laburnum, *Laburnum alpinum*.

The laburnum's late May to early June flowering could be followed by that of the flat, creamy white corymbs of an elder tree, *Sambucus nigra*. Again, they are deliciously scented but, unlike the laburnum, they are not poisonous.

The Exotic Garden

I find Mary Keen one of the most stimulating garden writers. She so often says what I should like to say myself. For instance: 'I love the crowded feeling of being surrounded by plants.' The jungle effect, one might call it, although maybe a real jungle would be rather too overpowering and threatening.

In the exotic garden with which I have replaced our rose garden, the formal paths now plunge through walls of lush vegetation. Foliage plays a major part, leaves being so much larger and lusher than flowers. Banana fronds (*Musa basjoo*) vie with the banana-like leaves of certain cannas: *Canna lutea* 'Musifolia' tells its own story, *C. iridiflora* has great green blades, edged with a tiny purple thread.

The paulownias (*Paulownia tomentosa*), stooled back almost to the ground in early spring, produce huge, heart-shaped leaves up to one metre across, and are furry to the touch. In contrast, tree of heaven seedlings (*Ailanthus altissima*), treated similarly, carry pinnate leaves, each perhaps 0.8 metres long, though I aim, by generous feeding, to get them longer.

Similarly pinnate, but with lacy divisions, is *Rhus glabra* 'Laciniata' (now clumsily renamed *R.* x *pulvinata* Autumn Lace Group). These last three are perfectly hardy, but make a tropical impression through the size of leaf, which hard pruning promotes. Castor oil, *Ricinus communis*, in purple and green-leaved forms, has palmate leaves. It is grown as an annual which we shall be sowing shortly. *Nicotiana sylvestris* has bright green paddle leaves supporting its spires of white, scented tubular blossom.

Dahlias are vital for the pure brilliance of their flower colours combined with beautiful shapes, and some have rich foliage, too. Canna flowers flaunt in hot summer weather. Close to the paths themselves, self-sown *Verbena bonariensis* makes a pierced wall of green stems and heads of soft, purple flowers from July to October. It is a see-through plant, not seriously blocking the view beyond, and it composes a theme throughout this garden. Still, we have to be strict with it, often cutting plants halfway back in mid-season, besides weeding out 99 per cent of its seedlings.

You weave your way through this vegetation, which encloses you up to head height and a little beyond, but never so high as to block out sunlight. I do make use of surrounding hedges, however, to give shade where it is appreciated, to begonias, ferns and streptocarpus (which delight in their summer airing).

One visitor, last autumn, was overheard to comment: 'This is a stupid garden. There are no vistas.' Well, the jungle effect does not ask for vistas. It asks for the satisfaction of immediate sensation. There are different ways of gardening. If you like to plunge, you can do so here.

On the other hand, there are occasions, I have to say, when I have not enjoyed the sensation of being crowded in. This happens in the garden that has simply become overgrown, without anything being done to control the scale. I remember visiting an old rhododendron garden in spring, where you slithered along greasy mud paths between the rhododendron trunks. These can be impressive in themselves, but any view of the blossom which their canopy was bearing would have needed to be taken from a helicopter.

Sometimes a large-scale rhododendron garden includes steep-sided ravines. Then there may be the opportunity to stand at a vantage point above and to look down on an undulating, heaving mass of magnolia blossom, say perhaps of the giant *Magnolia campbellii* itself, spilling rosy blossom and visible for once. Too often, it is way above your head, so that even when you have cricked your upturned neck, a dazzle of light or a lack of a highlighting background still prevents any possible appreciation of what you know to be there.

Such matters need to be thought of when planning for the jungle effect. How effectively wide you will allow your paths to be, is another question. Are wet legs or ankles a fair price to pay for the sensation of swishing through plants on either side? Sometimes, surely, yes, if there are alternative paths wide enough to allow comfortable passage without a soaking.

One of my favourite bamboos (and what could be more jungle-contributing than a bamboo?) *Himalayacalamus* (*Arundinaria*) *falconeri*, has glossy, olive-green canes at this time of year, when they stand mainly upright. But later on, under the weight of its elegant foliage, it will splay outwards, bowed by light-reflecting raindrops (or it may be dew). The jungle strikes back. But the sun may be shining and one soon dries off. Children would be delighted. It would be sad to lose all their spontaneous feeling in stodgy maturity. And I doubt that children are strongly aware of vistas.

Succession Planting: The Theory

One of our principal objects in the flower garden must be to keep the show going over as long a period as possible. A succession of interest and display is what we're after, at least from early April to the end of October, but not forgetting winter, either. At no point shall there be a lapse, a hole in our armoury. A continuous thread of successions, one highlight being immediately taken over by the next, is our aim.

No single group of plants can possibly achieve this, but to make use of the whole gamut of what is available to us, we shall adopt the mixed border concept. Shrubs will provide a permanent structure and the feel of continuity, but an all-shrub border quickly bores. Trees may demand too much space, if allowed to grow freely, but trees cut back annually and enjoyed for their young growth, sometimes also for the colouring of their winter stems, are far more controllable.

Herbaceous perennials are more flexible than trees or shrubs, yet still retain their virtues as anchor plants. Some may have an extended season, but most have one big climax, which can tie in with other mixed border ingredients, such as more ephemeral annuals or bedding plants.

These perennials generally have to take a deep breath as they swing into action in the early part of the year, and there is no better way of bridging this period than with spring bulbs. These can often be threaded through and between the individual clumps that together comprise a group. Not that all perennials require grouping. A singleton or double-ton may provide telling accents, especially if the plants in question have an individuality of habit that would be lost in a group. (We should forget the myth that odd numbers forming a group are good, even numbers bad; a doubleton, side by side, or one in front of another, may be just what you want.)

Bulbs, say tulips, can flow in rivulets, in this direction or that, often

77

between perennials of different kinds, and this in itself will promote the idea of our border being a tapestry, with many interweaving threads. This is far easier to see on the ground than to convey on a plan. I would always prefer to make up my mind on the spot about how to do my weaving, rather than be bound by any plan. We want to know which plants we'd like to see near to one another before starting, of course, and have them ready to hand, but after that, a measure of ad-libbing will give us a sense of exhilaration.

A word of warning, here. One and one and one and one adds up to a rash. Singletons are for the plant with individuality. Groups are for those that are clubbable types, shining in a party with plenty going on around them.

Self-sowers must be brought into the picture. We can never predict exactly where they will place themselves, but it is bound to be somewhere original and welcome some of the time. The other 99 per cent can be weeded out.

We can continue the spring bulb theme in summer, to an extent. Gladioli channelled through herbaceous peonies come to mind, but this role is largely taken over in summer and autumn by tender perennials that like to be bedded out. Cannas and dahlias are prime examples and will take our successions well into October, unless, in our anxiety to avoid the howling winds that batter these islands, we have foolishly chosen to live in a frost hollow. A case of Scylla and Charybdis.

Cannas and dahlias have tuberous roots and can take a rest in the dark, in winter. So can tuberous-rooted begonias. But for other ideas, we can look through the contents of greenhouses. Many of the plants we normally associate with pot culture can be turned out for a few late summer and early autumn months, and will go crazy with delight on finding themselves with a free root run.

Climbers, both annual and perennial, can be grown up poles, reaching for the sky, or over strong-framed shrubs. If a shrub cannot take its entire weight, some of it can be shared by a pole or peasticks put in alongside.

Our tapestry would be sadly incomplete without the contributive gaiety of annuals. We can either raise these from seed ourselves or, nowadays, buy them as plantlets. These annuals shout with delight, intent on cheering the world with colour and sheer joie de vivre. They are the icing on the cake and are infinitely obliging, both in planned plantings or for filling gaps. They have the freshness of the ephemeral. 'Here we are,' they sing, 'back again. Aren't you delighted to see us?' How could we not be?

These mixed border successions provide intense life and activity over a long period and the story is not over in winter. First, there is the inherited framework of handsome skeletons. Snowdrops are ideal in many places that have been released by deciduous shrubs, with all that space going for free now the leaves are off. Primroses and violets come into their own, and there are hellebores and winter aconites, all ready to take advantage of the so-called dead season – not dead in the least, but carrying us triumphantly forwards.

The more experienced we get, the better shall we play the game of continuity. Successions are a perpetuum mobile and we are the spinners of the wheel.

Succession Planting: Bulbs

With our sights always focused on getting best value over a long season – the ethic of 'I'm not greedy but I like a lot' – we constantly plan so that two plants of different seasons can share the same space without getting in each other's way.

Bulbs are often ideal for this purpose. Most will flower in spring before deciduous shrubs, and before many perennials have rubbed the sleep out of their eyes and become active. *Crocus tommasinianus*, say, will flower in February; it self-sows and will make a colony among the stems of the suckering dwarf almond, *Prunus tenella*, or around the crowns of the August-flowering willow gentian, *Gentiana asclepiadea*. The prunus will flower in May and the gentian in August.

Once the bulbs disappear, you may be afraid of chawing into them with a spade while they are dormant. The answer to that problem is they will be protected from damage by the proximity of the plants around which you have sited them. Suppose you planted winter aconites around your hostas, which works really well. The hostas' leaves will form an umbrella around the aconites snoozing underneath, just where you wouldn't dream of getting busy with a digging tool.

Japanese anemones, flowering from July on, are ideal hosts. Among them, I plant hyacinths, which often flower in February and then right through March. Later, *Allium cristophii*, with its big globes of stiff mauve petals, takes over. Its leaves, as with many alliums, are apt to die off before the flowers are fully out, but you'll be prevented from seeing this by the anemone's developing foliage.

Border phloxes come into leaf in very early spring, and no interference should hinder their development, but a small, wild snowdrop without big floppy leaves will serve you perfectly.

At the back of a deep, one-sided border, you might be growing big perennials. But something like the 2m yellow daisy, *Inula magnifica*, is late in leafing and can be interplanted first with snowdrops and then with tulips. Remember that while your border is comparatively empty, you can see to the back of it without hindrance, so quite small bulbs and hellebores will show up there, always provided that the flower colour is light. Dark colours need to be seen close to.

Some hardy cranesbills have a long, late-flowering season, but lend themselves to being planted around for early effect. Around the bright purple, dark-eyed *Geranium* 'Ann Folkard', which eventually has a great spread, we can grow quite strong bulbs such as camassias and Dutch irises. As these go dormant, the geranium takes over full command. Again, the pink geranium 'Mavis Simpson' has a long, late season but is less vigorous, so around that we have February-flowering, purple *Iris reticulata* interplanted with a late-ish snowdrop, the well-named 'Tiny'. There are some *Crocus tommasinianus* here, too.

But an early-flowering geranium such as G. *albanum* can itself be the first excitement in a colony of the late-developing *Hedychium densiflorum*. After flowering, the geranium copes with the canopy of the hedychium. This is a hardy member of the ginger family and makes a dense mat of fleshy rhizomes at the soil surface. The spikes of flowers, in July, are biscuit-coloured; its variety 'Assam Orange' is deeper orange and more exciting.

Eupatorium purpureum 'Atropurpureum' is a strong, 2m perennial with flat heads of purple flowers in high summer. It performs well at the back of a damp, one-sided border. You can interplant the clumps (if space is left) with tulips for an early show, but it is also feasible to overlay the tops of the eupatorium crowns themselves with low, creeping violets – the dog violet, *Viola riviniana*, works well.

The danger of including daffodils as early fillers is that the foliage of many of them is too coarse and obsessive, but some of the smaller kinds will serve us well. The *Narcissus cyclamineus* hybrid 'Dove Wings', for instance, gives early interest among clumps of *Hemerocallis* 'Marion Vaughn'. Both have strap leaves, but those of the later-flowering day lily take over from the narcissus, which is anyway not in the least coarse.

A good and unusual turn-and-turnabout act is *Narcissus tazetta*, an early flowerer, planted with the late-developing but long-flowering *Eucomis bicolor* (0.7m). This has thick stems of starry flowers crowned by a topknot of leaves, pineapple-style.

It is a lot of fun, stretching your wits and experimenting all the time. At the end of it, there'll never be a day in the year when your borders aren't worth looking at, even when under snow.

Succession Planting: Self-sowers

Gardens that give space to self-sowers have a comfortable, personal feel. These plants fill a gap and are wonderful accessories in our overall aim of keeping the show going.

Many people are frightened of self-sowers, thinking that, if allowed, they will lose control and that their garden will look a mess. So they apply thick mulches to prevent this. What they are missing!

However, a balance does need to be maintained. In a garden overrun by fennel, you'll be able to see nothing else by midsummer, though it is still nice to have a few of them growing in awkward cracks, between a wall and paving, say, where you wouldn't be able to plant anything yourself. I don't like to see *Alchemilla mollis* taking over, uncontrolled. It gets trodden on and bruised.

You need to think of self-sowers as allies that need to be controlled. You'll probably be weeding out 95 per cent of them. That's all right. Those that remain will do their job all the better for not having too much competition. The purple-leaved strain of orach, *Atriplex hortensis*, grows to 2m, casting quite a bit of shade. Just one of it, rather than 10, will do the job nicely.

So, in spring, let's be cheered by primroses – the wild kind. Their pale yellow colour shows up well at the back of a border and nothing will be competing with them for height when they are flowering in March–April. They are good fillers under deciduous shrubs, too, making use of the light, but able to cope happily with darkness when a canopy of leaves is overhead. Violets extend the season in the same way.

You may grow your own wallflowers, but they won't be flowering till the end of April. If you can leave some self-sowns between a hedge bottom and a lawn, where there is often a gap, they will last for years and start flowering as early as December. Antirrhinums, too. But they love to grow in uncemented walls, becoming hardy perennials in such a position and flowering much earlier than those you have raised from seed. I know an example, in Northumberland, where this has happened. It is on a bend in the road and is such an eye-catcher that any gardener-driver is liable to become a little dangerous at that point.

Deciduous ferns, such as the common male fern *Dryopteris filix-mas*, leaf out quite late, growing tall rather than wide. Allow a few forget-me-nots (myosotis) among them. Honesty, *Lunaria annua*, also makes a great companion in spring, and puts up, if necessary, with shade and a dry position. It self-sows like crazy, but the seedlings are easily spotted and thinned out.

The Welsh poppy, *Meconopsis cambrica*, in yellow or orange, is a great filler among deciduous shrubs, such as hydrangeas or the tall, late-flowering *Clerodendrum bungei*. The poppy is perennial, with quite deep roots and generally a second flowering. To keep control, you need to be on the spot when it is running to seed. Just grab all of its top growth and tug. It will break away cleanly from the roots.

Opium poppies, *Papaver somniferum* (often given a less suggestive name such as 'peony-flowered poppies') are annual self-sowers that work well among perennials. Start with a good strain and, over the years, most of its progeny will retain their original character. I have had a double pink one for as long as I can remember, and it still comes back. Any that are below par, I pull out when they reveal themselves. Sometimes these poppies germinate in autumn and survive the winter, making huge, earlier-flowering plants.

So, don't mulch but tickle your compost in with the tips of a garden fork. When the seedlings appear in their thousands, be ruthless about thinning them out. If you grow the lime-green *Smyrnium perfoliatum*

(1m) as a follow-on to early-flowering hellebores, you can see where they are quite early on and thin accordingly.

Many hellebores are themselves good self-sowers. The great advantage of our native stinking hellebore (don't worry, the stench is perfectly innocuous), *Helleborus foetidus*, is that the plant is evergreen, with handsome foliage. It tucks itself in among other border plants, looking comely all summer without getting in the way, and then, when everything else is dormant, providing us with sheaves of green, purple-edged bell flowers in the new year.

If you will but work with your self-sowers, controlling yet learning from them, they will provide great back-up in your goal of having a garden that always looks positive.

April

Taking Risks

We are now into the season for planting dangerously: that is, with desirable plants which are on the borderlines of hardiness for where we live. Every gardener worth his salt and with a grain of adventurousness takes risks. We hear enough from the pessimists with their dire prognoses on the effects of global warming, but they say nothing about the upside. There are many shrubs from which we can get years of fun (not to say thrills) despite their reputation for being tender.

A friend living near Stamford, in Lincolnshire, writes to me, saying, 'My *Coronilla glauca* "Variegata" (trained along the wall under the lounge window) has been flowering all winter. Does it ever stop?!' This is a gangling, pea-flowered shrub (officially *C. valentina* subsp. *glauca* 'Variegata') with airily white-variegated pinnate foliage and coronets of bright yellow, scented pea flowers. It has no business to be alive, let alone flourishing, in my friend's locality, but there you are. There is also a pale yellow variant, 'Citrina', if you prefer soft yellows, while *C. valentina* (0.4m) itself is of a dwarfer, denser habit and can be grown as a low shrub away from a wall. It also has a very long flowering season. Behind it you might grow the somewhat taller (1m) *Olearia stellulata*, often sold as *O.* x *scilloniensis*. Its small leaves are a slightly grey green, but are totally obliterated when the bush is smothered by pure white daisies in spring. The olearias come from New Zealand, a few from Australia. All are evergreen (like most tender shrubs) and many are worth a go.

For a large, sheltered, reasonably sunny space, I recommend *Azara serrata*. It has glossy, oval leaves and lots of rich yellow, fruit-scented blossom in May. Within the same space, you could include a true blue ceanothus. There are no shrubs to compare with these and the breeders have made a splendid job of improving them for garden purposes. They grow wild near to the Pacific coast of the United States, but although you see them in quantity, their colouring is never a match for the intense blues of some cultivated varieties. May is the peak of their flowering season and names to look out for include 'Puget Blue',

'Concha' and 'Cynthia Postan'. If trained to a sunny wall, their vigorous growth should be regularly trimmed back after flowering. Don't leave this job for several years and then have a major hack-back; they don't like being pruned into old, bare wood.

In any sheltered corner within an enclosed town garden, C. *arboreus* 'Trewithen Blue' (5m), of near tree-like proportions, will make an exciting early-flowering feature. It will be in full flower now. But for rather later – June flowering – a favourite of mine is 'Skylark', glossy-leaved, a good blue and not outrageously vigorous at 3m. Even later, starting in July and still evergreen, there are 'Autumnal Blue' and 'Burkwoodii'.

Feeling blue: it's almost peak flowering time for the ceanothus, whose cultivated varieties, such as 'Puget Blue' (above), are even more dazzling than those that grow wild in America.

Sowing Seed

This week, I aim to sow most of the seeds that start off in pots, plugs or trays. The days are long, the light is strong and there's plenty of sun heat – when there's a sun. Nature is on my side, and needs minimal help. I use no artificial heat for any seeds sown from April on.

Some plants require a long growing time before they flower: antirrhinums, for instance, and tuberous-rooted begonias.

For carnations to flower the same year they need to be sown early – say, in February – and aquilegias also take a long while to make strong plants. But if you haven't sown these early, when the use of artificial heat would have been necessary, there are other ways. You can sow the begonias in June, bring on the small tubers till they go to rest in autumn, store them dry, then bring them back into action in the spring and they'll be in fine fettle for a glorious display next year.

Antirrhinums will make very strong plants for next year if they are sown in late August and overwintered, separately potted, in a frame. Sweet scabiosa benefits from the same treatment. Annual carnations can be sown in October to flower the following year, and the border types, such as 'Florestan', can be sown in the next month, and seedlings lined out for the summer to make strong plants to go into their flowering positions (interplanted with tulips) in the autumn. Aquilegias, given a second year to grow on, will make magnificent plants.

Unless you take your sweet peas seriously, with your eye on a flower show, they can be sown any time up to the end of May. True, their flowering season will start late, but does that matter? You cannot expect it to last for more than six weeks, anyway. The main thing is to keep mildew at bay, with regular, protective sprayings.

We have been experimenting with annual poppies – a group notorious for disliking any sort of root disturbance. You can sow direct in their flowering positions, but much larger plants, with greater staying power, are obtained if given individual treatment. Take, for example, Thompson & Morgan's Angels' Choir poppies or the 'Ladybird' poppy – crimson red with a large, black blotch at the base of each petal. Broadcast seed thinly over a plug tray and thin the seedlings to one in each plug. That's best, but if you're neat-fingered, you can lift and separate the seedlings, when tiny, and prick them out into another tray of plugs. The first method, however, gives stronger root action.

This can be done in April or, for the strongest possible plants, in early autumn for next year.

I prefer to sow delphinium seed in March, but if sown now, you will still get strong plants for setting out when large enough (beware slugs) and to flower in August and September. That will give you the chance to rogue out any that are malformed, the wrong or a dirty colour or badly spaced along a distorted spike. Be severe in your selection, as seed strains yield a good deal of rubbish, yet a few really nice delphiniums. These can be saved to plant out next early spring – February.

We are always being advised not to move delphiniums in the autumn, because their roots are fragile and will easily break away from the ball. As they are dormant, they cannot make good the damage. This is true, but, if you are aware of the danger and the move is to be made swiftly, in your own garden, it can be done successfully in autumn, thus freeing the piece of ground where the seedlings were growing on. Again, take mildew precautions during the growing season.

We do not sow our tenderest annuals and bedding plants until May. Such are zinnias. Their seed germinates within four days, so they quickly make strong plants if the weather is right. The same happens with morning glory, *Ipomoea* 'Heavenly Blue', and with its climbing relative,

Ipomoea lobata. They are miserable if subjected to any suggestion of cold weather, their leaves turning yellow and looking pinched. Sow them late and don't plant out until June.

We were rather proud of ourselves last year, for making a success of Coleus hybrids, grown for their colourful foliage, but we didn't plant them out until the beginning of July. That still gave them enough time to make large plants, and their display was great from mid-August for more than two months. Sow in early May, therefore, and bring the seedlings on individually under glass protection.

Bedding dahlias that are sown in early May will flower from early July on, and are most useful for taking over from biennials such as foxgloves or Canterbury bells. Or from early-flowering perennials, such as pyrethrums, which can be moved out of the way, once flowered.

Cleome, the spider flower, grows quickly, but hates being cramped or held back. You can sow that any time from now until mid-May. Bring on the seedlings individually and plant them out just when you can see they need it. Then, they'll make huge, branching, long-flowering plants, each a metre high and across. You won't need many of them.

A curly-leaved parsley, for example 'Bravour' from Unwin, makes an excellent border ingredient of the liveliest, freshest green, to contrast with blue or orange flowers, for instance. Sow a pot of that in early May and bring on the seedlings in individual pots.

Plants in Unusual Places

When plants do unusual things in your garden, they often deserve to be encouraged. Walls, especially dry walls but any walls in which the rendering is crumbling a little, can be a source of great excitement.

We usually grow the 2m-high *Campanula pyramidalis* as a pot plant for indoor display in its August season, but in a public garden, which is where you least expect to see anything uncontrolled, I was once delighted to see one or two self-sown plants of this campanula in the cracks of a wall at Hampton Court.

Then, near Philadelphia city a couple of years ago, I spotted an outhouse with a sloping roof on which an opuntia had established itself.

It looked so happy, despite the winters there having far colder spells than we expect in Britain. Opuntias are cacti of the prickly pear persuasion, which make flattened pads covered in tufts of prickles (to be treated with respect); some of them, as evidenced there, are amazingly hardy. I can't wait to do something of this kind on my own premises, but am somewhat lost to know how an opuntia is to get a toe-hold on any of my roofs, and also how then to provide it with enough sustenance to live. (I have not been very successful with house-leeks.)

There is a long, wooden bench-seat in our garden, which is sheltered from wind and catches the midday sun. It is ideal, in late autumn and early spring – even in winter, if the weather is right – for enjoying a pre-lunch drink with friends. (The best time for champagne, Sir David Scott, then in his 90s, told me, is at 11am on a Sunday, when everyone else is in church.) Between the paving in front of this seat and the lawns either side, little strips of scented white violets, *Viola odorata*, established themselves years ago, without seeking anyone's permission; drinks time, mid-March is when I most enjoy them.

There are so many examples; you will have your own. The shrubby *Paeonia delavayi* is a pretty ungainly piece of goods, with thick stems to 2m and a short spring-flowering season. But the flowers are deep maroon and, although not large, they are rather nice and attract comment, so there must be something about them. Yet I scarcely feel this to be a plant deserving to take up border space. However, it has, in two places, established itself in the dry-stone walling surrounding our sunken garden and there it seems ideal, doing no harm to anyone.

Nearby, a red hot poker seeded itself in the same way. Who would be so crazy as to suggest kniphofias for dry-wall planting? But it was the plant's own choice and it has survived for many years.

Then there is the variegated *Arum italicum* 'Marmoratum' that a bird sowed in the crutch of an old wall-fig tree. Quite absurd, but charming, too.

My mother loved this relaxed kind of gardening. She was always planting snowdrops in odd places, and one of those has seeded itself into a crack in a dry wall. She also planted cyclamen seedlings – the autumn-flowering *Cyclamen hederifolium* – into wall cracks. They survive for years and their tubers look, when dormant, like toads. Eventually, they tend to lose support from behind and drop out.

My father liked everything to be just so and in its right place. So if a

Daphne mezereum, for instance, sowed itself in a step riser, I would, as a child, say to my mother 'we must protect it from Daddy and the gardeners'. On our sitting-out terrace, a seedling *Daphne tangutica* appeared some 20 years ago. There wasn't room for it to develop a stem between the paving cracks, so we chipped a corner of stone away for it and it still thrives.

Even more surprising, on the same terrace, was the appearance of a seedling *Azara microphylla*. This large shrub grows up a wall from the terrace below, and it is flowering as I write, wafting a delicious scent of hot chocolate. Till the seedling appeared, I never even knew that the parent made seeds, but I have since seen a few of them, looking like small white pebbles.

Of course, any garden in which no self-sowns were ever eliminated would quickly become an uncontrollable mess. But this seemed a special case, and the seedling, for which we again made space by chipping some stone away, is now some 5m high and I have allowed a travelling *Wisteria sinensis* to twine itself into the azara's branches.

It is easy to be gimmicky in your garden, and to earn a reputation for being a character because of the startling etceteras that you fit in, but if such additions are non-living things, I find they pall in the end. The plants themselves are what count for me. And when one of them does some strange antic, I'm on the watch; they make me laugh, and sometimes they persuade me to indulge.

Whether you do indulge or say 'enough' is for you to decide. It's your garden, isn't it? That's the whole point of having one. However, I'm glad to say that Fergus Garrett, who runs the garden for me, is generally of the same opinion as I am. It was he who suggested I write on this topic.

Greeny-Yellow Foliage in Spring

One of the most attractive features of spring is the fresh greeny-yellow of young leaves in certain plants. There is the rush, *Luzula sylvatica* 'Aurea', with low hummocks of coarse foliage that is at its brightest early in the year. Make full use of it then, as the colour fades and it ceases to be noticed.

'How shall we use it?' is the question gardeners should be asking themselves, because a garden is not just a collection of plants, but needs to present a picture. We enjoy the lungwort, *Pulmonaria saccharata* 'Frühlingshimmel', which is low and clumpy. It flowers at just the right time – pale blue with a touch of mauve included, too. Another is the herbaceous perennial *Euphorbia griffithii* 'Dixter', whose foliage on the young shoots is bronze. It will presently provide shade around it.

Valeriana phu 'Aurea' is another favourite of the early season, with fresh, lime-green foliage before it has reached any height to speak of (it flowers, nondescriptly, at 1m or so much later on). Blue and yellow make an obvious and effective contrast, and with the valerian we have x *Chionoscilla allenii*, a delicate-looking, scilla-like bulb. It might be tempting to slip in some bulbs of *Scilla siberica* 'Spring Beauty', but their colouring is so intense that they would dominate and kill the subtle valerian. Too much subtlety is a yawn, but I like it on my own terms. That's one of the great things about gardening: you can change the rules to suit yourself.

Take a good look at hemerocallis shoots early on when they are still low snouts. Some are a mouth-wateringly fresh greeny-yellow, and there is no vestige of sprawl in them yet. I can't recommend any particular variety, because so many of mine came to me unnamed from friends, and have none of the muscular, butch elements so many breeders strive for. They're charming in spring with any delicate, lightweight, white narcissus.

Bowles's golden sedge, *Carex elata* 'Aurea', is a plant to treasure, its colouring changing in unexpected ways. Quite early in the season, it does nothing much except flower very discreetly. But then the colour you were waiting for develops in the leaves and lasts several months. It is an accommodating plant, equally happy in shallow water or a moist border. I'd place it at the front of a border full of moisture lovers whose foliage is their strongest asset.

Finally, I must mention a summer-flowering perennial cornflower that combines yellow and blue in the same plant: *Centaurea montana* 'Gold Bullion' has lime-green leaves and blue flowers. Nature has done our thinking for us.

Planting in Pots

The air outside our porch is heavy with the scent of hyacinths. I grow lots of them, unforced, in pots, but there are plenty more in the garden to offer snatches of scent as one goes around.

Tulips and daffodils take over from them, and give a long season between the different varieties. *Narcissus cyclamineus* 'Jetfire' is as nice in a large pot as it is naturalising under meadow conditions, where it quickly clumps up, or as bedding among single white *Arabis alpina* 'Snow Peak'.

'Jetfire' has the unusual characteristic of a trumpet, intensifying rather than fading its orange colouring as it ages, as do the cups of most narcissi. And it flowers for a good three weeks rather early in the season.

The arabis should be raised from seed, sown now in a pot and grown on during the summer for bedding out in October. There are two rather late-flowering Jonquilla-type narcissi that I have found good for pot work: 'Suzy', which is deep yellow with a small orange cup, and 'Pipit', which is very pale yellow.

From mid-March, tulips make a grand display in pots or troughs. That can continue well into May. The shorter-stemmed kinds are best for the early part of their season, when strong winds are all too frequent.

By the same token, if the site is draughty avoid early flowerers with a large expanse of petal – hybrids of *T. fosteriana*. T. 'Purissima' (cream, fading to white) and 'Yellow Purissima' (a very clear, non-aggressive shade) are two I would not be without although choosing a sheltered spot. When growing the shorter-stemmed tulips – greigii hybrids, for instance – in containers, choose shallow examples, considerably wider than they are deep, so as to achieve good balance.

A deep container planted with short bulbs, polyanthus or wallflowers looks silly. In summer, such a situation can be rescued by including cascading plants that will spill over the rim. The softly felted grey foliage plant, *Helichrysum petiolare*, planted next month when the bulbs are finished, is ideal. The yellow, coreopsis-like *Bidens ferulifolia* is another. *Petunia integrifolia* is a cascading charmer, prolific, with quite small flowers in a shade of soft magenta. You buy it as a plant and keep it going from cuttings. Of seed strains, 'Purple Wave' is excellent, with a wide-spreading habit. It is so vivid a purple as to be nearly magenta. A new seed strain offered by Thompson & Morgan I intend to try is called 'Super Cascade', which can be obtained in separate colours or as a mixture.

Climbing plants in containers are effective for giving height, and they can be trained up brushwood to the desired height. For the spring, *Tropaeolum tricolor* is unbeatable. It has a twining habit, with small, palmately divided leaves setting off pixie-hat-shaped flowers, each with a long spur, rich, pure red, yellow and near-black around the rim.

If you buy one now, it will soon become dormant, but it will make fleshy tubers, which should be repotted in August and watered to get them started. Growth up a new set of twigs will continue throughout the winter under frost-free glass and flowering lasts for a couple of months each spring.

Looking ahead to summer, there are several climbers whose seeds you can sow now. *Lathyrus chloranthus* is a pea with lime-green flowers. Quite unusual. Also pea-flowered is *Dolichos lablab*, which is purple in the best forms, its unripe seed pods also purple. The morning glory, *Ipomoea tricolor* 'Heavenly Blue', is best not sown till early next month, as it is so sensitive to cold. *I. (Mina) lobata* is a close relation, though its flowers, in red, yellow and white (the colour changing with age), are tubular, borne in racemes.

Certain campanulas are wonderful pot plants, but you need to be thinking about them a year and a bit ahead. Sow now and grow the seedlings on, overwintering them in a cold frame.

Best known, though seldom grown as a pot plant, is the 'Canterbury Bell', *Campanula medium*, which makes a magnificent plant when given individual treatment. Colour varies between white, pink, light blue and purple. The trouble with a mixture is that you tend to get a heavy preponderance of one colour.

Single-flowered kinds are the most elegant, but if you insist on more colour for your money, there are doubles and cups-and-saucers.

The most striking campanula for pot-work is *C. pyramidalis*, in blue or white. Known as the 'chimney bellflower', it was traditionally stood (the plants 2m tall) in the fireplace when no fires were required during its August flowering season. It carries long spires of saucer-shaped flowers and, although hardy, is best brought indoors as soon as the first blooms open, to prevent their pollination by bees. Unpollinated, each flower will remain in condition for three weeks; pollinated, only for three days. It is much the same with all campanulas.

C. incurva and *C. formanekiana* are two other splendid biennial species to grow as pot specimens. Sow now and obtain large rosettes of furry foliage by the autumn, then pot on as the increase in plant size dictates. They will flower at midsummer next year, the *C. incurva* with large, ice-blue, upward-facing bells and the *C. formanekiana* with smaller and more refined ones of much the same colouring.

Tulips

We are now into the high season for tulips – and what a joy they are, especially when responding to the warmth of sunshine and opening wide to reveal those extraordinary colours and designs so often to be seen at the bloom's centre.

There will be a tulip competition at the RHS show in Westminster at the end of the month, but it can be guaranteed to be a non-event. It is curious that whereas narcissi have always received great attention within the Society, tulips have remained the poor relations. One theory I have heard to explain this is that the Dutch have done so much work on tulips that the RHS felt themselves upstaged and therefore looked the other way.

And yet tulips have far greater scope for development and variation than narcissi. I would add that they have far more personality. Narcissi are po-faced, always looking in the same direction, always predictable, never changing in response to sunshine or cloud, to warmth or to cold. This makes them reliable exhibition material; you know where you are with them. Whereas tulips are wayward and fool – or dazzle – you with all kinds of antics. Like the characters in a Dostoevsky novel, you never know quite where you stand with them.

I am growing more tulips than ever this year. There are always places to be found for them if you look, though you may not be ready to plant them straight away. It was after Christmas before we had planted our last, but tulips are very forgiving.

There are two ways of growing them as garden plants (we also grow them in containers, of course): either as spring bedding, in which case the bulbs will need to be lifted to make way for a summer sequence, or as permanencies among perennials or near to deciduous shrubs.

If your tulips need to be lifted while still in full growth, don't replant them hoping they won't have noticed the disturbance. You can't fool a tulip. Knock most of the soil off their roots and lay them on racks in a cool, airy shed. There they will withdraw nutrients back from stems and leaves into the bulbs. When sere, finish the job; pull out the withered stems, rub off any remaining soil from the bulbs and store them somewhere mouse-proof for the summer. We hang them in net bags (labelled) from a horizontal pole between two cross-beams. Squirrels would not be foiled, but mice are. At some stage (in that wet weather that never seems to materialise), we sort through our bulbs, separating those that are (or look) large enough to be used again for bedding next year from those that aren't. We don't throw these away, but line them out to grow on and be used again for bedding the year after.

If you retain old bulbs, you give them the chance of 'breaking' and of making for you those remarkable stripy tulips that feature in all the old Dutch flower paintings and were so highly regarded at that time, but which it has become illegal to sell, because we now know that 'breaking' is caused by virus infection. Like eating of the tree of knowledge, we can no longer live in happy ignorance. The viruses are still there and can never be eliminated, but we now go through the motions of shutting the stable door and pretending that the horse hasn't bolted, while knowing full well that it has.

So, if we want broken tulips (and who wouldn't?), we must let them occur on retained stock in our own gardens – which will happen sooner rather than later (the viruses are spread by aphids, which are ever with us), although always with unpredictable results. I haven't the space to go further into the subject here but you should certainly read Anna Pavord's fascinating monograph, *The Tulip*, for the full story. She writes with restrained passion and with a great deal of research behind her.

The second way of growing tulips, as border permanencies, is full of possibilities, as you discover more ways in which to use them. I grow a lot of border phloxes (*Phlox paniculata* and its cultivars); my heavy soil suits them. They need replanting every three or four years, but this gives me the opportunity of running tulips between their clumps and thereby pepping up an area in spring that would otherwise be rather dull. We did this with a late-flowering orange (flushed pink) tulip called 'Dillenburg', which is now coming up for its third season. And where there was initially one bulb, there are now clumps of several. Any gardener will appreciate how satisfying, not to say flattering, this is. The tulips really like us; hurrah!

But how shall we act when we really must rejuvenate our phlox plantings? That cannot for much longer be delayed. We can do it in the autumn, but cannot contemplate pulling the border to pieces until November, as we pride ourselves on our lively October garden. By November, the tulips will already be making strong new roots and the check would be serious. The answer is that we shall lift them during the summer, while their tops are still visible but they are fully dormant; then store them until we are ready to plant in November. Stored dry, they will remain dormant.

In other parts of the border, the tulips never need disturbing, as they are among perennials that detest disturbance. For instance, we have had the Darwin Hybrid 'Red Matador' with *Eryngium* x *oliverianum* for 30 years, and the tulip clumps are enormous.

Succession Planting: Bedding Plants

The flexibility of bedding out is what makes it exciting. It allows us to change our minds and expect almost immediate satisfaction. Nothing wrong with that, surely?

Bedding is apt to get a bad name because of the wretchedly mindless examples we see in public places. But at home, it gives us wonderful scope for variety. Lively and not so much with a song in its heart but an uninhibited shout of joy.

The most satisfying way to use bedding is to fully integrate it with plants of other kinds. Perennials or shrubs as neighbours will help both it and them. They provide substance; bedding will fill in the gaps but also send out its own messages of variety and liveliness. We can plant concentrations of bedding plants but allow them to wander at the edges in an exploratory mood, trickling through their neighbours. 'What's going on here?' they seem to ask.

Some perennials leave gaps when they have flowered. Oriental poppies perform in May–June, but what then? They lend themselves to being cut to the ground and the gaps we deliberately leave between plants can be filled with bedding – cannas, for example. Though in fact the old-fashioned scarlet *Papaver orientale* is so deep-rooted and obliging that we can actually plant on top of it – marigolds being suitable here. The giant fennels, Ferula, are imposing from the time their green appears in midwinter till they have flowered, in June. Then a blank. Again, bedding to the rescue – cosmos develops fast – and we can also interplant with tulips to flower before the fennel, whose leaves will act as a background.

Sometimes, our choice of bedding allows for three displays. At others, only two. For example, if we bed with *Dianthus* 'Rainbow Loveliness' (how can we deny ourselves its scent?), or some strain of *D. plumarius*, say, their territory will only be released for a possible follow-on in early summer.

The game of successions will start in early spring, with quite small things – primulas, primroses, polyanthus, anemones and auriculas, arabis and aubrieta. All sorts of bulbs, too. The scene is theirs because there is, as yet, little competition from the large-growing stuff. Small things can be clearly visible across even a deep one-sided border. A surge of colour is brought to a climax with tulips. These can either be replaced later on or, if they are worked in among the crowns of perennials arranged in groups (I would say clumps, only that sounds rather stodgy), they can remain there permanently, in nobody's way.

Come May, there are wallflowers. I always think this moment is epitomised by Siberian wallflowers – not the gentrified kinds in soft pastel shades, favoured by timid gardeners for whom bright colours are frightening, but the brilliant, clear orange that an uninhibited Siberian should be.

We can have an early summer show, which many gardeners omit, instead talking about the 'June gap'. It needs a bit of planning, that's all. Annual poppies are perfect. We have a special weakness for *Papaver commutatum*, the ladybird poppy, but other poppies or near-poppies (eschscholzias, *Hunnemannia fumariifolia*) are easily organised from early-autumn or early-spring sowings. It's the same story with the snow-white

Ammi majus and blue larkspurs, which go so well together. Also cynoglossums (*C. amabile*): the blue kinds are especially rewarding. Year-old plants of long-spurred aquilegias are great to fill this gap, the pale yellow *Aquilegia chrysantha* being especially elegant – perhaps interplanted with *Allium hollandicum* 'Purple Sensation'.

Then the summer show, planted out late June to early July and carrying us forward to the very end of the growing season. Here we have zinnias, sown at the turn of April–May (no heat required more than the sun's in a cold frame). What a thrilling blaze the giant kinds make. There are marigolds in many sizes and to suit all tastes; they have enormous staying power. Rudbeckias, including black-eyed Susans, are invaluable for getting into their swing in July and going on, boldly. Nothing flimsy about them.

Queening them all are dahlias, with cannas as a second string if reasonable heat can be expected. With global warming, this is increasingly likely. Dahlias come in many shapes and sizes and colours, and never fail to give an in-your-face display. Even the simplicity of singles makes a lovely show. We'll never reach the end of the capabilities of dahlias. My message is forget what's fashionable, and go for lots of colour and enjoyment of a good wallow.

Succession Planting: Climbing Plants

Climbers are invaluable adjuncts to keeping the show going. Their most obvious use is in conjunction with spring-flowering shrubs. Spring is the season when the majority of shrubs flower, but they tend to be lumps of inertia after that. Rhododendrons are the most obvious case: a blaze of colour followed by 11 months of sullen nothingness. Answer: drape some summer-performing climbers over them.

A classic example is *Tropaeolum speciosum*, the flame nasturtium. It has tuberous roots that run around and will do a terrific job all through the summer, particularly in areas where the climate is damp, cool and affected by mild south-westerlies blowing off the Atlantic. I have to warn you, though, that under a dry hedge in the eastern counties it will be useless, and it won't put up with much lime, either.

That is a special case, but hardy clematis, if satisfied at the root, can be grown anywhere. The most useful are those that flower on their young growth from mid-June to October, classified under the names 'Jackmanii', *viticella* and *texensis*.

The vigour of the clematis must be sensibly matched with that of the host plant, so that the one does not swamp the other. An example that generally works really well is C. x *triternata* 'Rubromarginata' over one of the winter-flowering *Mahonia* x *media* cultivars. The host must be given a number of years in which to become fully established with a solid framework. These mahonias can get leggy if not pruned, so they should have long growths shortened back in early spring. This makes for solidity that will take the weight of the clematis, which has a flush of deliciously scented blossom for a few weeks in July–August, after which it can be cut hard back, almost to ground level. The mahonia is then back in business.

One useful dodge with a climber whose entire weight would be too great for any given host is to place a stake strategically so that part of the climber can thread through the host, while the rest can be tied to the stake, creating a pillar of blossom beside it. There's one quite aggressive perennial climber that I nevertheless like to use at the back of my deep, one-sided border. This is the deciduous everlasting pea, *Lathyrus grandiflorus*, which we train up a curtain of pea sticks so that it reaches into the branches of pollarded silver willows above it. The pea has brilliant magenta flowers for many weeks, but then makes way for the willow, *Salix alba* var. *sericea*. The pea is wicked because it suckers, but we are still in command of it.

I have said nothing yet about what goes on underground. The climber must have sufficiently moist and not too rooty soil in which to explore, otherwise it cannot be expected to do its job. Under mixed border conditions, the ground will probably be well manured for the other contents, but if you plant in more open conditions, say against a tree, life may be less easy. Plant your climber well away from the base of a tree and lead it with string or insulated wire to reach the host, after which its weight will be carried from above.

We have a large, greedy cherry tree; spring-flowering, of course. I planted a vigorous climbing rose well outside its branches, but led it up and into the cherry on wires, which took some years, as the grass meadow in which they grow is highly competitive for moisture, so we

101

kept a cultivated and well-mulched area round the base of the rose. It is up there now and gives blossom in July, just when the cherry is at its dullest (except that it fruits and is appreciated by the birds).

John Treasure's garden, in Shropshire (Burford House Gardens), exemplifies the use of clematis within a traditional planting of heathers and conifers. When I saw it, summer-flowering clematis enlivened winter- and spring-flowering heathers by creeping horizontally among them. But where they encountered a vertical conifer, up into it they went.

In a mixed border, annual climbers may be the answer. For instance, where delphiniums have finished by mid-July, the red and yellow *Ipomoea lobata*, brought on in pots or plugs, would be just right as a follow-on. It is also a good filler after your *Alstroemeria ligtu* hybrids have done their stuff. Pull out their old stems and plant on top of them. Ditto your two-year-old *Verbena bonariensis* plants, which are early into flower but finish early. *Ipomoea lobata* makes an excellent follow-on, but will need a discreet stake. Succession gardening, you see, stretches the art of craftiness.

Clematis

One of the most delightful conceits for creating a happily integrated garden is to encourage clematis and other climbers to mantle shrubs that might otherwise look a bit dull in their off-season. This will allow you to grow more clematis than would otherwise be possible if you confined them to walls and fences. It is the way clematis grow in nature, we rightly reassure ourselves, and if shade at the roots is what they most like then their hosts will automatically provide it.

All this is true, but we also need to remember that no garden situation is static. Even if we plant with the idea of good-neighbourliness, the chances are that one of the protagonists will try to get the better of the other. It all looks charming initially, but at the end of the season we may discover that murder has been committed.

So a correspondent asks me for a solution where a clematis has flourished but, in one season, has killed or maimed a rhamnus, a choisya and two roses. She tries to close every easy escape that I might resort to in my reply. 'There are only so many tripods, posts and vertical supports that one can accommodate in a garden,' she protests.

And if I suggest she should grow large-flowered clematis as being less vigorous than the C. *viticella* types, well, she prefers the latter, thank you very much. So do I. They have a far longer flowering season than the earlier, large-flowered hybrids, and have a more natural habit of growth.

But as to there being limited scope for posts and vertical supports, I don't see it. An upright post takes up virtually no lateral space at all, and it makes use of vertical space that would otherwise go to waste. The ideal is to cut later-flowering clematis hard back at the end of the season, and to tie or train its new shoots to the post in the following year. The post will take all the clematis's weight, but if there is a nearby shrub over which it can negligently fling the odd vine, a delightful picture will result without any damage being done. In addition, you'll have a column of blossom up your post and everyone will be happy.

If you do allow a clematis to grow over a shrub, you must ensure that it is the right clematis – that is, not too enveloping and creative of darkness beneath it; and that it is the right sort of shrub – in other words, one that is of stiff habit and able to stand added weight on top of it without collapsing.

An ideal example for a number of years in my garden has been of *Clematis* x *triternata* 'Rubromarginata' growing over the top of *Mahonia* x *media* 'Buckland'.

The mahonia, which flowers in December, has a very strong, chunky framework because, every three years or so, I lop it back all over (right now is the ideal moment) to prevent it from becoming leggy and, in my eyes, ungainly. It breaks freely from the bare wood so exposed, and its flowering next winter is unaffected.

The clematis is a hybrid between white C. *flammula*, whose delicious airborne scent it inherits, and purple C. *viticella*. There are purple margins to a pale-centred flower. It is extremely prolific in its July–August season, but without producing very much foliage. So, as soon as it has flowered, by the end of August, we cut back all that flowered growth and the mahonia is freed for the next nine months.

No vertical post is involved in this case. But in another, I have the June to July-flowering Viticella hybrid 'Etoile Violette' growing up a fairly short chestnut pole – short because the clematis is quite near to the front of a mixed border. The clematis got there by accident, I have to admit, its roots being in some old potting soil with which we topped the border up. At the time, we didn't realise that a living clematis was being included, but we soon did, and we didn't like to discourage it. Well, it grew with a vengeance and killed a couple of daisy bushes, *Olearia* x *scilloniensis*, before we appreciated that the situation was critical and provided the post.

Next door is an extremely strong and stiff Hybrid Tea rose, the pink 'Paul McCartney'. Some of the clematis strays harmlessly on to that and, as the clematis itself is purple with a white eye, the team works excellently.

The July-flowering 'Perle d'Azur' is one of the best summer-flowering, near-blue clematis around, but it has tremendously long internodes that give it a rangy habit. It is quite a heavyweight. 'Prince Charles' is far shorter-jointed and less consuming of space. Its flowers are of the same colouring, but a lot smaller – however, as is always the case, size is compensated for by the numbers of blooms produced. So here we have a prolific clematis of moderate growth and I grow it over the clear pink-flowered *Hebe* 'Watson's Pink'. Thanks to mild winters, this is 1.8m high. Its texture is rather soft, but it copes well and the two colours are charming together. I dare say the situation will have to be reviewed – I fancy that the hebe would benefit from a hard cut-back itself – but we constantly need to adjust. Nothing tragic about that.

As for growing something through my own enormous yet by no means stiff Mexican orange, *Choisya ternata*, to pep it up after its May flowering, I have *Berberidopsis corallina*, an evergreen climber with pendant clusters of rich red flowers in summer. It is not easily pleased, but seems to respond to heavy mulching. If it succeeds in smothering my 50-year-old choisya, I'll join in its triumph.

Perennial Favourites

Spring is the best time to plant a range of perennial fillers with the merit of flowering for a very long time. They may be short-lived, they may not be winter-hardy, but they grow quickly and give value. Some of them have come up in the gardening world in recent years, with a good deal of hybridisation and muddle over their naming.

Argyranthemums were at one time best known for the Paris daisy, then classified as *Chrysanthemum frutescens*, much used, as it still is, in the window boxes planted up by institutions in London. It is a white-flowered daisy with dark green leaves. Of greater interest is the fine, glaucous-leaved A. *foeniculaceum*, again with white daisies, on a strongly bushy plant.

The best strains flower pretty continuously through the summer – worth mentioning, as many argyranthemums have a tendency to turn green and purely vegetative when the days are at their longest. They need a 12-hour night, at least, if they are to make flower buds in any quantity. Generally reliable in its flowering is the soft yellow 'Jamaica Primrose', while 'Vancouver' is deep pink and gives an impression of doubleness, with a central cushion of enlarged florets, a condition known as anemone-centred.

Osteospermums, once known as dimorphotheca, are also in the daisy family and they, too, have a tendency to become vegetative at the height of summer, though breeding has aimed for a long, uninterrupted flowering season. If your plants should die suddenly and unaccountably – not to say disobligingly – in the middle of their flowering season, they will have become victims of a soil-borne fungus. Apart from sterilising the ground – not easy for the amateur gardener – the only remedy is to grow them in an unaffected part of the garden, hoping it will remain that way.

The one I have grown for many years is O. *ecklonis* var. *prostratum*. This has white daisies with a blue disc and bluish reverse to the rays. When flowering freely, it is quite dazzling, being opened wide by sunshine. When old growth survives the winter (about half the time),

105

flowering will be at its freest in May, but a decent crop continues into autumn. Of similar colouring, but with rather smaller flowers and on a more compact plant, is 'Weetwood'. 'Lady Leitrim' is another white (slightly grubby), which is particularly hardy and long-lived.

O. *jucundum* is a reliable survivor, making a large, loose mat, smothered with pinky-mauve daisies having a blue disc. If it becomes unruly, cut it hard back halfway through the season.

'Blackthorn Seedling' is compact and has deep pink flowers. It is a variety of O. *jucundum*. 'Stardust' impressed me, being upright, free over a long period and bright pink. The well-known 'Whirlygig' is blue and white, each ray pinched in at the centre. 'Pink Whirls' is, unsurprisingly, a pink version. Of soft yellow colouring and bushy habit, 'Buttermilk' is a charmer when well suited.

Diascias have come up in the world. They have hooded flowers resembling nemesias. There is a marked tendency to salmon-pink colouring and a sprawling habit. They flower and flower, which leads to weediness halfway through the summer. Even though they will still be in flower, cut them back to within 8 or 10cm of the base in July, and they will bear a freshened crop a few weeks later.

In a sink, sometimes with the blue, loose-textured *Lobelia richardsonii* for contrast, I grow the reasonably compact *Diascia* 'Ruby Field', which is deep pink. *D. rigescens*, anything but rigid, is large-flowered with long racemes in salmon pink. It is very showy, tender and coarse-grained, but exciting until you tire of it. 'Blackthorn Apricot' is biscuit-coloured, which makes a change, as do 'Lilac Mist' and 'Lilac Belle'. They are fairly hardy, but young plants give the best account of themselves. Quite often, they'll layer themselves, and you can renew your stock from these layers.

The showy penstemon hybrids that we grow for bedding will sometimes last for three years before they need replacing with young stock. Old plants are best cut hard back at this season and will be at their peak in July. 'Garnet', for instance, is vigorous to 1m and of a brilliant colouring – reddish purple verging on magenta. But that's a clean, useful shade if its strength doesn't frighten you.

The best red I have seen in recent years is 'Chester Scarlet'. That sailed through last winter. 'Evelyn' is petite, with slender flowers on slender racemes – clear pink, fairly dwarf, the leaves fine and grassy. On a larger scale, 'Hidcote Pink' is tall at 1m, free-flowering with fair-sized pink funnels. In 'Alice Hindley' (not at all hardy), the mauve funnels are large on a tall plant. 'White Bedder' (sometimes misnamed 'Snow Storm') is of medium height and the best in that colour.

Perennials as Bedding Plants

A whole range of perennials can be used as bedding plants, although we might not normally think of them as such. They make our gardening far more flexible, but we must have some back-up area in which to let them develop.

Michaelmas daisies of most kinds can be brought on in seclusion. They contribute nothing to a border in summer, but we shall be grateful to them come the autumn, when we can give the plants a heavy soaking and transfer them to replace earlier performers – annuals, very likely – that have fizzled out. Water them in heavily, and off they'll go. Outdoor chrysanthemums can be treated in exactly the same way.

A Michaelmas daisy with a difference is *Aster* x *frikartii* 'Mönch' (0.8m), which flowers non-stop from late July to October. If you take cuttings of its young shoots now and then, grow them on in pots, they'll have made flowering plants by late summer and can be moved into the display bed. They team up particularly well with a black-eyed Susan (*Rudbeckia fulgida* var. *deamii* or var. *sullivantii* 'Goldsturm'), which has bright yellow flowers with a black central cone.

If you have a stock plant, you can take cuttings from that now, and line them out when they've rooted or pot them individually. Alternatively, if you have a large stock plant, split and line that out now and transfer it to the bed when the space is vacant.

Perennial lobelias are very much to our purpose. If starting from scratch, sow seed now of *Lobelia* 'Fan Scharlach'. They won't make large plants this season, but can be grown on in the usual way, lifted in the autumn and bedded into a cold frame for the winter, or over-wintered under a greenhouse bench. Their resting state is in the form of leafy rosettes at ground level. Get these moving next spring, split them if large enough (this is also the treatment for established colonies), and grow them on either in pots or in open ground until they are on the point of flowering. They can then be moved to their display sites.

Anthemis tinctoria, a species with bright or pale yellow daisies, is one of my favourite perennials for bedding. Young plants are easier to handle than old, and they flower for much longer. If left in situ, old plants tend to become tall and unwieldy and to go down to mildew, so take basal cuttings from mossy ground-level shoots in winter or very early spring. Grow them on and bed them out in May. They will flower from early July until late autumn at 0.7m. Each plant will have only one stem, needing one cane and a single tie. You'll need to dead-head once during the flowering period. Very rewarding.

I love long-spurred aquilegias, but they do have a limited season, finished by late June. Rather than have them cluttering up an important site for the rest of the summer, we often cut them back after flowering and transfer them to a reserve plot to grow on in discreet retirement, bringing them back to their display area in autumn. They can be interplanted with spring bulbs. Although easily raised from seed, seedlings take quite a while to mature, so you may like to grow them on, out of the way, until the plants are large enough to make an impression.

All this may sound like gardening made difficult, but it is so worthwhile if you have an important display area – a border seen from the house, maybe – and want to keep it at full stretch for as long a season as possible.

Planting between the Roots of Trees

Dry shade is a recurring problem, but there are different kinds. There is the predictable shade from buildings all around you, there is the seasonal shade from deciduous trees, and there is the shade beneath evergreens, which is the heaviest.

Under difficult circumstances, you must give the plants of your choice a good start; they in their turn must then be able to cope without further cosseting. Where trees are involved, whatever you plant will quickly be invaded by tree roots.

Obviously you can't cut big tree roots, but you can find spaces between these and create pockets of decent soil with plenty of organic matter added. Rather than aiming at a uniform sheet of one kind of plant, it is better to vary the plant content, with different shapes and colours.

Euphorbia amygdaloides var. *robbiae* is always a great ally, with its year-round rosettes of dark green foliage. It is shrubby, with green flowering spikes in spring. After flowering, you can cut these down, making room for fresh growth. It has a mildly suckering habit that builds into a colony.

The advantage of Welsh poppies, *Meconopsis cambrica*, which may be orange or yellow, is that they self-sow and do some of the work for you. Once they have had their first flush, in May, sweep the lot away (they break off cleanly at ground level) and you can rely on them to grow again.

We may think of ferns as moisture-loving, but some are amenable to drought conditions, in particular the polypodies. I have a particularly soft spot for *Polypodium* 'Cornubiense', which is a bright and cheerful green. It goes well with the solid, dark green butcher's broom, *Ruscus aculeatus*, of which you must get the hermaphrodite form so that crops of its cheerful red berries are assured. These will last year round.

The variegated-leaved *Arum italicum*, often known as 'Marmoratum', is deciduous but with a long season, from autumn to May. It gets bird-sown in a charming way – seedlings appearing in unexpected places. *Epimedium pinnatum* subsp. *colchicum* is reliable evergreen ground cover. When it looks tired, by February, the whole colony should be razed to the ground, as the coppery young foliage that follows is a spring attraction and accompanied with pale yellow flowers. Dry shade can be interesting and we don't need to wring our hands over it.

Sunflowers

Yellow daisies, many of them called sunflowers, can give our borders a great boost from midsummer on. They epitomise the light of later summer and autumn, and have a richness all their own. Many unenlightened gardeners will say, with disgust, 'All that yellow', but the general popularity of this class of plant is being recognised in trials during the next few years of perennial Helenium, Heliopsis, Helianthus, Inula, Solidago (golden rod), Coreopsis and Rudbeckia, which are being run at the RHS Garden, Wisley.

Many Helianthus, the traditional sunflower, are annuals. Of the perennials, I have often written about *H. salicifolius*, principally as a most unusual foliage plant. 'Capenoch Star' is a splendid, long-flowering border perennial, 1.3m tall and requiring no support. It has a disc of enlarged, tubular florets, known as anemone-centred. 'Lemon Queen' will soothe the nerves of those who find bright yellow difficult. On a 2m (rather floppy) plant are borne an abundance of small, pale yellow daisies from late August on. The sometimes inconvenient height of this plant can be reduced (as with many perennials), by lifting and replanting each spring.

Heliopsis have smooth leaves and, by and large, grow no taller than 1m. Their colouring is the richest shade of golden yellow imaginable. Varieties such as 'Summer Sun' (correctly 'Sommersonne') have several rows of petals. Heliopsis take time to settle down, and should not be submitted to competition by near neighbours.

Helenium have a profusion of small daisies in yellow or bronze, or a mixture of the two. The central boss of florets is prominent and the rays tend to hang downwards. Their heights vary from 0.6m to 2m, and some are quite late flowering. For my money, I would go for the old variety 'Moerheim Beauty' (bronze, 1.2m), which starts to flower in early July and can then be relied upon (especially if dead-headed) to produce a second crop in September. None of the later-flowering kinds can do this. There is a fairly recent, and so far unidentified, disease of Heleniums (which I am glad not yet to have met), causing root rot in the dormant season.

The other genus of sunflowers with a prominent central disc is the cone flower, Rudbeckia. (Echinacea is closely related to this, but pinkish.) One of the most useful is *R. fulgida* var. *sullivantii* 'Goldsturm' (0.7m), of wiry, branching habit, with rich yellow, black-centred daisies. 'Black-eyed Susan' is one of its popular names, also applied to other rudbeckias. In moist soil, this is excellent for lighting up shaded positions. *R. fulgida* var. *deamii* more prolific, but later flowering – September.

The green-coned 'Autumn Sun' ('Herbstsonne') (2.5m) may be an inconvenient height, but is less floppy if grown in an exposed situation.

It has a long, late-summer flowering period and is a wonderfully luminous shade of yellow. Plenty of moisture is needed for this.

Inula vary greatly in height. *I. magnifica* (2m) is well named, but there are inferior clones around. On a nobly wide-branching plant, it carries big daisies with long rays. This is reasonably self-supporting, and I grow it as a late feature in a meadow area. *I. hookeri* (1m) is a rampant perennial, but with flowers of great delicacy.

The buds are twisted into a spiral and open to finest yellow rays, with a hint of green. *I. orientalis* (*I. glandulosa*) (0.4m) is similar as to habit, but smaller, with orange-yellow daisies.

Avoid elecampane, *I. helenium* (2m), which is sold to those with herb gardens. It has miserable little daisies. We should want our herbs to look nice. Solidago are mostly called golden this and golden that, but are as yellow as they come.

Best Coreopsis is C. *verticillata* (0.5m) with stiff stems and feathery leaves. It makes a colony with its bright yellow rhizomes. Go for the type-plant, rather than the 'Grandiflora' or the 'Moonbeam'. There are several Coreopsis with 'Sun' in their names, such as 'Golden Sunrise' (0.4m), some of them raisable from seed. Again, in our climate, a proportion of the seedlings will flower in their first year, while others remain vegetative until the second season. They are the most pungent and dazzling shade of yellow imaginable, but need to be dead-headed, as they cling to their old, brown petals.

Spring Scent

Flower and plant scents are with us all year round, and though most are pleasing, a few are disagreeable. But then, opinions differ in this respect.

Many people's eyes moisten, as they exclaim, 'Ah, box! How that takes one back', and a vision is conjured up of granny in her bonnet fossicking among the granny's bonnets that have seeded at the bottom of the box hedge. That particular smell summons no nostalgia in me, but then I have always gardened where I still am. It needs a break and a move for the pangs of nostalgia to be evoked, and I can do without them. Last year, everyone's box bushes flowered like mad in April – quite an event, in its small way – but I've seen no signs this time.

The heavy, immoral scent of *Osmanthus delavayi* is our forte at Dixter just now, and it continues to waft over half the garden long after the white blossom has browned. Trim the bush over as soon as it has flowered, and it will flower all the better next year. O. x *burkwoodii* is similar, but hardier, and its leaves are coarser.

At about the same time, we can enjoy a group of viburnums, whose fragrance comes close to that of carnations: *Viburnum carlesii* (dull leaves all summer) V. x *juddii*, V. x *burkwoodii* (semi-evergreen one wishes it would make up its mind) V. x *carlcephalum* (the showiest and insufferably coarse). They have closely packed, domed heads of white flowers, with more or less of pink in the bud, and have a delicious scent of pinks until you approach too close and wish you hadn't. These make large shrubs which are passengers for 50 weeks of the year, so use them sparingly.

Daphnes are a subject all to themselves. Perhaps the most rewarding is *Daphne tangutica*, an evergreen and, in my experience, long-lived and not subject to the lethal daphne disease. It is not a particularly elegant shrub, but wonderfully scented from evening to morning. There are two flowerings: the first in April, the second over quite a long summer period. A metre high, the bush may spread a good deal wider.

D. *tangutica* Retusa Group is far more compact and slower growing. As an investment, it is the better plant, though it does take a long while to fill out.

Azara microphylla is wafting a mouth-watering smell of chocolate as I write. It has aspirations to make a tree, but it may get clobbered by a hard winter. The foliage is neat. Larger is A. *serrata*, whose flowers make puffs of deep yellow in May, and it is excellent (and fast growing) against a sunny wall, although it bulks forward quite a bit. The scent is of fresh fruit salad.

Another foody scent is that of gorse, *Ulex europaeus*, which may flower at any season but is most free now. It is too rough a subject for polite gardening but the double-flowered form makes a tremendous show, each bloom providing twice as much colour as normal. The scent is of coconut. Another yellow, pea-flowered shrub, which may flower generously in autumn (and even in winter, if mild) but which reaches a climax now, is *Coronilla valentina*. It seldom grows taller than 0.5m and has a strong, warm, sunny smell.

Of fruit blossom, the strongest is the pear's, which is sickly sweet and unlike anything else. I love it.

The deciduous species of Elaeagnus flower now or very soon, my favourite for fragrance being *E. umbellata*, though its foliage is somewhat dull. *E. angustifolia* is just as strong, if less prolific, and has the advantage of silver-grey foliage, especially in 'Quicksilver' (syn. Caspica Group), whose scent is almondy.

In the evergreen *Clematis armandii*, the scent is of vanilla – it is cloying, but how nice to be cloyed. This is a vigorous species that can look rather awful if allowed to hold on to its old foliage indefinitely, so give it a hard pruning immediately after it has flowered. And never mind if, at the same time, you remove young shoots as well. Plenty more will soon come along.

Wallflowers . . . and more nostalgia. If you don't want to grow them for bedding every year, keep a few old plants where they won't be in the way, under a hedge bottom for example. I was picking bunches of these well before the end of March. The Siberian wallflower, with its bright, clean, orange colouring (loathed by the weak-stomached), flowers a little later, being at its best in May, and has a different scent, albeit one that is just as good.

You don't really expect a pleasant scent from euphorbias and, indeed, that of *E. characias* is curiously musty, not unlike the typical azalea scent but less sweet. The cypress spurge, *E. cyparissias*, however, is honey-scented on the air and, like tiny crystals, has the light-catching sparkle common in certain spurges when the sun is on them. Its columns of linear leaves are pretty, too, and they turn bright autumn reds, though it is a grand coloniser (i.e. watch it). The big, shrubby *E. mellifera* is, as its name indicates, also honey-scented but its flowers are drab. It is a magnificent foliage shrub in its youth, but it needs shelter and is best replaced after a heavy flowering from its own seedlings. Old specimens become scruffy.

Of course, we have been enjoying the fragrance of many narcissi, especially those of the Tazetta and Jonquilla groups. But the best comes last: the poet's narcissus or pheasant's eye, *Narcissus poeticus* var. *recurvus*, is so rewarding to pick for the house, where it can be combined with trusses of an early lilac.

Fast-growing Shrubs

Mobile-home owners need quick results from a garden they do not expect to own for more than three or four years. There are some shrubs which, if planted now, will give surprisingly satisfying results even in the year of planting. By next year, they will start to look as though they intend to take over, and the year after that, they will have done so. It is all a part of the jungle syndrome.

The mallow, *Lavatera olbia*, alias *L. o.* 'Rosea' or plain 'Rosea', is an obvious candidate, being a fast-growing 'tree' mallow with a succession of pinky-mauve flowers from late June to autumn. The pale pink 'Barnsley' is a quieter-toned version of this, but tends to revert to the old 'Adam' from which it derived, with bright pink creeping in. These will reach two metres by the end of the season. Shorten them back by half in November, and by half again in spring, to stop the wind from breaking them up.

Similar results will be obtained from the 'tree' lupin, *Lupinus arboreus*, which carries upright candles of pale yellow (sometimes white) flowers in early summer. Trim it as soon as it has flowered. It has a delicious scent and its bright green foliage is a cheerful winter feature.

The Spanish broom, *Spartium junceum*, has rush-like stems and quite large, scented pea flowers, which are bright, but not aggressive, yellow. If hard-pruned in spring, it will flower from July. If unpruned, flowering starts in June but ends earlier, and the shrub will get leggy and need a stake. That goes for quite a number of the brooms, notably *Cytisus multiflorus*, widely, though incorrectly, known as *C. albus*. This is the Portugal broom, and it presents its innumerable, small white flowers along wands which, in bulk, look like a firework display. To prolong its life and mitigate its legginess, shear off all its flowered shoots immediately after flowering in June.

Of the many fast-growing brooms, the April-flowering *C.* x *praecox* is my favourite, because its habit is naturally more compact, though it still benefits from a cut-back after flowering. This is soft, primrose yellow, with a sharp, rather disagreeable scent (you can't have everything).

Some say *C. battandieri* smells of pineapple, others of fresh fruit salad. The yellow flowers are gathered into short, dense columns and the trifoliate leaves are silvery with soft felt. Trying to train this to a wall, as many do, is a mistake, as its growth is too exuberant to keep it in without heavy pruning, and that eliminates much of its potential flowering. Give it a place in the open and plenty of space. A good partner would be *Solanum crispum*, which carries clustered mauve potato flowers with a yellow centre.

Sunshine and free drainage are the prerequisites of the genus Cistus. Its members are all baskers in the maquis country of southern Europe and most of them have a warm, gummy aroma, free on the air, even in winter. Flowers open at sunrise and shatter in the early afternoon, if the weather is hot. If wet, they just look bedraggled.

'Peggy Sammons' and *C. x skanbergii* are both soft pink, the latter spreading but low-growing. *C. x purpureus* is tallish and an exciting magenta with dark central blotches. *C. x cyprius*, with its large white flowers and central maroon blotches, is my favourite. The leaves are quite a feature in winter, turning the colour of oxidised lead, and the plant sprawls but reaches a height of 2m. Halimium is closely related, but in cheerful yellow. *H. lasianthum* subsp. *formosum* is a low-spreader with grey leaves and small, but numerous yellow flowers, dotted with maroon spots, one at the base of each petal. From there, you go down to Helianthemum, the sun roses, which make dense mats and come in a wide range of colours, sometimes double.

Ceanothus are quick off the mark, the earlier flowering kinds being evergreen. They are not always very hardy, but this is the ideal moment to get them established and their hardiness is often worth risking. The best have clear blue flowers. I recommend 'Puget Blue', which is May flowering, and 'Skylark', at its best in June. These may need staking, but if you buy a plant that has not become root-bound in its container, it has a better chance of standing securely on its own legs.

C. thyrsiflorus var. *repens* is tough, with a spreading habit that suits a position at the top of a retaining wall. It is not the cleanest or most intense shade of blue, but is impressive, nonetheless.

The summer-flowering ceanothus are deciduous and the sort of blue that seems in need of a dusting. Most vigorous is the pale 'Gloire de Versailles'. Deepest and least vigorous is 'Henri Desfosse'. Between these, for colour and vigour, is 'Topaze'. Allow a summer-flowering clematis such as 'Etoile Rose' or 'Gravetye Beauty' (red), to sprawl among them, near to ground level.

Buddleias, forms of the butterfly bush *Buddleja davidii*, must clearly be included, though I am fond of B. *fallowiana* var. *alba*, which has felted grey leaves and small spikes of white flowers over a long season. The normal white-flowered buddleia, such as 'White Profusion', looks horrible on fading brown. 'Pink Beauty' is the best in that colour. 'Lochinch', with fallowiana blood in it, is an excellent lavender and greyish-leaved plant. 'Black Knight' is too clumsy of habit, but 'Dartmoor' is a dramatic purple and graceful.

Dahlias

Planning for autumn in spring is even more important than planning for spring in autumn. The excitement of spring, with bulbs, flowering trees and shrubs followed by poppies, peonies, irises and roses, pretty well takes care of itself. But there is a danger of a horrible falling-off in flower power from July onwards, just when the garden is at its most pleasant to linger in.

Dahlias provide an answer to this dilemma: their colours can be soft or brilliant, and their shapes and sizes are varied enough to please all tastes. There is no need to moan that summer is past when you see the first dahlias in bloom. I can assure you that they have no influence whatsoever on the advancing season, nor on the discomforts or dangers of chilblains or frostbite. The sooner they start blooming, the better value you will have from them.

That applies particularly to a variety such as 'David Howard', which has a tremendous capacity for keeping up its abundance of bloom for month after month. Not much more than a metre tall, it is small and decorative, with dusky orange flowers and purplish leaves. Fergus Garrett, my principal confederate, yesterday dug up a really healthy clustered tuber of this variety that we'd inadvertently left in the long border over winter. It had developed from a batch of cuttings taken in early May last year. Not using any heat other than the sun's, we get around to these jobs a couple of months later than would serious commercial nurserymen, but this did not deter 'David Howard', and for early bloom we had overwintered tubers that had been boxed up in old potting soil and kept in the cellar.

Not everyone has a cellar, I know, and those who have one might use it for other purposes, but tubers are not difficult to manage provided they start off good and strong. The main aim is to prevent them from shrivelling, keeping them cool but reasonably frost-free. You can leave them in the garden, if pushed, and will often get away with it.

From late-struck cuttings or from seed not sown till the end of April, you will have plants in readiness to replace earlier performers such as foxgloves, sweet williams, Canterbury bells, aquilegias and Siberian wallflowers. Or use them to follow lupins, treated as biennials, the seed for next year's plants being sown now.

'Grenadier' is a thoroughly reliable and early-starting small, pure red decorative plant, given me by a friend in Nottingham. On the whole, I've chosen varieties from an RHS trial ground, the nearest to me being at Wisley. Any dahlia grown there has to be made available to the public, and addresses will be supplied by the RHS, on application. Some suppliers, such as Butterfields, at Bourne End, Buckinghamshire, and Aylett, at St Albans, Hertfordshire, have no mail-order service. You have to collect, by arrangement. For mail order, I have found Halls of Heddon (Heddon-on-the-Wall, Newcastle-upon-Tyne, NE15 0JS) most obliging and satisfactory.

An excellent dwarf bedder, though it takes time to get into its stride, is 'Ellen Huston', a rich orange, small decorative with bronze leaves. 'Orange Mullett' (Aylett) is not much taller, at 70cm. Again a small decorative, its flowers are soft orange, with just a hint of pink, and the leaves green.

In 'Chiltern Amber' (Butterfields), the leaves are very pale green, well in tune with soft, pure orange, small decorative flowers, borne at 1m or a little higher.

Halls has 'Wittemans Superba', 1.5m tall with substantial, deepish-red semi-cactus blooms borne on strong stems and presenting themselves proudly. 'Alva's Doris' (Aylett) is a small, bright, true red cactus, while for vibrant reddish purple, the small cactus 'Hillcrest Royal' (Halls) is hard to beat. I mixed it with the green-and-white-striped grass *Arundo donax* 'Variegata'.

Water lily dahlias, which are decoratives with fewer petals and an elegantly informal look, are well represented by the soft pink 'Pearl of Heemstede' (1m), which I thought teamed successfully with the purple foliage of the castor oil seed strain *Ricinus communis* 'Carmencita'. I also want to get the clean and prolific 'White Ballet' (Butterfields), admired at Wisley. One of the oldest favourites is the pale, acid yellow 'Glorie van Heemstede' (1.5m).

Collerette dahlias are single, but with a collar of small petals, sometimes of a different colour, between the disc and the main row of petals. We grew the 'Dandy' mixed-seed strain last year and found all but one of them so pleasing that we have saved their tubers to do another stint. But a named collerette that is very pleasing is the pale yellow 'Clair de Lune', 1.2m tall, the collar also yellow. That looked well next to the pale green cones of the annual *Bassia scoparia* f. *trichophylla*.

Dahlias are amazingly resilient to wet weather, standing up to it without rotting, unlike chrysanthemums. Their leaves are apt to be coarse, though far less so when the flowers are on the small side. 'Bishop of Llandaff' is famed for its purple, deeply fern-cut leaves supporting small, semi-double red flowers. Even the deepest-dyed of anti-dahlia snobs allows a place for that.

Grey Foliage

The accepted protocol for the use of grey foliage plants is to put them with white flowers, as in the Sissinghurst example, or with pastel shades – soft pinks, mauve (always called lavender or lilac), cream and palest yellow. There is no need to limit them in this way. Think of them, for a change, as an exciting contrast to highlight bright colours.

There are certain practicalities to bear in mind. Greys, at least in our climate, tend to sulk in shade. They are at their palest and most glittering in bright sunlight. Then, again, their high season is summer and autumn. In winter, beneath grey skies, they generally look glum (there are a few exceptions), while in spring they will not have recovered from a hard cut-back, which is normal treatment for shrubby greys. Or, if herbaceous, their new leaves will not have assumed the luxuriance that will characterise them later on.

An early plant to settle into a state of pristine greyness is *Anthemis punctata* subsp. *cupaniana* (*A. cupaniana*). Making a loose mat of grey, pinnate foliage, it becomes a dazzle of white, yellow-centred daisies in the course of May. It can be used for bedding, interplanted with tulips, or as a foreground companion for a fairly densely planted group of tulips. Whichever tulip you decide on, it needs to be late flowering. The orange 'Dillenburg' would be my choice, or the strong (but not hard) yellow 'Mrs John T. Scheepers', which has elongated, egg-shaped blooms.

The parrot, 'Texas Gold', would also be suitable. It starts green and yellow, the green phases itself out and, in middle age, the petals become orange around the margins.

One of my favourite greys is the semi-tender *Senecio viravira* (*S. leucostachys*). It has a rambling habit, which becomes increasingly pronounced as the summer progresses. Set a bit of brushwood among its (brittle) stems, and it will hoist itself up to a metre (more, if it survives the winter). The leaves are a double comb, particularly pale if the soil is not rich. This goes excellently in front of a group of alstroemerias. Among the modern hybrids, two that I can recommend are Princess Grace (0.8m), which is orange-red, at its best in late July (though the season tends to be extended) and Princess Carmina, warm, brick red, at its best in late August. Being rather short (0.5m), it is best in front of the senecio, rather than behind. But you can juggle the senecio around from year to year.

Of much the same hardiness, or lack of it, but fast-growing, is *Artemisia arborescens*. It is a soft, loose-textured shrub, perhaps 1.5m tall, and looks good in the company of yellow sunflowers.

Buddleja 'Lochinch' has grey leaves and long, pale lavender flower spikes. As with other summer-flowering buddleias, you can control its time of flowering to an extent by how and when you prune it. For late flowering, prune to within a foot of the ground and at the end of April. It makes an admirable backdrop for a strong and sturdy red hot poker, such as *Kniphofia uvaria* 'Nobilis' (2.5m). If you had the cream plumes of *Artemisia lactiflora* (2m) in the same team, that would look spectacular through August. The purple-leaved form of orach, *Atriplex hortensis* (2m) is a self-sowing annual, which you will never be without, once introduced, and it is protean in its ideas of where to site itself.

One that we liked last year was behind a colony of blue (grey-blue, really) lyme grass, *Elymus arenarius* (0.8m), which it drooped over. Both are foliage plants. The lyme grass, be warned, is a ferocious spreader. The pure red *Lobelia* 'Queen Victoria' (1m), with purple stems and leaves, needs highlighting, and I would suggest either *Senecio viravira* or a form of the somewhat hardier *S. cineraria*, such as 'White Diamond', whose height can be contained to 0.4m by a hard cut-back each spring. Since they are on the borderlines of hardiness, it is wise to lift your lobelias at the end of each season and overwinter them under cold glass.

In our exotic garden, where we specialise in late-summer luxuriance, it is surprising what a good contrast to such lushness is made by a few groups of *Artemisia* 'Powis Castle' (0.7m), a grey, pretty well hardy shrub with finely divided leaves. Give it a hard pruning, fairly late in spring, when signs of growth can be seen low down on last year's stems, to which one can safely cut back.

This looked good in front of the pink-striped New Zealand flax (Phormium), called 'Dazzler' (1.5m). The strong contrast, in this case, is mainly of form. Nearby, we have a pink-flowered Canna, 'Louis Cayeux' (1.5m), whose smooth, broad leaves provide yet another contrast.

Some plants provide their own colour contrasts between flowers and leaves. There is a familiar example in *Brachyglottis* (Senecio) 'Sunshine', often grown for its grey leaves alone, so that certain owners are maddened by the swathes of yellow daisies that it produces, in late June, from silvery buds.

They should be welcomed. The shade of yellow is good – sunshiny, indeed – and pruning can be delayed until after the display.

Meadow Planting

Natural and assisted natural meadows are at their most beautiful during the next two months. The secret for their success and the maintenance of a varied content is poor soil. If the soil is rich, you might as well cultivate it. A meadow on rich soil encourages the coarsest plants to take over and to squeeze out all the less aggressive, and they include the ones that interest us most. If you have a lawn that you're not proud of and that you've failed to feed, you could allow it to become a meadow and it would be ideal for the purpose.

Management does necessitate cutting the grass two or three times a year otherwise it will become hopelessly tussocky. Hold off the first cut for as long as your nerves can bear the untidiness of the last weeks, as it is then that your plants will be ripening and shedding their seed. The whole point of a meadow is to give the plants you want a start, but that they should be of a kind that will thereafter spread without assistance – generally by self-sowing. The ideal time for your first cut will be in the last week of July or the first half of August.

At least one more cut will be needed right at the end of the growing season, so that the turf is nice and tight for displaying snowdrops and winter crocuses in the new year. It is with them that the fun begins. You don't want anything fancy in the way of snowdrops; the common kind will not only clump up by natural division of its bulbs, but will self-sow freely. A little shade is best, as turf tends to be thinner in shade and that suits the snowdrops.

Crocuses cope well with a dense sward and like full sunshine, which opens their blooms wide even if the air is still chilly. Most crocuses (but not the Dutch yellow) self-sow; the chubby March-flowering Dutch hybrids in shades of white, mauve and purple, increase freely, making a thrilling carpet of blossom in time. At least a month earlier are all the different colour forms of *Crocus chrysanthus*, the mauve *C. tommasinianus* (outstandingly prolific), and the rich orange *C. flavus*. If you can get hold of plants of any of these crocuses and snowdrops from another gardener now, before their foliage has died off, it is an ideal planting time and the ground is still soft.

Plant just one bulb in each position, and give them some potting compost in their own holes, to get them going. Plugs of turf are most easily removed with a long-shafted bulb planter, operated with your foot from a standing position.

The European dog's-tooth violet, *Erythronium dens-canis*, is a great success in the same sort of turf which snowdrops like: mauve-pink, Turk's-cap flowers in March and beautifully purple and green marbled leaves. That clumps up; after a few years you can split the bulbs apart immediately after flowering to spread them around.

It goes well with the miniature trumpet daffodil, *Narcissus minor*, bright yellow and only 15cm tall. Try to keep the coarse daffodils and narcissi out of your turf, as they are too domineering. The hoop-petticoat daffodil, *N. bulbocodium*, is of just the right scale, and the pale yellow form, *N. citrinus*, self-sows excellently. Sources for everything mentioned can be found in *The Plant Finder*.

On wettish (but not stagnant) soil, the snake's-head fritillary, *Fritillaria meleagris*, with purple, checkered bells (white, in the albino), will self-sow and build into impressive colonies. That's in April, and don't be sniffy about dandelions; they look wonderful in spring sunshine. Buttercups come in a range, the first to flower being goldilocks, *Ranunculus auricomus*, which likes it damp. The field buttercup, *R. acris*, is my favourite of the others, tallish and excellent on dry soils. Buttercups look splendid with red clover and plenty of fresh meadow greenery.

Cowslips are in their prime in April–May and especially happy on chalk and lime soils. Wood anemones, forms of *Anemone nemorosa*, flourish in turf as well as in woodland, and flower more freely where sunshine can reach them. Blue-flowered kinds make a change from the usual blush white.

It should never be forgotten that grass is the most important element in a meadow. You should enjoy a rich assortment, from the early-flowering sweet vernal grass to the June–July flowering pinkish-purple haze of common bent, designated a poverty grass because it will flourish on the poorest soils.

Native flowers will dominate in May and June, particularly the yellow-daisied Hawkbits, Hawk's-beards, and Hawkweeds – a desperately confusing lot but very jolly and following the sun around as do the ox-eyed daisies, which go so well with them.

A foreigner worth introducing for its clumps of deep blue stars on 38cm-tall spikes is the North American *Camassia quamash*. That self-sows well and is much remarked upon in my garden in May. At the end of that month, the magenta spikes of *Gladiolus byzantinus* are in striking contrast to all the other flowers.

From mid-June to mid-July, the meadow cranesbill introduces large patches of blue – always a precious colour. It is easily raised from seed and should be grown on in a row till strong enough to plant into turf. Another blue wild flower for this late period is the tufted vetch, *Vicia cracca*. Of a scrambling habit, it will climb any fence or hedge within reach, making curtains of colour.

Bulbous irises, *Iris latifolia*, will bring this season to a glamorous conclusion.

May

May Borders

When I am in the middle of spring, I find the idea of a spring border very appealing. There are so many wonderful ingredients that it would be good to get together. I do not think that spring-flowerers should be allowed to dilute the impact of a garden's or border's principal season later on. By the same token, a border of spring flowers would inevitably contribute little in summer or autumn, and this too should be accepted.

I would have the border include some low shrubs, and a couple that are currently inspiring immediately come to mind. *Coronilla valentina* (0.3m) makes a low hummock (I like to plant two or three together, integrating an undulation of hummocks) and is so smothered with little clusters of bright yellow, sweetly scented pea flowers that scarcely any foliage is visible.

Behind this, and in contrast, I would like a favourite rosemary, the fine-leaved one called 'Benenden Blue' (0.7m). It has a fairly spiky habit, making a series of spires, and is smothered for many weeks with rich blue flowers – the best in this respect of any rosemary. Like all of its kind, it tends to splay apart with age, but this can be regulated a little by tipping some of the longer shoots back after flowering.

You might include a clump of a dozen or so white tulips around here – the lily-flowered 'White Triumphator' is elegant. Many spurges are spring-flowering. If I had to select just one for this border it would be the clump-forming *Euphorbia polychroma* 'Major' (0.3m), which flowers much more persistently than *E. polychroma* straight and makes a bold dome of yellow-green, flowering heads.

This colour goes particularly well with scarlet and orange – *Anemone x fulgens* (0.2m), say, or the scarlet lily-flowered tulip, 'Dyanito'. Another cooling-off flower is biennial white honesty (1m), *Lunaria annua* var. *albiflora*, which has quite a statuesque, broadly spire-like habit. It self-sows, which will keep you guessing where to expect it next year. So does *Smyrnium perfoliatum* (1m), which never fails to attract attention and, with its bright lime-greeny-yellow colouring is an ideal companion for the honesty. It takes time to establish this as a self-sowing colony, but once you have passed that stage it will be a question of rationing its spread.

In my garden, the spring self-sower to beat all others is forget-me-not, myosotis. We never allow these to become overcrowded or starved-looking (Fergus is hot on the yearly application of surface mulches of either mushroom compost or, where its alkalinity would be unsuitable for lime-haters, finely ground and well-rotted bark, which is considerably more expensive). Where you have a lot of self-sowers in a border, there is a temptation to leave things alone, but that results not only in overcrowding but also in neglect of the soil's condition, which needs constant enrichment with organic matter.

Blue is everyone's favourite colour, and even bluer than forget-me-nots is their perennial relative, *Omphalodes cappadocica*, of which the deepest, richest blue cultivar is 'Cherry Ingram' (he was a doyen of the gardening world who died in 1980, aged 100). A clump-former that you can divide after flowering (enriching the soil at the same time!), it has a long flowering season.

It likes moisture and, given that, will take a lot of shade. One might grow with it one of the less gaudy polyanthus primroses. The laced kinds (which can be raised from seed) have great charm. One in my garden has flowers so dark as to be near black, but each petal is rimmed with bright yellow.

Bleeding heart, alias lyre plant, alias lady in the bath, *Dicentra spectabilis* (0.7m), is one of the most delightful spring flowers with arching racemes from which dangle lines of pink and white, heart-shaped flowers. There is also an albino version, in which the leaves are a notably pale green and another clone, 'Gold Heart', in which the pink flowers are daringly combined with yellow-green foliage.

Next to this, I should be tempted to have a smallish daisy bush, *Olearia* x *scilloniensis* (1m, prunable after flowering), which is smothered with white daisies, now. It is a little on the tender side, however, but the current run of mild winters is worth banking on for the sake of a bit of extra fun.

Of the earlier-flowering cranesbills, one that I enjoy is *Geranium macrorrhizum* 'Bevan's Variety' (0.3m), which has magenta-coloured flowers. That goes well with a dwarf Jacob's ladder, *Polemonium* 'Lambrook Mauve', a most obliging clumpy plant that, after it has flowered, you can divide and resettle in improved soil every few years. The flowers are open-funnelled.

A clump of Spanish bluebells (*Hyacinthoides hispanica*) in the vicinity will not come amiss, either, but do make sure they are not allowed to self-sow, as they can become quite a weed in a border setting and, with their lank foliage, they look weedy, which is even worse. I grow a virtually non-seeding variety called 'Chevithorn', but I don't know who is offering it.

Of the perennial violas, *Viola cornuta*, in a deep, violet-coloured strain, is most rewarding. But its albino form, Alba Group, is arguably even better, flowering again in September if its flowered growth is slashed back in June. That enjoys moisture and rich living. It has the companionable habit of growing into and through its neighbours.

Birds in the Garden

Many gardeners are bird lovers, and gardening certainly gives you the opportunity to watch them from the corner of your eye. So long as you go steadily about your job, without making sudden, uncalled-for movements and observing the birds without appearing to, they will feel comfortable in your presence and will treat you as they would a sheep or cow. That is the greatest compliment.

A garden rich in variety, containing shrubs of different heights and density – some against walls, others in the open – with plenty of seed- and fruit-bearing plants, will attract a wide range of birds, without any conscious effort on your part. It is the kind of garden we should want, anyway.

Ours is far fuller of birds than the relatively untamed countryside around. And yet there are fewer of many species than there were 30 or 40 years ago, and the reasons are complex. I do not pretend to understand them all myself.

I'm certain that house martins' nests used to abound on certain of our buildings; they have been gone for many years. More recently, swallows have become scarce. I realise that we now have three cats permanently and officially around, while those belonging to neighbours are certainly no respecters of boundaries; but swallows, by nesting higher in open-sided buildings, can steer clear of them.

Yet when it comes to their gathering season, at the turn of August and September, the hundreds that used to sun themselves on our roofs are totally absent. I believe they find a dearth of insect food. Certainly, I am far less bothered by flies in my kitchen during the summer than I used to be. Modern farming practices are responsible for that. On the whole, we must be pleased, but there are always less welcome side-effects.

We tend to be selective about birds we like and those we resent. Personally, I detest the sight of a bullfinch – or of bullfinches, rather, as they always feed in parties. In the days when they abounded, there was a wide range of shrubs and trees that it was pointless to try and grow. Plums were regularly stripped of flower and leaf buds. It was the same with many cherries. *Prunus* x *subhirtella* was reduced to writhing, leafless branches. No forsythia blossom, kerria, weigela, exochorda, nor apples (except Bramley, which was spared, for some reason). It was a long list. But then, in the early 80s, bullfinches disappeared from the region where I live and I have joyfully returned to these excluded plants. Bullfinches are beautiful, but handsome is as handsome does.

I welcomed the return of the sparrowhawk after its near extinction by aldrin and similar farm chemicals (later banned), but those who deliberately feed birds and enjoy the feel-good sensation of seeing the creatures regale themselves at the table provided are usually loud in their wails of protest against its resurrection.

The fact is that we find it difficult to accept nature in the raw. We want it on our own terms. Those terms will vary according to our interests. 'I fed it all the winter and now it's eating all my fruit,' you hear in protest against a blackbird. What did you expect? Shouldn't the blackbird's song be compensation enough? Apparently not.

May Sowing

Come May, I think about sowing and planting all sorts of the more tender plants. Zinnias – the big, dahlia-flowered kinds are a great excitement when the summer goes right for them – will germinate in four days, if sown now in a close frame where the sun will warm, but not burn, them.

They are said to loathe root disturbance; that is not my experience at all. But, to give them their best chance, it is a good idea to pot them individually at an early stage and to keep moving them into ever larger pots, until the weather (which really means the nights) has genuinely warmed up – they can then be planted out in late June. If grown unchecked, the seedlings will branch naturally and not need stopping.

The chimney bellflowers, *Campanula pyramidalis*, that we display each August in large pots in the house, always arouse admiration and, sometimes, envy. They grow 2m tall, and make ropes of blue or white blossom that last for a number of weeks, so long as bees cannot reach and pollinate them.

They're easy to grow – if you do the right thing at the right time. For next year's display, sow now, barely covering the tiny seeds. Prick out the seedlings into a tray, and from there pot up individually. Then continue potting on (using a strong compost, John Innes No. 3, or its equivalent), in three stages, until, by the end of August, the plants are in their final pots – which could be five litres.

This can be done on the assumption that the plants are hardy, and I overwinter them in a cold frame. Stand the pots out in a sheltered spot next summer, so that wind can't get into them, and give a stake to each pot and a tie to each stem, some time in June. As soon as the first flowers open in late July, bring the plants indoors. As they'll be discarded after flowering, light will not be an important factor, but dying leaves will need to be stripped off the bottom of their flowering stems.

I sow cucurbits now – gourds, squashes and, most important, ridge cucumbers that will be planted out on the compost heap.

I don't bother with marrows, which have little flavour, nor courgettes, which are most easily bought the right size when needed. If you grow your own, they need picking every day, otherwise they become marrows in no time.

Eucalyptus for bedding out next year can be sown this month or next. The best species for their ornamental juvenile foliage are *E. globulus*, which grows more quickly and will be 3m or more tall at the end of the season, if bedded out next May. Or, *E. gunnii* has smaller, neater leaves and less coarse growth (I'm not saying that coarse growth isn't exciting, in its way). The latter will make a pretty-well hardy, evergreen tree, if required to, moving over to its adult foliage, which is narrow and willow-like, but tough of texture.

Another gum that you might consider as a smallish specimen tree is *E. niphophila* (correctly *E. pauciflora* subsp. *niphophila*).

It has a silvery trunk and its leaves glitter when struck by low sunlight. You want to establish these gums before their roots have had the chance to become pot-bound, otherwise they'll never be reliably wind-firm.

In borders, this is a good time to mess about with the perennial *Salvia uliginosa* (2m), which is pale blue, and *S. guaranitica* 'Blue Enigma' (2m), which is deep blue; its cultivar 'Argentine Skies', however, is pale blue. As the winter was mild, these will probably have survived. Young stock will flower well the first year, if you take cuttings of young, basal shoots when less than 10cm tall.

Some of the calceolarias are pretty hardy. My sub-shrubby 'Kentish Hero' and 'Camden Hero' (both in shades of warm brown) have each survived. Hardiest of them all, though a pretty brash shade of yellow, is *Calceolaria integrifolia*, which has a tremendously long flowering season.

In the same family are diascias, which have become very popular in recent years and have a long season, especially if cut back halfway through it to make them compact again. Most of these are pretty hardy, given the style of recent winters, though the largest of them, *Diascia rigescens*, is not.

Salmon is their predominant colouring, but if you aren't crazy about salmon shades – and I'm certainly not – there are several variants, such as 'Lilac Mist'. I am also impressed by 'Redstart', which really is red.

They all tend to sprawl around at 0.2m–0.3m, and are really most productive if renewed annually from cuttings, which can be taken from soft growth now. They may even be 'Irishman's' cuttings, with a few roots already attached.

A pleasing shrub that flowers for some six weeks at this time of the year is *Piptanthus nepalensis* (2m). It has short racemes of substantial yellow pea flowers among dark, trifoliate leaves, while the young stems (it can make 1.5m of new growth in a season) are dark blue-green and glossy, not unlike a young bamboo cane. It has a reputation for slight tenderness that I believe is undeserved; the best I have seen were in Perthshire. But the protection of a wall somewhere nearby does seem to help; east or west will do. Full sunshine is not necessary. Sometimes, a branch or branches will die unaccountably, but they will renew themselves from ground level.

Young Foliage

Young foliage in spring gives us some of our best opportunities for mixed-border effect. When it is green, the shape and surface gloss will be the main contributors. Thus, the jagged, palmate shape of delphinium foliage, although a feast in itself, will combine well with oriental poppy leaves, which are pinnate, having deep indentations and a furry, dew-holding surface.

The gloss on bunches of smooth, broad colchicum leaves gives an amazing sense of thrust. One bright green leaf that stands out in bunches is that of *Angelica pachycarpa*, which is pinnate and little more than 0.5m high. Buy your first plant and thereafter save your own seed, as it often dies after flowering.

The giant fennel *Ferula communis* will be around 1m tall for the next month, and produces a few huge, intricately divided leaves in an undulating cushion. Grow it from seed and, once established, it will be permanent.

Grey is best represented now on plants that will run to flower later, such as the thistle *Onopordum acanthium*, which is spectacular in the run-up to flowering at midsummer but sadly disreputable after that.

A 1m favourite with me is the biennial *Salvia aethiopis*, currently still in the stage of a low rosette of deeply indented, silver-furred leaves. A similar, more frequently grown species (but without the jags) is *S. argentea*. Sow seeds of these two now for next spring's display. *Artemisia ludoviciana* – which grows to 1.2m tall – is still quite low, making a tangle of fine, perennial rhizomes above which silver foliage combines with the blue of self-sown forget-me-nots. They happily invade the colony.

There are two variegated forms of biennial honesty in which the foliage is particularly effective as they come in to flower in spring. To get them self-sowing true to type, they need to be kept separate from plain-leaved honesties, which is difficult in a small garden. In *Lunaria annua* 'Variegata', the heart-shaped leaves are splashed white all over, although most pronouncedly towards the margins; the flowers are mauve.

In *L. a.* 'Variegata' 'White-flowered Form', also called 'Alba Variegata', the white variegation is more distinctly zoned around the leaf margins, creating a pattern. But the flowers are also white and so do not always show up too well against this background. I like them both, but there is much dissension from members of the public, who often hold strong views on the kinds of variegation that they find intolerable, and those, the neatly zoned, which they can take on board.

The variegated comfrey *Symphytum* x *uplandicum* 'Variegatum' is widely accepted because the broad, cream, marginal zone is so distinct. It is marvellously fresh in spring. But when, in a few weeks' time, it has flowered, it should be cut to the ground, because the second crop of foliage is as good as the first.

There are so many hostas with handsome foliage in spring – before the slugs and snails have got at them or their freshness has tarnished – that choice should be an individual matter, but you will undoubtedly find that your opinions as to which are the best for you will keep changing, which is a good thing. 'Frances Williams', one of the most popular, is at least fresh now, but its glaucous leaves' lime-green marginal variegation can become horribly raddled as early as June in many gardens, especially in time of drought.

Hot sunshine combined with drought is the bugbear of the majority of golden-leaved shrubs and plants. My elder *Sambucus racemosa* 'Plumosa Aurea' is ravishing now, copper fading to yellow, and this foliage colouring is always most impressive on specimens that were hard-pruned in winter, which prevents flowering and channels its efforts into larger, lusher leaves. But come the hot weather, it is only too liable to scorch.

With these golden-leaved plants, a balance between too much or too little exposure to sunlight is critical. Too much and they scorch; too little and the colouring is weak, more pasty green than gold. Keep trying and, where possible, make sure the roots are never short of water.

The evergreen *Euonymus fortunei* 'Emerald 'n' Gold' (1m, but spreading) never lets me down and is bright yellow all over just now. Even better is 'Silver Queen', which is normally green-and-white-variegated, but soft yellow on its young leaves.

Purple foliage is fresh and not too heavy in spring. In some cases, as with the purple-leaved hazel, *Corylus maxima* 'Purpurea', it becomes a grubby, greenish purple on ageing, though clones vary in this respect and the best results are always obtained by cutting the shrub hard back every few years. 'Royal Purple' is the best cultivar of *Cotinus coggygria* to grow simply for foliage, and that should be pruned by shortening all growths back every winter.

Among perennials, the herbaceous *Clematis recta* 'Purpurea' is subtle on its forest of young shoots. The top and undersides of its young leaves are different colours – purple and silvered purple. *Euphorbia dulcis* 'Chameleon' is charming in youth too. The top of its developing inflorescence hangs a little, revealing a paler, softer purple on the underside. The yellow loosestrife *Lysimachia ciliata* 'Firecracker' is rich, uniform purple on its young shoots, which make a striking background for late yellow tulips.

Plants for Paving Cracks

Paving cracks colonised with little plants add a touch of magic to the garden. You start them off and thereafter they do their own thing.

There's the violet cress, for instance, *Ionopsidium acaule*, with scarcely any height at all but capable of making white, violet-tinted ribbons – it's only an annual (why should one always be demeaning annuals with 'only'?) but a self-sower. The so-called blue-eyed grass (not a grass at all), *Sisyrinchium angustifolium* (15cm), is a born crack plant, with dusky blue flowers that never open wide till lunchtime. They'll be ready for you when you take your coffee out after you have eaten.

And then there's the purple-leaved, bright-yellow-flowered *Oxalis corniculata atropurpurea*. It is a nuisance in pots in the greenhouse, where it will self-seed and compete with other plants, but in paving it is a welcome charmer.

The New Zealand *Acaena novae-zelandiae* is a mat-forming crack plant that makes burrs after flowering, and these turn bright carmine before ripening. New Zealanders hate acaenas – they call them biddy-biddy – because the burrs work their way into socks, sheep's wool and anything else that will give them a hitch to pastures new, but you won't find the one I'm recommending a problem.

A bit of height here and there, where the plants won't get in the way, makes for variety. *Verbena bonariensis* (2m) blocks nobody's view. The same goes for the wand flower *Dierama pulcherrimum*, sometimes rather nauseatingly called angel's fishing rods. It is a great plant if you clean up its dead foliage in spring, its tubular magenta flowers (they also come in pink) dangling from 2m arching stems in July. The 2m *Campanula lactiflora*, with panicles of mauve bells in summer, had the idea of seeding itself into my terrace from another part of the garden. I control its height by pinching out the leading shoots quite early on; it is a great favourite.

How to get started? First make sure that there are no perennial weeds, such as couch, in the cracks. Use a systemic weedkiller if necessary. Run a screwdriver or similar tool along them to make an open channel. Make a mixture with your seeds, in a seed compost such as John Innes, brush it in and water with a fine rose. Or fill the cracks with a soil-based sterilised seed compost only and stand pots of the desired plants on the paving so they can ripen and drop their seeds. (The Mexican daisy, *Erigeron karvinskianus*, 15cm, is great for doing this.)

Trying to establish ready-grown plants seldom works. Once you start experimenting, you'll get carried along. Just see.

Pruning Spring-flowering Shrubs

Many spring-flowering shrubs can, or should, be pruned now, as soon as their flowering is past. This will give them time to make and ripen new shoots on which next spring's flowers will be borne.

There are the early-flowering spiraea, such as S. *thunbergii* and S. x *arguta*, loosely known as bridal wreath or bridal veil. With no pruning, the bushes become scraggy. Old branches can be taken right to ground level, but those that are showing strong, young, leafy shoots can be pruned back to these. At the end of the task, there should be no remains of recently flowered shoots. If you want a low shrub, prune the whole lot to the ground (there is considerable job satisfaction, here). But, rather than weaken it unduly, do this only every other year or every third.

Kerria japonica can be treated like this, one way or the other. The double kerria is often ridiculously tall and lanky, and there is no need for this. Forsythia – oh dear me, forsythia. How many hideously mangled examples of this does one see around? Well, never touch it in autumn. It should be now, if at all. Best is to prune selectively, removing the oldest branches in their entirety, but leaving the shrub a loose outline, which is what suits it. Pruning into balls and blobs looks pretty frightful, even though it does endorse that there's a man around and that everything's under control. If there isn't the space for a freestyle forsythia, plant something smaller.

Winter-flowering *Jasminum nudiflorum* is usually trained against a wall (it doesn't have to be) and it will flower on a north aspect, which is handy. But, unpruned, it gets terribly stringy, so go over it with shears. A well-cared-for winter jasmine is a picture in December.

Russian almond, *Prunus tenella*, and others like it that flower in April on young shoots made the previous year – such as *P. triloba*, *P. tomentosa* and *P. glandulosa* – should be cut back very hard after flowering, otherwise they'll carry a lot of unproductive old wood and only flower on top of this. You want to encourage a forest of young shoots.

Osmanthus delavayi and *O.* x *burkwoodii* (both evergreen) similarly benefit from a clip-over immediately after flowering. This encourages far more young shoots than they would otherwise produce, and young shoots will be the flower bearers next year.

If these, why not forsythia? you may wonder. Forsythia is a far coarser shrub and deciduous. Ball treatment doesn't suit it. In osmanthus, it does; in fact, it looks better than a disorganised, unpruned specimen.

You might feel the same about *Choisya ternata*, the Mexican orange. It doesn't have to be pruned, but looks well if it is and as you would need it to be, either side of a door entrance. Prune with secateurs rather than shears; the latter cut through leaves as well as stems, and this looks brutal when the leaf is a fair size.

Choisyas may get too hot and turn yellowish in blazing sunlight. But in the north, they need all the sun they can get to make them flower well. In the south, they'll often flower a second time in autumn. But you mustn't delay cutting them as soon as the spring flush has finished.

The spring-flowering tamarisk, *Tamarix tetrandra*, is a wonderful sight for a brief spell in May, with all those wands lined with deep-pink blossom from end to end.

But it is a large and ungainly bush. I shouldn't recommend regular pruning, but when it becomes a you-or-it situation, get going with a saw the moment its blossom has faded, and be a butcher, for once. Next year's flowering may be slightly affected but not nearly as much as if you prune at any other time.

Repeat-flowering roses are very flexible. Largely you can prune them to suit yourself. If you'd like them to flower in early August, prune heavily now. I, on the other hand, have bushes of an old-fashioned polyantha called Madge, which makes clusters of divinely scented, shell-pink rosettes. They were already so full of flower bud when I contemplated pruning in late March that I decided to let them flower (which they are, now), before I prune. Their second flowering will be in September.

It is quite another matter with once-flowering roses – no pruning should be contemplated that will affect their one-and-only contribution. After that, in July, you can get busy removing flowered wood.

What do you do about rhododendrons and their dead heads? Some people make a virtue of removing them all. In large establishments and institutions, this may take weeks to complete and involves much step-ladder work.

However, I do not believe that virtue is necessarily its own reward. If the bush clings to its old flowers and looks a fright, dead-head it by all means, so that it no longer offends you, but stop pretending that the job is necessary, or even desirable, for the shrub's sake.

It will make no difference to its performance next year. If it is one of those obliging naturals that flowers every year, it will flower whether you dead-head or not. If its strength is set back by flowering, it will be set back anyway, whether you dead-head or not.

The delay to its making new shoots on branches that are flowering will either inhibit or not inhibit its next year's flowering, whatever you do about those seed heads. So, if they don't look too bad, relax or, for preference, get on with some of the many other garden jobs that are clamouring.

Experimenting with Colour

There are all sorts of little dodges for gaining the best effect from the plants we grow. About now, we are sowing wallflowers for next spring's display. They join the brassicas in their seed bed outside and are subsequently lined out, some 25cm apart, to make fat plants. Don't grow mixtures; they include too many colours and, visually, cancel each other out. Choose which colours you want to juxtapose (two or three will probably be enough in any one year), grow them separately, then combine them when bedding out in autumn.

If the colours are of comparable strength, such as orange and lemon yellow, I usually make adjacent, informal patches side by side. But if one colour is dark, and the other bright and light, I make single-plant splashes of the bright colour (it might be 'Cloth of Gold') in a matrix of the dark, which might be purple or brown. That would entail three plants of the dark colour to one of the bright.

Here at Great Dixter, I like tulips with my wallflowers, but in separate patches, among or behind them. This is because wallflowers are basically scrawny plants, easily blown sideways in the wind. If massed, they hold one another up and become a single, undulating carpet.

Another scrawny plant, which I yet like to grow, is the summer-flowering annual, *Helenium amarum* (30cm). It has masses of small yellow daisies over a long period, supported by very bright, light green, linear leaves. That loses its scrawniness if massed. It combines well with the substantial bronze red *Gaillardia* 'Red Plume' – one plant of that to two of the helenium, in adjacent blocks. I should warn that you don't get much seed of the gaillardia in a packet, so two packets of that to one of the helenium.

Ladybird poppies, *Papaver commutatum*, have great appeal, with their crimson flowers, each petal with a large black basal blotch. Never think of plants in isolation; always think of how to combine them effectively with something else. In this case, you might use the annual or biennial (according to when you sow it) *Cynoglossum amabile*, in one of its pure blue-flowered strains. But in a mixed planting I should have two plants of the cynoglossum to one of the poppy (both are roughly 0.5m high), as the poppy's flower is much the larger and makes the stronger impact.

On the other hand, you might combine it with *Omphalodes linifolia*, which is a little shorter and has small, dead-white flowers above grey leaves. White stares, so in this case I should bed with the same number of each component, mixing them evenly. We raise both poppy and omphalodes in modules, then pots, so as to be sure of strong plants for bedding out. Experiments of this kind are fascinating and can be changed annually, which is a way of prolonging your own life in terms of experience.

A piece of bedding out that I admired in the Logan Botanic Gardens at the south-west tip of Scotland, and have since imitated, was a mixture of the tender perennial, grey-leaved *Helichrysum petiolare* with the bright yellow, coreopsis-like *Bidens ferulifolia* – this is also tender, so now is just the time to get such a scheme planted.

Both plants have a sprawling, widely spreading habit and the units can be planted almost 1m apart; they will soon be interlocking. As the bidens is such a bright yellow, you need far less of it than of the helichrysum. One plant to three would be enough. This is an easy and effective way to cover a wide area of ground. They will not give you any height to speak of, however, so you may need to think of a taller background: blue agapanthus, perhaps.

I love red 'geraniums', not in mindless, solid blocks, but in touches to liven the scene. So, perched above my sunk garden, I have four large terracotta pots planted up about now for the summer, the ingredients varying but always including a *Helichrysum petiolare* (again) and a red or orange 'geranium'. One loses the names (meaning that I have lost the name), but we keep it going from autumn-struck cuttings overwintered under glass.

A combination that we found most satisfying, but which needs planning (sowing seed now to flower, as biennials, in a year's time), was of Canterbury bells (*Campanula medium* – a single-flowered strain) with the scarlet *Lychnis* x *haageana*. The latter is half the height of the campanula but of a very strong personality, so that roughly equal numbers of each worked out right, planting the Canterburys first, rather widely spaced, and then interplanting the lychnis.

You can still buy Canterburys in separate colours – pink, white, mauve (called blue) or purple, but in practice we used a mixture of the four and it worked admirably. All this, I have to say, was totally unorthodox, so we (Fergus and I) were overjoyed by the result.

This year, we have combined the lychnis with *Campanula primulifolia*, which is campanula blue. I have not grown it before. Flowering will be in June. Come and see what you think.

Mulching

There seems to be an increasing tendency to avoid personal value judgements. Instead of giving a personal opinion, based on personal experience or research, which I have done all my life (though I have, with further experience, often revised, even reversed, my original viewpoint), the fashion now is never to state where you stand on any question. (Though there are notable exceptions, such as Anna Pavord, Carol Klein and Stephen Anderton.)

This playing safe may keep you out of trouble, but it makes for extreme boredom. I noticed it a good deal when hearing an American lecturer on gardening, who showed streams of photographs without ever a hint of whether what was in them was worthwhile in any absolute sense. One comes away with a sense of frustration and unfulfilment.

Go for it, I would plead. By all means say that you are merely giving your personal opinion and that anyone is welcome to disagree, but then disclose unashamedly where you stand. Avoiding commitment is a kind of disease, and it leads to drab greyness.

In last month's issue of *The Garden* (the journal of the RHS), there is an article on mulching that a friend of mine found extremely irritating. It provided a mass of facts, many of which were just common sense and a waste of space, but did not even go into the question of whether, for the ordinary gardener, mulching is necessarily a good practice at all.

Some gardeners go mad on bark mulches. They cover every scrap of exposed soil, so that you simply cannot get away from the stuff. But no one seems to have considered the possibility that it is hideous to look at. To say so would be a value judgement and that, it seems, is not on.

We, at Dixter, do not mulch our borders at all, for well-considered reasons, one of which is that doing so prevents the germination of self-sown seeds. *The Garden*'s mulching article, however, simply assumes this to be a good thing. True, our weed seeds have the chance to germinate, but so do the seeds of many self-sowns that we welcome. I believe that, in parts of my garden, 25 per cent of the plants you see are self-sowns, and these are largely responsible for its overall air of comfortable relaxation.

Don't imagine that all this means we have let things get out of control, however. If, for most of the year, you have a good cover of plants that you want to see, weeds get an ever-decreasing look-in. We use herbicides; we even hand-weed – and why not? But the overall plant cover makes very little of this necessary.

Planting Garden Steps

When putting steps into your garden, never be mean about their width. In fact, make them as wide as you can, so that plants can take over in the corners on either side. And don't cement the risers: leave cracks into which small plants can colonise. There'll be some hand-weeding to do, but that can be done comfortably by kneeling two or three steps below the risers that you are working on.

Among the most modest and least competitive plants for steps is *Arenaria balearica*. Its tiny leaves make a mossy carpet, above which pure white flowers – borne singly now, on thread-fine stalks – appear like stars at dusk, 2cm above the mat. It also likes damp and shade.

Small ferns are excellent in shade, the most appropriate being the spleenwort *Asplenium trichomanes*, whose narrow, pinnate fronds spread themselves like the limbs of a starfish.

Equally diminutive is the rusty-back *A. ceterach* (*Ceterach officinarum*), with crenate leaf margins and brown scales on the underside. The size of hart's tongue ferns, *A. scolopendrium* varies depending on what the roots find to live on. In the corners of your steps, where debris collects, they may form sizeable tufts of their evergreen fronds.

Erinus alpinus is a miniature, rosette-forming plant that is often to be seen colonising the cracks in old walls. Generally of carmine colouring, it can also be a richer magenta or pure white, which shines out best under shady conditions.

It seeds itself most agreeably, and its season starts shortly.

Another consummate self-seeder is the Mexican daisy *Erigeron karvinskianus*, though it doesn't like too cold a climate. Rejuvenate your plants by cutting them back in spring and they will produce a long succession – from May for the next six months – of white daisies that change to pink as they age. Its preference is for sun, but it will also grow in shade.

Still with step risers in mind, *Campanula portenschlagiana* (*C. muralis*) will run discreetly along the cracks, and never bulk inconveniently forwards. Flowering shortly, it bears campanula-blue bells in profusion. Once that performance is over, grab all visible growth in both hands and tug. It will break cleanly away at the base, and the colony will make fresh foliage from there. In the corners of the risers, you could accommodate the more vigorous *C. poscharskyana*; 'Stella' is the best choice of clone, being slightly less aggressive and having more intensely coloured blue star-flowers. This species is adept at plastering its annual-flowering shoots against a vertical surface, so it would be ideal if there was a wall adjacent to the steps, on which to make a curtain of blossom.

Where there is sufficient space, I allow the ox-eyed daisies *Leucanthemum vulgare* to seed into my steps from the neighbouring meadow. They have a wonderful freshness at the turn of May into June. Although they stand 0.5m tall, order is restored as soon as the display is fading by employing the grabbing technique described above.

Wallflowers (*Erysimum cheiri*) should be allowed a niche at one or other end of the steps. Dribble some seeds into the detritus that collects in the corner, and they will do the rest, self-sowing from year to year, though individual plants will, given the chance, last for several years. Whatever colour they start out at, they will eventually settle down to a kind of bronze yellow – similar to the colour of the wild plant.

Red valerian, *Centranthus ruber*, wedged into steps where space allows, looks fine in June, and will do so again in September if the first growth is cut back after flowering. Red or white are the best colours, the mauvy-pink sort being on the muddy side.

As a plant and in the wrong place, valerian can be dodgy. Its roots and rootstock are strong and thick, and may damage the fabric they are growing through. Still, I can find a place for some of them.

An enthusiastic plant that I am reluctant to allow in my steps is lady's mantle, *Alchemilla mollis*, which seeds itself everywhere.

It looks really nasty once it has been trodden on, and where is a more likely place for that to happen than in step risers? However, a welcome self-appointed coloniser at both ends of our curved, Lutyens-designed steps at Great Dixter is the spring-flowering spurge *Euphorbia amygdaloides* var. *robbiae*. Its lime-green columns are held above rosettes of dark, evergreen leaves. All this should be removed at the end of its long flowering season, and others will take their place.

Steps are often arranged to have on either side a ramp, on which a plant may be grown that will bracket outwards a little, and so break the hard line. Ideal for this arrangement is the shrubby, grey-leaved *Convolvulus cneorum*, whose every mound is thick with blush-white convolvulus flowers in terminal clusters – now, or very shortly, and often with a second crop in autumn. It is none too hardy a plant, but the dry, perched position suits it ideally.

Vegetables in a Small Garden

Even in a very small garden, you will want to grow a few herbs and vegetables; the question is, which of those you like is it sensible to include? Definitely not a globe artichoke. True, it is very ornamental at its best, but it looks terrible once harvested and you'll be fighting over who is to eat it, as only one main globe, or two smaller ones, will be borne at a time. After you've been saying 'You have it, darling', 'No, you have it', for a few days, it will have become too large and coarse, anyway, and won't be eaten at all.

Other vegetables are ornamental at their best and are often grown for that very reason, but if you cut one, it ruins the symmetry of your design; yet if you don't cut any, what a waste. On the whole, I recommend being hard-headed and practical on this subject. A few tomato plants can be grown against a sunny fence or wall, or up a post in a sunny, open position. Choose a variety of what is known as 'indefinite growth' – not a bush tomato, but the normal, tall-growing kind, which fruits over a long period and occupies otherwise wasted vertical space. For flavour, I should choose 'Sungold'. The smallest tomatoes are often the sweetest in our climate, but this one is not absurdly small. The greatest snag about tomatoes is that they will fail on you if grown repeatedly on the same piece of ground. That goes for many vegetables, in fact. You must think ahead on how to switch things around.

You may be able to manage a small patch of lettuce (maybe inter-sowing them with a colourful radish). 'Little Gem' is small, neat and crunchy, and has the best flavour of all. Sow some around now. But for late summer and autumn, a leaf lettuce, non-hearting, is easiest to manage. 'Salad Bowl' is typical. There are also red-leaved kinds that look pretty in the garden, though I always think they look a bit wan once you get them inside. This type of lettuce is very slow and reluctant to bolt, which is a great advantage. Its stem keeps elongating, but it goes on producing new leaves, which you pick individually. It has pretty, frilly margins, too. The overriding disadvantage is that it is flabby and entirely lacking in crunch. Sow some now and they'll keep on cropping into November, if the frosts hold off.

Dwarf French beans take up little space and are very productive, if you keep picking them. They hate cold ground, so there couldn't be a better moment for sowing a few than right now. I was impressed last year by a variety called 'Masai'. It has small (stringless, of course) beans in great quantity, and they are reluctant to grow large, old and coarse.

I don't care about runner beans myself, and they cast a lot of shade, though the red flowers are pretty. Three or four plants will provide an abundance of beans. They are a particularly English delicacy.

I am very fond of cress in a sandwich or salad – much better flavoured than mustard (which is actually rape). This is best sown a couple of weeks before you mean to start eating it, on the surface of a seed compost in a seed tray. Never cover the seed, or the compost will spoil your sample, getting mixed into the leaves. The seed will be liable to dry out. Guard against this by enclosing the box in a clear polythene bag for the first few days. Land cress is very different and has a strong, coarse flavour. It is very hardy and will overwinter from an autumn sowing.

Planting Partners

Never grow plants in isolation – however well they may be doing, half the potential pleasure they should be giving will be lost unless you have paid attention to their surrounding neighbours. Green foliage, if interesting of its kind, may be quite sufficient for some plants. But a background of dark, bark mulch – however pleased you may be to have it – can look quite dismally negative.

Avoid such a potential eyesore by getting your borders looking full as early in the season as you can. Teamwork is the object that has for long been worked out in spring bedding, where a carpeter provides a setting for bulbs: tulips, most likely. You underplant with myosotis, bellis, pansies, polyanthus primroses, wallflowers, or with something less usual – doronicums or arabis, perhaps – and the tulips are highlighted in a way that they would not be if surrounded by bare earth.

That there should be a team at work becomes most important when one of the partners is itself of a particularly dark colouring. Many gardeners get excited over dark-flowered Lenten roses – hellebores – but unless you are very close to them, or have them pointed out to you, they can easily remain virtually invisible and non-contributing. They need help, first by removing their tatty, old foliage before flowering commences, and second by interplanting them with some light-coloured, early-flowering bulb, such as snowdrops or scillas.

I have been given, from a pedigree source, an unusually fine form of *Fritillaria pyrenaica*. Not that I am a fritillary nut, who is prepared to give my all to the successful cultivation of a range of an often tricky species. But if they will thrive and increase in my garden without being much bother, I am, naturally, delighted to enjoy the results (who wouldn't be?). The outstanding feature in the particular strain of *F. pyrenaica* that I was given, so far as I can make out, is that almost the entire flower is as close to black as you will find – black bells nodding at a height of 0.3m. All very classy, but visitors need to have it pointed out to them.

I have tried to enliven my fritillaries by planting a neighbour – the grape hyacinth, *Muscari armeniacum* 'Blue Spike' – and it seems to be working.

A similar example, but this time with foliage, is *Clematis recta* 'Purpurea'. When it flowers in June, this looks like any other *C. recta* – a huge froth of white blossom supported by dark-green leaves – but in spring, this purple-leaved form is so handsome and distinctive that there really seems little point in growing the normal green-leaved kind. But you don't want to see that wonderful purple surrounded merely by well-mulched, or manured, or simply wet soil, as this would utterly fail to highlight the star of the moment. A smattering of other leaves – such as the young foliage of *Allium cristophii* or (a favourite of mine) the hairy, pinnate leaves of young oriental poppies – should be quite sufficient to do a highlighting job.

It recently struck me (indirectly; it was actually a companion who made the observation) that the cushions of purple foliage made by *Euphorbia dulcis* 'Chameleon' are rather wasted in the run-up to flowering. A narrow-leaved tulip such as *Tulipa sprengeri* (the latest of all to flower) would look excellent among euphorbia clumps, provided it was planted a little further apart than it might otherwise be. The tulip, whose flowers are bricky red, settles down to make a colony and needs no further attention once established.

The low-cushion-forming *Veronica peduncularis* 'Georgia Blue' has rich, deep blue flowers in spring, but seems a trifle dead – as blue so often does – without a nearby contrast. The one I am working with at the moment is the late-flowering, miniature *Narcissus* 'Hawera', a miniature triandrus hybrid, cluster-headed in bright yet pale yellow. The taller *N.* 'Thalia', with its pure white flowers, is admirable for pepping up the amorphous hazy blue of *Brunnera macrophylla*.

Shrubs should be given just as close attention. Where you see great sweeps of one kind in mass plantings – near factories or superstores or in public open spaces, for instance – no sort of thought seems ever to be given as to how the next sweep should correlate with the last, except with regard to height. Such questions as colour, leaf size and shape are equally important, however, and that applies also in the privacy of our own gardens.

After all, shrubberies can be excessively boring features for most of the year, when the constituents are considered purely for their flowers. The compact cherry laurel, *Prunus laurocerasus* 'Otto Luyken', can be a big yawn when herded 20 to 50 at a time and without related plantings, but it is an excellent shrub nonetheless. Its growth – which is easily controlled by occasional pruning – is neat without being stodgy; its leaves are smartly cut and glossy; it flowers with white candles in spring and often again in autumn. Yet, if a garden designer suggests introducing even one such plant, his client is likely to exclaim with disgust at its being 'that overplanted thing'.

It pays to look at it a little more dispassionately. Next to mine, I have another (over-) popular but contrasting shrub, *Thuja occidentalis* 'Rheingold', which slowly builds up a cone of fine-textured scale-leaves and whose colouring is always changing through the year, from old gold in the coldest weather to lime green in summer. I think it works well with 'Otto Luyken', and the surrounding plantings can be as different as you please: red hot (or orange or yellow) pokers – kniphofia – might be a possibility.

Staking Tall Plants

The needs of our plants require attention almost every day at this season, while growth is so rapid. Staking is one of them. What does one stake and is it worth the effort? I think it is.

Aware of our congenital laziness, plant breeders have produced replicas of familiar species, so dwarf as to require no support. *Campanula lactiflora*, one of the tallest of the genus, may easily soar to 2.1m, but has been reduced in the cultivar called 'Pouffe' to no more than 23cm. Many annuals, notably marigolds, have been similarly served. A large flower on a short plant, as you find in the Inca Series of African marigold (*Tagetes*), looks totally unbalanced. Whereas large flowers on a large plant, such as the F1 'Toreador' strain, look splendid. They don't even need support.

But even if support is necessary, does the supply of it need to cause outright anguish? Tall plants generally have style. In a typical *Campanula lactiflora*, each panicle of blossom will comprise two or three hundred of its bell flowers. Nearly all of this is lost in the dwarfened version. And it simply is not true that small gardens (if such is your lot) have no space for tall plants. For fewer of them, yes, but those few will be more impressive than the tiddly many. So, if you have a group of two or three July-flowering pink hydrangeas, one plant of a tall *Campanula lactiflora* among or to one side of them would be a great addition.

For support, use a couple of bamboo canes and some discreet soft string (fillis). Secure the string to one cane with a non-slip clove hitch, leaving a considerable length at the free end. Take this to each principal campanula stem as you reach it and twist it round that stem before proceeding to the next. When you reach the second cane, make another clove hitch. And so on till you return to where you started, where you'll finish off with a reef knot.

There are a number of commercial supporting devices, some better than others. The one I least like, because it always shows, is the hoop on a leg (or more than one leg). Link Stakes, however, are excellent, and their green colouring (green is a difficult colour to make seem natural) really does blend. Your support system, after all, should aim to be so discreet as not to show at all, once plant growth has reached its peak and flowering has started. These stakes are available in different lengths.

Early support is required by alstroemerias, which flop readily and by the August-flowering *Aster sedifolius* (*A. atris*) whose shoots resemble a gypsophila's when young. Eventually (and you need to anticipate) it will grow 90cm high and very top-heavy. But if well supported, it will make a lavender mauve quilt tightly packed with its spidery blossom.

The herbaceous *Clematis recta*, despite the uprightness suggested by its name, is one of the floppiest plants in the border, but, if well supported to 1.8m, will present a huge cloud of tiny white blossoms at the turn of June–July, excellent for cutting. The variety to grow is 'Purpurea', whose foliage in spring is rich, yet cool, purple. I hate the moment when support has to be provided, because it looks so handsome before this stage is reached. I like it behind the hairy foliage of oriental poppies in April. Later on, it makes a good background to their scarlet flowers.

Whether the stems of these poppies should be given support is always a question. If not provided, a shower of rain may splay all the stems outwards, so that the centre of the plant looks as though a fat cat had been lying in it. Short lengths of cane with string taken from stem to stem while they are still upright can make all the difference; support here is not required high up, but about halfway up the stems.

With some perennials, the stem is quite stiff and thick, but apt to sway over at the base from top-heaviness. Many of the eryngiums are like this. You can use short canes and make your ties less than halfway along the stems. The same with *Lychnis chalcedonica*, whose domes of scarlet blossom open in early summer.

Many border phloxes need no support but one of my favourites, the archetypal *Phlox paniculata*, which has given rise to all the exciting derivatives, grows up to 1.5m high, even in the dry south-east (a foot taller in Scotland), and its stems are on the weak side when topped by its lilac panicles.

Anticipation is the watchword, where it is known that plants will require support. Once they have been laid low, their stems will quickly curve upwards, and it will be impossible to make them look natural with subsequent support.

Cottage Gardens

Fergus will today be speaking to a cottage garden society. This makes me wonder, for a start, what a cottage garden is and what the people who so named it had in mind. Is it a woolly, sentimental concept, conjured up by the well-to-do middle classes, of the simple, unspoilt life of the working class, and the gardens tended by them in their spare time? Something of that, I think.

There would be honeysuckle twining around the porch and a cohort of stately hollyhocks standing in front. Very nice, too. There would be lots of self-sowers and a generally relaxed feeling – not too much organisation. The only straight line would be London Pride along the path from front gate to cottage door. An elderly lady in a sun bonnet would be tending her borders of thoroughly mixed contents – a real creative garden jumble.

Such a garden probably never existed, but the idea of it has romance. It ties in with the notion that the past we have lost was delightful and so different from the horrible present which, alas, we cannot get away from.

Our concept of an imaginary cottage garden may be false, but there's no reason why it shouldn't take on a life of its own. The danger is that it is no better than a mess that becomes messier as the season progresses. That it is simply an excuse for being sloppy.

Carol Klein is the ideal protagonist for the best of cottage gardening. She understands that it needs to include some sort of bone structure, places and features where the eye can rest as a change from massed detail. You see this year after year in her Chelsea Flower Show exhibits.

Beth Chatto, in the years when she used to show and regularly win top awards, gave us a relaxed, cottagey effect, but the display was planned in great detail. Nothing was left to chance and she gave herself a mass of alternatives before deciding exactly what she would use.

I have to admit that even my long border at Dixter has been referred to as an overgrown cottage garden, which I actually take as a compliment because it conveys the element of relaxation that it needs to make the eye comfortable. We allow some self-sowing – but only some. The way we thread groups into and through one another so that the plants appear to have put their own ideas into the weaving of an overall tapestry makes its strongest contribution to the cottage garden element.

To sum up: the cottage garden is a fake, but it gives pleasure and should be encouraged wherever it occurs.

May Bulbs

After the tulips and narcissi finish, several bulbs act as very useful – not to mention attractive – fillers in our borders until the mainstream of perennials reach their prime.

The genus Camassia, from North America, is clearly closely related to our bluebells, but it carries spikes of blue, mauve or white starflowers instead of bells. At 1m in height, some of these, such as C. *leichtlinii*, may be a little apt to flop under border conditions and, having perfectly naked stems, don't lend themselves to discreet support. But they are ideal under meadow conditions, where grass stems give them the necessary support without further effort on our part.

The colour varies somewhat, and can be a weak shade of greyish-blue, but 'Electra' is sufficiently strong-coloured and will also make a bold, upstanding clump in the border.

As this sort of bulb leaves a complete gap when summer has truly arrived, I place it where the gap will automatically be filled in by neighbours. For instance, in this case, by *Geranium* 'Ann Folkard', a cranesbill that gathers strength slowly: from nothing in early spring, it gradually takes over a large area with its lime-green, deeply cut foliage and long succession of bright purple, black-centred flowers.

The white forms of C. *leichtlinii* do flop, in my experience, and the biggest flopper of all is the extraordinary double white, each of whose blooms looks like a tuberose's. A flower to be gawped at rather than assimilated to normal border conditions. My favourite camassia is half the height of these and usually a deeper, richer blue. This is C. *quamash* (it is edible, and, to me, quamash suggests the sound of scrunching bulbs). It is ideal for naturalising in rough grass, where, if you don't cut the grass too early, it will ripen seed and self-sow over a period of years. It grows either side of my front path and always arouses interest.

So, under similar circumstances, does the early-flowering *Gladiolus communis* subsp. *byzantinus* (1m), whose flowers are brilliant magenta. That shows wonderfully under meadow conditions, but it is also an excellent subject for border infilling in early summer. The corms increase rapidly, so you can spread them around in early autumn. Another charming May–June-flowering gladiolus that can be scattered through a cottage-garden-style border and will maintain itself happily through the years is 'Robinetta' (0.5m), which is coloured cherry red.

The 1m-tall *Allium hollandicum* (A. *aflatunense*) 'Purple Sensation' carries boldly showy hemispheres of rich, purple flowers and can be used in several ways. As a permanency in an undisturbed position, it blends especially well with the rosy-mauve umbellifer, *Chaerophyllum hirsutum* 'Roseum', which is like cow parsley, but coloured. The allium will self-sow if allowed to. I tend to use it as a bedding plant, lifting and drying off the bulbs soon after they have finished flowering. It is nice under-planted with the double pink campion, *Silene dioica* 'Flore Pleno', but also shows up dramatically against a permanent planting of lime-green *Euphorbia palustris* (1.2m), which is a strong-growing perennial for damp soils.

Allium cristophii (0.7m) has a larger globe and a longer season, as its pinky-mauve petals are stiff and long retained. This invaluable bulb is another self-sower. A successful use for it is in a colony of Japanese anemones. These develop quite late, so the allium provides early interest among the anemones' developing foliage; and when the allium's own leaves are dying off they are discreetly masked.

Quite a different allium is A. *moly* (0.2m), low-growing and with umbels of bright yellow flowers in early June. We have that between clipped yew topiary and lawn, where it doesn't get in the way at all, and I find that it combines strikingly with spikes of the spotted orchid *Dactylorhiza fuchsii* (0.5m), which is mauve.

The groups of bulbous irises that we call Dutch, Spanish and English (none of which hail from Holland, Spain or England) all flower in May and June. I do not find that the Spanish persist as well as the others, but these will continue indefinitely. It is a question of finding places for them. The Dutch are in interestingly mixed colours within each bloom, including blue, purple, yellow, brown and grey. They have quite a seasonal spread between them, and will pep up some rather uniformly low ground-cover plant, as among a border or swathe of catmint. They'll give height and sinew to a planting of June-flowering cranesbills, such as the bluey-purple *Geranium himalayense* or 'Johnson's Blue'. I also like them among aquilegias, which flower around the same time.

The English iris, derived from *Iris latifolia*, have notably wide-spreading falls and somewhat reduced standards. Their colour palette ranges between purple, mauve, grey and white, but they are obtainable only in a mixture nowadays. These are the latest bulbous irises in flower; late June and early July being their season. In a border, they increase prodigiously, and I have them forming a ribbon between double rows, comprising a hedge, of the Michaelmas daisy *Aster lateriflorus* 'Horizontalis' (1m). After flowering, the irises' dying remains are concealed by the developing aster hedge.

When we need to replant, surplus iris bulbs are scattered through meadow areas, where they maintain themselves very well through the years.

Canna

Cannas add a flaunting whiff of the exotic to the summer garden and we should be thinking about planting them in the next few weeks. Unlike dahlias (which have other virtues), canna foliage is among their greatest strengths – broad and shiny, often beautifully striped and, with a tendency to stand rather upright, great at transmitting sunlight, especially early and late in the day.

The silken flowers, which are often brilliantly coloured, are good, too, though rather pathetic in rough, wet, mouldy weather. Under such circumstances, we don't feel much better ourselves, so let's bank on a tropical summer.

Often, the flowers are ostentatiously spotted – red on yellow, for instance. That fidgets me, but you may love it. For those of a nervous constitution, there are discreet, softly shaded cannas. Grow these, if you instinctively loathe cannas but want to show how open-minded you are.

Most gaudy flowers earn a bad name for themselves through no fault of their own, but because they are clumsily used. As dot plants, standing a metre above the surrounding beddings, they look awful. Or in huge, mindless drifts of one variety, as I saw them along motorways in Georgia, USA. Some unknown creature had decimated their foliage, which is precisely what happens when you herd large numbers of the same plant together.

Get your cannas into mixed plantings of a similar mood and roughly similar stature, and make bold groups of several plants of the same variety together. Their heights vary from 1m to 3m, so there is plenty of choice. The palmate leaves of castor oil bean, *Ricinus communis*, make a good contrast and are especially effective in a purple-leaved seed strain such as 'Carmencita'. Dahlias make excellent companions and so does the bright orange, zinnia-like annual, *Tithonia rotundifolia* 'Torch' (1.5m). The 2m tobacco plant, *Nicotiana sylvestris*, is also excellent, if you can keep it free of mildew (a recent scourge of nicotianas). It has long-tubed, white flowers and bright green paddle leaves of great presence.

Cannas, generally, have green or purple leaves. *Canna indica* 'Purpurea' (2.5m) has fairly narrow, purple leaves and, because of its height, their translucence is especially effective. The small, orange-scarlet flowers are pleasing without knocking you backwards. Best of the tall, purple-leaved kinds in my garden is 'Wyoming', which has large, brilliant orange flowers.

You could grow it with a yellow sunflower such as 'Monarch', which is perennial. Then tone down with the deep blue *Salvia guaranitica* 'Blue

Enigma' (2m). Add some small, decorative, apricot-orange Dahlia 'David Howard' (2m) and you'll have the crowds sucking their teeth.

Purely for foliage effect, grow C. 'Musifolia' (3m): green with a purple margin and veins, and leaves of an immense size (though not as large as a banana's). Another very large-leaved canna is C. *iridiflora* (1.5m) – green with a very thin, purple margin. There is something voluptuously satisfying about this canna, when it is well fed and watered. Unlike the rest, whose inflorescences are always stiffly upright, in this species they arch over, and although the flowers are only of moderate size, they are a beautiful shade of cherry red.

I have a soft spot for the cannas you can grow in shallow water, although they do equally well on terra firma. The prototype is the soft yellow, spidery-flowered C. *glauca* (2m), which is in totally good taste (should such matters concern you). From it is derived 'Erebus' (1.5m), which has an even bluer leaf and salmon-pink flowers that make a good show. I grow a potful of each of these in my sunken garden pool.

Do remember that cannas are exceedingly greedy, and give them a really nourishing compost. Their thirst is well-nigh unquenchable, once they are growing strongly, but go easy on the water when they are coming out of dormancy and before they have a strong new root system.

The stripy-leaved cannas are quite something, especially with sunlight behind them. Most self-proclaiming is one going around by various names, including 'Durban' and 'Tropicanna'.

The leaves are purplish, but striped bright pink. It is not a tall canna but will reach 1.5m when in flower, and the flower colouring is orange. So it is in 'Striata' (1.5m), which also has other, somewhat more confusing names, but is green and yellow striped. Get plenty of lush foliage around these cannas and they will blend in perfectly well, but are best sited at a border's margin, where their entire height can be savoured.

Cannas have thick, fleshy, storage rhizomes and their cultivation is much as for dahlias. If you leave them out through the winter, with a thick cover of protective material such as fern fronds, you will often get away with it and, when you have surplus stock and can afford to take risks, do that.

But it is safer to lift the rhizomes once the foliage has been frosted and store them in a cool but frost-free place. We box them up in old potting soil and water occasionally during the winter, just enough to keep the rhizomes from shrivelling.

Move them out into the light in spring, earlier or later according to what warmth (if there is any) you can give them. Plant them out when they are growing strongly, and this is a good time to split the rhizomes, if you want to increase your stock. However, be warned that the young shoots tend to be brittle. If you accidentally snap them off, there'll be no one to blame but yourself, which is always a galling situation.

June

June Gardens

Most garden lovers, asked which is their favourite month, would say June: it has all the sparkle and freshness of early summer, and is still full of hopefulness. When it comes to it, they will certainly find grumbles – too hot, too cold, too wet (turning the old roses mouldy), too dry, always something – but on 1 June, all is happy expectation.

If we talk about the June gap, it is because we rely heavily on bedding out, and the changeover from spring to summer bedding leaves us with a hiatus. On the other hand, if ours is a spring garden, heavily dependent on flowering shrubs, there'll be sighs of a different kind. It all depends on how we organise things.

Here and now, we can enjoy the cistuses, those aromatic shrubs from the Mediterranean that present us with a fresh crop of their ephemeral flowers every morning. Some of the most flaunting of the perennials also reach a peak: peonies, oriental poppies, bearded irises, delphiniums and there'll be the first of the day lilies.

Cranesbills, the huge array of hardy geraniums, make a tremendous contribution, those that have a single flush doing it in early June. The magenta *Geranium psilostemon*, with its black eye, especially appeals to me.

Some excellent alliums develop, notably *Allium cristophii*, with large globes of stiff mauve stars that gradually fade but still keep their shape. Given a chance, they'll self-sow and you'll find yourself with a colony.

Many of the largest-flowered clematis hybrids, some of them double, put on a show in June. They might make minor subsidiary contributions later, but now's the time when they truly flaunt themselves. Vulgar, lacking in subtlety, did I hear someone say? But surely a little vulgarity is in order, from time to time. There comes a stage when good taste begins to nauseate.

One of the things I enjoy most about my borders in June is the masses of lush foliage of different sizes, shapes and colourings. Any coloured flower, even the brashest scarlet oriental poppy, can be safely let loose among that. Or the magenta *Gladiolus communis* subsp. *byzantinus*: I like it with a blue or purple bulbous Dutch iris. Both die off after flowering, but later-performing neighbours will easily fill the gap. Border phloxes, for instance.

As I like early colour as well as late, I am inclined to fidget, impatient for the next change. I'll enjoy a big swathe of lupins, usually in two contrasting colours. We'll have raised them from seed sown a year ago, planted out in autumn and interplanted with tulips, for an early display. But when the lupins have finished, we throw them out (harvesting the now dormant tulips) and replace with dahlias, cannas and suchlike. Once lupins have flowered, there's no disguising the fact that they look hideous.

Obviously, this caper is not for those who have 'anything for a quiet life' as their motto. But if they enjoy visiting gardens, they may see how I enjoy my own style of unquiet.

Poppies

I have yet to meet anyone who disapproved of poppies, of the genus Papaver. Their very fragility seems to recommend them, as does their generous way of opening, early in the morning, throwing off the boat-like double cap, which is the calyx, and quickly expanding from crumpled chiffon to gorgeous perfection.

These poppies epitomise early summer in all its freshness. Although their season may be brief, it is intense and, in the case of the annual kinds, we can extend it by making successive sowings. Some of the annuals make the strongest plants if sown in the autumn and many, once established, will continue to self-sow through the years.

Such is the case with the opium poppy, of which there are many named strains and selections – though opium is never mentioned, in case it should give us the wrong idea. The plants are handsome weeks before flowering, with smooth, glaucous, wavy-edged leaves. Self-sowns that managed to overwinter will make huge, cabbagy plants.

The flowers may be single or double in a range of pink and red shades, although, typically, they are mauve. I am keen on experimenting with contrasting colour combinations, but was slightly disconcerted one year when a patch of brilliant orange *Anthemis sancti-johannis* found itself in partnership with self-sown, double pink opium poppies. They looked so healthy and pleased with themselves that I was helpless, but soon got to like the juxtaposition.

The great thing about these poppies is the huge quantities of tiny, granular seeds they produce. Seed merchants can afford to be generous with them and this makes it easy to practise direct sowings.

Still, it is worth pointing out that poppy seed can be sown under controlled conditions in a pot, if you are careful. When the seedlings are still only at the seed-leaf stage, they can be gently transferred, individually, to plugs, and later planted out from these without further root disturbance.

One of our favourites among the annuals is the 'Ladybird' poppy, *P. commutatum*, which can be sown in the autumn and in the spring for later displays. The bowl-shaped flowers are rich, crimson red with a large black blotch at the base of each of their four broad petals. They start flowering in May and we thread the plants through all sorts of border plantings.

Another that we treat like this is the Angels' Choir mixture from Thompson & Morgan – which was ultimately derived from our scarlet field poppy, but in this strain there is every possible colour except scarlet, which has been eliminated. If you save your own seed, you will find that scarlet will creep back and eventually dominate, unless you are ruthless. The flowers in this strain are double, and their colourings are in a wide and most seductive range.

Last year, we enjoyed a Turkish species, *P. tauricola*, with glaucous leaves and soft red, quite sizeable flowers that have telling black blotches. Unfortunately, the public liked them, too, and we lost every seed pod. As these were still perfectly green and unripe when taken, nobody stood to gain. A poppy with its seed head is still rather handsome, but stalks without the head look terrible and I have to follow up, almost daily, with secateurs to tidy up.

Grown as a biennial (you could sow it now), *P. trinifolium* is an extremely attractive foliage plant in its first year, making a perfectly formal rosette of hairy, deeply cut foliage. This is rather inclined to collect too much water at its centre in winter and to rot, but, if it survives, it flowers from May on, with an upright, branching inflorescence. The flowers are apricot orange and last the morning.

This colouring is seen quite frequently in a number of poppy species. Another that I'm fond of is a perennial that can be raised from seed, *P. spicatum* (syn. *P. heldreichii*). The plant is pale, silvery green on account of a dense covering of soft hairs. The flowers are arranged in threes along an upright raceme. They seem to open haphazardly, but the centre of one of each trio comes out first. Morning, again, is its brief flowering period.

Yet another apricot-flowered species is *P. rupifragum*, whose flowers arise singly on long stalks from the base. It is perennial and seeds itself almost too freely.

I prefer the loosely doubled form offered by Chiltern Seeds. *P. pilosum* is similar.

Of course, there are the well-known Iceland and oriental poppies, but I thought I would devote myself, on this occasion, to some of the less publicised kinds.

Pondside Planting

Most well-designed ponds allow for marginal planting, or, if formal, for containers within the pond itself. The sword-like leaves of irises, with their vertical thrust, are especially effective. Best are the forms of *Iris laevigata* (in shades of blue, purple and white). The white-variegated 'Variegata' is clean and bright – the best variegated iris I know. Its flowers are blue. For yellow, our own native *I. pseudacorus* does a wonderful job in May–June, but can be embarrassingly vigorous. Here, again, its 'Variegata' variant comes to the rescue. Its glory (though it also flowers) is its pale yellow variegation in spring, which gradually fades to green.

The colour blue is always at a premium. You should include the water forget-me-not, *Myosotis scorpioides*, the cultivar I grow being 'Mermaid'. These myosotis get going in late spring, but go on and on. The yellow eye is quite a feature. Canadian pickerel weed, *Pontederia cordata*, does wonders for us in late summer, with arrow-shaped leaves and spikes of blue flowers. It contrasts well with a spear-leaved buttercup, *Ranunculus lingua* 'Grandiflorus', which has a long season but is extremely vigorous, so watch it.

The skunk cabbage, *Lysichiton americanus*, seeds itself pretty freely when happy. It is a dramatic plant, with bright yellow arum flowers in March–April, followed by large, lush leaves. No smell to worry about. Arum lilies are a must: their white flowers last for three weeks and have a great presence in the garden from May on. Their glossy leaves are another asset. They will welcome partial shade, but are not out-and-out hardy. I think one should also have the kingcup, or marsh marigold, *Caltha palustris*, which flowers in quite early spring. In a garden setting, the double 'Plena', packed with glossy yellow petals, gives best value.

The fern to go for is the stately royal *Osmunda regalis*, which reaches a metre or more when happy. It has an incredibly long season of beauty: bronze fronds unfurl in spring, changing to bright green, which shows up at a distance (if you have seen it wild in Ireland, you'll know what I mean), then to warmest rufous in autumn. Another beauty, among foliage plants, is the undemanding *Cyperus vegetus* (correctly *C. eragrostis*), which is related to the Egyptian papyrus, and has heads of narrow leaves on top of 0.6m naked stems.

Some plants look as though they should be hanging over water, but are actually happiest in normal, well-drained garden soil. This may easily go up to a pond margin and will be a good site for the wand flower or angel's fishing rods, *Dierama pulcherrimum*. It flowers in high summer, with arching stems carrying little chains of, typically, magenta bells, though the colour varies from quite light pink, intensifying.

Small Trees

Recently, I considered the possibilities of a garden without borders. Today, I should like to discuss which small trees would be suited to a mixed border. When you make a border, it is generally best to have it as deep as possible from front to back (supposing it is one-sided), or across (if an island). A small tree (or a shrub that will become one in time) will give body and structure to the scene.

In such a situation, don't choose a tree, such as a birch or cherry, that has greedy, surface-feeding roots as these will seriously inhibit other plants you want to grow underneath it. A fruiting tree might be good if, like most plums, it enjoys the fairly rich soil conditions that we encourage our borders to have. Pretty, rosy-skinned 'Victoria' is the great favourite, both for eating raw and for cooking, and it does not need a pollinator. But I find its flavour insipid. I am much more enthusiastic about a round, black culinary plum, 'Rivers's Early Prolific', which often ripens its fruit in late July, before wasps become a pest. But it needs a pollinator: 'Victoria' would do, or even a plum tree in a neighbour's garden, if it flowers at the same time.

The crab apple 'John Downie' makes an ornamental small tree with its white blossom and glossy, oblong fruits, which are red on the sunny side. They ripen in early September and are the best for crab-apple jelly. A small horse chestnut, little larger than a bush, is *Aesculus* x *mutabilis* 'Induta'. It always draws appreciative notice when flowering (in May), and its leaves are ornamental, too.

Hawthorns make charming small trees, both in flower and in fruit. Sometimes, as in *Crataegus laciniata*, they are desired for their grey foliage. This would be my top choice in many situations, and it has splendid orange haws in late September. If your soil is not too limey, an acer, or Japanese maple, may be best. *Acer palmatum* 'Sango-kaku' (alias 'Senkaki') is deservedly a favourite, with pink young stems throughout winter and fresh, green maple leaves that turn yellow in autumn. We enjoy a maple of quite tight-growing, upright habit, *A. palmatum* 'Shishigashira', which changes to rich bronze in November.

If you want an evergreen, the almost prickle-free holly, *Ilex* x *altaclerensis* 'Golden King', is excellent; its leaves are broadly margined with gold, making it luminous from a distance. We trim ours annually, to form a column. The strawberry tree, *Arbutus unedo*, is another possibility. This develops a red-tinted trunk with the years, and its waxy, white flowers open in late autumn. Sometimes, it makes small, strawberry-like fruits, but I wouldn't count on it.

Dianthus

Most dianthus may be had in bloom from May to autumn, but the cottage garden kinds, that touch us most closely with their gusts of airborne scent, belong to early summer. The most typical derive from

D. plumarius. They have pink or white, ragged-edged single flowers, often with a maroon zone near the centre and the foliage makes glaucous mats.

When established in a retaining wall, plants can last for many years. They love chalk or mortar rubble, light soil and a basking position. On heavy clay soil they are seldom a great success, although all right if frequently renewed from cuttings. Old plants in some cases, even if they remain healthy, tend to become shy-flowering with age, so renewal is the more important.

Cuttings of leafy, barren shoots can be taken at any time from spring to late summer; now is as good a moment as any. Make a cut across the shoot, just below a node, so that the cutting is 5cm or 7.5cm long. If it is rather leafy, make a further cut, against a hard surface (or between your fingers and thumb, if you know what you're doing), so as to shorten back the foliage by about one-third. Dibble into a very light, gritty compost, water and place the container in a cold frame where there is plenty of light. Don't keep it without ventilation for longer than a week or two or the leaves will be inclined to lose their natural, waxy coating and will rot.

'Mrs Sinkins', which came out in 1868, is still one of the most popular pinks for edging paths. Double white, but with an incorrigible habit of splitting its calyx, which gives it an overblown look – but who cares? The scent is terrific.

So it is in another old-fashioned path edger, 'Sam Barlow', this being double white with purple at the base of the petals.

You should really choose your pinks by eye (and nose), when they are flowering. A favourite of mine is the single pink 'Inchmery', which is excellently scented. Laced pinks, such as 'Dad's Favourite' or 'Laced Joy', are a delight, with blackcurrant-purple petal margins and similar colouring in other parts of the flower.

The larger, longer-flowering hybrids between pinks and carnations include the immensely popular, salmon-pink 'Doris'. With its simpering, toothpaste-advertising smile, I find 'Doris' repulsive, but I am in a minority of one. 'Haytor White' I go for with enthusiasm – a fully double, almost carnation-sized flower of good scent and long season. An excellent buttonhole flower.

The price of a long season is apt to be a looser habit, so that plants become scrawny after two or three seasons and need to be renewed. You should bone up on what's around. The *RHS Plant Finder* will clue you up on sources and the result will be a nicely labelled parcel through the post. 'Kesteven Kirkstead' is a single white with a maroon zone and the plant has a good habit.

There are seed strains of pinks. 'Spring Beauty' is one of the oldest; good, but I wish it was better selected for colour, with fewer mauvy-pink flowers. They are mostly double. Another seed strain, the Highland hybrids, are singles in shades of pink and carmine, with a dark zone at the centre of the flower. You can sow the seed in late spring to bring strong plants on for flowering the next year.

I line out the young plants in a reserve area and move them to their flowering positions in the autumn.

I think they are best treated as bedding plants, throwing them away after they have flowered, as the plants make few vegetative shoots to carry them forward for another season. Treated as bedders, you could interplant them with bulbous Dutch irises (a late-flowering blue variety would be suitable) to give height to your planting.

One dianthus that I can never be without, and which I raise annually from seed, is the strain called 'Rainbow Loveliness', derived from *D. superbus*. It has single, deeply laciniated flowers, giving a raggedy look and in colours from white through pinks and mauves to a quite deep reddish-purple. The wafted scent is incredibly sweet, even syrupy.

From a spring sowing, the plants would be in flower before they had made a decent size, since their habit is anyway on the thin side. I find it best to sow in late summer and overwinter the young plants, singly potted, in a cold frame.

Seed is ripened by the end of July, so it is easy to keep your own stock going by sowing it fresh.

Mule pinks are, as their name suggests, sterile – hybrids between pinks and sweet williams. They are green-leaved. Early spring is a good time for taking cuttings of young shoots. The flowers are double and sizeable, in loose clusters. 'Emile Paré', with salmon-pink flowers, is one of the best known and is scented. Don't keep old plants, as they become virtually barren.

More Colour Combinations

Fergus and I enjoy bright colours but quieter ones are a pleasure, too, as contrast. One of the combinations that I enjoyed a little earlier was the magenta *Gladiolus communis* subsp. *byzantinus* with red ladybird poppies, *Papaver commutatum.*

This is a near-hardy gladiolus from southern Europe, but it varies a great deal in colour and you may find it difficult to locate the brilliant one I am writing about. It must be a cultivar, as it doesn't set seed but multiplies rapidly in a border from offsets (small corms or bulblets that grow off the parent). Beth Chatto offers it, and I hope she's not fed up with being asked for it. Dan Pearson wanted it for his 'meadow' area at Chelsea, but was supplied with a different species. Its vital colouring looks especially lively among green meadow grasses, and we plant it there.

The ladybird poppy is a crimson annual with a black blotch at the base of each petal. It is very showy and Fergus raises a lot of it in pots, either sowing in autumn or in early spring. He plants them out lavishly, and I've never met anyone who wasn't thrilled by them. You have to visit them each morning to savour the newly opened blooms.

Our lupins have done well this year, having not been afflicted by the wretched lupin aphis. If that turns up, you have to spray against it several times. I like to choose my lupin colours. This year, we have pale yellow and red. We sow about now, line the seedlings out in separate rows and, in late autumn, plant them where they are to flower next year. By then, they will have flowered a bit in their rows and we can rogue out those we don't like.

These lupins are treated as bedding plants. We interplant their groups with tulips, and lupin foliage makes an ideal background to these. After the lupins have finished (very soon now) we destroy them, at the same time lifting and saving the tulip bulbs, which will be sorted through some rainy day for the largest, which we will use again next year. The display area will then be planted up with summer- to autumn-flowering things, often of a flamboyant nature, notably cannas (such as 'General

Eisenhower') and dahlias (such as 'Bishop of Llandaff' and 'Ellen Huston').

So this one area works hard for us, providing three seasons of display. We shan't grow lupins there the next year, as we like a change. Bedding offers endless scope to experiment – this is a high-maintenance garden and gives us a lot of fun and opportunity for discussion.

Muted Colours

Some colours are old-fashioned. We think of Victorian matrons and the rustle of taffeta skirts in their connection.

In respect of flowers, the short-spurred columbines, *Aquilegia vulgaris*, known nowadays as granny's bonnets (though I believe this cosy appellation to be of quite recent adoption), set the tone exactly. In various shades of lilac, mauve, purple and sort-of blue, their colours never jump at you. Even when white, they are a muted shade of white.

I have been delighted this year with a seed strain called 'Magpie', that has given perfectly uniform results. The leaves were suffused with purple before the buds matured, and associated cunningly with the young, crispy foliage of sea kale, *Crambe maritima*, which are also near to purple before fully expanding. The aquilegia's flowers are purple and white – white with a hint of purple, not staring. If you don't like magpies (I do) you can call it 'William Guiness' and be correct.

Another old-fashioned-looking plant is the Jerusalem sage, *Phlomis fruticosa*. Its evergreen leaves are dusty grey and the whorls of hooded, labiate flowers a dusky shade of yellow – not a quarrelsome yellow at all, though they make their mark in a mixed-border setting. This is a shrub and I have had my plant for more than 40 years. Never much more than a metre high, it has spread-eagled, so that all sorts of other plants, often self-sown, grow between its limbs. At some point, it needs dead-heading, though the dust that it then gives off makes many of us cough and choke most painfully. Give the job to someone who doesn't notice or do it when the plant is wet.

Auriculas come in a range of old-fashioned colours and shades, including brown and ochre, as well as purples and mauves. The seed

Christopher Lloyd with head gardener, Fergus Garrett, standing under Malus floribunda

Looking towards the house from the Lower Moat:
wood anemones, primulas and buttercups growing wild

Spring in the High Garden:
'If I could have only one
spring flower, it would be the
tulip; if I could have only one
type of tulip, it would be the
lily-flowered because of its
elegance; and if I could choose
but one of those, it would be
"Queen of Sheba".'

Christopher Lloyd
chopping herbs in
the kitchen at Dixter

Euphorbia in front of
aubrieta: 'The key is
never to think of plants
in isolation, but always
in some combination.
That's where the art of
gardening comes in.'

Dahlia 'Wittemans
Superba': 'Red flowers
backed up with flatteringly
supportive neighbours.'

In the vegetable garden: Christopher Lloyd holding his dog, Canna,
and leaning against the compost heap over which he has grown gourds

'I love bright colours, so dahlias and cannas provide most of these.' Orange flowers – single-flowered dahlias combined with the large flowers and purple foliage of cannas – grown amidst verbena which 'makes a pierced wall of green stems and heads of soft purple flowers'. In the background, one of the bananas which are a feature of the Exotic Garden

Pears 'Doyenne du Comice',
the favourite dessert pear of
Christopher Lloyd's father,
who bought Dixter in 1910

The Long Border in autumn

Storm clouds brewing over the Peacock Garden. English irises grow between the rows of the aster hedges

Frost in the Peacock Garden, with topiary and aster hedges

strain of so-called alpine auriculas, offered by DT Brown, has given me excellent results. After three years, I am splitting the crowns into separate rosettes. They can be bedded out like polyanthus, but look better on their own rather than as a carpet to bulbs. Their flowering season lasts for two months from late March. Out of season, plant them out of sight in a moist position, which can be partially shaded.

Wallflowers, *Erysimum* (*Cheiranthus*) *cheiri*, should be sown now for next spring's bedding, and the old-fashioned colours will be found in such strains as brown 'Vulcan', 'Blood Red' or 'Purple Queen'. These mix well with a bright colour, like those in 'Cloth of Gold', but the latter, being assertive, should not be planted in a higher ratio than one in three. You can sow your wallflower seed in a drill outside, but if the weather is dry, water the bottom of the drill first.

The seedlings may need protecting from flea beetle with a spray. When large enough to handle, line them out to grow on into bushy plants, which will be better than any you'll get in the marketplace.

Many of the old roses that were bred before the lively modern pigments came in are in muted shades of mauve and purple. 'William Lobb' is one such, in the moss-rose category, 'Veilchenblau' (Violet Blue) among the ramblers.

Another rambler, *Rosa banksiae* 'Lutea', with trusses of neatly doubled flowers in May (June in Scotland), is a soft, kindly shade of buff yellow. This rose likes shelter but is extremely vigorous. You should plant it only where there is plenty of space, and tie in its long young shoots. Don't prune them – this is a rose that takes a few years to settle down to the business of flowering. In one instance, in east Scotland, it took nine years to gestate, but was regular after that. Pruning of a mature specimen consists of the removal of old growths that have flowered several times. As the rose is virtually thornless, this is a far less painful exercise than handling the 'Mermaids' and 'Albertines' of this world.

An annual that has come into prominence quite recently is *Cerinthe major* 'Purpurascens'. Growing 0.7m tall, its leaves are gun-metal grey, while the bracts and tubular flowers – not unlike a comfrey's, for this belongs to the borage family – are purple. We have some pots of it outside our porch, and muted though the colouring is, everyone notices this plant.

It flowers for ages, but by far the best results are obtained from an early autumn sowing, overwintering the individually potted-off seedlings under just frost-free glass.

Another annual, *Salpiglossis*, has trumpet flowers that are intricately patterned, but specialise in calm bronze, browny orange, purple, dusky blue and pinky-lilac shades. Sometimes, to be honest, the colours are too muddy and get thrown out. I like to grow this flower as a pot plant for display. For that purpose, an early April sowing is soon enough.

Bronze seems to be the most natural colour for chrysanthemums, and it goes with their characteristic smell, which epitomises autumn. All-the-year chrysanths are a ghastly mistake. Flower arrangers would do well to ban such hackneyed flowers from their repertory.

Garden Scent

This season's muggy weather, known to gardeners as good growing weather, is also ideal for bringing out scents, both of flowers and of plants.

If the scent of sweet peas matters to you more than glamorous appearance, you want to turn to the Grandiflora types that prevailed before the large, frilly Spencers became the rage a century ago, reigning supreme ever since. Old-fashioned Grandifloras – typically purple, but the pink-and-white 'Painted Lady' is still available – are the only kind I grow. Their fragrance is astonishing.

Most of the evergreen sun roses, Cistus, are midsummer-flowering. Each bloom normally lasts a day, but there is a profusion of them. Any that are gummy to touch will be aromatic. My favourite, C. x *cyprius* (1.5m), is white with maroon blotches at the centre. In winter, the dark green leaves are the colour of oxidised lead.

With the milder climate we've lately been enjoying, *Pittosporum tobira* has been a success in many gardens. Its clusters of white flowers open in early summer and are deliciously fragrant. Better known is the neat-leaved *P. tenuifolium*, which will make a small tree, although it can easily be clipped as a hedge. That has small, chocolate-coloured, powerfully fragrant flowers – akin to cocoa but not altogether pleasant at close range. It has a number of variegated forms.

Day lilies, *Hemerocallis*, should, in my opinion, be sweetly scented, though many are not. The yellow-flowered kinds are the most reliable in this respect. Early-flowering *H. lilioasphodelus* is of ancient cultivation and amazingly free-flowering, but becomes a bit of a mess at the height of summer, so I like to fit in a clump here and there, where they won't get in the way. Showy and having a much longer season is 'Marion Vaughn', a real winner with bold yellow flowers. It's good in front of the tall mauve *Phlox paniculata*. This class of phlox has a scent all its own, that is lovely on the air.

Philadelphus, the mock oranges, are mostly strong on the air, though some have practically no scent. The early-flowering *P. coronarius*, one of the strongest, has several forms that are equally good for their leaves. The golden-leaved 'Aureus' tends to scorch on its flowering branches but not on its young growth. So prune out the flowered shoots as soon as flowering is past. The white-margined 'Variegatus' looks light and airy. Its white flowers do not show up well, but they have all the fragrance you could wish for.

Perhaps my favourite is 'Sybille', which has none of the coarse growth of many, but arching wands whose height is easily kept to 1.5m by removing flowered shoots.

Euphorbias

Euphorbias are so strongly structured that they always stand out in a garden setting. Always, that is, apart from the petty spurge, which is an annual weed, almost devoid of character.

Most euphorbias are perennial, whether shrubby or herbaceous, with a woody base. But there are at least two biennial species of note. *E. lathyris*, the caper spurge, grows boldly to 90cm and draws attention to its presence with its dark green foliage in two ranks. But it sows itself too freely and generally in the wrong place – and it does not ward off moles, as advertised.

On the other hand I'm very fond of *E. stricta*. This hardy species will colonise in Northumberland as happily as in Sussex and it is admirable in paving cracks where an element of starvation brings out the red colouring in its metre-tall flowering stems. It is easily controlled when in the wrong place so there's a lot going for this species.

Boldest of the shrubby spurges is *E. characias* subsp. *wulfenii*. Don't be content with straight *E. characias*, green, with a dark frog's spawn eye. It lacks the personality of *wulfenii* which, in its best forms, stands out from a great distance, with bold, lime-green inflorescences set off by rich, slightly glaucous, evergreen foliage. It is compulsively photogenic.

That usually grows to 1.2m. *E. mellifera* can, in a sheltered corner, grow considerably taller but this is a tenderer species. Worth risking, however, as its light green foliage, clustered into extended rosettes, has the kind of presence that every garden needs. The flowers are insignificant to look at, but in their April season they waft a strong honey scent.

The name mellifera tells this story but another species, *E. cyparissias*, gives off the same scent, though I have never seen it alluded to in print. This is the cypress spurge, whose foliage is arranged in a brush similar to the juvenile foliage on a conifer. It is a creeping plant, only 30cm high and makes a beautiful colony, in a sunny position, with massed flowers in vivid yellow-green.

They sparkle in the sunshine, and this is another endearing character in many euphorbias. There must be a glistening dot of nectar at the centre of each flower, when the light – especially low light – catches it, it sparkles like a sliver of glass. Planted in the right place, you'll love this species; it colours brightly in the autumn before disappearing for the winter. But it is invasive, so you mustn't grow it near precious things.

Another notable sparkler is *E. palustris*, whose name indicates its preference for wet, stodgy soil. It is the freshest thing in my spring garden, with quite bold flower heads closely arranged on a perennial plant that is 60–90cm high when flowering, but grows to 1.2–1.5m in the course of the season and may flop on to its neighbours. Best, therefore, to plant around it winter- and spring-flowering bulbs.

Most widely known of the spring-flowerers is the hummocky *E. polychroma*, which is particularly brilliant greeny yellow at the height of its April season. This looks good with red flowers, such as *Anemone* x *fulgens*. The display is relatively short-lived; not much more than two weeks, at its peak.

So perhaps, if space is limited, one should give preference to those euphorbias, of which there are quite a number, which flower for a long period. Heading this group would come *E. seguieriana* subsp. *niciciana*. Again, it makes a hummock, about 40cm high. Its leaves are almost needle-fine, the flowers in small but numerous heads, bright yellow-green and remaining fresh from May till autumn.

The penalty for this overextended profusion is that plants are liable, after a few years, to flower themselves to death. I sometimes get the odd self-sown seedling, but it is safer to take cuttings while the plant is still young enough to carry bright green, non-flowering shoots. Non-flowering this year, but flowering next. At the front of a border, this spurge will look good with a tufted flowering grass such as *Pennisetum orientale* or *P. villosum* (raised from seed).

E. sikkimensis is long in flower with a useful late summer to early autumn season. It is a suckering perennial that makes a colony. Perhaps its best moment is in late winter, when its young shoots are a warmly inviting shade of coral red (brighter than *E. griffithii*, which is otherwise similar at this stage). The lime-green flowers of *E. sikkimensis* are borne at 1.2–1.5m and my chief grumble against this species is that, in well-nourished garden soil, it is a flopper and it is difficult (though not impossible) to support unobtrusively. On rather poor soil and in an open situation it grows shorter and more sturdily.

My overall preference, however, would be for the fairly lately introduced and named *E. schillingii*. This flowers from July to September. It doesn't run but makes a clump, 1.2m tall, with bold inflorescences nearer to yellow than to green. It is an excellent border perennial and mixes particularly well with blue lacecap hydrangeas. As good and with the same season is *E. longifolia*, another clump former. Its sharply angled bracts, which are the showy element in the inflorescence, give it exceptional definition.

Philadelphus

From early May to late July the mock oranges, Philadelphus, are in bloom; the ideal in one's own garden would be to walk from the orbit of one into that of the next with only a small gap in which to take breath. Their fragrance is carried generously on the air, and is of that kind which suddenly assails you en route when you are thinking of something entirely different. These are good moments, and they are the essence of summer.

Although beautiful in flower, mock oranges are not generally beautiful shrubs, so you can scatter them about singly, sometimes in the background, sometimes nearer the foreground, for their heights vary from 3.6m to a mere 90cm or 1.2m. Strong spikes of blue or purple delphiniums look wonderful among the cascading branches of a Philadelphus.

The mock orange flower is nearly always white, though not infrequently flushed purple at the base of each petal, as in 'Beauclerk', whose 7.5cm-wide single blooms are among the most dramatic on a large specimen. There are a number of double-flowered varieties, and although the individual blooms do not stand up to close inspection of their somewhat dot-and-carry form, they give an overall impression of bounty. The extra blossom weighs the branches into arcs and swags.

'Virginal' is the best-known large-flowered double. I had it for many years but its gaunt habit, and a propensity to shy flowering unless given the sunniest of positions, persuaded me to give it up. 'Burfordensis' is another that is unnecessarily stiff in habit. I have the double 'Enchantement', which grows to 1.8 or 2.4m, and there are some charming 90cm- to 1.2m-high doubles, such as 'Boule d'Argent'.

Of a graceful, widespreading habit but only (as a rule) a few feet high is 'Sybille', which has single flowers, purple stained. The single 'Manteau d'Hermine' is probably the most popular of the dwarf mock oranges and deservedly. The flowers are creamy white and richly scented.

The quality and strength of mock orange scent varies considerably. In *Philadelphus incanus* there is very little at all, but it is a beautiful late-flowering species, continuing to the end of July and notable for its greyish foliage.

One of my favourite mid-season mock oranges is *P. delavayi* var. *calvescens*, alias *P. purpurascens*, in which the cupped flowers are enclosed by a purple calyx. This touch of colour gives the bush (it grows quite large) an air of distinction.

Although foliage is not generally the mock orange's strongest feature, there are exceptions, especially in the European species, *P. coronarius*, cultivated in Britain, since the sixteenth century, if not before. The flowers of this species are small and cream rather than white, but they are early in bloom, often by early May, and exceptionally powerful in their scent. Rather than the type plant, you should grow 'Aureus' or 'Variegatus'.

'Aureus' has vivid lime-green foliage in spring and early summer, and although it flowers freely, there is a strong case for treating it as a foliage plant by shortening all its growth quite hard back each winter. In that case the young leaf wands, which will be freely and vigorously produced, will look their most handsome and will seldom scorch, which is the main fault in 'Aureus' when given standard pruning treatment. Even before it has finished flowering, the small leaves on flowering branches turn brown, a condition aggravated by hot sunshine and dry roots.

'Variegatus' is not strong-growing, but is one of the prettiest shrubs when its white blossom combines with heavily white-variegated leaves in late May. This, too, has a tendency to scorch.

The correct and regular pruning of mock oranges is important if you are to retain a comely shrub, not a vast thicket consisting largely of dead wood and taking up a quite undeserved share of garden space. If yours is such, either inherited from a previous owner or allowed to develop by you through benign neglect, order can still be restored. There is no cause for despair.

The main principle in pruning any philadelphus, and other shrubs of similar habit – deutzia, dipelta, weigela, keria and abelia, for instance – is to remove all flowered wood and leave the young shoots intact. You can either do this immediately after flowering – which is probably best as long as you don't break too many fragile young shoots while you're plunging around – or in winter, when there's more time for such ploys and when, the leaves being off, you can better see what you're about.

The flowered branches are easily recognised, even in winter, because they have a mass of side shoots which bore the flowers. Young growth consists of whippy, unbranched wands of a deeper brown than the old wood. So you remove the flowered wood, making your cut just above the point where a strong young shoot arises (take no notice of weak young shoots).

If there are no such shoots, this must be a tired old branch and you can remove it at ground level by sawing rather than cutting through with a blade.

One golden rule is never to prune out the tip of a young shoot; be sure to always leave the entire wand intact throughout its length. It will then flower along its entire length. If you tip it, weak leafy shoots will be produced below your cut, unbalanced and undesired.

But what to do with your overgrown monster? Make up your mind, for a start, that you will almost certainly need a bath after tackling it.

173

You will find there are no strong, wand-like young shoots in such a neglected veteran. You must induce them. Remove half the bush, selectively sawing out the oldest, largest branches. Make each saw cut as close to ground level as you can otherwise the stumps you leave, besides being useless in themselves, will get in the way of your making other cuts.

What remains then will still not be beautiful, but you will have enabled light to reach the centre and bottom of the bush so new young growth will be made in the next growing season – particularly if you feed generously with a mixture of bulky organic manure as a surface mulch, and some general fertiliser applied in spring. Generous watering in times of drought will also help.

Next year, you can set about removing the rest of the old bush, so that from the third year you'll be following a normal annual routine.

June Jobs

Flowers come and go so swiftly at this season that it needs an act of concentration to take them in while they are there. Cistuses and their relations – Halimium and Helianthemum (shear these over after their first flush, otherwise they'll go bare in the middle) – must be seen in the morning, as they generally shatter at midday.

Watch the alliums. If you like them to self-sow, as I do *Allium cristophii* in particular, leave their faded flower heads, which are generally ornamental anyway. With chives, however, it is easy to have too many. Take a large pruning or kitchen knife and slash all their top growth to the ground; it will sprout fresh shoots within the week. A. *neapolitanum*, left to itself, is too prolific.

Grab all the shoots on a clump between both hands and tug sharply. They will separate cleanly from the bulbs and you can now fill the gaps around them with summer bedding. The allium will start to grow again in October.

Lupins will be going over soon, if not actually gone. (I hope you took action against the revolting lupin aphid, as soon as spotted.) To an extent you can coax them on by removing the central spikes and allowing side spikes to continue the show. Last year, as with many perennials, my lupins flushed with an entirely new crop of blossom in July. More often, however, they go down to mildew by then and look a wreck.

You could plant annual climbers to clamber over them – *Thunbergia alata* (black-eyed Susan); *Rhodochiton atrosanguineus*, with its purple lanterns; *Ipomoea quamoclit*, or morning glory (*Ipomoea* 'Heavenly Blue'). I treat my lupins as biennials and throw them out when flowered – raising a new batch from spring-sown seed if I want to repeat them the next year. This method requires a stock bed in which to grow them on – likewise other biennials such as wallflowers, sweet williams, foxgloves and mulleins.

The same goes for Canterbury bells, *Campanula medium*. We are at the height of the campanula season, now. Canterbury bells do not flower for very long, but if you have only a few plants and they are close to where you often pass, you can pinch out the individual faded blooms and a second crop will be borne later on. Cup-and-saucer types and doubles provide more colour for your money, but the singles are colourful enough and much the most elegantly shaped.

Among the earliest campanulas in flower is the biennial C. *patula* (from Chiltern Seeds), and you should sow that now for next May. It has gracefully loose sprays of open bells in typical campanulas blue.

I am combining that with the old verbascum variety called 'Gainsborough', which has open panicles, and is 1m tall, with soft yellow flowers. This is often twice the height of some campanula, but, being a see-through plant, there would be no need to think in terms of shortest at the front, tallest at the back. These perennial verbascums come readily from root cuttings, and so do oriental poppies. You could take these now: the season is not critical, but the sooner you make your cuttings, the sooner you'll have strong plants.

Scratch around the base of established plants and you will find thickish, fleshy roots. Extract long pieces of these, remembering which end is top and which bottom. Cut them into 10cm lengths and insert them with the top just covered in light soil on the shady side of a building – somewhere easily watered. Alternatively, use a cold frame. Leafy shoots are apt to be made before new roots, so don't be in a hurry to move the young plants until they are properly established.

Among the prettiest effects in my garden just now is a mixture of the pure white *Ammi majus* and the light, open spikes of a larkspur – 'Blue

Cloud', or something similar. The ammi is a kind of biennial Queen Anne's lace (this sounds rather better than cow parsley).

For best results, in both cases, you should try to sow in the autumn and overwinter the young plants under cold glass. Plant out in April from 10cm pots. The ammi will grow to 2m or more, and the larkspur a little less, but it is nice to mix the plants. Again, they are of open, see-through habit.

Gladiolus byzantinus, which is now designated G. *communis* subsp. *byzantinus*, was at its best at the turn of May–June, and in its most brilliant form most often seen in cottage gardens. It is magenta on the inner segments, but somewhat warmer carmine purple on the outer. It is a striking plant, 1m tall, that can be fitted in almost anywhere, as it takes up little lateral space and dies away soon after flowering. So, if border phloxes, for instance, were its neighbours, they would quickly fill the gap.

This gladiolus sets little or no seed, but is prolific in making small corms, which can be grown on. Lift clumps now, replanting in early autumn, as growth starts in winter. This species looks dramatic in meadow conditions, where its colour is a wonderful contrast with the green of fresh grass and yellow of field buttercups, *Ranunculus acris*.

If you buy your corms, you are, unfortunately, liable to get a strain with considerably weaker mauve-pink flowers. So, watch your sources, keep your eyes open and, if really necessary, beg.

Serial Planting

24 June, Midsummer's Day, and many gardens may be judged to have reached their peak for the year. Their shrub roses are in full blow; the Hybrid Teas and Floribundas – depending on when and how hard they were pruned – are not far off it. Must a slow decline from now on be a garden's fate?

In many cases, it is, but what a shame to accept it. Only now can we rely on the evenings being warm enough for a soirée without the need to don extra layers. Only now has the sharpness of spring truly yielded to a beguiling, 24-hour-long softness in the air. So why allow it to be wasted on a scene of ever-increasing slovenliness and decay? It need not be so, but the decision is up to each of us.

In the first place, we need to be vigilant over upkeep. Dead-heading may seem a chore, but it makes all the difference to appearances. Kniphofias whose pokers have run their course look terrible if simply left to decay visibly. The larger-flowered day lilies really need to have their dead heads removed every morning if the newly opened blooms are not to be seen in a sordid setting. Many roses are even more obtrusive. If you cannot cope with this situation, admit it and grow fewer of these delinquents.

Lupins run to seed – their spikes are easily removed – but their foliage will almost certainly become unsightly with mildew. Our solution at Dixter is to grow them as biennials, sowing seed for next year now and chucking out the flowered plants now or very soon. That leaves us with a clean space in which to enjoy new plantings for the rest of the summer, such as dahlias, zinnias, or gaily coloured coleus plants, all of which can be raised in readiness from May sowings.

Even easier would be bedding nasturtiums, which need not be sown till this month, as they come on so quickly. Poke a couple of seeds of comparatively compact bedding types into a number of pots and the plants will be ready to bed out when you want them.

Always think ahead, even when you are ordering seeds in the winter. Around now, we are planting up our exotic garden in readiness for an exciting August-to-October display. True, you need some greenhouse space in which to bring many of the plants on, but a lot of British gardeners have that.

If your delphiniums are soon threatening you with a wreckage of cut-back stems, plant some annual climbers to grow over them. Morning glory, *Ipomoea* 'Heavenly Blue', offers a fresh revelation every day. As charming in its way is *I. quamoclit*, better known as *Mina lobata*, with racemes of tubular flowers graded through red to yellow and white. But one of the best is *Rhodochiton atropurpureum*, with garlands of purple bells over a long season. Best policy with that is to sow it in September and bring the seedlings on under glass.

Dahlias, of course, are a wonderful mainstay from July on. There is such a range of different kinds that even if you loathe some of them there must surely be others that will please you. Late-struck cuttings will provide plants that are just right for planting out now, to replace biennials such as foxgloves and sweet williams.

I grow early-flowering chrysanthemums in a row. They are seedlings (you can either sow in spring or save old plants). When we can see their relative heights, and colour enough in their buds to gauge how best to group them, we move them to replace annuals, perhaps in late August or in September. Given a good soaking before and after the move, they take it without flinching. So do Michaelmas daisies.

Perennials and shrubs must play their part. Hydrangeas have, between the different kinds, a tremendously long season that has already started. Some varieties flower almost continuously, both from shoots off last year's old wood and from young shoots made this year. You can help them with generous waterings (feeding is better reserved for the run-up to flowering) and by dead-heading the earlier trusses.

The border phloxes – most of them cultivars of *Phlox paniculata* – flower in July and August. We are interplanting them with tulips for earlier interest. Some phloxes – generally the earliest flowerers – give a repeat performance. So do other perennials, such as *Helenium* 'Moerheim Beauty' and *Salvia* x *superba*. But a dead-heading in between crops will greatly help.

There are certain stalwart bedding plants with a long flowering season. They are great allies, though it can happen that you get bored with them. Some marigolds I can do without, but there are others making big enough plants to have personality; they make good living companions. And you'll need fewer plants. Choose your fibrous-rooted bedding begonias (*Begonia semperflorens* types) carefully. Those with a free habit are the easiest to integrate into mixed plantings.

Among ageratums, by far the best as a freely growing, long-flowering mixed border plant is 'Blue Horizon'. Grow it yourself from seed, next year.

Sowing Biennials

Biennials are those plants which need two growing seasons between seed germination and seed harvest. Many of them flower in early summer and thereby fill the gap between spring bulbs and summer bedding.

Their disadvantage may be that, if they die off in July, you need to have done a bit of advance head-scratching on how to follow them for the rest of the growing season. This is not difficult, but anything is better than leaving their corpses – of sweet williams, for example – to spoil the appearance of your borders from August to October.

On the question of when to sow the seed of biennials, much depends on whether or not they are liable to flower in the year of sowing, as though they were annuals. If they do this, they may not be of much use in the following year, when they should be performing. Sweet williams, traditional Canterbury bells, foxgloves and biennial mulleins such as *Verbascum olympicum* will never flower in the year of sowing. If you sow them early, say April or May, you will enjoy the largest plants, capable of putting on the finest display, and avoid their flowering at half-cock.

The brilliant orange Siberian wallflower, *Erysimum hieraciifolium*, however, and the mauve *Erysimum linifolium*, which behaves similarly, can flower prematurely after an early sowing. The next few weeks is when to get busy with them.

There are several biennials that are best sown now. A spring sowing of the Iceland poppy, *Papaver nudicaule*, may give you flowers the same year, but you can obtain far larger and longer-flowering plants from a summer sowing. These poppies sometimes attempt a second season, but it is better to start again. The horned poppy, *Glaucium flavum*, is as delightful for its scalloped, pale grey foliage in its first year as for its yellow flowers in its second. This grows wild in the shingle along our coasts. Possibly even more attractive is the form called *fulvum*, whose silken flowers (they last for only a day) are burnt orange.

A must among the sages is *Salvia sclarea* var. *turkestanica*, whose big, furry leaves support a strong flowering spike (1.5m) in shades of soft, rosy-mauve. The plant has a strong, catty smell when bruised, so you and your cats are advised not to roll in it. *S. argentea* is grown chiefly for its palest grey, woolly foliage and is happiest on very dry, well-drained soil. Even better, in my opinion, is the similar *S. aethiopis*: its leaves have wide indentations and its flowers, at 1m, are white.

There are several kinds of biennial honesty, *Lunaria annua*, which it is as well to keep separate from each other if their self-sown progeny are to retain their identity. Typically a strong shade of purple, there are two variegated kinds: the mauve-flowered 'Variegata', in which the leaves are mottled and streaked haphazardly in cream, and the white-flowered 'Alba Variegata', in which the white variegation is more distinctly zoned. Then there is the pure, white-flowered var. *albiflora*, with plain green leaves, at 1m or more.

Not dissimilar, apart from its night scent, is sweet rocket, *Hesperis matronalis*, which is typically mauve, but seed of the albino, var. *albiflora* (2m), is what I normally grow. It lights up a shady situation.

Talking of disorganised variegation, this is never more hectic than in the tree mallow, *Lavatera arborea* 'Variegata' (1.5m). The seedlings may start plain green, but the variegation becomes increasingly widespread and intense, reaching a maximum in the early summer of its second year. Although quite woody, the plant usually dies after flowering, but also self-sows.

The deadly poisonous henbane, *Hyoscyamus niger*, often included in a herb garden's poisonous section, makes a low rosette of clammy, hairy foliage in its first year (though the seeds often lie dormant for several years before germinating). In its second, the villainous, sickly yellow funnel flowers, veined purple, look every bit as wicked as they are. They open in succession on a branching inflorescence, up to 1m, and the seed pods are persistent, excellent for dried flower decorations. Altogether, a rather fascinating plant.

Some perennials – those that are grown from seed and are at their strongest as young plants – can be grown as biennials and discarded after flowering. Such is *Anchusa azurea*, whose blue flowers obviously relate it to borage, though it will grow 2m tall. When setting out young plants in the autumn, I make cuttings from its fleshy roots, each about 8cm long. These are tied into a bundle and plunged upright into gravel or light soil to overwinter. In the spring, when they are sprouting, they are lined out to make strong plants for the next season. Having flowered, and as they become straggling, we replace them with dahlias or cannas.

Herbaceous lupins, *Lupinus polyphyllus*, are excellent grown from seed and treated as biennials. Having lined them out to grow, in the summer, we bed them in the autumn and interplant them with tulips, for which the lupins' foliage makes an excellent background. The lupins' own display will have been completed by the end of June, and this year we are replacing them with large-flowered zinnias, sown in early May. But there is a wide choice of alternatives.

July

The Garden at its Peak

If I am asked, 'When is your garden at its best?' I reply, 'Now, today,' but if the question is pleasantly accented, my reply is, '9 July' (or sometimes 12 July, in a late season).

A great many perennials reach their peak around now. On my heavy soil, phloxes are in their element, especially if we can get around to giving them a good soak in the run-up. Between the different varieties, their season is quite two months long. *Phlox carolina* 'Miss Lingard' is already a range of long conical white peaks before the end of June, but most of the heaving eiderdown phloxes can be attributed to *P. paniculata*, which also has the best scent.

The names of most of mine have never reached me, as my original stock came from friends' gardens, where they were obviously growing healthily. A clean bill of health is essential when starting out with phloxes – much more important than the exact shade of colour.

Some of the earlier-flowering kinds will put on a worthwhile second display. That is one of the plus points with *Helenium* 'Moerheim Beauty', which will bloom again in September, if you dead-head the first flush. It is a warm, bronzy orange and I grow it near *Salvia* x *superba*, which is purple, with a reddish-purple calyx. It is, in my view, the best by far in this group of perennial sages, having great staying power. Again, it flowers a second time in September.

Next to my salvia is a patch of pure scarlet *Lychnis chalcedonica*, whose domed flower heads contrast with the sage's spikes. The lychnis has one flowering that lasts for three weeks at most.

It's a similar story with the fiery-red *Crocosmia* 'Lucifer'. That has bold, ribbed sword leaves and the flowers present themselves proudly. I allow the magenta-flowered *Lychnis coronaria* (its leaves and stems are a soothing grey) to seed itself among or close to 'Lucifer', if you find that too contentious, I recommend the sea holly, *Eryngium* x *oliverianum*, as a quieter partner that benefits from a lively neighbour. It is blue, with the colour strongest on its stems below the spiky inflorescence.

Astilbes are a reproach if not liberally supplied with water. I have rather gone off the general run of them, as their season is so short. 'Superba', often called *Astilbe taquetii* 'Superba', is one of the best, flowering for longer and having excellent foliage. And I enjoy its self-sowing habits. 'Professor van der Wielen' is another self-sower that comes true, and its white plumes are graceful – not stiff, like many astilbes.

Astilbes are good in partial shade, as are astrantias. *Astrantia maxima* is a bold shade of pink, and its running rootstock can be allowed to wander among thin-textured shrubs.

Of the greeny-white forms of *A. major*, 'Margery Fish' (*A. major* subsp. *involucrata* 'Shaggy' when correctly identified) is one of the punchiest, but these astrantias' self-seeding habits are a nuisance, as the bastards are generally inferior to the parent. 'Ruby Wedding', well grown, is by far the finest of the red-toned varieties, needing sunlight to bring out its deep, rich colouring.

I am a staunch supporter of yellow daisies. *Telekia speciosa* (*Buphthalmum speciosum*), at 1.5m, opens from buds with intricately overlapping bracts to form a branching candelabrum, then fades to black, which looks good in winter if not swept aside.

Inula hookeri has soft, spirally swirling buds that open at 1m to palish-yellow daisies that are very popular with butterflies. Its rootstock runs a little and may need curbing at the margins. *I. magnifica* lives up to its name, with the largest bright yellow daisies on a 2.5m plant. It copes well with turf and makes a handsome ingredient in rough grass.

Shrubs play an important part in mixed borders, and those that flower now are especially to be valued. Hydrangeas are among the favourites, high marks going to *Hydrangea arborescens* 'Annabelle', with large, pure white buns over a long period.

Roses are good if they can be absorbed into their surroundings. You must not be aware of stiff, stick-like legs. At the front, 'The Fairy' is one of the best, with its neat, shiny leaves and flowers of a pure shade of pink. Like the single pink 'Ballerina', it isn't at all stemmy.

Clematis should certainly be included, the most valuable being those that flower on their young wood and can be cut hard back at the end of the season. Most of them are reaching a climax now. I have the purple *Clematis* 'Jackmanii Superba' making a column up a 4m pole, behind a 2m daisy with shiny leaves and large heads of small flowers, *Senecio doria*.

Yellow, biennial mulleins are in this part of the border, too, their positions varying a little from year to year. *Verbascum olympicum* makes a splendid 2–3m candelabrum, and is effective when allowed to move to the front of a one-sided border.

The cranesbills that I favour in July are the double blue and double purple forms of *Geranium pratense*. The blue one, 'Plenum Caeruleum', contrasts happily with a prolific, small-flowered yellow day lily, *Hemerocallis* 'Corky'.

Dry Conditions

Everyone is predicting a hot summer; perhaps it is with us already. This raises burning questions for the gardener – water for the plants being the most urgent of them. Hosepipe bans are already in operation in many parts of the country.

Many people imagine that the planting season ended with spring and won't return till autumn, but this is by no means the case. The warm conditions of summer are excellent for establishing a great many plants, always provided that sufficient water is available to give them a kick-start.

Cultivate the planting ground thoroughly and incorporate plenty of well-rotted organic goodies. Firm this ground by treading on it. When digging each hole that will receive a plant, make sure it is large enough to take the plant comfortably and without any cramping. Hold the plant in the hole at the right level with one hand and tip in enough water (I turn a can of it upside down) to fill the hole. As the water drains away, fill the hole with soil. You shouldn't need to compress it.

In this way, the plant is given a good start with water at its roots. The most frequent mistake is to complete planting before you water, and to imagine that a sprinkling right at the end is sufficient. In fact, this surface watering dries out almost instantly. On heavy soil, it is also apt to seal the surface, so that subsequent rains cannot penetrate but run off. Get the water in where it's needed – at the roots – right at the start.

Some plants' water requirements are greater than others. You can plant, as Beth Chatto has in her gravel garden, with drought-resistant plants that hail from countries where rainfall is minimal and desiccating winds all too frequent. Woolly leaved plants are drought-resistant, as are those glaucous plants with waxy leaves, which protect them from water loss.

Cistuses can put up with droughty conditions; so can verbascums, brooms such as *Spartium junceum*, lavenders and many others. Succulents, too. They have inbuilt water reserves, requiring only occasional replenishment. We bed out tender cacti and succulents for the summer. Even so, you should not get the idea that succulents never need watering. They do, and thoroughly, once in a while, but if this is done at the start, when planting, there'll be little to worry about during a drought.

Choosing the Right Rose

Over the years, I have severely cut down on the number of roses that I grow. The many disadvantages of herding them into gardens or beds of their own are only too plain to see. This way of growing them is almost a reflex action when starting a new garden – a feature that is taken to be a necessity. Of course, it is nothing of the kind and leads to all sorts of troubles, including pests and diseases, in the same way as herding a great many people together does.

But to be altogether without roses would also be unthinkable and, by scattering them through my garden so that they keep company with other plants, I can take fullest advantage of their assets while avoiding the pitfalls. Of course, they still have to be pruned and most of them are out for your blood, but it is assumed as an example of natural and undisputed heroism on the gardener's part that he or she should put up with these insults uncomplainingly. To emerge covered with bloody scratches is regarded as a virtue; you can even wear them with pride to a party; they are a topic of conversation.

Quite a number of my roses date back to the time when our garden was made, some 90 years ago. 'Albéric Barbier' came out in 1900. It is still one of the most popular climbers, with its healthy foliage and abundance of fully double, creamy-yellow flowers. A pity it doesn't shed its faded petals.

When it is at its best, I still love 'Irish Elegance', a stiff pillar rose with single blooms, which are particularly shapely as the furled bud expands into an open flower. They are of peachy colouring, and two good crops can be relied upon if the first is dead-headed. Our plant shows no signs of weakening and I am pleased to note that Vita Sackville-West grew it at Sissinghurst, too, where it still exists. And it was she who gave me my cutting of 'Mrs Oakley Fisher', now a 1.5m-tall bush with single, rich apricot flowers above purple young stems.

My parents planted two very large beds of the China rose, 'Comtesse du Caÿla', which (or who) came out in 1902. They were largely decimated in the 1947 winter, but six or eight of them remain and are widely appreciated, with their loosely doubled, deep salmony flowers, which are scented like China tea.

My healthiest 'Perle d'Or' is only 50 or so years old, from a cutting I struck – striking rose cuttings is one of the most satisfying aspects of propagation. It is a large bush, almost 2m tall and has two huge crops of its miniature Hybrid Tea flowers, buff-apricot-coloured and most richly hued when the weather is cool.

As a large shrub, I value 'Cerise Bouquet', whose flat, fully double flowers are borne on long, wand-like, arching shoots. They are of an almost startling cerise colouring and have the most distinctive feature of prominent bracts below each bud.

Collecting Seed

Collecting ripe seeds and growing plants from them is one of the great joys for gardeners. But there appears to be widespread ignorance about which seeds are worth collecting, and what condition they should be in to make the exercise worthwhile.

Every day at poppy-flowering time, our visiting public at Dixter remove a couple of dozen seed heads immediately the petals have been shed. I have to follow up and remove the stalks, as they look awful without anything on them. But the embryo seeds will not be ripe for another couple of months, perhaps. So it is a complete waste of time, as well as being a nuisance.

You must wait until the seed capsules are turning brown, but not for so long that they have already spilt or forcibly ejected their contents. Pansies and violas need to be caught at just the right time, because, on a warm day, the valves of their seed heads will open explosively and most of the contents will be lost. There are many similar cases: alstroemerias, for instance.

I pick these as soon as I see them changing colour and put them in a cardboard shoebox, covered with a single sheet of newspaper, placing this behind a sunny window. All the exploding then happens in safe confinement. It is the same with broom and sweet pea seed pods.

And with euphorbias. One way with these, as also with hellebores, is to tie a nylon stocking end or a piece of horticultural fleece around the capsules, which are clustered in a terminal head, so as to make a bag, thereby safely securing your quarry.

If seed is perfectly ripe on collection, I put it straight into a pay-packet envelope, appropriately labelled, and store it in a cool, dry place forthwith. If still damp, I dry it off on that sunny windowsill.

Some seeds have a very short period of viability and should be sown within a few weeks of ripening. Fleshy seeds shrivel if kept dry, so they want immediate sowing. With peony seeds – for instance the yellow *Paeonia mlokosewitschii* – if you sow at once, a leafy shoot will be produced in the following spring. If you delay at all, the seed may make a root in the following year, but its first shoot will not appear until the year after. Unless the seeds have been stored so as to keep them plump, those of peonies that you buy (and others that are similarly fleshy) will be dead before you receive the packet.

Many umbellifer seeds (belonging to the cow parsley family) have a short life and should be sown in the same autumn as they ripen. Hellebores must be sown quickly. Don't coddle the seed containers: in many cases, frost is needed to break the seeds' dormancy. So, in deciding how to treat the seeds that you have container-sown, consider the plant's natural habitat (there are many reference books to help you). If they come from a climate with hard winters, put the containers where frost can reach them.

Seeds enclosed in pulp, such as berries, should have the pulp washed off before sowing and then be sown immediately. Daphnes are a case in point. *Daphne tangutica*, *D. pontica* and *D. mezereum* all come well from seed, which will germinate the first spring if washed and cleaned, sown forthwith and kept in a cold frame.

Some of the maples grown from seed germinate better if sown a little before they are ripe. It is always worth having a go with *Acer griseum*, which has beautiful, warm brown, peeling bark, excellent autumn colour and makes a fine small tree. It may seed abundantly, but is notorious for poor germination. Still, if you sow hundreds of seeds, outdoors and protected from mice, even a couple of seedlings will probably give you satisfaction.

Ripening this month is *Dianthus* 'Rainbow Loveliness'. I treat this as a biennial, collecting and sowing the seed as soon as it is ripe and getting germination quickly. Seedlings are pricked out and then, if there's time (and for best results), potted individually, overwintered in a cold frame and then planted where they will be required to flower in the spring. They'll be blooming through May and June.

July is a good month for sowing pansies and violas for next spring's bedding – or for winter flowering, if you sow appropriate kinds. From the previous spring's flowering, you can now have ripe seed with which to put your plan into operation. A warning here: if you are growing open-pollinated varieties, you'll save seed from the best plants and go ahead. But if they were F1 hybrids, the progeny will be useless. That's how professional seed-growers make money.

Some plants find it difficult to ripen good seed in our climate and need a good, ripening late summer and early autumn to achieve this. Many composites (of the daisy family) provide examples. I collect the seed of my cardoons, *Cynara cardunculus*, to grow for sales, but they may ripen good seed only once in four or five years. The upside is that the seed keeps well and often remains viable for that long, allowing me to sow it in batches as required. But plants from which you want good seed should not be irrigated from above, thereby making their developing seed heads soggy and liable to moulds. Something I have to remember with the cardoons.

Fuchsias

There are 20 closely printed, double-column pages of fuchsias in the *RHS Plant Finder*. This, and the British Fuchsia Society's activities, suggest the existence of a great number of fuchsia fanciers. Where they all lurk, I do not know. Fuchsias are generally treated as conservatory flowers, though their pots are often brought out for a summer airing, and impressive displays of standard fuchsias are sometimes seen outside.

But if I see a stand of fuchsias at a flower show, I am nearly always aware of a certain monotony not found in, say, begonias or cacti. They just haven't changed much over the years. Larger flowers bring larger leaves, and it is the dullness of their foliage en masse that is partly responsible for the yawn.

But actually, their unchanging quality is an endearing feature. When I go through the lists of names, I find that those I knew half a century ago are still available. 'Scarcity', although a fairly unexciting variety, was a name that always caught my fancy. Why was it so named, and by whom? And who thought of 'Display'? – a simple and obvious name, but more evocative than most, and appropriate, too, as its mauve skirt is widely flared beneath the pinky-red sepals.

'Uncle Charley' always seemed to have a roving eye. The upcurved sepals bring the petals into prominence in a far more effective way than the same colouring – deep pink and mauve – in 'Tennessee Waltz', although that has survived as a hardy perennial in my long border, entirely uncared for, over several decades.

But it starts too late, which is the trouble with many fuchsias when they are treated as hardy plants. A great number of varieties are, in fact, hardy, but our summers are too short for them. By the time they start to flower, autumn is upon us.

In some ways, if it remains open, autumn suits fuchsias in the garden. Once their growth is there, they are happy with cool weather and moisture. And in autumn, we need not worry about the damage caused by capsid bugs, the bugbears of fuchsias in the summer garden, which attack the growing shoot, distort it and prevent it from making flower buds.

In some shy-flowering fuchsias, I don't believe this is the trouble. The vigorous, hardy, red and purple 'Mrs Popple', for example, never starts to flower in earnest for me until late September, even when given protective sprays earlier on. 'Madame Cornélissen' is another that shines only in October, but what a beautiful fuchsia. For once, there is no hint of coarseness in its leaves, while the contrast of red and white is exceptionally clean.

Enthusiasts for the flower alone are apt to neglect its possible uses as a garden plant. Some, I admit, seem to suggest no particular combination. I am fond of 'Lena', which is outstandingly hardy and, although herbaceous outside (as most are), has a long flowering season from early July on. The rather modest sepals are flesh white, but the voluminously doubled skirt is purple. Being heavy-headed, the stems arch to the ground, so a position near paving suggests itself. Other than that, I have no bright ideas for its placement. 'Tom Thumb', on the other hand, is easily matched. It makes a little 30cm bush of small, red and purple flowers that go excellently with a bright green, polypody fern, such as 'Cornubiense'. Both enjoy moist conditions.

'Genii' is a tremendous stand-by, and such a good-looking plant. The redness of its young stems and main leaf veins are presently emphasised by the redness of the flower's calyx, while the leaf blades are luminous lime-green. That makes a good plant in the course of a growing season and I like it placed near golden marjoram with a plant of blue perovskia overhanging from behind.

In late summer and early autumn, red fuchsias also team up well with the pure blue of hardy plumbago, *Ceratostigma willmottianum*, and the lower, but spreading *C. plumbaginoides*, which also has the asset of rich red autumn foliage colouring. And I must do something to rejuvenate and improve my stock of 'Dollar Princess', which is both hardy and early in flower. The red sepals make a tightly cramped rosette of doubled petals. The corner on which I have it always attracts the attention of the snatchers of cuttings, who often leave nasty snags behind. Why can't they carry a knife, like any self-respecting gardener?

One of the attractions of fuchsias to amateur growers is the ease with which they can be propagated from soft cuttings. If you are short of material, internodal cuttings, using only one node at the top of a length of stem, is perfectly adequate. And fuchsias are a pleasant reminder of childhood – one flower is easily transformed into a beautifully dressed fairy, while the popping of fuchsia buds is a pleasure I have yet to grow out of.

Climbers for Trees

We are often asked which climbers would be suitable to grow into trees to pep them up. This is not so simple to answer. The vigour of the climber must be a match for that of the tree, and conditions at the climber's root must not be dry, dark and starved, as is often the case.

First, the tree. It must be of a moderate size, not a forest tree such as an oak. Something like an apple, pear or cherry, whether fruiting or ornamental, would be suitable. So would a conifer, though not one such as Leyland cypress that needs regular clipping. A tall Scots pine with a naked trunk can be turned to account if you can manage to hoist the climber high enough to reach into its branches. It will need help on the way, probably with wires. Once up there, it will support itself from above.

The climber must have decent conditions at the root. To this end, it may be wise to prepare its planting area beneath the tree's outside branches, supposing that one or more of these come fairly close to the ground and at a distance from the trunk. Again, you can lead the climber up by string, rope or wire. There will be most light outside the tree, which will help the climber.

Planting it in turf, whether mown or rough, is often a tough proposition, as grass is greedy and also mops up available moisture. That has been my trouble in attempting to get the rambler rose 'Treasure Trove' (John Treasure's 'Kiftsgate' seedling) through a large, fruiting cherry in our old orchard. We can feed and mulch it, but cannot reach it with water when its needs are greatest. It has never taken off.

If you can plant your rose in a cultivated bed, it will have an excellent chance. We have done that with our 'Kiftsgate', an ultra-vigorous white rambler, deliciously scented in its July season, which grows over a damson tree. The rose's weight would soon bring the tree down, however, if we did not practise some pruning. So we do, in winter, removing the previous season's flowered wood, and a very unpopular task this is.

Ivy climbs trees and you probably won't have to tell it how. Once the ivy settles down into a shrubby, flowering condition, it can be a very agreeable feature, especially when flowering and alive with insects in the autumn. But it also makes an ideal background for an extra climber, planted to go over it. In my case, this is *Vitis coignetiae*, a vine that, if you get a good strain, takes on brilliant crimson autumn colouring. Mine has at last, after years of sulks, got the idea. The sulks were my fault for inadequate feeding and watering. Just how long the host-playing ash tree will put up with its attendant sprites is another question, but an ash has the advantage of a thin-textured crown of foliage, which allows light to percolate.

Wisteria is as vigorous as any climber we can grow in Britain, and is especially suitable for a tallish tree, from which its blossom can best be appreciated along horizontal branches. The species with longest blossom is *Wisteria floribunda*, which is mauve, but even more effective is its pure white cultivar 'Alba'. Best for scent, however, is the mauve *W. sinensis*, obtained from a reliable source, for you must not buy a seedling, however tempting its low price. It is likely to take many years to start flowering and then to be a very weak shade of mauve. You should get a layered or grafted plant of the clone that was originally introduced from China early in the last century. This one frequently has a second, lighter, flowering in August.

The only clematis with vigour suitable for a fair-sized tree is *Clematis montana*, or one of its close relations. The colour will be pink or white and the flowering season, in May, may coincide with that of pink or white blossom on its host.

There are vigorous honeysuckles suited to small trees. One of the well-coloured forms of *Lonicera periclymenum* will, according to variety, also provide the most pleasing night scent when in flower, and often in spasms between May and October. *L. japonica* 'Halliana', with white flowers ageing to cream, is even more vigorous and evergreen. It flowers continuously for four months from late June and has a strong, rather sickly sweet scent. It flatters those with a weak sense of smell. Similar, but more elegant, is *L. similis* var. *delavayi*.

The most colourful climbing honeysuckles have no scent but make up for it with their grand display, and they are also tolerant of a good deal of shade. Such are the yellow *L. tragophylla*, apricot-orange *L.* x *tellmanniana* and bright red *L.* x *brownii* 'Dropmore Scarlet'. They have a limited flowering season in early summer.

The self-clinging *Hydrangea anomala* subsp. *petiolaris* can make a wonderful column of white blossom up the trunk of quite a tall tree. But its success will depend on conditions at the root, without excess competition for nutrients and moisture. To give it a good start, it can be planted in a box of good soil above ground and against the trunk. Then comes the moment of truth, when the tree finds the good soil.

Perennial Planning

Perennials are not, on the whole, strongly designed. Many tend to be hazy and structureless. Gypsophilas, for instance, linums, most lychnis, cranesbills, asters, day lilies, spiderworts, phloxes . . . I could run on.

But some are helpful in this respect, and they will be especially valuable in perennial borders where you don't want shrubs. It would be better if you would keep an open mind on this question and grow a shrub among perennials if it seemed to you to look right in the context, but I shall here suppose that perennials, and perennials only, are your aim.

Anything spiky with an upright thrust will look purposeful. Eremurus, the foxtail lilies, for instance. Their colours range from white through pale pink and yellow to soft orangey shades; their heights from 1m to 3m, and their season covers, between them, all of May and June. No one of them flowers for very long. They have fleshy roots and need good drainage. They like alkaline soils and are exciting to look at. Dying away completely from view in late summer, you need from the start to think of replacements in their vicinity.

Verbascum chaixii (1.5m) seeded itself among mine, which was a good idea. It has more or less unbranched spikes of yellow or white flowers with purple stamens at the centre, flowering in July. All verbascums have a strong presence but some of the best are biennial. These self-sow.

Kniphofias, the red hot pokers, are strongly spiky and always make an impression, although not one that everybody likes. Their strap leaves can be rather messy, as are those of day lilies and tradescantias, but are a distinct asset in *Kniphofia caulescens*, where they are glaucous and borne in rosettes. This is quite a variable species, some strains flowering in June, others not till September, in a soft orange-red. In 'Little Maid'

(1m or less), the pokers are creamy white and prolific over quite a long, late-summer season, especially if you replant fairly frequently.

I like the September-flowering 'Torchbearer' (2m), because there is quite a lot of green in its yellow colouring. Among the fieriest and most aggressive, but a fine landscape feature, is the August-flowering *K. uvaria* 'Nobilis' (3m). That is orange-coloured.

I count phormium as evergreen perennials, and their fans of tough leaves are generally the principal asset. But some flower regularly in early summer, spiky at first, rather like a heron's neck and beak; then branching as the muted, greenish-yellow flowers develop. Hardiest and most reliable, in my estimation, is *P. cookianum* 'Tricolor' (2m in flower, half as high in leaf). The strap leaves are curved and combine strips of purple (at the margins), green and cream. The flowering stems in June are generously borne.

When flowers or leaves are borne in whorled tiers, they always agreeably draw attention to themselves. Thus, in *Veronicastrum virginicum* (1.5m), whose spiky flowers are a rather dusty purple, and the more popular white 'Album', there is a great build-up beneath the flowers of whorled lance leaves. In *Phlomis russeliana* (1.2m), the tiered whorls are of dusky-yellow labiate flowers, which show up at a distance as strong shapes.

On the other hand, the flat, cow-parsley-style corymbs of many umbellifers draw our attention in a different way, and they often have a branching inflorescence that is strong on presentation. Among the handsomest are any species in the genus Ferula, the giant fennels. They have wonderfully dissect foliage but rise, on flowering, way above this, often to 3m, the domed flower heads themselves being greeny-yellow. Any ferula will give pleasure in the first half of the year and flowering will be most generous if the plants are well fed, although in nature they may grow on arid, hungry slopes. In this respect, ecology is not the best guide.

Alliums, with their domed heads above naked scapes, make themselves noticed, especially the larger-headed kinds, such as *Allium giganteum* (1m), which is lilac-mauve, and *A. cristophii* (60cm), whose globes of spiky stars start a light shade of purple. That seeds itself right through my borders, and it is the best way to see these alliums. On a recent visit to Germany, I was impressed by the strong clumps of *A. multibulbosum* (1m), with flowers in white domes. *Multibulbosum* does sound a bit threatening, however, as though it might take one over, as some alliums do.

A panicle of blossom can make a good impression from a distance. Red valerian, *Centranthus ruber*, does this, whether red or white, but I would avoid the rather dirty pink-red strain. It is a great self-seeder, but it is best to cut back the first flush of blossom now, before it has sown itself everywhere. In our southern counties, there will be a second flush in September.

The moisture-loving rodgersias are grown mainly, I suppose, for their bold foliage, but some of them flower most handsomely, with large panicles, if grown in good soil. *Rodgersia podophylla* (1m) is a shy flowerer but most of the others are pretty free, generally white but sometimes pink, as in certain strains of *R. pinnata*. The inflorescence dies tastefully over a long period.

Last mention shall go to the wonderfully structured cardoons, *Cynara cardunculus* (2m), with their widely branching candelabrums of mauve thistle heads. Grey, divided leaves are handsomer still, early in their long season.

Coarse Plants

This is the season when coarse plants luxuriate. The late Henry Mitchell, whose weekly columns appeared in the *Washington Post* and have been published in book form, hit it right, when writing of daturas, the angel's trumpets, that all 'are inherently coarse, with large leaves, usually hairy and weedy looking'. Their flamboyant beauty has 'the usual excitement that accompanies unembarrassed coarseness. I often think that daturas, tithonias and tropical weeds of that sort were the original "If you got it, flaunt it."'

Well, daturas, most of them now termed Brugmansia, can be planted safely in the garden now, or stood out in pots, but they do enjoy the free root run. Under dry conditions, they can be martyred by red spider. They grow rapidly and their pendant trumpets, heavily night-scented, are borne in distinct flushes – some say at the full moon, which sounds romantic and as it should be, but is not borne out by my experience.

B. suaveolens is the usual white kind, while *B.* x *candida* 'Grand Marnier' is soft beige.

Tithonia rotundifolia, originally from Mexico, but now a cheerful annual weed in much of the tropical world, is closely related to zinnias, but grows to 2m. Its soft, hairy leaves are heart-shaped, and the plant, if you get 'Torch' and are not fobbed off with the dwarf, untypical 'Goldfinger', puts on enormous bulk in a twinkling, carrying sombrero flowers in purest, dazzling orange. If you are wilting in a spell of humid, torrid heat, remember that plants such as this are revelling in it.

At a low level (0.3m), consider the perennial *Farfugium* (once *Senecio*) *japonicum*. In Japan, you will see it straight, with plain green, orbicular leaves and yellow daisies in October. Here, it does not flower and you will probably choose to grow one of its variegated-leaved kinds. In 'Argenteum', the leaves are broadly streaked in white, but my heart goes out to 'Aureomaculatum', whose leaves are covered in large spots of yellow, faint on their first appearance, but growing in intensity as they mature. Some people loathe this sort of variegation, and think they are being witty when they ask if it has been sprayed with weedkiller.

But, if grown well, with plenty of moisture, rich soil and some shade, it is clearly a picture of rude health.

You could grow it alongside one of those foliage begonias that are normally seen as pot plants.

Begonia scharffii (syn. *B. haageana*) is one of the easiest and most effective, with bold, hairy, lopsided leaves, red on their undersides. About 0.6m tall and covered for months on end with sheaves of flesh-pink blossom. The lower-growing 'Burle Marx', named after the great South American landscape architect, who was also a plantsman – a rare combination – is another house plant that is amenable to garden cultivation in the warm months, having rounded foliage that is deeply veined, wrinkled all over and bronze-tinted.

Echium pininana is a blue-flowered bugloss that has naturalised in the botanic garden at Ventnor, on the Isle of Wight, where it may be seen flowering in May, with 4m-long spikes, assembled in large colonies. This looks excitingly grotesque. After flowering, the plant dies, but self-sows. For most of us, it must be treated as a tender foliage plant, and, really, its big rosettes of long, hairy leaves – perhaps at a height of 1m – are a feast in themselves and arguably more handsome than the mature, flowering plant.

The hardy *Petasites fragrans* is known as winter helioptrope, flowering in January. With its running rootstock, it is a pernicious weed in the wrong place, and so is its giant cousin, *P. japonicus* var. *giganteus*, with orbicular leaves up to 1.5m across, on 2m stalks. It makes large colonies, and there are suitable places for such plants, so long as we know what to expect, and site accordingly.

So now I have acquired a tender, apparently woody plant, *Senecio petasitis*, with similarly orbicular foliage, but softly felted and with scalloped margins. I have no idea what to expect of its behaviour, but it looks exciting. Always yield to temptation when you feel waves of it overcoming you.

I have been given an unrooted cutting (now rooted in a close frame) of *Dahlia imperialis*, which will make a branching tree to 5m, with thick, hollow stems when well suited. It needs to be regarded as a luxuriant foliage plant. The flowers, which I have not seen, do not appear (if at all) until the very end of the growing season. They are pale mauve, only 10cm across, but borne in great numbers. I shall give my plant a place of solitary honour in what was once a cattle drinking tank, and see how it responds.

The last example is the fig 'Brunswick'. It has the largest leaves, handsomely indented, and was the variety often recommended by Lutyens in the Edwardian gardens he designed. Mine is one of these, and we have five specimens. The figs are sometimes produced in a generous crop, and they are two or three times the size of any you see marketed. Edward Bunyard, in *The Anatomy of Dessert*, describes this as 'a large and rather gross-looking fruit formerly known as the Madonna, but, upon the arrival of George I, it was re-christened. It is not recorded if His Majesty accepted this as a compliment, but it has a certain Hanoverian lustiness, and so the name has remained.'

Ornamental Grasses

There is currently a great vogue for ornamental grasses. A craze always tends towards distortion, with highest praise for plants that may not deserve it. But these grasses deserve to be in every garden.

Do not be so carried away by them that you want to grow them in covies. Nearly all have a similar long and narrow leaf. If massed, they cancel each other out. Very often they look best if standing apart from other plants or, in a mixed border, seen head and shoulders above the surrounding vegetation, so that you can admire the shape and presence of each grass as an individual.

Molinia caerulea 'Transparent' (2m) is a see-through grass. If placed near the edge of a border, you have the chance to let it act as a filter to plants behind it. The closely related 'Windspiel' is equally imposing. It gets better and better through the autumn, as its honey colour intensifies, but in mid-November, all its growth suddenly breaks off at the base, which is a little disconcerting.

Some of the earlier-flowering grasses have a very long season. One is *Stipa gigantea* (2m). I love to sit on a low wall near mine and see the veiled form of blue *Campanula lactiflora* (2m) behind it. Although near to a corner, this grass is not right on it, otherwise people damage and bend its stems as they walk by.

For smaller gardens, *Miscanthus nepalensis* (1m) seems to be ideal, with its pretty flowers and long season. It is better than M. *sinensis* 'Yakushima Dwarf' (1m), which has a dumpy carriage. We are not yet certain how hardy M. *nepalensis* is, but last winter it presented no problems.

Calamagrostis x *acutiflora* 'Karl Foerster' (1.8m) is amazingly versatile. When flowering in early July, it is purple, soft and fluffy. Afterwards, its stems stiffen and gradually bleach to pale fawn. It is beautiful right through to the following March, when all should be cut down low. Truly rewarding.

Everyone falls headlong in love with *Pennisetum setaceum* 'Rubrum' (1m) the moment they see it, but it is tender and a challenge. Reddish in colouring, it flowers with amazingly long, drooping 'tails'. If started early, it flowers into late autumn. But old plants must be lifted in early October, shortened by a third, potted and kept growing (sparingly watered) under well-heated glass throughout the winter. Then, in spring, you can split it and plant out when the weather has really warmed up. It is an irresistible beauty, but captious, as beauties so often are.

Plants for Ponds

However small your pond, it is nice to have some plants flowering in it. Beware of water lilies (Nymphaea), which are apt to take over the whole pond surface. If you can't see any water, there's little point in having a pond in the first place.

Certain cannas are particularly well adapted to growing in shallow water. Their prototype is *Canna glauca*, with glaucous (bluish) leaves and yellow flowers. 'Erebus' is particularly good, flowering abundantly and salmon-coloured, but there are a number of others. 'Ra' is a strong yellow.

Houttuynia cordata 'Chameleon' has a running rootstock and is a bit of a menace in a border, but if grown in a pot and plunged in shallow water, not only is its bright variegation heightened but it's perfectly under control.

Insectivorous plants are fun. We grow the yellow *Sarracenia flava*. First it flowers handsomely, then it makes its insect-catching pitchers. We grow it in shallow water at the pond's edge for summer but, come autumn, stand it in a dish of shallow water for winter under an open-sided shed.

Thalia dealbata is another insectivore, 2m tall with insignificant little flowers which do, however, catch small insects by closing over and ingesting them when they land. The main point of it is as a hardy foliage plant with striking glaucous leaves, although it is best replanted in a pot each spring. Shallow water or a damp flowerbed suit it equally.

Cyperus papyrus, the Egyptian papyrus, is quite easily grown from seed and easy to keep through winter under mildly heated glass. Other species, such as *C. involucratus*, the umbrella plant, are popular on indoor windowsills. Bring it out in summer and plunge in shallow water at the pond's margin. *C. longus* is a hardy native in which moorhens like to nest. It needs space, but *C. eragrostis* (syn. *C. vegetus*) is only 50cm high, hardy and equally happy on land or in shallow water.

The autumn-flowering *Schizostylis coccinea* 'Major' has crimson, bowl-shaped flowers and is normally treated as a border perennial, but it will grow in shallow water as a marginal plant. *Iris laevigata* loves shallow water. It can be blue, purple or white. But my favourite variegated iris is *I. laevigata* 'Variegata'. The white contrasts brilliantly with the green.

July Jobs

July is when the borders begin to look a mess, so you need to take them by the scruff and pull out all those self-seeders that were delightful in May and June but have now had it. If you can stop some of the self-seeding, you'll be saving yourself a lot of trouble later on. Often, however, as with forget-me-nots, there's really nothing to be done about it.

Pull out the opium poppies, the herb robert and various wild cranesbills; also evening primroses that look weedy, along with teasels that are far too prolific. Likewise fennel, which develops a tough root very quickly from seedlings. The same applies to lady's mantle, *Alchemilla mollis* – as soon as that begins to look bedraggled, cut the whole lot back, leaves and all, and it will return and look fresh again before many weeks have passed.

That, too, is the best treatment for aquilegias – preferably before they have seeded, but you may be too late to prevent that by now. Anyway, cut them back, including the leaves, and decide which are dispensable – digging them out, as they make aggressive neighbours.

I always find myself with too much astrantia, which has a tough rootstock that requires effort to be rid of. Seedlings are rarely as good as their selected and named parents. 'Shaggy' is a favourite, with big, green bracts. 'Ruby Wedding' is the best of the deep reds, while 'Sunningdale Variegated' has lively cream variegation in spring, but becomes a dull dog later on. Don't let it seed around.

When you have two shrubs, or a shrub and a perennial that look good flowering together, you can often manipulate the timing so that they coincide, but it can be tricky getting it right. Last year, I was pleased that my double pink Hybrid Musk rose, 'Felicia', flowered in front of, and at the same time as, the warm purple clematis 'Victoria' on a trellis behind. It is a less heavy purple than 'Jackmanii', but of the same type. This year, the rose is a couple of weeks too early for there to be much overlap – but had I pruned it harder, or later, its flowering would have been delayed by the desired two weeks.

Another combination, more by luck than by judgement, is working just right this time around: the deep mauve hebe 'Midsummer Beauty' with the Spanish broom, *Spartium junceum*, which is a bright, clear yellow of a less hard tone than our native variety. The hebe makes a large bush, 2m high by more across, and it will flower well again in the autumn if you can be bothered to dead-head its first flowering. Its spikes are long and sweetly scented.

The broom has a wonderfully strong, sweet fragrance. It flowers on its young wood, and you can manipulate when this happens by pruning lightly or hard, early or late (the end of April is late), the second alternative in each case resulting in later flowering.

A cool, moist, early summer is kind to plants whose foliage is apt to scorch when it is hot and dry. Rodgersias, with their bold, rugged leaves (almost impervious to the attentions of slugs and snails), have never looked happier. *Rodgersia podophylla* can be susceptible, but this year is going through its natural cycle: its palmate leaves, each leaflet shaped like a webbed foot, start purple, become green, but then soon develop a pink flush around the end of June. This intensifies until autumn, when it really flares up, before dying.

Then there is the *Aralia cachemirica*, a vigorous, pinnate-leaved perennial that makes a bold foliage feature, two or more metres tall, and revels in the kind of summer most of us loathe. I water it from time to time, but its leaves will still die off prematurely if the weather becomes scorching. If not, it makes big, arching inflorescences of tiny, umbellate flowers, these being succeeded by black berries subtended by purple stalks and stems.

The pink variegated form of box elder, *Acer negundo* 'Flamingo', is delightful on its young foliage, but if left unpruned becomes a large, dull bush with nothing to recommend it from summer onwards – but cut hard back each winter and treated as a 2m feature, new growth with the desired pink colouring will continue throughout summer. It doesn't want to be blazed upon unremittingly; watering the root helps keep it happy.

We ought to be thinking about autumn bulbs now. Among the latest-flowering of the bulbs that we plant in autumn is the June–July-flowering *Brodiaea laxa*, as it is still listed, though it is now designated

Triteleia laxa. At 30cm, it bears an umbel of rich blue, funnel flowers. With me, it is looking particularly good with the bright orange annual daisy, *Osteospermum hyoseroides* 'Gaiety'.

The bulbs increase quickly and, having spare stock, we have tried them in meadow turf. You can't judge whether a new feature works well in the first year, but in its second, which this is, the bulbs are doing well, the blue flowers in excellent contrast to more normal meadow ingredients, including the grasses themselves.

An Early Morning Walk

A walk in the garden around seven in the morning is, I find, a mixture of pure enjoyment and sharp reminders of things that want doing.

Scents are good early on, especially from the late Dutch honeysuckle, *Lonicera periclymenum* 'Serotina'. It is important to get this true to name. The flowers should, just before opening, be a very rich, dark red. This clone is not always the easiest to propagate from cuttings, and nurserymen over the years have been inclined to take a short cut by using an inferior but more easily propagated clone. The original came from a wild Dutch source, so it may be imagined that plenty of alternatives grow in nearby Holland.

Before long, I come into the orbit of *Dracunculus vulgaris*, the dragon arum, with its very large, deep purple arum flowers and a jet-black, club-like spadix at its centre. It is a magnificent plant, especially as the foliage is also handsome, but on the day of opening it has a powerful smell of rotten meat, which attracts pollinating blowflies. Next to my colony, I have two large beds of sweet-smelling pinks, seed-raised, so I move from the orbit of one to the other, making sure I'm doing this in the right order.

During the dry weather, we are watering a lot, using overhead sprinklers. In each position, we give them a couple of hours, on average. It is important, though, to make sure that plants which might collapse under the weight of water are well supported (either with brushwood or with stakes and ties). Supports are never beautiful, so we do this as late as we dare.

The double blue and purple cranesbills, *Geranium pratense* 'Plenum Caeruleum' and 'Plenum Violaceum', need support, but those that flowered in June, such as G. *himalayense* and G. x *magnificum*, we cut to the ground. They soon refurnish.

Stipa calamagrostis, flowering now, collapses under its own weight and needs assistance. Actually, we find that if we cut this back to 20cm at about the time it is coming into flower, it grows again quickly enough to give us a display in the autumn. That ties in well with chrysanthemums and other natural autumn-flowerers. By far our favourite helenium is the repeat-flowering, bronze 'Moerheim Beauty' (1.2m), but that needs a bit of support.

As do the taller forms of *Campanula lactiflora*, which are by far the most stately. Again, make sure you buy the best, as height and colouring can vary greatly. 'Prichard's Variety' (1.5m) is a rich, deep blue, when correctly named, and is, I think, the most serviceable for most purposes. It would look good in front of the shrub rose, 'Cerise Queen'.

Another good companion would be the everlasting pea, *Lathyrus grandiflorus*, with its handsome magenta flowers. It is a herbaceous climber, to 2m or so, and quite a traveller in its root system, but you can cope with that.

Summer Climbers

Herbaceous and annual climbers can be the icing on the cake in our summer gardens. They can twine among other plants and give us unexpected but pleasant nudges.

Nasturtiums are the most familiar example. They sow themselves year after year and, whatever colours they started, are likely to end up their characteristic, no-nonsense nasturtium red, excellent in its way – for instance threading through the mauve, August-flowering *Aster sedifolius*. The semi-trailing, semi-double yellow 'Gleam' hybrids are favourites of mine.

At Dixter, we use a lot of *Mina* (*Ipomoea*) *lobata* as an annual to climb among perennial plants in our mixed long border. Its clusters of orange and yellow tubular flowers have a long season until first frost – especially useful, we find, to cover cut-back stems of delphiniums, when they have finished flowering, from July onwards.

The everlasting pea, *Lathyrus latifolius,* has no scent and should not, as it often is, be called everlasting sweet pea. It is a staunch perennial climber that dies down in winter and grows to 2m–3m in summer. Naturally a villainous mauvy-pink, the white 'Albus' can be grown as a separate colour and is excellent for covering a stiff shrub – perhaps a shrub rose.

Black-eyed Susan is a name applied to a number of plants, but I associate it with the climbing herbaceous perennial *Thunbergia alata.* You can get this in a mixture, but by far the best is the natural bright orange with a black eye. It is best in a hot summer.

Given a warm, sheltered, but not necessarily sunny, position, *Bomarea caldasii* is a reliable climbing perennial, twining up to 2m or more. With me, it dies to the ground in winter and thereafter carries just a few stems topped by a generous cluster of orange, alstroemeria-like flowers.

Dicentra scandens is a herbaceous climber that you forget all about while it is dormant, until suddenly it turns up again, threading its way through any plants that happen to be near it.

A hardy herbaceous climber that I should mention rather as a warning than a recommendation, unless you are confident of its siting, is *Thladiantha dubia.* This is a member of the cucumber family, covered in yellow flowers in September, but a real thug. Its tuberous roots explore everywhere and make new colonies. I hate being told that such and such a plant is a challenge, but this one certainly is.

Positioning Plants

With so much looking its best this month, there is ample opportunity to plan which plants might set each other off to advantage. And though there is no close season on moving plants around, it's advisable to do so after they have flowered, so giving them time to settle down and make new growth before autumn.

The golden rule is to water them heavily a day before the move, and again immediately after or during it – I refer to the latter as 'puddling in'.

Place the plant in a roomy hole, then quickly fill the hole with water from an upturned can and, as the water drains away, fill the hole with soil. This is because if you water after planting and restoring the soil, some of the water may run off instead of soaking in. Much, of course, depends on the quality of your soil – if there's a considerable area to be planted, Fergus, the head gardener at Great Dixter, often prefers to complete the planting and then put on the sprinkler for half an hour.

Looking very striking here this month has been *Anthemis tinctoria* 'Grallach Gold' with *Geranium pratense* 'Plenum Violaceum', both of them more than a metre high. The anthemis is a clean, piercing yellow – the best of its kind if you enjoy strength in this colour. The daisies fold their rays back overnight. The cranesbill has neat, rosette-shaped flowers.

From a hard spring cut-back, perennial bedding penstemons are at their peak in July, and the loose, cherry-red racemes of 'Drinkstone' are an excellent match for *Salvia* x *superba*, with stiff, upright purple spikes a metre high. Third in this team, with me, has been a mistake. The flat-topped corymbs of *Achillea* 'Moonshine' are good for shape, but the shade of yellow is too bright, and the softer 'Taygetea' or 'Anthea' are what's required.

A good foliage group has been accidentally promoted by the self-sowing, purple-leaved strain of orach, *Atriplex hortensis*, next to *Helianthus salicifolius*, which is a clump-forming perennial. Both of them are well over 2m tall.

Right at the end of the season, the helianthus has yellow, black-centred daisies, but its main point is as a foliage plant. The narrow leaves droop and make columns of fresh greenery, not unlike those of the Egyptian papyrus.

You can add to this combination as you please, and I enjoy the somewhat shorter *Telekia speciosa* (*Buphthalmum speciosum*) with yellow daisies in front. Later summer and autumn is a great season for yellow daisies. For a September–October display, we have planned to have the pure blue *Salvia guaranitica* 'Blue Enigma' (2m) with one of the largest-flowered of the perennial sunflowers, *Helianthus* 'Monarch'. A spot of disbudding of side shoots (as with exhibition dahlias) will give rise to larger blooms still. I am not exactly recommending this practice, but it is rather fun to experiment with a plant's capabilities.

The somewhat lax habit of *Geranium psilostemon* is well suited to partnering it with plants of stiffer habit into which it can thread its way, thereby gaining both height and support. Some yellow-flowered verbascums will do this job, and I enjoy the combination of yellow and brightest magenta when, as in this case, the actual flowers of both components are small. Those frightened by the strength of this geranium's colouring are apt to settle for the softer-toned clone, 'Bressingham Flair'. Shame on them. Just go for it with the real McCoy. It is a marvellous colour.

So too is *Lychnis coronaria*, 'Abbotswood Rose' being pretty enough but no real improvement. Magenta flowers are here set off by grey leaves and stems, a combination that can't be improved upon and splendid in front of a patch of *Crocosmia* 'Lucifer' (1.5m), which is as pure and fiery a red as they come.

Pink and blue is a soothing combination, and I have it with *Hebe* 'Watson's Pink', over part of which there is a mantle of the 'blue' (not pure blue, of course) *Clematis* 'Prince Charles'. This is of a more compact habit and smaller-flowered than 'Perle d'Azur', but the same colour.

Roses and clematis are a classic combination, and I can recommend the Hybrid Musk 'Felicity', which is pink, in front of a backdrop of 'Victoria', which is similar to 'Jackmanii' but of a less heavy purple colouring – a colour, moreover, as pleasing when fading as on the newly opened flower.

If you want summer-flowering clematis to make a spectacle, don't forget the old but ever-effective dodge of planting a couple of the same variety within a metre or so of one another. They will intertangle and appear to be one exceedingly successful and floriferous specimen.

We are bang in the middle of the season for perennial phloxes, those derived from *Phlox paniculata*. The mauve-flowered species is by itself well worth garden space, although, at 1.5m, it is taller than most and probably in need of support halfway up the stem length.

It makes a froth of smallish flowers and has great elegance. I like it with the pale yellow, long-flowering *Hemerocallis* 'Marion Vaughn' (1m).

I grow great quilts of phlox because they love my heavy soil. I try to make sure that they have plenty of water at the root before they come into bloom, as overhead watering at that stage can bring on premature blossom fall.

As a break from pink and mauve phloxes, and in the middle of a large colony, I have *Hydrangea arborescens* 'Annabelle', which carries flattened domes (not quite so high-pointed as the phlox panicle) of white blossom at the same time and at roughly the same level.

Summer Pruning

It's pleasant to loll around at the height of summer (an iced drink within easy reach), and to enjoy the fruits of your autumn, winter and spring labours in the garden. But where's your conscience? In case you'd forgotten you had one, there's always a killjoy like me around to remind you of things to be done. So I'll get that off my own conscience before pouring myself another drink.

I particularly have in mind summer pruning. Much of this can be left till winter, but there are advantages in getting busy with some of it now; even in taking two bites at the cherry and completing it when the leaves are off. But while they're on, you have before you a shrub's summer appearance without having to bring your powers of imagination or recollection into play.

A number of privets will have just finished flowering. If you want the swags of black fruit that may follow, leave well alone for the time being. But if you remove the flowered branches now you'll be opening up the bush, letting light into its centre and encouraging the production of strong, young vegetative growth.

In a golden-leaved privet, this is the plant's principal role anyway. Some people go over them with shears and treat them as solid lumps of colour. I prefer a selective treatment, using secateurs and saw to remove only old, flowered branches. Your specimen is then allowed more grace, shapeliness, and personality. A favourite with me is *Ligustrum* 'Vicaryi', with sizeable leaves, greenish-yellow and brightest where exposed to most sunshine.

Some of the elders (Sambucus) with variegated or coloured leaves are grown entirely as foliage plants and should receive a hard cut-back each winter. Others are magnificent at their late May and June flowering. Even *S. nigra* 'Guincho Purple' (alias 'Purpurea'), though grown largely for its dark foliage, is a splendid flowering tree/shrub. These flowering kinds do benefit from regular pruning, which entails the removal of flowered branches and the retention, at their full length, of strong, unflowered young shoots. Leave this pruning till the winter if you like, but if you do it now you'll prevent the ripening and self-sowing of all those fruits. Elder seedlings can be a nuisance. And by pruning now, more energy will be channelled into the young branches.

Unpruned elders eventually become a dense, amorphous mess wherein all the growth is weak. And that holds for many summer-flowering shrubs requiring constant rejuvenation. You may argue that they don't receive it in nature and still get along all right. However, under ideal cultural conditions, most shrubs and trees are a vast improvement on their wild counterparts. And if constantly renewed, they live longer and are healthier.

Many gardeners grow once-flowering roses (which they like to call shrub roses or old roses, though all roses are shrubs and many of the apparently old kinds are modern) as though they were never in need of pruning. How wrong they are. Take a look at yours now and you will see young, unbranched shoots among the flowered branches. These will produce the best of next year's crop and need encouraging by the removal of the old and the tired. Humans are expected to look after their old, however tiresome, but the same principle should not be applied to plants.

Pruning of these once-flowerers is by thinning, not by shortening back. Leave the young shoots full length and they will flower next year along that entire length in magnificent, arching swags. But the thinning-out process allows light to enter the centre and base of the bush and thereby encourages the production of new growth from low down, which is where it comes strongest.

So also with philadelphus (mock orange), deutzias, weigelas and shrubs of similar habit – dipelta, kolkwitzia – all those that perform best on the wood they made in the previous year.

Tree lupins, *Lupinus arboreus*, are short-lived shrubs and little more than three years can be expected of any one specimen. We depend on them to carry on the line by self-sowing. But if you remove the spikes which are running to seed immediately after flowering, a second crop will quite often come on in September. The pink flowers of *Spiraea japonica*, of which there are some 30 different kinds, turn brown on fading. When removing these, prune the whole shrub. Two- to three-year-old growth will be very branched and weak. Cut this out, either back to a strong, upright, unbranched shoot or (if there isn't one) to ground level, leaving no stumps. Tall, unbranched shoots merely need their flower heads removing. They'll make new side shoots and may flower again in October. Varieties such as 'Goldflame' and 'Golden Mound', grown principally for their colourful foliage, can be treated in the same way. They'll refurnish with young leaves later in the season and you won't need to prune them at all next spring.

Bamboos can have their old canes thinned out and removed at any season but this is a marvellous moment for taking pieces off an established clump that you want to increase. Get well back into the colony and use a saw, if the going is too tough for a spade, to chop through the underground horizontal rhizome.

Looking After a Meadow

Anyone who has lately been looking at their piece of meadow with despair, and wondering what on earth to do about it, has my sympathy. If the grasses are coarse, they will have collapsed and will by now be looking a complete mess.

There is no straight and simple answer to the way such an area should be treated. If the soil is poor, the grasses will be fine, like the common bent, *Agrostis tenuis*, which is a pink haze of its own blossom right through July and is particularly beautiful when laden with dew. Where we have such areas – and they are most common in old turf, or in an area of starved lawn that has been allowed to grow into a hayfield – we delay cutting until mid-August, which will allow time for its latest-flowering plants to have ripened and distributed their seed. Among the late flowerers are meadow cranesbill, tufted vetch, the blue-flowered *Triteleia* (syn. *Brodiaea*) *laxa* and, if you have been lucky with them, the spotted orchid, *Dactylorhiza fuchsii* (whose seeds are liable to blow in on the wind).

We have one area of lawn turned meadow that has no bulbs in it, and we cut in September. We cut it again in February. And that's it. But if the soil is on the rich side, a different treatment will be called for. Plant it up with spring bulbs – crocuses, snake's head fritillaries, narcissus – and give the first cut in mid-June. Then cut it tight (removing the mowings to compost) at frequent intervals right into November. This will reduce the vigour of the contents and eliminate any docks or nettles that may be there. Then leave it until the following June.

There are possible variations on this treatment. In one area, which we cut tight for the first time in early July, we have the pheasant's-eye narcissus, *Narcissus poeticus* var. *recurvus*, in late spring, followed by a great display of field buttercups, *Ranunculus acris*. However, interplanted among these, at uneven but wide spacing, are clumps of the big yellow daisy, *Inula magnifica*, which is 2m–3m tall and flowers through July and into August. The grass around it therefore needs to be mown before this gets going, and before it starts to flop sideways, which will happen after heavy rain, but doesn't matter a bit, so long as the grass was cut first. When the display has finished, you can mow around it again and yet again, into late November, when the narcissus shoots may begin to push through once more.

On the whole, meadows succeed best in an open, unshaded situation, but if there is a small tree at hand, say a hawthorn (Crataegus), you can underplant with erythroniums (dog's-tooth violets) and snowdrops, and also with autumn-flowering *Cyclamen hederifolium*. If that is present, you can mow over the whole area before it starts to flower (very soon now), but not afterwards, as it will then have come into leaf.

If you include autumn-flowering crocuses and colchicums (they should be planted soon), cut your meadow before they start flowering in late August. You can cut them again after they have finished in late October.

August

The August Garden

Flower power will almost certainly be falling off in our borders after the second week in August, but the loss can be largely mitigated by careful planning. It is a shame, then, that so many gardeners seem to give up once returned from their summer holiday. After all, the garden should remain enjoyable until the end of October. So, this week, let's consider what August has on offer in the way of shrubs and perennials. I'll leave out the bedding plants so that the subject doesn't sprawl unduly.

Among the shrubs, there are eucryphias, with white flowers and a mass of red-tipped stamens at the centre. The deciduous *Eucryphia glutinosa* is one of my favourites, but it must have acid soil, while *E.* x *nymansensis* 'Nymansay' has larger flowers, once it gets settled in, and sheets of them every year. Bees love it for its nectar. It is easily trained to form a quite narrow column, which will reach to 10m, but that is after many years. Do give it a heavy soaking as it comes into flower, otherwise the blooms are apt to wilt and will not last so long.

Summer tamarisk, *Tamarix ramosissima* (3m), has bright green growth and is covered with spikelets of pink blossom for quite a while. To enable you to use it in any mixed border, you should prune it hard each winter. There is a super elder, *Sambucus canadensis* 'Maxima', which flowers on its young wood after all the other kinds, and from which you can make elderflower cordial. If pruned back each winter, it will make creamy, flat-topped flower heads the size of dinner plates.

Of early-fruiting shrubs, *Rosa moyesii* has long, scarlet hips; these are particularly bright in the 'Geranium' cultivar. It should be grafted, but short cuts are sometimes taken by raising it from seed – though if you do this, you run the risk of your 'Geranium' never setting fruit at all. The rugosa roses, if not double-flowered, carry magnificent clusters of globular, tomato-like fruits from August onwards. Greenfinches sometimes take a fancy to their seeds.

The guelder rose, *Viburnum opulus* 'Compactum', can be kept to 2m if its fruit branches are removed regularly in winter. It is hung with clusters of glistening red fruit, which ripen quickly and seem to have no attraction whatsoever for birds.

Last month, Japanese anemones started their long season, which goes on until mid-October. 'Honorine Jobert' (up to 1.5m in moist soil) is the nicest single white – the singles are better formed than the doubles. Of the pinks, I like 'Hadspen Abundance' (1m), but there are many others, such as the rather charming double, 'Pamina' (1.5m).

There is a long succession of pokers to choose from, one of the best for August being *Kniphofia uvaria* 'Nobilis' (2.5m), which sports orange flowers over an extended season. On a smaller scale, Beth Chatto's 'Little Maid' (0.5m), with cream-coloured spikes, has a long, prolific season.

This is a great season for perennial sunflowers of the genus Helianthus. 'Capenoch Star' (1.5m), with its medium-sized, bright yellow flowers, has an enlarged, anemone-flowered centre. It is self-supporting and long-flowering. 'Lemon Queen' (2m), with soft, yellow colouring, does need support. The flowers are small but become progressively more numerous into next month. Then, too, 'Monarch' (3m) reaches its peak – it has very large yellow daisies for a perennial sunflower, and black-centred. To get the largest blooms, disbud a few stems so as to leave the central flower to receive all available energy. The effect is gorgeous and a touch dramatic, especially when seen against a bright blue sky.

Most of the best rudbeckias, annual or perennial, are late-flowering. *Rudbeckia fulgida* var. *sullivantii* 'Goldsturm' (0.7m) is a deservedly popular black-eyed Susan of compact, branching habit. It will bring light into a shady place, but does need plenty of moisture.

R. fulgida var. *deamii* is more prolific and even better next month, when I like to contrast it with a 'blue' michaelmas daisy, such as *Aster* 'Little Carlow' (1.5m). The aster for now, and continuing untiringly into October, is *A. x frikartii* 'Mönch' (1m), though it can be a martyr to slug damage in winter. It has quite large daisies, and you might contrast it with a later-flowering crocosmia, say the bright orange 'Star of the East' (0.8m).

Verbena bonariensis (2m) is of rather sparse habit, so it can be grown at the front margin of a border without blocking your view. It is a soft shade of purple with dense heads of tiny flowers. From late June, it becomes increasingly free-flowering for three or more months.

Don't leave foliage out of your calculations. Some of the forms of

Miscanthus sinensis just keep on getting better. The fountain-like, white-variegated 'Variegatus' (2m) can stand above its neighbour as a solo beacon, or there's the yellow-striped 'Strictus' (2.5m), of upright habit, which I prefer to the comparable 'Zebrinus'.

Blue

For a great many people, blue is their favourite colour. True blue flowers are at a premium and, of course, I like them myself. But I sometimes find blue tricky to handle – it has a way of being recessive and of not showing up sufficiently from a distance.

I've had quite a large bedding-out area with double, orange-pink opium poppies (*Papaver somniferum*), orange calendula marigolds and then, among and in front of these, to calm things down, a large interplanting of love-in-a-mist, the true blue *Nigella damascena* 'Miss Jekyll'. And bless me if, from a distance, the blue disappeared entirely and all one saw was a wall of nothingness.

I think blue needs greater emphasis by being more concentrated, not diffused, as in love-in-a-mist, by the plant's misty element. That density is to be found in *Anchusa caespitosa*, a fairly short-term annual I was using at the same time. It grows only 20cm high, but makes a brilliantly intense, mid-blue display that draws the eye just as much as if it were scarlet.

I find *Cynoglossum amabile* 'Firmament' (35cm) tremendously effective, if I have grown it well. It belongs to the borage family (like the anchusa) and is quite a light yet penetrating blue. Grow it either as an annual, from a spring sowing, or as a biennial, sowing it later this month, though the seedlings are not entirely hardy and will need cold-frame protection in winter. They will then flower in May.

Eryngium x *oliverianum* (0.8m), one of the sea holly tribe, is a deep-rooted perennial that flowers in July and is intensely desired by all who see it – seen close to, its flowering stems are an incredibly intense, metallic blue. This plant would melt into the landscape at any distance, but it is saved from this by a dramatic structure of a central dome of small blue florets surrounded by a bold, spiky ruff, forming a collar of bracts. The blue stems are just below all this. They must be in full sun, to bring out the colour. I like it as a contrast to bright yellow or scarlet perennials: say, the yellow *Coreopsis verticillata* (50cm) in front and a scarlet *Crocosmia* 'Lucifer' (1m) behind.

Few shrubs are blue-flowered, but some of the May-flowering, evergreen ceanothus are startlingly so: 'Cynthia Postan', for instance, or 'Puget Blue'. They need a bit of shelter – for example, close to the sunny side of your house – and can be trained against a house wall, pruning and tying them into it immediately after flowering. No one could possibly miss that astonishing eyeful of their favourite colour, even if they're merely driving past it.

Cranesbills

My borders get great support at this time of year from a number of hardy geraniums – cranesbills – having a roving habit. They keep on growing and flowering, and in so doing they manage to find their way into all their neighbours. Thus they infiltrate, and thereby make a powerful contribution to achieving the aims of any artistic gardener, namely the creation of a tapestry, a fabric of foliage and of flowers through which no canvas – soil, that is – shows through.

There are a great many of these cranesbills to choose from, and their numbers just keep increasing, not least because this is a fashionable flower that invites breeders to work on it. An advantage of this rambling category is that they have a phenomenally long season – in some cases, this may mean that their habit becomes too wide-spreading and sprawling, but if they do so, just cut the whole plant right back, mid-season. It will soon refurnish and flower again as a more comely unit.

But *Geranium* x *oxonianum* 'A.T. Johnson' is almost too vigorous, and is therefore often used on its own as ground cover, which is boring. Its colouring is an insistent pinky-mauve, with darker veins.

If you get just one plant, it will do a good job if put close to a shrub into which it can climb. 'Wargrave Pink' is similar, but a little less vigorous and a warmer shade of salmon pink. I have it wandering into lacecap hydrangeas, Bluebird and 'Blue Deckle'.

The chalk-pink G. *endressii*, from which these two derive, is less aggressive than either, and its colouring shows up best in part shade. I am pleased with a new partnership I have made, running through two bushes of the elegantly white-flowered *Hebe parviflora* var. *angustifolia* (0.7m), sometimes known as 'Spender's Seedling'. They form a cornerpiece on my long border.

G. x *riversleaianum* 'Russell Prichard' (which can't be said without a hiccup, so just remember the last bit) is one of the greatest of all cranesbills – on its own terms. It is not absolutely hardy, although I usually assume that it is and get away with it, but it is definitely short-lived, which is perhaps the penalty of flowering non-stop from late May to late autumn.

You should take a few cuttings of shoots off healthy, young plants sometime during the winter, and then they can be struck in a cold frame. The foliage is softly hairy, and has a hint of grey, while the flowers are vivid light magenta. I have it, principally, mingling with the grey foliage of *Artemisia ludoviciana* 'Silver Queen', but this year it is also associating with the purple *Verbena rigida*, and with some mixed verbena hybrids that we grew from seed. 'Mavis Simpson', which has smaller, and clear, pinky-mauve flowers, also belongs to this group and is a weaver. This is the one for you if your nerves are not strong enough to take 'Russell Prichard'.

'Dilys' is fairly new to me; its flowering gets going lateish, but runs on; it's always good to have fresh-looking plants in the second half of summer and autumn. The deeply cut leaves are a lively shade of green and the flowers bright rosy-mauve. Where I use the word mauve in my colour descriptions, many writers, especially those of nursery catalogues, would no doubt call them rose or by some other adjective that omitted mention of the blue element that is nearly always present in cranesbills, but this hint of blueness is nothing to be ashamed of. Of course, when they want a geranium to be unadulterated blue – which it never is – they will omit mention of the pink element which makes the flower mauve-blue, or blue-mauve. Such is G. *wallichianum* 'Buxton's Variety', more often known by the alliterative 'Buxton's Blue', which trips off the tongue. Anyway, whatever you call it, this is a thumping good cranesbill: mottled foliage and a saucer-shaped 'blue' flower with a zoned white middle and very dark anthers at the centre. The colouring is a rather dirty mauve if the weather is hot in July, when flowering starts, but steadily improves.

There are several other forms of G. *wallichianum*, all of them worth growing. One of them is called 'Syabru'. I have been told how to pronounce this name, but invariably forget and get it wrong. Whatever, it is mauve, veined deep purple and has a purple base to each petal. I love the magenta, dark-centred G. *psilostemon*, but its flowering is mostly completed by mid-July. I once saw it threading through an early-flowering, yellow verbascum and am trying to emulate that. Magenta and orange or magenta and bright yellow are exciting combinations. However, for those of you who turn weak and wobbly at the very mention of magenta, there is the gentrified version called 'Bressingham Flair'. Have nothing to do with it, I would say; I mention it only to be fair.

'Ann Folkard', on the other hand, is a winner. It is a hybrid, with G. *psilostemon* as one parent, and its colouring is almost, though not quite, as bright. It could pass as purple. It is smaller-flowered, but has a very long season, during which it is apt to grow enormous and swamp many of its neighbours. You need to prepare for this by surrounding it with brushwood, under which circumstances it will rise to 1.5m and be reasonably contained. The acid, greeny-yellow tones of *Euphorbia schillingii* make a satisfying companion, as does a pale yellow achillea.

Drought-tolerant Plants

If we knew that hot summers, parched gardens, and water restrictions were to be the norm, we could plan accordingly and grow drought-resistant plants. Likely as not, however, it will be chilly and wet next year and the phloxes and hydrangeas will beam their approval.

We have to hedge our bets and grow some of both – but with the emphasis on drought-tolerant plants where soil is light and dries out quickly; on moisture-lovers where it is heavy.

We can also increase the range of plants we grow by manuring and mulching the light soils with abundant organic matter while lightening heavy ground with a liberal dressing of coarse grit (a builder's merchant is the likeliest source for this).

Plants with fleshy roots or fleshy leaves are always well adapted to water shortages. Sedums, the stonecrops, are an obvious example of the latter. *Sedum* 'Herbstfreude' is a wonderful standby whether green in summer, bronze red in autumn, or brown in winter, it always looks pleasing. *Sedum spectabile* 'Brilliant' is a clearer shade of pink. It attracts butterflies as well as bees but its August–September flowering season is shortish.

'Ruby Glow' is a near prostrate variety for the border margin, deep plum red, while *S. telephium* subsp. *maximum* 'Atropurpureum' is rich purple in all its parts, although the flowers are paler. It grows 60cm tall and looks splendid with grey foliage.

Fleshy-rooted plants are a less obvious group because you cannot normally see their roots, but they delve deep for moisture. Such is the sea holly, *Eryngium maritimum*. It deserves to be a more popular garden plant. Among the best is *E. x tripartitum*, with a mass of small blue spiky heads. *E. x oliverianum* is bluer still with metallic blue stems and large flower heads. It grows 90cm tall and needs no disturbance once established. Stocks are always in short supply so order early.

The globe thistles, Echinops, are comparable but poor relations. There are so many really handsome thistles, and all are drought tolerant. One of the lowest is the carline thistle, *Carlina acaulis*, with large, whiskery, white thistle heads (beloved of bees and butterflies) on 30cm stems in late summer. The tallest is *Cynara cardunculus*, the cardoon, with magnificent greyish cut leaves in spring and early summer, and lavender-blue flower heads at 2.4m in August.

Even as quite a young seedling, fennel makes a long tap root. The purple-leaved *Foeniculum vulgare* 'Purpureum' is a beautiful clump-forming plant with lacy foliage and pale yellowish flowers. Do cut them down before it sheds its seeds. If you have a huge crop of seedlings you can bed them out this autumn, among and as a foil to late-flowering tulips, especially a tall yellow tulip such as 'Niphetos'. After the display, cast them out.

Seakale, *Crambe maritima*, is good though too many pests batten on to it for my liking: flea beetles, cabbage white caterpillars and a small grey weevil work on mine. Still, the 90cm domes of honey-scented white blossom are delicious in May. Cut it down after flowering and it will be a foliage plant for the rest of the summer.

Try the unusual *Asclepias tuberosa*, especially if you live in the southern half of England. It is a fleshy-rooted, July–August-flowering perennial, 60cm tall with flattened heads of orange or bronze-orange flowers of beautiful construction. *Dictamnus albus*, white- or purple-flowered, has a strong lemon scent and dark green pinnate leaves. It will grow 90cm to 1.2m tall if it likes you. Its winged seed pods are beautiful and, while still green, you can set light to the oil vapour that collects around them at the end of a still, hot day. Hence the name, burning bush.

Most of the aromatic plants, whether shrubs or herbs, are richly endowed with essential oils and these help them avoid desiccation during hot, parched summers.

The Cistus tribe is wonderful in this respect. I love the gummy smell of C. x *cyprius* and the leaden odour of its foliage in winter. The large white, maroon-blotched flowers in early summer are among the most handsome. The vivid magenta of C. x *purpureus* is another good one while C. x *corbariensis* makes an attractive bush with neat, wavy-margined leaves that turn purple in cold weather. Pink buds open into smallish white flowers in amazing profusion.

Myrtle, *Myrtus communis*, is a similarly aromatic plant deserving the warmest spot you can give it. After three hard winters in a row, my 75-year-old plant was on its way out, but the last two winters have enabled it to regain its strength. It stands 1.2m to 1.5m tall again (from zero, two years ago) and has just produced a crop of its wonderfully scented white blossom.

Lavenders are all drought-resistant. The lavender cotton, *Santolina chamaecyparissus*, is so often used for low hedges, although I think *Helichrysum splendidum* is hardier and more attractive for this purpose. *Santolina pinnata* subsp. *neapolitana* is my favourite in this genus, with rather long, double-comb leaves. Plants should be cut hard back every spring to avoid flowering.

We are in the realm of the greys, now, and all are hot soil baskers. *Artemisia* 'Powis Castle' is one of the most valuable, because it never attempts to flower and that, in a grey foliage plant, is a great asset. It has feathery leaves and is hardier than most. My favourite, *Centaurea gymnocarpa*, is not very hardy, but the plants are in their third summer and I take precautionary cuttings in the autumn. Get a good clone and don't grow it from seed.

Red Hot Pokers

Red hot pokers – kniphofias – are more often orange than red: the colour of glowing embers. This, together with their strong outlines, adds zest and life to the garden. They are not restrained. Their flowering season is extended, according to variety, but I think of August as being their high point.

This month, we enjoy the largest and most flamboyant of them all, *Kniphofia uvaria* 'Nobilis'. Rising to well over 2m, it has quite an extended season and I love it in my principal mixed border, with the lavender spikes of *Buddleja* 'Lochinch' and the flattened domes of *Eupatorium purpureum* 'Atropurpureum' behind, and pink border phloxes in front. Quite an eyeful. There are greens around to soften the impact of orange with pink, notably the elegant columns of foliage from *Helianthus salicifolius*.

Truly red, though with just a hint of unexpected pink in it, is *Kniphofia* 'Lord Roberts'. This is half the height of the other kind, flowering towards the end of the month. The spikes are long and tapering. The rich red 'Samuel's Sensation' is sensational, though it is not always an easy one. The popular 'Little Maid' was bred by Beth Chatto.

Kniphofias are easily raised from seed. They take a few years to reach flowering size and the varied results are fun, though there is always a danger of rating them higher than they deserve because they are your own babies. 'Little Maid' is quite dwarf, at less than a metre, but prolific over a long period, especially if you can be bothered to split and replant at frequent intervals. The colour is cream-white.

K. caulescens (1.2m) is rather extraordinary, making rosettes of glaucous leaves, which are a principal reason for growing it. The stems become woody, so it is almost a shrub. Its flowering season varies according to the strain you are growing. One of mine flowers in June, the rest in September, the colour being soft orange. A colony of this makes a lively feature and looks especially well in gravel. A small but worthwhile improvement is to pull off the old dead leaves at the base of the live rosette (while steadying the stem, so you do not remove the whole thing).

Another striking kniphofia of the same type is *K. northiae*, which has the largest rosettes and broadest leaves of them all. Often, the rosettes fail to multiply, which I find disappointing, but when they do, forming a cluster, they are spectacular.

I am fond of 'Torchbearer' (1.8m), whose season is late September. It is a greenish shade of yellow and I have it near the pink domes of *Hydrangea macrophylla* 'Ayesha' (one of the many examples of yellow going well with pink). The season of orange *K. rooperi* is centred on early October. A customer whom Fergus was serving objected that it looked like a short penis. 'It may be short and stumpy,' said Fergus, 'but it comes late.' He sold her several plants.

Later still, and arriving in a great rush of blossom, is *K. linearifolia*. You might object to having to wait so many months for your reward, but in fact the foliage earns its keep by being a very bright green. The flowering coincides with the glistening young plumes of the pampas grass, *Cortaderia selloana*. That makes a good background. Fresh flowers arriving late have quite a lot to be said for them.

A main objection to the pokers is the space taken up by their long, lank evergreen foliage. Generally speaking, where the leaves have no particular asset, I think plants should be sited well back in a border, so that they are masked by plants in front. To what extent is it safe to tidy their foliage without prejudicing their health? you might wonder. I think it is best left through the winter, when a border's appearance isn't too important anyway. In spring, old leaves may be shortened by about half, or pull them off altogether. The crowns are a great roosting spot for snails, it is worth remarking.

The hardiness of kniphofias, most of which come from South Africa, is not entirely secure, so it is unwise to mess about with them unduly in the autumn. In spring, they can be propagated by division. Most of them require very little attention for years on end – just a regular mulching and feeding. There is a horrible bacterial disease that sometimes afflicts kniphofias, entirely rotting them, accompanied by a foul smell. Sometimes you buy this trouble in, so beware. There is nothing to be done about it except to destroy your stock and not replant in the same spot. Generally speaking, though, pokers are backbone plants that will give character to your garden.

Summer Evening Scent

When I put flowers into a visitor's room, I always include something that smells nice. In my own bedroom, this is quite unnecessary, as its open windows are above great draughts of scent reaching me from outside our porch entrance.

You need to be at that distance from some of the pongier liliums; notably, just now, the 'African Queen' strain of trumpet lilies. These are in very agreeable shades of buff yellow, and their scent is a little too overpowering at close range but welcome at a distance. The other big waft comes from a self-sown honeysuckle, *Lonicera periclymenum*, which is clambering over an ancient *Cotoneaster horizontalis*. Honeysuckles of the woodbine type are freely bird-sown but, if you are starting from scratch, you'll want to procure a well-coloured clone, and the late Dutch 'Serotina' is, when properly named, very dark red on the outside of its flower buds.

You may need to select your plant personally, as it is in, or about to, flower. There is inferior stock around of less intense colouring, but easier for the nurseryman to propagate.

The honeysuckle of the moment, in my garden – and it will have a second flush of blossom in the autumn – is *L. similis* var. *delavayi*, which is seething all over with creamy blossom that is powerfully fragrant at night and in the early morning. It is halfway up a tiled roof, which must mean that it has found anchorage under some tiles, which means trouble later on, when the honeysuckle's wood thickens and lifts the tiles. For the moment, I choose to look the other way, which is legitimate, seeing that I have to pay the bills. These climbers don't have to be given something to climb over; they also make excellent free-standing bushes. Space-consuming, they may be, but if cut hard back in the early spring, they'll still flower on their young wood, though rather later in the summer.

One of my favourite bushes in August is *Itea ilicifolia*, an evergreen with rather thin-textured, glossy leaves. It needs shelter and, given that, may grow up to the second storey of your house. Mine, in a more open site, is nearly 3m high and is now hung with pendant racemes of varying length, of tiny, pale green blossom, deliciously lemon-scented at night. It is a quite unusual and arresting sight, certainly not flamboyant, but not in too mousily good taste, either.

This is so obviously a season of scents that I have a list of 22 different kinds in front of me, not including nicotiana – it is under something of a cloud since becoming, in the past few years, a martyr to downy mildew, which will completely destroy your plants when reaching their peak. Closely related to nicotiana is a little-known hardy perennial (listed by nine sources in the RHS Plant Finder, however), Jaborosa integrifolia.

So far, it is trouble-free. It is a ground-groveller that makes a colony, in time. Elliptical leaves are pushed, singly, out of the ground, and with them – also singly and almost stalkless, though with a long tube – nicotiana-like white flowers. They have a swooningly powerful night scent. Something of a fun plant; with a name like that it has to be.

I will confine myself to night scents in this piece. Most of the day lilies open their buds in the morning and, if scented – look to the pure, yellow-flowered kinds for that attribute – theirs is a daytime scent. But some, not many of them in cultivation, open in the evenings, close in the following forenoon and are night-scented. Such is *Hemerocallis altissima*. You might call it spindle-shanks, because its naked scapes rise to 2m and they are apt to get twisted among their neighbours. Not that that really matters. The flowers are smallish, pale yellow and the plant has charm. I like it, anyway.

Of the fragrant, climbing jasmines, we have the pink, June-flowering *Jasminum* x *stephanense*, which is of moderate vigour and flowers abundantly, but only for a few weeks. *J. officinale* is the usual white-flowered summer jasmine, but we grow its extra-vigorous form, *affine*.

Its vigour is exactly comparable with that of the May-flowering *Clematis montana* group, and if you grow them together, neither will kill the other and you'll have a succession of blossom. *J. o. f. affine* is sometimes accused of being shy (meaning shy-flowering, not that it blushes in public), and that may be so in its early years, especially if you have to cut it back a lot to keep it within bounds. But once in a settled condition, I find that its flowering is both long and loud. I do prune it fairly regularly in the winter, when its leaves are off, removing all old, flowered growths that have clearly had their day. They'll be on the underside of its new stuff.

226

Daphne tangutica, which is evergreen and just about the easiest of all daphnes, is night-fragrant. A point to appreciate about it is that, although its main flush of blossom comes in April–May, it always gives us a generous second flowering in July–August.

Petunias of the less sophisticated kinds have a delicious night scent. Even the highly bred strains (of which breeders would be surprised to hear that scent was a petunia attribute at all) have by no means altogether lost it, though it should be looked for in the blue, purple and white strains, not in the bright pink and least of all the reds.

Some of the ginger group, species and selected clones of Hedychium, are almost overwhelming – nocturnal scent factories, notably the not quite hardy (except, that is, in Cornwall), the yellow H. *gardnerianum*. It is an excellent cold conservatory pot plant.

In the garden, any with white or pale yellow blossom are likely to be fragrant, for instance H. *densiflorum* 'Stephen'.

Summer Bedding

We are at the height of the season for summer bedding, so it's not a bad idea to consider what we expect of our bedding plants. Speaking personally, I don't really enjoy beds carved out of a lawn and looking thoroughly self-conscious. Open jam tarts, my mother used to call them. But if that is what you like, then you'll be aiming for a blaze of colour.

You'll easily find what you want at the garden centre, where most of the plants on offer are already flowering. However, the chances are that the life of such plants will be short. Their dwarf habit means that they have little capacity for making new growth. The initial explosion of colour has no follow-up. There are exceptions. Many begonias, for instance, have astonishing resilience. The dwarf rudbeckia (black-eyed Susan) called 'Toto' keeps up the display for many weeks.

I like to integrate my bedding in a mixed border with hardy perennials, shrubs, bulbs and anything else that will look nice in their company. For this purpose you need a bedder that won't look dumpy in the context and will integrate well with its neighbours, which a compact plant will not.

Take the bedding type of verbena. There are many seed strains that make dense little units and a carpet of colour, but they do not spread or integrate. However, the natural habit of a verbena is very spready. It will send out horizontal shoots which, on meeting a plant taller than itself, will rise and thread through it. So you find yourself with a kind of tapestry, which looks wonderful.

One year, I had a tall rudbeckia, 'Indian Summer' (1m), with rich yellow flowers and a black cone behind a lavender-mauve verbena called 'La France'. Neither looked anything at the time of planting out, so you could not indulge in instant satisfaction. Nor would they be on offer at a garden centre. But both, once they got going, had a long late-summer and autumn season. The verbena, planted in front of the rudbeckia, grew up into and through it – and, as you may imagine, the mauve with the yellow looked pretty good.

Verbenas of this kind are kept going by propagating them from cuttings taken in the autumn, and then overwintering them under frost-free glass. Other good varieties are 'Homestead Purple' (very bright), 'Silver Anne' (soft pink) and 'Sissinghurst' (bright pink).

Cosmos are long-flowering, and their height varies from about 0.7m to 2m, according to variety. A tall white one that I always grow is 'Purity'. Sown in May, it makes an easy replacement for foxgloves. The 'Sonata' strain, in shades of pink, carmine and white, is excellent and long-flowering at a mere 0.7m, while 'Dazzler' (1m) is a particularly intense crimson.

You may have to raise some annuals from seed. Two low-growing ones that I enjoy together are Gaillardia 'Red Plume' – double and intense orange-brown – and Helenium amarum, which has thread-like foliage of the brightest green with a succession of small, yellow daisy flowers.

Some of the taller annuals will need a stake (a cane is easiest) and a single tie, but it is quickly and simply done. I like large-flowered, double zinnias: they are now at their peak, but grow 1m high and will need that stake. These plants are not too tall for the small garden – you just need fewer of them, that's all. But there are some excellent dwarf zinnias, too. In the Profusion series, I find 'Orange Profusion' very effective and long-flowering, each plant making a substantial bush. 'White Profusion' is good of its kind, too.

One really tall annual (2.5m) that you might have to grow from seed is Persicaria orientalis. It starts flowering in July, and reaches its peak in

September, with masses of drooping, deep pink spikelets. It fits in well with late-flowering, deep blue aconitums, and will also overlap with the tall, purple-leaved orach, *Atriplex hortensis*. If you let that self-sow, you will have it for ever. But why not? Surplus seedlings are easily removed.

One bit of summer bedding that I love to work into a mixed border context is the orange *Canna* 'Wyoming' (2m), which has big purple leaves, with the small decorative dahlia 'David Howard' (1.8m), which has darkish leaves and an abundance of apricot-orange, fully double flowers over a long season. It must be – and fully deserves to be – one of the most popular dahlias ever raised.

Attracting Butterflies

My garden is currently harbouring a large number of butterflies, although not nearly so many, nor as many species, as 50 years ago. Still, it is good to see them. When we set out to grow butterfly plants – ones on which they will suck nectar – we tend to think the impulse altruistic, whereas it is, in fact, entirely self-indulgent. We just like to see those pretty insects around us and to feel that they are, somehow, ours. There's no harm in that, though sentimental butterfly talk can be a bit nauseating.

Most notable this year is the Painted Lady, which is not, alas, an indigenous species, though it breeds with us during the summer. Our winters nullify all its best efforts; it simply cannot survive them. All of which seems rather a wasted effort. Still, here they are, active and graceful, and I love to watch them. Their colouring is a soft, tawny orange with black-and-white trimmings. This morning, in my old rose garden, now planted as an exotic garden, there must have been 50 of them at one time.

We depend on an invasion from the Mediterranean region, and Painted Ladies became abundant over much of Britain in the first half of June. I saw them in Scotland, and friends in Wales have also reported seeing them. The brood that is now on the wing and looking fresh will mostly be home-bred, though more are doubtless arriving from abroad. Thistles are their food plant, but the imago loves to sup on nectar, particularly on *Verbena bonariensis*, which is the most popular butterfly flower I grow. Also on the flowers of Eryngium, notably on *E.* x *oliverianum* – the one with the steeliest blue stems.

Much, of course, depends on what you have on offer. All my buddleias were pruned late and, thanks also to the continuingly late season, are not yet in flower. They won't be long now. In September, the great attraction in my garden is the little-grown *Escallonia bifida*, which has huge clouds of white blossom for several weeks. The butterflies show up wonderfully against it.

I have not seen many Red Admirals yet, though they are around, and there are lots of newly emerged Peacock butterflies. They like my phloxes, and also the yellow daisies of *Silphium perfoliatum*, a 2m plant with great presence that I grow at the back of my long border. Another outstandingly popular yellow daisy is the 1m *Inula hookeri*. From the spiralling centre of a hispid bud, this emerges into a daisy with fine-spun rays of great delicacy. It's such an easy perennial, too, though its colonising tendencies need checking once annually. *Inula magnifica* is the giant of the genus, at 2–3m, but it's by no means coarse. We have established a colony to make discrete clumps in rough grass and it has a splendid presence.

Hebes are popular butterfly plants. There were Painted Ladies and Meadow Browns on them this morning. The blossom of 'Midsummer Beauty' is syrup-sweetly scented, but the butterflies seem just as happy on scentless varieties such as 'Great Orme' – just opening its slender pink spikes – and the dwarf, indigo-violet 'Autumn Glory'. These hebes are generous in their flowering, and the more so in many cases if dead-headed (a task on which even the most ignorant visitor who wants to be helpful can safely be let loose). They will often flower again, even into midwinter, if heavy frosts hold off.

The Small Skipper dodges about, though without sustained attention to blossom. The first Small Copper appeared in a meadow area of the garden in early May and I expect plenty more of them from now on, especially in Michaelmas daisy time. They are extraordinarily agile little butterflies.

There are fresh-looking Commas about, and they also like my phloxes. I cannot say they are numerous, but there is time yet. Hedge Browns are still plentiful, but I have seen no Speckled Woods as I do in some years, particularly from late-summer hatchings. They don't seek the sunshine but seem to find plenty to please them in my garden.

By this time last year, we already had a huge invasion, mostly from abroad, of large and small white butterflies, the ones which cause such trouble to our brassicas. But they also go for sea kale, nasturtiums, stocks and the spider flower, cleome. To date there are only a few, so maybe their parasites got the better of them between last year and this.

Of day-flying moths, Angleshades and the Silver Y are the most commonly seen, especially on my *Salvia* x *superba*. Their wings move with rapid vibration, which makes them appear ultra-busy. But their larvae eat a wide range of our plants without any apparent preference.

Also day-flying are the Hummingbird Hawkmoths. Their long proboscis enables them to hover at a considerable distance from the flower being supped at. In between hovering, they move to the next flower at incredible speed. A great fascination to watch.

Red Valerian is a favourite in June, but the verbena seems to please them as much as it does the butterflies.

Dahlias Revisited

When I first became enthusiastic about growing dahlias some 50 years ago, they were regarded as flowers that needed a place to themselves, and would not integrate with mixed or herbaceous plantings. All that has changed, and they are now seen as brilliant essentials for enlivening the shorter days.

We are always trying out new ones (new to us, that is) at Dixter, and Fergus has now been elected to the RHS Dahlia Committee, so it is small wonder that most of the new ones we try come from the trial ground at Wisley, which any dahlia fancier should visit in the coming weeks.

Dahlias are just about as malleable as tulips, and are ever ready to change their appearance from the more conventional ideas of how a dahlia should look. One of the oldest to break ranks was 'Bishop of Llandaff', enigmatically classed as 'miscellaneous'. It is fairly tall (1.5m), rich red, semi-single and has amazing foliage, not merely dark but deeply cut, almost fern-like. A great many new dahlias now have dark foliage. Its mundane leaves have always been the dahlia's weakness. I think dark leaves can be taken too far, but we shall see.

'Fascination' (0.5m), which already has an Award of Garden Merit, is classified as a dwarf bedding type combined with small water lily type, but I don't honestly think that classification means a lot where mavericks like this are concerned. Well, it certainly is dwarf and suitable for bedding. Its leaves are purple and highlight the flowers, which are an agreeable shade of fairly light mauvy-pink, semi-double and with broad petals.

'Art Nouveau' and 'Art Deco' are complete breaks with tradition. Again dwarf (almost too dwarf) and rather too congested at the start of the season to accommodate their medium-sized blooms; but height is gained as the season progresses. These two become increasingly exciting – the flowers are fully double (or nearly so) with in-curved petals, showing the darker reverse as well as the lighter pink or apricot upper side.

'Paso Doble' (1m) is classified as anemone-centred. The centre, in fact, is a large, fully double rosette, taking up as much space as the broad frame of rays. All are the same shade of pale yellow. The leaves are fresh green.

'Moonfire' (1m) is already a very popular bedding dahlia, with a single flower, buff yellow shading to orange at the centre. The disc is dark. This, as is the way with singles, sets seed abundantly and will stop flowering if not regularly dead-headed. Potentially, it has a long flowering season.

'Chimborazo' (2m) is a tall collerette dahlia, which you will either love or dislike intensely (provocative flowers are such fun). The outer frame of broad rays is deep red, while the collar of enlarged stamens is, in contrast, pale yellow. The disc is deep yellow. You cannot be bored by such a flower.

Combining Plants

When plants look well together, they seem to be enjoying each other's company, and that enjoyment rubs off on us. You might plant a patch of the lavender-blue Aster x frikartii 'Mönch' and it will flower quietly, undemandingly, from early August for a good two months. Just a little too quietly, perhaps, depending on your temperament; so you work in a few nasturtiums and their brilliance enhances and doubles up on the aster's own merits.

The summer's rains in the south have suited border phloxes and anyway they love my heavy soil. I have some bright pink ones in front of the white globes of *Hydrangea arborescens* 'Annabelle', new to me but evidently settling in. Though one is a shrub and the other herbaceous, they match up in the way they present their flowers.

Few of my phloxes are named; I've acquired pieces from friends over the years. Another, less brash, pink one, which I call Doghouse Pink (its owner lived at Doghouse Farm), shows up to 3D effect against the purple foliage of *Cotinus coggygria* 'Royal Purple'. The long, lavender panicles of *Buddleja* 'Lochinch' rise behind that. And I have also included the yellow candelabrums and spikes of two species of verbascum into this grouping. I think that looks smashing but many would avert their eyes. I garden to please myself.

One of my favourite phloxes is the species *Phlox paniculata*, from which all the garden varieties derived. It has none of their muscularity. Its mauve flowers are gathered into a light and airy inflorescence and it grows to a height of 1.2m or even 1.5m, so discreet staking is needed.

It looks good with the soft yellow funnels of *Hemerocallis* 'Marion Vaughn'. But I also have it against a backdrop of purple *Clematis* x 'Jackmanii Superba' (supported on a stout pole) and with the yellow cut-leaved elder *Sambucus racemosa* 'Plumosa Aurea' to one side. The purple and yellow contrast is by no means hectic. In front of the phlox is *Monarda* 'Beauty of Cobham', whose soft pink flowers are set off by purple bracts. All these plants need plenty of moisture at the roots, so the season has suited them well.

I do like privet blossom, even its sickly sweet scent. It's a part of summer. There are many good privets but they'll only flower if you go easy with shears and secateurs. The time to set to work with these is immediately after they have flowered. *Ligustrum* 'Vicaryi' is a softer greeny yellow than the usual golden privet and its leaves are larger. It has just been flowering in a huge mound of vegetation at the back of my border, where the candelabrums of wild teasels add just that element of backbone needed here. Of course, they are self-sown and it's just luck that they are there. Not entirely luck. With self-sowing plants, the gardener still has to exercise control by eliminating 99 out of every 100 seedlings, leaving the few that are well placed.

Another of my privets, *L. japonicum*, makes a much smaller bush at 1.5m or so. When that was covered in cream blossom the yellow daisies of *Inula hookeri* were flowering in front of it, 90cm tall and each daisy presented as a discreet unit. A good plant, though you need to watch its running rootstock.

Allium sphaerocephalon, a late-flowering bulb, is one of those plants which effortlessly looks important. Its elongated globes of purple flowers are carried on long (90cm), thin, leafless stems. When you get a lot of them together, they have a commanding, yet graceful, presence. You can use it in all sorts of ways and the bulbs increase quite quickly. It's good with a red penstemon, for instance. But I am enjoying it with a lower background of *Lysimachia ciliata*. This is a loosestrife with pale yellow flowers held like open lampshades. Again, its roots run into all its neighbours, so it wants watching. That's nothing new to the gardener.

Contrasts in foliage, form and colour can be just as effective and longer-lasting than dependence on flowers alone. An excellent sedge has the popularity-destroying name *Carex muskingumensis*. It makes 60cm clumps of bright glossy green, linear foliage, the leaves arranged in whorls of three. I have this growing out of the lower regions of a smoke bush, *Cotinus coggygria* 'Foliis Purpureis', whose leaves are not as deep a shade as 'Royal Purple' – that can be a little too aggressive, and it does not produce the smoky inflorescence which is a part of this species' charm.

Bright green foliage is comparatively rare at summer's end, and therefore the more welcome. You find it in the polypody fern, *Polypodium* 'Cornubiense', which has just produced its new crop of lacy fronds. That will make a 30cm-tall patch and I like to get a dwarf fuchsia near to and behind it. 'Genii' would be a good choice, its season of interest being so long, and its lime-green foliage set off by a red central vein and leaf stalk. The young stems are also red, while the red and purple flowers join the festivities with increasing freedom as autumn advances.

'Genii' is absolutely hardy. I cut my plants to the ground in January, which allows an innings to interplanted snowdrops. In another foliage grouping I have an interplanting of snowdrops (*Galanthus plicatus*) and the blue anemone which flowers in April, *Anemone nemorosa* 'Robinsoniana'. The plants they grow among are a cut-leaved male fern, *Dryopteris filix-mas* 'Linearis', and the large, furry-leaved *Bergenia ciliata*, which is deciduous. The web-footed leaves of *Rodgersia podophylla* also take part and all are overhung by a graceful bamboo, *Arundinaria falconeri*, which I keep in order by removing, each early spring, all its older canes, leaving only those thin rods which it made in the previous season. Sometimes a hard winter will prune it for me, and even more severely, but it always springs again from the base. So this damp corner, receiving only afternoon sunshine, is interesting for most of the year.

August Shrubs

An all-herbaceous border is lacking in strength and fibre. It is too flimsy, and that is where shrubs come in. But those that are looking their best in August, which is when you may want your border to peak, are none too numerous. I value them all the more. They may be chiefly valuable for their foliage but, if for their flowers, it is surprising what a large proportion of these are white. There is nothing wrong with that, of course colour can be found elsewhere.

The New Zealand hoherias are all white-flowered – not unlike cherry blossom, but the leaves are more mallow-like. One August-flowerer I particularly like is the vigorous *Hoheria sexstylosa*. It makes little impression in youth but improves every year, though it is sometimes wiped out with alarming speed by the coral spot fungus.

Eucryphia, also from the southern hemisphere, are all white-flowered. My favourite is E. *glutinosa*: it is deciduous, and its pinnate leaves colour well in November. The flowers contain lots of stamens, each tipped with red. It must have acid or neutral soil, but the hybrid, E. x *nymansensis* 'Nymansay', will accept some alkalinity. It is semi-evergreen, tall and easily pruned into a slender spire. Bees adore it.

Most of the hardiest hydrangeas are white-flowered and in bloom now. Perhaps my favourite is *Hydrangea quercifolia*, although I grow it chiefly for its handsome oak-leaf-shaped foliage. This takes on deep, burnished red tints in autumn, the colour lasting right into December.

H. paniculata has many cultivars, all white-flowered, although some, such as 'Grandiflora', fade pink. One I grow is 'Tardiva', which has a conical, lacecap inflorescence, with big sterile florets interspersed by a fuzz of tiny fertile flowers. These hydrangeas flower on their young wood, so you can prune them by shortening their old growth, either hard or lightly, according to the height you want the shrub to be.

H. arborescens 'Annabelle' is a similar one, with a long season. The huge flower heads are domed rather like a cauliflower. But the best August-flowering hydrangea is *H. aspera* Villosa Group, a flat-headed lacecap of intense lilac-mauve colouring, the centre blue. Bees collecting pollen from it accumulate a blue sac on each leg, instead of the usual yellow. This makes a large shrub with felted leaves and it only needs occasional pruning, by cutting out old, tired branches.

Buddleias are mostly colourful. Those that flower on their young wood, such as *Buddleja davidii*, are generally pruned back quite hard in early spring, but you can adjust the height of the shrub by the severity or otherwise of your pruning. Also its time of flowering. If you want to delay its flowering, so that it is timed for after your return from a holiday, prune it harder and later, say in early May. One of my favourites is 'Dartmoor', which carries heavy fans of purple blossom, rather than the usual spikes. They are all scented and attractive to butterflies.

If you stand in the right place, my 'Dartmoor' comes into the same picture as two other good, late-summer-performing shrubs. *Bupleurum fruticosum* (making a background to summer bedding) is a rounded evergreen that grows to 2m, but again you can control its height by spring pruning. The heads of its umbelliferous flowers are green. The other shrub is the green-and-white-variegated dogwood, *Cornus alba* 'Elegantissima' which, by hard early April pruning, I keep down to about 2m. It gives a light and airy impression right into autumn. Then, when its leaves have been shed, you can enjoy its carmine stems throughout the winter, so it is a dual-purpose shrub.

The summer-flowering tamarisk, *Tamarix ramosissima*, is an easy mixed-border shrub to manage for height, by the winter pruning of its previous year's growth. Its tiny, bright green leaves are all airy lightness through early summer, but develop a mass of spikelets of pink flowers now. Mine is growing above *Hydrangea macrophylla* 'Mariesii', which is a lacecap and comes pink on my more or less neutral soil, though it would tend towards blue if yours were acid.

I believe that privets are underrated. One that flowers with tremendous grace late this month, and into the next, is *Ligustrum quihoui*, with showers of white blossom. Its pruning should consist of annually removing its old, flowered shoots but leaving the wand-like young ones intact. *Ligustrum* 'Vicaryi' is a very superior golden privet, with larger leaves than the normal type and, if you go lightly with your pruning, an abundance of white blossom. Leave all its non-flowering shoots intact and remove those branches that have flowered as soon as they have finished flowering.

Phlox

Many perennials have flowered their heads off this summer; none more so than the border phloxes, cultivars of *Phlox paniculata*, which are everyone's idea of what a phlox should be. They make great quilts of voluptuous colour from late June on. All they require to get the best from them is well-nourished, humus-rich soil and plenty of moisture at their roots.

They must, however, start with a bill of good health. I find this easiest to ensure by begging a piece of one I like the look of in a friend's garden. They'll never know its name, so I call it after them or their house.

Phloxes make a mass, at about 1.5m, of brilliant, undulating colour. If kept well nourished, they may not need dividing and replanting often; you can judge this by the state of your colonies when they start into renewed growth in February. If replanting, choose healthy, quite chunky bits (not single shoots), so you get a decent show the same year. Some of the best have the capacity to flower twice, and generously both times if you enjoy the warmth of southern England. They do remarkably well in Scotland, but get going later, so their season is shorter.

I have a light purple one which I call P. 'Burgi' because it came from the family of Burgess: ma, pa and daughter. It starts in late June and continues virtually non-stop into October. One of my favourites is the soft mauve *P. paniculata* (2m) itself, my stock of which was given me from its American homeland. It is very graceful and generous, but does need support. There is also a white version. I find the so-called red phloxes (there is always a hint of pink in them) unsatisfactory. They lack vigour. You never see them in old gardens, which says something in itself.

I do wish we could get the real names for some of the old-fashioned stalwarts – my 'Doghouse Pink', for instance (from Doghouse Farm, on Stone Street, Canterbury, originally a pub, the Dog). It is in two shades of soft pink and full of charm. Next to it is a really brash, raw yet thoroughly effective one, 'Ladd's Pink' (after Edward and Sylvia Ladd). 'Long Border Mauve' (in our Dixter long border since before I was born) is a penetrating colour that shows brilliantly from a distance.

Phloxes give me little trouble, too. Mildew can be troublesome (though not at Dixter) and need a spraying. Eelworm can be a real menace but, if you start with clean stock and are careful about provenance, it need never come your way. I wish more of my plants gave me as little anxiety as the phloxes. They are a great joy in their season.

Evergreens

By late summer, it should be possible to assess the evergreens in our gardens. They provide obvious furnishings in winter, when there's little else on the scene. Spring is often their worst period; battered by months of rotten weather, they have not had time to recover. Spring, indeed, is the season of their principal leaf fall (much to the annoyance of the tidy gardener). Then comes the flush of young growth which, for a few weeks, may completely alter their appearance.

But by now, things have settled down and we can ask whether we have too many evergreens for the summer. Are they making the garden too heavy? Are they worth the wait? Many rhododendron hybrids would get my unequivocal 'no' to this last question; except in the largest of gardens, where long-term passengers don't get in the way. Think of 'Cynthia', 'Betty Wormald', 'Pink Pearl', or 'Purple Splendour': the price of two weeks' knockout display is 50 weeks of an excessively boring lump.

Their foliage is no help to these rhododendrons. But some species and hybrids have wonderfully enlivening leaves. In *Rhododendron* 'Sir

Charles Lemon', the leaves are a warm, rust colour on their undersides, and the young foliage is held like fingers pointing upwards, as though to draw attention to this most alluring feature. Its white flowers become a bonus rather than a necessity. Alas, it is none too hardy and it relishes the kind of Atlantic conditions that can be expected along the west coast but not in Essex.

The familiar so-called castor oil plant (a complete misnomer), *Fatsia japonica*, can never bore. Its big, glossy, fingered leaves have a splendid presence, especially in a semi-formal setting like a courtyard, where this strong leaf form can be repeated in the shadows it throws up. In a large, mixed border, it can form a backdrop for more lively summer flowers, whether Japanese anemones or the apricot-orange Turk's caps of *Lilium henryi*.

Viburnum rhytidophyllum, when well grown (it can look dejected, when not), is similarly a presence in its own right but can also highlight adjacent attractions. It is a fast grower with large, elliptical leaves whose glossy surface is stamped with a network of recessed veins (*rhytidophyllum* means wrinkled leaves).

The dirty-white flowers are no asset – unlike the clusters of berries. Ripening about now, they turn first red, then black, and there's a stage when both colours handsomely combine. But to get berries, you must plant a couple of genetically different seedlings side by side. You can plant them in the same hole if pressed for space. The hybrid 'Pragense' (raised in Prague) is similar, but with smaller leaves and is a smaller, laxer shrub.

I rate *Daphniphyllum* subsp. *macropodum*; a super evergreen shrub, up to 3m or 3.6m high, with a strong character that makes it stand out from a distance. Its smooth, elliptical leaves form rosettes, so flowers would be superfluous. The leaves' stalks and veins turn pink in late summer, retaining this colouring throughout the winter.

Another broad-leafed evergreen shrub (it can grow into a tree but it's better to start with a young specimen) is *Trochodendron aralioides*. Again the leaves, which are shaped like some mature ivies, are borne in rosettes, clustered around pale yellow-green young stems. The leaves are soap-smooth and thick, making them a pleasure to handle. Green flowers with stamens like the spokes of a wheel (*Trochodendron* means wheel tree) appear in May.

Variegated evergreens tend to deserve prominence. The holly, *Ilex* x *altaclerensis* 'Golden King', is the best year-round feature in my long border. It stands in the angled corner of yew hedging and is now, after nearly 40 years, beyond reach, even from a small step-ladder, but I trim its sides with secateurs to retain a fairly narrow column and a dense habit.

Another holly with spire-like habit and yellow marginal variegation of its sizeable leaves is *I.* x *altaclerensis* 'Belgica Aurea', more often listed as 'Silver Sentinel'. It isn't silver at all, but I suppose the alliteration is irresistible.

On a smaller scale, some of the *Euonymus fortunei* cultivars are a year-round feast. I would award first prize to 'Silver Queen', but you need patience as it takes 25 years to reach maturity. It is this slow growth that gives it its fine shape in the long run. There is little green in the leaf, which is broadly margined in white, though pale yellow when young in spring. For speedy growth, 'Emerald Gaiety' makes an elegant specimen bush, lively and fresh in green and white.

Variegated and coloured privets can be excellent features if not overdone. A whole hedge of golden privet is too much. My favourite, *Ligustrum* 'Vicaryi', has largish leaves of a variable yellow-green, the yellow being brightest where the bush (which I keep to about 3m) receives most light, at the top.

Late-flowering Perennials

I like to have plenty of later-flowering perennials to keep my borders looking fresh and lively. Of course, ones that look dull for months beforehand should be grown in limited numbers, but that is often not the case.

The two best-known border sedums, *Sedum spectabile* and 'Herbstfreude' (aka 'Autumn Joy'), both look promisingly energetic long before they flower. When at its best, I prefer the former – the clone to grow is 'Brilliant', which is a deeper, richer pink than the prototype. But be warned: it pales easily. We do a little roguing when this happens, unless we enjoy a mixture of the two. This sedum excels at attracting butterflies, but its flowering season is fairly short and the dying flower heads soon turn black.

'Herbstfreude', on the other hand, will intensify from pale (though always dusky) pink to rich ruby and then to a good shade of brown, which it retains through most of winter. It is definitely not a plant to cut down when you're in an officious, tidying-up mood. Once settled in, however, it becomes too tall for the weight of its inflorescence and splays open in a disagreeable manner. But you can prevent this by lifting your plants in the dormant season (take the chance to divide them, if they need it) and replanting them where they were. Breaking their roots sets them back so that their stems are shorter and thus strengthened.

This is a useful way to treat many perennials that have a tendency to grow taller than suits you. A good example is the August–September-flowering sunflower *Helianthus* 'Lemon Queen'. You can reduce the height of an established colony by up to a metre by not allowing it to become established. Lift (and divide) your clumps in winter or spring, and plant them back. Additionally, when they are still less than a metre high, pinch out the growing tips – just the central tuft of leaflets – as this will keep the plant well below 2m. It may still require support, but the small flowers are borne increasingly over many weeks and they are such a soft shade of yellow that even yellow-phobes will find it hard to dislike them.

They will not, however, so readily accept *Solidago rugosa* 'Fireworks' (1.2m), which is as bright a yellow golden rod as you'll find, though it has an excellent habit. Don't avoid it just because you think golden rods are lower class. Give it a try. A blue Michaelmas daisy, such as 'Little Carlow', would make a suitable companion.

Actaea simplex has great presence and, although 2m tall when flowering, it can be grown near a border's margin since its handsome, bipinnate foliage is at a low level, leaving the spires of white pouffes to soar without competition. There are purple-leaved strains, whose dark foliage is in even more striking contrast with the white flowers, but the intensity of purple varies greatly, so it is as well to choose your purchases (which will be quite expensive) by eye.

Like these plants, the rudbeckias also revel in moisture. I like a 0.5m-tall planting of *Rudbeckia* 'Goldsturm' – a black-eyed Susan with rich yellow, narrow rays – in front of my *A. simplex*. Another moisture-lover, though on a far grander scale, is *Aralia cachemirica*, a 2m perennial whose large pinnate leaves are a feature in themselves. The numerous umbels of tiny flowers are like those of an ivy (and they are related), but they truly come into their own when the purple-black berries ripen, and the stems and stalks also turn purple.

I had always regarded globe thistles Echinops as rather second-rate, with their coarse, pinnate foliage and a kind of heartiness in adversity (I expect to see them covered in bindweed, yet still smiling nobly) that becomes a little nauseating with familiarity. However, I think I am converted by the seed strain E. subsp. *ruthenicus* (1m). In only its second year, it is already a handsome plant with a boldly branching habit. Plant it out where it is to remain, as transplanting is often fatal. As the buds open into flowers, the silvery globe heads change to a truly intense shade of blue.

This is not to be gainsaid.

There are two species of allium that I find particular stalwarts late in the season. One, A. *tuberosum* (0.3m) or Chinese chives, is of upright habit and carries umbels of not dazzling, but decent white flowers for many weeks and seeds itself pleasantly along the margin of my long border. The other, A. *senescens* subsp. *montanum* (0.1m), is so short that it deserves an open, sunny position without competition. Its curved, greyish foliage grows in waves, twisting this way and that, and the flower heads are sizeable, numerous and mauve; popular with butterflies.

A bulbous plant with a long season – from August on – is *Zephyranthes candida* (0.15m). Its white crocus flowers are set among clumps of fresh green, rush leaves. The hotter the summer, the better it flowers – though it never seriously lets you down.

A Visit to the Exotic Garden

When the weather settled and became hot towards the end of July, I concluded (as I frequently do) that this year summer had come to stay. This gives one a feeling of almost excessive relaxation. I get up in the morning, wash, shave, put on my wristwatch and feel fully dressed, although I've not in fact even started.

The mood of dreaming summer is nowhere stronger in my garden than in the humid, enclosed area that we now call the Exotic Garden, although for more than 80 years it was a rose garden. Since Fergus came to manage things in 1993, there has been a transformation. The roses all went, bar a dozen or so (to show there was no ill feeling), and we now have plants of a kind that, on a warm morning, you can almost hear growing. I have to admit that, in the course of those eight years, we have built three more heated greenhouses to protect the tender plants in winter, but in such a good cause.

We planted up this garden in mid-June (I even denied myself a trip to Scotland, to show I was serious about this, because we were late on the job last year). From a June planting, things still take time to settle in, but now everything (except some of the huge collection of begonias that we like to try outdoors) is revelling. While other parts of the garden may be showing signs of strain, the Exotic Garden is flaunting itself.

Overtopping all else are three banana palms (*Musa basjoo*), with their great sail-like leaves. When the weather is really hot, each plant can produce a new leaf in 10 days (eight is the record). In banana plantations, the leaves are always torn to shreds, but if they are really sheltered, the tearing process is much slower. This species overwinters outside, though well wrapped up.

Big, imposing leaves are a feature of the garden. They are far larger than any flower and they are there to be admired for weeks and months, rather than an average flower's few days. Most glamorous is *Tetrapanax papyrifer*, with light green palmate leaves, the margins indented, the texture furry. By contrast, elephant's ears, *Colocasia esculenta*, is soap-smooth and beautifully veined. It rocks from side to side in the wind, and drips dew at the slightest occasion. Then there are spear leaves and pinnate leaves, and many other shapes and sizes. A broad-leaved tender grass, *Setaria palmifolia*, is a great favourite, with hard-textured, ribbed leaves.

But I love bright colours, so dahlias and cannas provide most of these. Cannas have the great advantage of combining imposing foliage with showy flowers. One of the best is going around as 'General Eisenhower' (the validity of the name is in doubt, but a plant without a name is useless): magnificent, sculptural purple leaves subtending bunches of brilliant crimson flowers. The best orange canna is undisputedly (at least I will allow no disputing) 'Wyoming', 2m tall. It has purple leaves, so it goes well with the stalwart and deservedly popular dahlia, 'David Howard', which is small, apricot-orange, decorative and prolific.

Many cannas display their leaves so that sunshine illuminates them from behind, thereby giving double value. The pink-variegated 'Durban' and yellow-variegated 'Striata', both striped, are excellent in this way, and both have orange flowers. For salmon-pink, 'Erebus' is unusual, as its leaves are conspicuously glaucous – bluish-grey. It is a generous flowerer.

Dahlias, by and large, have rather mundane foliage but make up for this with flower power. A new one is 'Davar Donna', a smallish semi-cactus of piercingly acid-yellow colouring. On the whole, I gravitate to the red, orange and yellow shades, though the purple 'Hillcrest Royal' (medium cactus) is a great favourite. Of course, we have to include the crimson 'Bishop of Llandaff', as its deeply cut, purple foliage is exceptional.

There is plenty of colour from other flowers. One that shouts like the loudest member of a football crowd is *Salvia involucrata* 'Bethellii' (1.2m), which is light magenta.

This kind of gardening is hard work but sheer fun. We can't help grinning with silly pleasure when we're in that garden. It lasts well into October.

Dogwood

If I had to single out the best shrub for year-round pleasure, it would have to be the dogwood, *Cornus alba* 'Elegantissima'. It doesn't flower, but it has everything else. I have two groups of three in the middle of a border. They are currently nearly 2m tall, and all light and airy, their green, oval leaves bordered with white.

They make an excellent background to anything I like to bed out in front of them, currently some bronze, early-flowering chrysanthemums. Into one group, a pink, late-June-flowering *Alstroemeria ligtu* hybrid (1m) sowed itself and was charming in its season. Another self-sown interloper that makes me smile is the July-flowering *Veratrum album* (2m), with broad, ribbed leaves and candelabrums of white, starry flowers.

The cornus is deciduous, but its young stems in winter are carmine and gleam in low sunlight. They are underplanted with quite tiny,

March-flowering bulbs – the little yellow trumpet daffodil, *Narcissus minor*, rich blue x *Chionoscilla allenii*, and a late-flowering snowdrop.

As soon as these have finished, at the turn of March and April, the dogwood is given its hard, annual cutback, down to about 70cm. The best colouring of its stems comes from young shoots, and this treatment ensures the brightest results. It also restricts the plants to a convenient size. They don't look much for the next few weeks; you may start to wonder if they'll ever get a move on. But they do, and will soon be arrayed with vigorous growth for the summer.

The bedding in front of them changes two or three times in the course of the season; this is an important area in front of the house. Between the groups of dogwood, there are colonies of white Japanese anemones, 'Honorine Jobert' (1.5m), and as they flower rather late, from July to October, they are interplanted with a large-headed mauve allium, *A. cristophii* (80cm). It is later engulfed by anemones, but is a great self-sower and easily established.

Another similar cultivar to *C. alba* 'Elegantissima' that you might like just as well (both have the RHS Award of Garden Merit) is the yellow-leaved 'Aurea'. It has all the same attributes except leaf colour. It looks excellent in the double mixed borders at Wisley, in early summer, with the rich blue cranesbill *Geranium* 'Brookside' threading through it. From the current geranium trial at Wisley, I should hazard that the similar but even more intensely coloured 'Orion' might be an even better choice.

A garden is a community with many intertwining threads.

Late Summer Plants

If flower power is falling off in our gardens during the next six weeks, the fault is partly due to the natural winding down of the season. But such an anticlimax can be avoided in future years.

First the annuals. Late sowings made in May can be raised in a cold frame or greenhouse. Backed by white Japanese anemones, I have a long bed in front of the house with groups of the dark *Amaranthus* 'Red Fox' and, in front of them, three kinds of dwarf, small-flowered zinnia.

'Tropical Snow' is white, 'Orange Star' is orange all through and, my favourite, 'Chippendale' is deep bronze with an orange margin. These are just reaching their peak.

Related to zinnias but making giant plants is *Tithonia rotundifolia* 'Torch'; each plant needs a cane and a single tie. Its brilliant, rich orange goes well with the *Nicotiana sylvestris*, which has luminous green paddle leaves supporting candelabra of long tubed, white, deliciously scented flowers. This needs sowing in March with some heat.

I'm crazy about 'Striped Marvel' among the tall marigolds; the single flowers are alternately striped in bronze and orange. It makes a lot of growth before flowering, but is ideal for the tail end of the season. In front of banks of hydrangeas, I'm growing May-sown *Malope trifida* 'Vulcan', a deep carmine mallow with translucent green slits at the base of each funnel.

Annual climbers soon to be at their best include *Mina lobata*, with red and white tubular flowers, and *Cobaea scandens*, with large, murky purple bells. To get it going, sow early under heat.

A climbing herbaceous perennial that I grow for display in pots outside my porch is the blue, campanula-like *Codonopsis convolvulacea* or, better still, *C. forrestii*, in which the centre of each saucer is zoned in purple and a thin line of orange. The display is also kept up with salpiglossis, from an April sowing, eventually moved into 18cm pots; and lilies. Pure white *Lilium auratum* 'Casablanca' will be followed by pink *L. speciosum* var. *rubrum* and that by the long white trumpets, purple on the outside, of *L. formosanum*, all sweetly scented in their different ways.

Shrubby plants which, if pruned hard annually, make huge leaves and look tenderly exotic, but are perfectly hardy, include the cut-leaved sumach, *Rhus glabra* 'Laciniata', and the furry, heart-leaved *Paulownia tomentosa*. We are also growing on some seedlings of tree of heaven, Ailanthus, with long, pinnate leaves, to be treated in the same way. The poker, *Kniphofia caulescens*, is semi-shrubby and has huge rosettes of glaucous foliage, especially imposing if the plants are divided into single crowns every second year.

I shall treat *Decaisnea fargesii* as a severely pruned shrub grown entirely for its dusky green, pinnate foliage. This has a lovely way of heaving up and down and swaying from side to side when the wind is blowing.

Strap leaves are in happy contrast to heart-shaped, pinnate, and palmate. I have the giant reed grass, *Arundo donax*, which annually makes 3.6m of height with its arching, blue leaves. The variegated form, broadly banded and striped in pure white, grows only 60–90cm in a season. It is a bit tender, but is perhaps the most beautiful of all variegateds.

Of flowering perennials, *Verbena bonariensis* is the most generous with its innumerable clusters of purple blossom. It grows 1.5m to 1.8m tall. I grow some late-flowering kniphofias, of which the tallest, at 2.1m, and most spectacular is the bright orange and yellow *Kniphofia uvaria* 'Nobilis'. Then there are the salvias, which deserve an article to themselves, but of the reasonably hardy perennials, the deep blue *Salvia guaranitica* and the light, sky-blue *S. uliginosa* are the stars.

Planting Autumn Bulbs

Among the first bulbs that we should be thinking about now are those that will be flowering almost as soon as they are planted, notably the true autumn crocuses. Colchicums are also loosely known as autumn crocuses, because they look similar, but they are not even distantly related, as becomes clear when their broad, glossy leaves appear in spring; they, too, should be bought and planted without delay.

As I write this, I have two wholesale bulb catalogues at my side – both from firms that will deal direct with the public. It pays to order £100-worth, as carriage and packing is then free, so pool your requirements with friends, or else go through your local horticultural society, which can also put through a bulk order at the same time.

The best crocus for autumn flowering is *Crocus speciosus*, whose heavily veined flowers help give it a bluer appearance than any other crocus. In contrast, the central stigma is brilliant scarlet. It is deliciously scented. Corms are £5 per 100, and, far from dwindling in the garden, they will increase. This is also the best autumn crocus for naturalising in grass. Its new leaves do not appear until the new year, so you can make a late-autumn grass cut after the crocuses have finished flowering. They usually bloom in late September.

Another autumn crocus on offer (cheap) is listed as *C. zonatus*, though correctly *C. kotschyanus* subsp. *kotschyanus*. It is pale mauve but beware, there are very shy-flowering stocks of it around. *C. salzmannii*, correctly *C. serotinus* subsp. *salzmannii*, is mauve with a well-shaped bowl flower. It flowers well if the corms have had a good summer baking, but as its foliage appears at the same time as its flowers and remains for months afterwards, it is most suitable in a border.

C. ochroleucus is a sweet little thing, but not very practical. The flowers do not appear till late autumn and run on into December. They are very small and white, with yellow at the base; charming when open to warm sunshine, but there is seldom enough of that commodity at that time to open them. I grow it at the front of a border and it increases obligingly.

Two or three other autumn crocuses that are not offered wholesale are worth seeking out. Good stock of *C. nudiflorus* is rich purple with sturdily upstanding blooms that flower in September and October. This one has stoloniferous corms that make it hard to handle in a harvested state, but once you have it there are no further worries and it will spread of its own accord into colonies, making it highly suitable for meadow conditions. The leaves appear in spring.

C. pulchellus is a delightful mauve October-flowerer that I have not yet tried under meadow conditions. I have it at a border front, where it self-sows. *C. medius* is a very rich mauve-purple and flourishes in Beth Chatto's gravel garden, although I have been less successful with it, probably out of negligence.

By comparison with autumn crocuses, the cheapest colchicums on offer are far more expensive. There is generally more substance in their blooms than in any true crocus, and usually, other than in the albinos, a flush of pink that you never find in crocuses. If grown in a border they soon multiply and you can work up your own stocks. There's something to be said for buying pot-grown plants that are already in flower, as then you can see what you're buying.

I order my lily bulbs now, though they are not generally dispatched until December, when planting conditions in the garden are pretty wretched. Really, it will be safest to pot most of them up, to keep them moist, but not wet, in a cold shed until growth appears in February or March, and then to transfer them to a cold frame or a greenhouse.

Essential to be planted in early autumn is the madonna lily, *Lilium candidum*, as this makes a tuft of basal leaves forthwith, which it carries through the winter before producing a flowering stem in spring. It is never suitable for pot work, and should instead be given a sunny border position, the bulbs planted only just below the soil surface. It is particularly good in chalk or limy gardens.

Another bulb that needs to be planted early is the crown imperial, *Fritillaria imperialis*, which is already flowering before the end of April, either yellow or browny-orange. Some gardeners find this easy under practically any treatment, while for others of us the bulbs are most often blind: they make leafy stems, but no flowers. Humus-rich soil seems a good idea, as does a sunny position. Sometimes you are recommended to plant the bulbs on their sides, so that they cannot become waterlogged. I must admit, however, that the crown imperial is not one of Mr Lloyd's more outstanding successes.

Ordering Next Year's Bulbs

Making the year's principal bulb order also involves thinking about how, and where, the bulbs will be used – whether in pots for display, in bedding-out areas, as ingredients in mixed borders or naturalised in rough grass.

To buy in bulk from a wholesaler is much cheaper than buying from retail outlets if the quantity you buy is of sufficiently high value. To this end, we pool our order with the requirements of our local horticultural society.

When you receive your order, keep the bulbs cool and make sure you quickly plant those that shrivel easily and those benefiting from early root action long before shoots become apparent. Of the shrivellers, dog's-tooth violets, erythronium, are notable. The European *E. dens-canis* is a favourite of mine. It makes low clumps and has pinky-mauve, turk's-cap-style flowers with chocolate-and-green-marbled foliage.

That naturalises well in rough grass. The pale yellow hybrid, 'Pagoda', is safer in a cool border or in open woodland conditions (how many readers have open woodland, I wonder?). That has hybrid vigour and carries plenty of pale yellow Turk's caps. Even better, I like *E. tuolumnense* (partly for the fun of getting my tongue around its name), which is bright yellow with shiny green foliage. All these are March-flowering.

Blue-flowered bulbs are understandably in great demand, and they show up especially well in grass turf, where they contrast tellingly with natives such as red clover and field buttercups. The North American camassia, which is similar in growth to a bluebell but with stars instead of bells, is particularly good. Best of these, for richness of colour, is *Camassia quamash* (syn. *C. esculenta*): not only does this clump up, but it seeds itself, provided you wait until late July for the seeds to ripen and distribute themselves before cutting the grass. It flowers in May.

Triteleia laxa (syn. *Brodiaea laxa*) does not flower until late June and early July, but needs to be planted the previous autumn. It has umbels of true blue funnels and looks very striking in a meadow, although, if you want to increase stock quickly and then transfer your gains to a meadow area, you should grow it under border conditions.

Snake's head fritillaries, *Fritillaria meleagris*, are native in wettish but not waterlogged meadows and they naturalise in turf well, in Scotland as successfully as in the south. You can buy them cheaply, but you may be disappointed in the results of your efforts the first year. Be patient: they take time to get going. These snake's heads spread by self-sowing.

Certain alliums are splendid for giving body to a border in late spring and early summer, when other perennials are of comparatively flimsy texture. It is a good idea to scatter them among different species, so that they create a running theme. *Allium hollandicum* (syn. *A. aflatunense*) (1m) is mauve, while 'Purple Sensation' richer purple; both mix well, flowering in May. 'Globemaster' does so slightly later, and is mauve with larger globes.

Of the easy kinds, *A. cristophii* (0.7m) has the largest spheres. They start flowering in late May, being lilac mauve then, but keep their shape, while gradually bleaching, through the summer. It sows itself liberally, if you give it the chance, and I value it for pepping up my Japanese anemones when they are only half grown. *A. giganteum* (1.8m) looks splendid rising from behind other perennials, having globes of intense mauve flowers. It may need topping up from time to time.

Eremurus (2m or 3m), the foxtail lilies, make a startling impression in May and June. They like a sunny position and good drainage, but it is best to site them in the middle of a border, where their dying foliage will remain unseen. One of the most vigorous is the well-named *Eremurus robustus*, which is a pale, flesh pink. *E. bungei* is late flowering, rich yellow, and much more petite than most. There are some excellent hybrid strains, such as Ruiter Hybrids, in compatible shades of pale pink, yellow, white and bronze.

Eremurus have fleshy roots arranged like the limbs of a starfish and are notably brittle. The sooner they are planted, the better (ie, now), as root growth starts early.

September

Gardening in Your Own Way

Political correctness is as rife in gardening as it is in other walks of our lives. Follow the fashion and you'll be listened to. Most such fashions, as it happens, are playing safe. Individuality has always been frowned on as crankiness. Let us examine the qualities that go to making the play-safe, PC gardener.

He – or, as often, she – loves to hark back. A haze of nostalgia, a whiff of stale potpourri is spot on. Hence the vogue for herb gardens (which ties in nicely with any natural propensity to slovenliness, most herbs being weeds at heart). Modern medicine is clinical, heartless, un-understanding. Just go back to those old remedies that great-granny knew and practised. Ah, they knew a thing or two in those days (but overlook that many died in infancy, or giving birth, or of some now rare but then common disease).

I grow herbs for the kitchen. I don't grow them all together in one patch, as that is inconvenient, some being annual, some perennial, some large (like our vast bay tree), some quite tiny. Herbs should be grown either because they are beautiful plants and also happen to be herbs, such as henbane, or because they are in regular use, such as lavender to scent our drawers or flat-leaved parsley to flavour every sort of savoury dish.

Further nostalgia, together with a reluctance to make the best of the present or to plan excitingly for the future, is evidenced in historicism; in the re-creation of old gardens using their original plans and, if traceable in records, the same plants as were used when they were made. If not traceable, then plants that were in use then. This is a safe game in which nobody can lose. Praise for sensitivity and diligence with loads of mutual backslapping is the order of the day. The National Trust excels in this and English Heritage is catching up, as it acquires more historic gardens.

Well, there is something to be said for preserving or re-creating examples from our past, but the danger lurks of a terminal paralysis setting in. Copying becomes a substitute for original thought and

255

creativity. The original owners of the gardens we seek to preserve were passionately keen to try out every new plant introduction, yet we insist on an act of fossilisation.

Going native with wild flower gardens or gardens consisting entirely of indigenous plants is another fad that comes and goes. It tends to be linked with a kind of pseudo-patriotic jingoism. You don't find this so much in Britain as in Australia or California, for instance.

Through accidents of our geological history, Britain's genuinely native flora is exceedingly poor, while our climate is ideal for growing a wider range of plants than is practical in almost any other country in the world. So we're not too crazy about sticking to our own flora, though wildlife gardens are enjoying a great boom. They are another good excuse for indulging a natural bias to untidiness. As long as you appreciate this and don't try to append highfalutin moral motives, the exercise is harmless, though 'ecological correctness' can become a wearisome way of trying to make plants obey your rules.

No subject is more beset with rules and taboos in gardening than the use of colour. This has social connotations and is closely linked with class. No one cares to be thought conscious of lower or upper classes these days, but everyone acts as though they existed. Thus, the lower classes, the owners of ex-council houses with front gardens, are portrayed as loving bright colours, red with yellow tulips, followed by a gaudy display of orange marigolds.

Therefore, the upper classes are distressed by all this. No orange for them; it is the one colour they cannot abide. Nor any of those dreadful marigolds, either. Violent (the adjective would be theirs) colour contrasts are in bad taste. Colour harmony is the thing, especially in pastel shades, soft and soothing. Silver and grey is best of all. It is all stiflingly self-conscious.

Readers will surely have met something called the Colour Wheel. I'd never heard of it until after my official education was at an end, but Gertrude Jekyll believed in its efficacy, which automatically confers the seal of upper-class approval. But just how are we supposed to use the Colour Wheel? I can well see that diametrically opposed colours are as different as colours can be and that adjacent colours have much in common, but what then? Are there colours that we must not use together? I think not. Well handled (ie handled by me), any two colours can be pleasingly juxtaposed. (I'm still talking about plants, though I believe that much the same is true of fabrics.) Or any three colours, come to that.

Your novice to upper-class, or upper middle-class, or yuppy-class, gardener will be terrified of doing the wrong thing, of growing the wrong plants, of combining them stridently and, worst of all, of being commented on adversely by 'friends' and acquaintances whom they regard as important.

Hence the asphyxiating boredom born of the good-taste gardener, who hasn't a fresh idea in his/her head (well, we all have to start from scratch at some point) or any desire to develop one (we are even more painfully aware of this among flower-arranging groups). They'll all be growing old roses, all have a white garden and the Lutyens-designed Sissinghurst seat. All will yearn for a potager (rather than a vegetable plot). White-painted trellises and arbours will be in vogue. The entire paraphernalia of upper-class fad fashion, in fact.

With more self-confidence and self-reliance there would come, perhaps will come, a wonderful sense of release. What all those other people are thinking and saying really doesn't matter, so long as you are making yourself, and perhaps one or two close friends, happy, as long as you are enjoying yourself and your plants in your very own garden. (Even if you are a paid worker in someone else's garden, you really have to identify with it as your own.)

And the more different colours and kinds of plants with their varying arrangement you can enjoy, the happier you will be in pushing out your frontiers of experience. Never stay still or you'll slip backwards. Never stop experimenting.

It is important not automatically to accept received ideas. Most advice would recommend against the use together of orange and pink flowers. And yet if you look at certain tulips, such as the parrot, 'Orange Favourite', there is a pink flush overlying the orange on the outside of the three outer petals, and it is quite magical.

I have a group, in my big mixed border, of a tall orange poker, *Kniphofia uvaria* 'Nobilis', behind a large quilt of pink (though not a pale pink) phlox. The wind blew the pokers so that some of them leaned directly over the phlox, giving it a nudge. And, you'll have to take my word for it, it didn't look bad.

All colours can be mixed if you don't get too busy and overexcited. Areas of rest will also be necessary. That is why I think scarlet oriental poppies look so good, during their early season, in a border that is otherwise nearly all foliage, the foliage of plants whose flowering is later than the poppy.

The big innovation in my garden over the past 18 months has been in the conversion of the rose garden into a garden that gives you the feel of high summer (extending well into autumn) with more than a touch of the subtropical thrown in.

Roses arouse strong feelings. Many people identify in themselves an affinity for roses. Criticise the rose and you are criticising them. Like many other flowers, roses have their charm, but have been artificially elevated in status. It is time their faults (many of them of man's own making) should be recognised as well as their virtues.

Our rose garden was designed by Lutyens and has remained more or less static for 80 years. Replant disease means roses can't be replaced on a piecemeal basis – which is my preferred method when a rose that has become weakly or one I no longer like is growing next to another that's strong and I do like – without also replacing a large volume of soil where it grew. This is extremely inconvenient and, anyway, the soil that has become tainted for roses is excellent for any other plant.

With the help of my energetic friend and co-gardener, Fergus Garrett, a complete change has been made. The new garden already looks fully established and it enthrals us and many visitors, too.

There are cannas, with their splendid leaves and flaunting, silken flowers; dahlias – why are dahlias unfashionable with the elite? (I could tell you) – for brilliant, clean colours; wonderful foliage plants, including a hardy banana; leaves of a stooled specimen of paulownia, 90cm across; the Egyptian papyrus; castor oil plants, purple and green – I could run on.

With a great many plants we are experimenting, as no books can give us the answers. For instance, I planted out my streptocarpus, Cape violets – usually regarded in this country entirely as indoor pot plants. How would they, in a shady place, like to be treated as bedding plants instead? They've loved it.

And so it has gone on, the tender mixed with the hardy, but always with a sense of exoticism and lush flamboyance. It has been and continues to be exciting – and it isn't fashionable.

Continuous Planting

'What's new?' asked my great-nephew Christopher Lloyd when he came to lunch recently.

Giving his question the broad interpretation (ie, new to my garden at Dixter), the first plant that came to mind was *Colocasia esculenta* (1m or more). This is a tropical aroid, allied to caladium, grown for its great heart leaves. Their stalks rise from the ground and, when the wind blows, the leaf blade swings. It is about 0.8m long, smooth and has a swirling, feathery venation. Drawn to a fine point at its downward-pointing tip, it not only collects dew but creates its own water supply from early evening on, so that a considerable puddle collects beneath each leaf in the course of the night. I cannot think why you almost never see it bedded out. In the winter, its fleshy rootstock must be stored in a frost-free place, to be started up again under warm, close conditions the next spring.

Also new at Dixter is a tender grass that I've seen often in America in tubs and bedded out, but never here. This is *Setaria palmifolia*. It has broad, hard-textured leaves, with fine points and sharp margins. The surface is handsomely ridged with parallel veins. It makes a low (0.4m) but wide plant, becoming a fine specimen in a very short time.

In the trial of perennial lobelia at Wisley, I admired the seed-raised Fan Deep Red (0.5m) strain, which makes a fat, bush plant and flowers for a long time from August on. Although the flower spikes are a sumptuous deep red, they are effective from a distance.

We raised this from DT Brown's seed and bedded it out with *Salvia farinacea* 'Victoria', which is another fairly late starter and of the same habit, but with deep lavender flower spikes. The lobelia can be treated as an annual or as a tender perennial, it being risky to leave the plants out to overwinter.

With late-flowering bedders like these, which come in fresh in August and will continue through until late October, you feel that the garden has been given a face lift and provides an exhilarating setting for the good weather that is so often there to be enjoyed in late summer and early autumn.

We are often advised that September is the month to clear away the bedding plants that have flowered all summer and to tidy the garden in preparation for the winter. As the annual bedding plants finally fade, it's time to clear them away and replant with bulbs and spring-flowering bedding.

Steady on, I would plead. This is indeed a commonly held view, but it is, I feel, unnecessarily pessimistic.

A well-husbanded garden with a back-up area for raising a succession of plants will treat autumn as a continuation of summer. The difference is that the annuals and bedders to be enjoyed then will not feature in garden centres, because they are not performing at the time when these outlets are geared to catching the public's attention. All the more reason for raising our own plants.

Another genus in this category is rudbeckia, of which the seed strains that can be grown as annuals have come into prominence in recent years. New to us this year is 'Indian Summer', and it is a corker. We sowed under cold glass on 15 April, and in early July the bedded-out seedlings still looked unpromising. But then they got the skids on and made a terrific show from mid-August on. Each bloom is quite 15cm across, rich yellow and with a large, black central knob. There are 13 rays to each daisy, and their margins are incurved, at first, but later rolled back. The flowers are beautifully poised on long stalks, the entire plant being a metre tall.

The display is backed up by late-flowering perennials.

Incidentally, I have found that rudbeckias in which the rays are clear yellow – so that they contrast with a black or a green cone – are far more telling than those with shades of brown mixed into the yellow, so that the disc or cone ceases to be a focal point.

Browallia are generally considered as conservatory or hanging-basket plants but we have grown B. *viscosa* (0.5m) as a bedder for the past two years with considerable success, and that comes into its own from August onwards. With a nice branching, yet bushy, habit, the flattened, irregular flowers (2.5cm long) are deep lavender, while the upper, notched, petals have a white spot at their base. I haven't combined it with anything special, but the scarlet *Alonsoa warscewiczii* should make a nice companion.

We keep trying different begonias – even those varieties that are normally treated as house or conservatory plants – out in the garden to see how they like being bedded out for a few months.

Our greatest success so far has been with *Begonia scharffii* (*B. haageana*), with dark, furry leaves, purply on the undersides. It has surpassed itself as a flowering plant, with large, loose panicles of shell-pink blossom. However, the old favourite, *B. metallica*, with its dark, green-veined leaves overlaid with a metallic gloss, seems highly promising for both foliage and soft pink flowers.

Eupatorium

There is currently an interesting trial of Eupatorium (Hemp Agrimony) at the RHS Garden, Wisley. I didn't think I could get worked up about them until I saw this. The way we look at plants depends largely on how we grow and present them, and we are now increasingly realising that perennials often have much more to offer if we rejuvenate stock frequently, perhaps every year. So it is with this trial. The plants are all young, vigorous and well spaced and you have to think, 'Why have I been missing out on this?'

Here we see sturdy, base-branching perennials rising to a flat-topped platform of tiny composite flowers, with purple the predominant colour. Height may average 2m. Insects, particularly butterflies, adore them, but the dusky purple 'Flore Pleno', which is double, is less popular and clearly has less nectar on offer.

Eupatorium seed heads look good in winter, even after the seeds have blown away. Some may self-sow with inconvenient freedom. *Eupatorium cannabinum* 'Album' (1.2m) is pearly, not white, so it fits comfortably into any scene. *E. purpureum* subsp. *maculatum* 'Album' (2m) is upstanding with an open texture. It has the not unusual combination of a darkish leaf with white flowers. Best of the lot was *E.p.* subsp. *maculatum* 'Riesenschirm' (1.5m), with dark, well-presented stems and bright purple flowers: an impact plant.

E. rugosum 'Chocolate' is a foliage plant. It is dark purple but the leaves catch the light, which has a leavening effect. *E. capillifolium* (1.2m) is a very different foliage plant. Its numerous stems spring vertically from ground level and the foliage is a fine, bright green. A colony of it is worth the space. In New England, where summers are warmer, it flowers, which is a mistake: it should be enjoyed for its foliage only.

Although not in the trial because it is woody, E. *ligustrinum* has many attributes of the herbaceous eupatorium, such as popularity with insects. It flowers at various seasons and needs tidying over when its trusses have browned. Cold weather may hit it back, but after a series of mild winters, mine is a 3m bush. One way and another, eupatoriums have much to offer, especially to the late summer garden and a mixed border.

Serial Planting for Autumn

The sad fact is that many gardens look a shambles in the late autumn – a second flowering on some roses (leaves already stripped by rust and black spot), and that's about the sum of it. Which is our fault, not the season's. But this week I am writing about how to make your garden look worthy of a visit from friends.

There is no need to cut down everything in sight, apart from shrubs, of course. But all dowdy remnants that can no longer give pleasure should go. The tarnished silver of *Eryngium giganteum* (Miss Willmott's Ghost), for instance; the over-prolific, self-sowing purple orach, *Atriplex hortensis*, now changed from red to brown; likewise *Alchemilla mollis*, which probably looks a wreck – yet if the whole plant had been shorn back in early August, it would now be covered with a new crop of young leaves. I make these latter form a background to colchicums, which are now in bloom. If there is too much self-sown honesty or fennel or teasels, most of that goes, too, leaving just a few as winter skeletons.

Follow-on bedding is a great idea for enlivening the autumn scene. This year we had dwarf lupins, a seed strain called 'Gallery Mixed', bedded out late last autumn, at the same time interplanting them with tulips, as young lupin foliage makes a handsome background to those. We removed the whole lot in early July (the bulbs stored, the lupins discarded), and replaced them with African marigolds and a mauve bedding verbena (propagated from cuttings), 'La France'. The marigolds, in orange and yellow, are fully double and in two strains: 'Jubilee Mixed' and 'Treasure Trove'. They make big plants and can be bedded at 0.8m intervals, each plant given one stake and a tie when large (you may be more sheltered than we are).

Now, these were not sown till 18 May, and they came into flower in late August, just when needed. By timing your sowings, you can manipulate the peaking of your displays.

In the same way, we sowed Thompson & Morgan's dahlia collerette 'Dandy Mixed', also on 18 May, and those seedlings followed another earlier lot of summer bedding. We also (largely because we don't get around to the job earlier) take late cuttings from dahlias that we overwinter in store. They produce plants that may not be bedded out till late August, but we are seldom afflicted by frost before November, so the young plants have a good innings and they look fresh when other dahlias may be tiring.

Begonias are great value, and we are especially pleased with a tuberous-rooted strain called Dragon Wing we received as plugs on 10 May. It has single, intense red flowers and handsome, glossy foliage. We shall save the tubers from that.

Some seed-raised annuals have a prolonged season anyway. *Ageratum* 'Blue Horizon' is one of our greatest standbys, growing to 0.5m and mixing well with yellow annual rudbeckias, or with begonias. *Salvia coccinea* 'Lady in Red' (0.5m) is a great seed strain, and will carry two flushes of blossom in most years. It looks good with the bluey-purple *Salvia farinacea* 'Victoria'. There is a very long-flowering annual that I always grow, called *Cuphea* 'Firefly' (0.3m), with dusky, pinky-red flowers on a nice bushy plant. We save seed from that from year to year.

Grown in pots, you'll still be enjoying heliotrope: a scented kind such as 'Chatsworth' or 'Princess Marina'. Or there's the untiring blue *Convolvulus sabatius* (save your old plants, splitting them a little next spring), which has a cascading habit, as do nasturtiums. We make fresh sowings of them, one seed or two to a pot up to late July. Zonal pelargoniums ('geraniums') are a wonderful standby, and I turn to them for spots of scarlet and vermilion where highlights are needed. You must keep them fresh by regular dead-heading and by rubbing out the dead centres of flower heads that still have life left in them. Remember that single-flowered kinds stand up to wet weather better than doubles.

I must have lilies in pots, to bring forward in their season, and

September gives us the *Lilium speciosum* hybrids and the white trumpet *L. formosanum*, which is quick from seed.

Some perennials are very long-flowering, so you don't have to feel they are keeping you waiting for too many months before they perform – as do some Michaelmas daisies. But *Aster* x *frikartii* 'Mönch' (0.5m), with large, lavender daisies, is exceptionally generous, blooming from late July to October.

Japanese anemones have a similarly prolonged season. I have one long-lasting combination with pink *Anemone* 'Hadspen Abundance', yellow, deeply cupped *Hypericum* 'Rowallane' and an umbrella above them of *Rosa glauca*, with bluish leaves and hips in dangling bunches, which colour now to deep red. I prune this regularly by removing all the flowered wood in winter, leaving only the long, straight new canes, which will flower and fruit for me next year. The shrub is constantly rejuvenated in this way, and never becomes outsize.

Some shrubs give us a second flowering, notably hebes such as 'Midsummer Beauty'. The cherry laurel, *Prunus laurocerasus* 'Otto Luyken' is doing it this year, and I have hopes of the Mexican orange, *Choisya ternata*.

Late-flowering Shrubs

Flowers to surround ourselves with in late summer and autumn deserve a special vote of thanks. None more so than the shrubs, because there are not many of them.

Itea ilicifolia was a favourite with me last month, and it flowered particularly well, quite undeterred by last winter's cold, though it benefits from a sheltered position. It is evergreen and the holly-like leaves to which its name refers are thin-textured, with marginal prickles that don't prick. The flowers are green, borne densely in drooping racemes, and they smell most deliciously of honey at night and early in the morning, when they are visited by small moths.

Another green-flowered winner – a bright, yellow-green that shows up well at a distance – is *Bupleurum fruticosum*, which is one of the few shrubby members of the parsley family (Umbelliferae). It too is evergreen, and it makes a domed specimen. The only pruning required, when you want to tidy up, is the removal of flowered shoots. It is covered with umbels of blossom, which are attractive to wasps and flies, for many weeks.

It is not an easy shrub to root from cuttings, although it appears to produce plenty of suitable material. Seed is the answer but, as with many umbellifers, it must be sown fresh. It took me years to find that out.

Most escallonias are serviceable without having great distinction, but *Escallonia bifida* has plenty and makes a tremendous impression in the September garden. Its flower panicles are pure white, making a perfect background for the colourful butterflies which besiege it. This is a large shrub requiring warmth and shelter. I use it as a background for red dahlias.

Broad-leaved evergreens tend to lack hardiness, and myrtle, *Myrtus communis*, is another such. It well deserves the best place you can give it against a warm south wall. Mine is next to a garden door, which is open for much of the time and the myrtle's spicy scent is wafted through the house. Its white flowers consist largely of a cushion of stamens. In hot years, like 1995, they are followed in November by a crop of handsome purplish-black fruits. A cock blackbird, resplendent in its new plumage, usually takes up residence in mine at that season.

Instead of being in flower by mid-August, *Clerodendrum bungei* has held back till now in this year's late season, but it brought its old wood intact through last winter, which is the important thing, otherwise it may fail to flower altogether. So a sheltered position is needed for this suckering sub-shrub, though sunshine is not particularly important. It can make a handsome colony among trees. Its dark green leaves are large and heart-shaped, the flowers being borne terminally, in a domed corymb. They are deep carmine in bud, opening to a rich shade of pink, very sweetly scented on the air and again popular with butterflies.

Abelia x *grandiflora* is such an obliging and undemanding shrub that you might rather take it for granted, which would be a mistake, as it well repays good feeding, regular pruning in spring by the removal of tired old branches and a place in the sun. It carries a long succession of small, blush-white, trumpet flowers, borne in sprays. When the trumpets have dropped, there remains a persistent, pinkish calix, giving a flush to the whole shrub.

There are other abelias, such as 'Francis Mason', which is golden-variegated, and A. *chinensis*, which makes a large shrub, scented on the air.

A. *floribunda* flowers earlier than the others, with drooping funnels in bright magenta, but that requires a warm wall. I have seen it flourishing in Easter Ross, however. The one for my money is A. *schumannii*, which carries a largely undeserved reputation for lack of hardiness. Mine is flourishing in a sunny border – sheltered, it is true, but some distance from any wall. The flowers are a definite shade of pink, with a touch of mauve added in.

Hydrangeas are staunch allies from early July on. Given an open autumn, you'll see them winning prizes in the floral competitions at the Royal Horticultural Society show in London, late in October or early November. The white hortensia, 'Mme Emile Mouillère', is one of the best for continuity over a long period. 'Ayesha', with shiny, incurved sepals, pink or blue, according to your soil's acidity, has a long season too, but is not one of the hardiest and needs protection.

But the star performer, with one flush of blossom in late August or early September, is *Hydrangea aspera* Villosa Group. Getting the right plant is all-important, as it is often confused with the inferior H. *aspera* 'Macrophylla'. It is a lacecap, the outer ring of sterile florets being a strong shade of lilac mauve, while the small, inner florets (visited by bees, which collect blue pollen from them) are pure blue. This makes a large shrub, that should only be pruned by the occasional removal of tired old branches. The leaves are furry.

The big snag here is not winter hardiness, but spring frosts on expanding young shoots, which are apt to flush before it is safe to do so. At its best, this hydrangea is a wonderful, airy confection of fluttering blossom.

Pots for Porches

There is a community of pots on either side of my porch entrance, and they are making a lively display. They face north-east, so lose the sun mid-morning, but they're sheltered from our prevailing south-westerlies. Here are some of the ingredients.

First, the foliage plants, which provide texture and a setting for the flowers. *Davallia mariesii* is a low, creeping fern, which laps over the edge of its container.

It makes a pattern of well-dissected foliage and colours in October before shedding. Similar is *D. m.* 'Stenolepis', though the leaves are a darker shade and it is evergreen. These are almost hardy and spend the winter under a greenhouse bench.

Aeonium arboreum is a shrubby succulent, which makes large formal rosettes of fleshy leaves. They are green, but I also have the purple 'Atropurpureum'. *Agave americana* 'Variegata' looks like a fleshy-leaved yucca and is splendid in green and cream. *Pseudopanax lessonii* is a shrub with palmate leaves variegated in green and gold. It is undemanding, but needs frost-free conditions in winter; no more. *Euryops pectinatus*, another shrub, was covered in bright yellow daisies in the spring, but deserves to retain a position for its silvery, pinnate foliage. In complete contrast is the hardy New Zealand sedge, *Carex buchananii*, with a hair-like tuft of arching brown foliage.

Of flowers, there are two climbers, growing up brushwood. *Codonopsis forrestii* has open, campanula-blue bells or saucers, with darker marking near the centre. It belongs to the Campanulaceae family. It dies down in winter, but perennates with tubers, which you repot in spring. *Sollya heterophylla* is a charmer, hung with quite tiny, light blue bells all over. Don't trust it for hardiness.

Bidens ferulifolia appeared on the scene only a few years ago but is now ubiquitous, especially in hanging baskets. It has a sprawling habit and flowers continuously for months on end, with coreopsis-like yellow daisies. It is a good yellow and the flowers are a pretty shape. The rather newly arrived *Petunia* 'Purple Wave' has a similar habit and will infiltrate neighbours over a wide area. It is the brightest purple imaginable and remarkably weather-resistant. You can grow it from seed or strike it from cuttings, which you should take now.

I also have two small-flowered begonias: *Begonia sutherlandii* is deservedly popular, with elegant, brown-speckled foliage and soft orange flowers. It is pretty hardy, and as the tubers are easily stored in winter there is no need to test it. Although good for flowering in shade, it should be got going in the sun to begin with. Then, when flowering has started, you can move it into shade. 'Flamboyant', an old variety, has brilliant red, single flowers in great abundance on a fairly compact plant. There are many other begonias, normally given greenhouse treatment, that will enjoy a spell outside. *B. fuchsioides*, with tall sprays of fuchsia-like pink flowers, is one that I want to try after seeing it so used at Iford Manor, near Bath.

Solanum aviculare can be grown quickly from seed. It is a soft shrub, with large, deeply jagged leaves and purple disc flowers. These are followed by egg-shaped (and poisonous) fruits which ripen orange and look like costume jewellery. Sometimes I also use *S. rantonnetii*, which has similar flowers – though they are slightly smaller, there are more of them. This is a woodier shrub, which tends to be rather too leafy in its youth, but it makes a fine show if brought on in a greenhouse (it is easily trained as a standard, like a fuchsia) and set out when flowering has started.

The common myrtle, *Myrtus communis*, with pouffes of white, scented blossom, is excellent and flowers freely in a pot from an early age. The shrubby *Mimulus aurantiacus* (M. *glutinosus*), has a pleasantly spraying habit but is brittle. Its flowers are a soft orange, while in M. *puniceus* they are rich copper.

Convolvulus sabatius (C. *mauritanicus*) has a mildly sprawling, rather than a climbing, habit. Feed it well, and it will flower over a long season with near-blue funnels that change to mauve later in the day. It is almost hardy.

There are many annuals that are suitable for pot presentation, and they can make impressively large plants when given individual treatment. Looking ahead to next year, sow now some cornflowers, love-in-a-mist, viscaria (as this Lychnis is listed by the seed houses – it looks rather like flax, in shades of pink and blue), *Lavatera trimestris* (the annual mallow), and the white, grey-leaved *Omphalodes linifolia*, which looks like a gypsophila that has acquired a pedigree.

Since July, I have been enjoying a mixture of Salpiglossis, which resemble tall petunias with intricate flower markings. You will get fine plants from an April sowing. We also potted some red *Cosmos bipinnatus*, which are flowering generously. Fresh for autumn are pots of annual aster *Callistephus chinensis*. In a two-litre pot, they will make fine base-branching plants, but choose a strain that makes a good plant and has a range of colours. I find 'Princess' or 'Super-Princess' ideal. The flowers are double, with centres of tubular florets – what's known as anemone-flowered.

Autumn Planting of Shrubs

I like to get as much planting done in autumn as I can, preferably while the ground is still warm and encouraging to new root production and before dormancy sets in. There may be a temptation to delay until spring, but the danger of drought and the pressure of 'things to do' often pushes planting down the list of priorities.

Here is a fairly random selection of hardy shrubs that you may like to consider (the frost-tender ones had better wait until next year).

The best-known Osmanthus, O. *delavayi* and O. x *burkwoodii*, both carry their fragrant white blossom in spring. O. *heterophyllus* flowers in mid to late autumn and is equally scented on the air. It is a handsome, evergreen bush with small, holly-like leaves – the sort of evergreen that is a good defence against noise and neighbours, although not generally much more than 2m high.

Another wonderfully fragrant autumn-flowering evergreen is the greeny-grey *Elaeagnus* x *ebbingei* (3m), well known to flower arrangers for its foliage as it makes a sober foundation upon which to build an arrangement of colourful varieties. It, too, provides a sound defence against wind and noise, but you would be advised to keep it in the background as there is an element of dullness about it.

For January blossom to cheer you up, I suggest a bush cherry, *Prunus incisa* 'Praecox' (3m), whose blush-pink buds open to white blossom. You can prune it to the desired size by cutting branches of it for the house, just as the buds are colouring. This will obviate the habitual wailing when a frost blights the blossom just as it is reaching its peak.

The weeping, willow-leaved pear, *Pyrus salicifolia* 'Pendula', is very popular. It is over-planted, in fact, and I find it a big yawn. It never wants to grow upwards to make a decent, small specimen tree, and the shoot has to be supported by means of a strong pole that is then, itself, tied to the tree's trunk. However, in its defence, it does have rather nice grey foliage. But I suggest trying the deciduous *Elaeagnus angustifolia* instead. This has narrow grey leaves, but instead of weeping it makes a small tree, smothered by May in tiny, deliciously scented blossom.

Meantime, if, like me, you have a soft spot for the pear tribe, even if they are not the fruiting kind, you might like *Pyrus nivalis*, a small tree whose white spring blossom is seen with silvery, young foliage.

If you can cope with an unfriendly shrub, then the double form of common gorse, *Ulex europaeus* 'Flore Pleno', is well worth a place in the garden. It has double the flower power of the single kind and an abundance of the expected coconut scent. If a gorse becomes unruly, you have only to cut it down. It will be totally rejuvenated by young shoots.

I am fond of *Ribes speciosum* (1.5m), which is a flowering gooseberry, rather than a currant. It tries to be evergreen, but has a slightly disconcerting way of losing its foliage at summer's end. A new crop, glossy and bright, is soon produced. In spring, its tubular, rich crimson flowers hang in rows on the underside of each branch, and are reminiscent of fuchsias.

A strange member of the berberis family is the evergreen *Nandina domestica* (1m), whose large leaves are elegantly subdivided into slim lances, which are coppery when young. There are a number of dwarfened and 'colourful' cultivars that I find entirely repellent, but the type plant is charming and carries panicles of white blossom in August. Although hardy, it grows better in a climate with hot summers. Then it flowers earlier and sets handsome crops of red berries. Even without these, it is worth growing. Some describe it as being similar in appearance to bamboo, but actually it is nothing like it.

The trouble with philadelphus is that the green-leaved varieties look dull when not actually flowering, and one or two of them will be sufficient for most gardens. You want to be sure that the variety of your choice is heavily fragrant, because that is half the point of all mock oranges. For a small garden, I would recommend 'Sybille' – 1.5m, if regularly pruned. The smallish, fragrant white flowers are produced in abundance in June–July, on gracefully arching branches. I should prune it when the leaves are off, removing all the flowered growths. Feed it well, and you will be rewarded with many new, unbranched shoots. Don't tip these; leave them their full length.

Physocarpus opulifolius is a vigorous shrub, but is best grown for foliage, which is yellow in 'Dart's Gold', deep purple in 'Diabolo'. You prune it heavily each winter, which rewards you with wand-like shoots the following summer. There'll be no flowers, but they're insignificant.

'Diabolo' in a sunny position makes a fine background for red, orange or yellow flowers. Height can be kept down to 2m.

Alders tend to be overlooked in favour of birches, but there are some most interesting kinds. *Alnus glutinosa* 'Imperialis' and 'Laciniata' both have deeply cut leaves, giving them lightness and grace. They will make small trees (you can prune for the desired height) and are tolerant of boggy conditions.

Marigolds

There is often confusion about what we mean when we talk about marigolds. We may be thinking of the pot marigold, *Calendula officinalis*, from southern Europe. There has been a trial of these at Wisley this year and they made a brilliant display, their main colour based on orange. Their petals are edible and look good used with blue chicory flowers to decorate a salad. They self-sow freely, but the quality of the bloom deteriorates over the years. For a quality display, we rejuvenate our stock annually. We like 'Prince Orange' it has a bold, upright habit.

Calendulas are hardy and grow quickly from a March sowing outside, direct where they are to flower. They can also be sown in autumn.

More popular by far are Tagetes, the so-called African (*T. erecta*) and French (*T. patula*) marigolds, which hail from Mexico. So does the delightful little *T. tenuifolia*, which makes a long-flowering ball of tiny blossoms, orange or yellow. We are growing 'Tangerine Gem' this year.

African marigolds include the big chaps with double flowers rather like a sponge. They are yellow, light orange or intense orange (the best). When they make a big, branching plant, a metre or more high, they look very handsome, the flowers set off by lacy foliage. 'Jubilee Orange' is one of the best strains. 'Simba' (Swahili for lion), also called 'Ragged Reggie', makes a fine, showy plant a metre or more high, with orange, ragged-petalled flowers and a green centre. It shows up at a distance.

As often happens, breeders have concentrated on producing large flowers on a dwarf plant – an explosion of colour on a totally unbalanced plant. I should avoid, therefore, the Inca and Discovery series.

French marigolds, single or double, comprise the biggest selection:

bronze and orange, often mixed in the same flower. 'Cinnabar' was one of my favourites but was withdrawn: single-flowered bronze with a thin orange margin. So I have saved my own seed and allowed it to become a larger, less dwarf plant.

Single-flowered 'Striped Marvel' makes a fair-sized plant with alternating rays of bronze and gold. This is good but the breeders have tried to dwarfen it in 'Mr Majestic'.

I love the brilliant all-orange, single, dwarf 'Disco Orange', and mix it with the bright green, frilly parsley strain 'Bravour', backing them with the fairly dwarf 'Cosmos Sonata White'. Marigolds are a mainstay of our autumn borders, and we can endlessly experiment with them.

Ground Cover

Ground cover is quite an obsession with many home-owners. They may not be committed gardeners, but they know that something needs to be done – and the less work it involves, the better. The market, of course, is ready to supply these abundant and lucrative customers with the goods.

To a committed gardener, it can be a depressing scenario. But one can also take a positive view of ground cover, so that, besides doing a job, the plants give pleasure, too.

On each of the four corners of our formally designed Barn Garden, I have specimens of the evergreen shrub *Osmanthus delavayi* that are now nearly 50 years old. With time, space has developed beneath their lowest branches. Under one of them, I grow a lungwort, *Pulmonaria officinalis* 'Sissinghurst White', which flowers in early spring. My idea was that the white flowers would show up well in a darkish situation. I should probably do better with *P. rubra* 'David Ward', which gave such a good account of itself – but as a foliage plant – in the recent pulmonaria trial at Wisley. The leaves are very pale green, with a broad, white margin. They remain in good condition for months in summer and on into autumn, as long as the plant has plenty of moisture and is not beaten upon by the sun.

Under another, I have *Euonymus fortunei* 'Sunspot', whose evergreen, oval leaves have a narrow, yellow flash down their centre. It looks cheerful, even in dark conditions. This year it is carrying quite a crop of berries. When ripe, the case enclosing the seed bursts open to reveal an orange or scarlet interior.

Under a third, I have the variegated form of greater periwinkle, *Vinca major* 'Variegata', with fairly large leaves that are boldly cream-and-yellow-variegated. It spreads by runners, but the best treatment is to cut the whole colony flush with the ground in late winter. This has a rejuvenating effect, and is the right treatment for many vincas and for other kinds of ground cover, too.

The old-fashioned rose of Sharon, *Hypericum calycinum*, becomes quite presentable if shorn to the ground each March – use a strimmer. The flowers it produces on its young growth will be more numerous and show up better.

With *Epimedium pinnatum* subsp. *colchicum*, a favourite of mine, the old leaves make decent cover throughout winter, but then become tatty. Strim them in early February and enjoy their bright yellow flowers in March–April, which will be joined by coppery young foliage.

The lady's mantle, *Alchemilla mollis*, is a great goer and self-sows, soon forming a dense colony. It has delightful hairy, scalloped leaves, which hold raindrops like quicksilver, followed by sprays of light green flowers. But its bad moment comes at the turn of July and August, when it becomes tired, brown and bedraggled. A strim-over then will be followed by a pristine crop of new leaves for September and October, after which it becomes dormant; weeds scarcely have a chance.

The best ground-cover cranesbill is *Geranium macrorrhizum*, which is more or less evergreen, though the leaves do colour highly when their time comes to die. This flowers in late spring and early summer and there are a number of colour forms. If you are planting a considerable area with it, I can recommend making large, informal, adjacent patches of the different kinds. But even this obliging plant will benefit from being lifted, split and returned to improved soil from time to time.

Though many ground-covering plants are excellent weed-excluders, they cannot compete with perennial weeds established before they were planted. Get rid of these first, even if it takes a whole year to do so. Spray Roundup on their foliage when they are growing strongly. A month or two later, where some regrowth has occurred, spray again and perhaps even a third time.

Another point: many plants will tolerate and grow reasonably well in shade, but will flower (if that is what you want them to do) far more freely in sun. Some foliage plants react in the same manner. The ivy, *Hedera helix* 'Buttercup', which has yellow foliage when grown in a light position, will turn pasty or even green in deep shade. Others that are variegated may retain their variegation very well in shade, lighting up dark places with it.

A plant such as *Rubus tricolor*, with glossy, evergreen leaves, will thrive as ground cover in sun or in shade, but will become an unsightly, tangled mess if never cut back. The same applies to that aggressive dead-nettle, *Lamium galeobdolon* 'Variegatum', which has marbled leaves in two shades of green and which will choke everything in its path. But there are places even for a plant such as this, so cut back all its toe-tangling growth in early spring and then, before the next crop of leaves develops, enjoy its spikes of hooded yellow flowers.

Teasels

We got rid of all our teasels last month, as soon as they'd finished flowering. They immediately turn brown and look depressingly wintry. As always, there are masses of seedlings from which to choose a few for next year. Theirs is a truly architectural shape and a fine presence so long as they remain green and fresh. This is our native *Dipsacus fullonum*, which you find in woodland clearings sometimes, also on marshy banks. The flowers, in July, are mauve and popular with insects.

One of the few hardy members of the pineapple family, Bromeliaceae, is *Fascicularia bicolor*. It is a fun plant, making rosettes of stiff, spiny-edged leaves in a hummock. When one or more of these rosettes is minded to flower, in autumn, the whole of the centre turns red and it opens out to reveal a disc of tiny baby-blue flowers, which wink with the drops of nectar that they produce. This lasts for only a few days, but will have been worth it. The plant doesn't require much moisture and we have one on a sloping tiled roof, where it is very happy. Whenever it rains, it receives drips from the roof above. It is best to remove rosettes that have flowered, to make space for others that haven't.

Eryngium giganteum is popularly known as Miss Willmott's Ghost, perhaps because she was pale and prickly. It is said that the Garden Society of England was made all-male so as to exclude her. The plant is monocarpic, dying after its June–July flowering but leaving a great many seedlings, which need to be rigorously thinned. Some will be virus-infected and never do any good. Chop them out as soon as identified. The leaves of infected plants are thin and ill-looking. They won't actually die unless you remove them.

Houttuynia cordata is a creeping hardy perennial with white flowers that is good for colonising difficult dry banks. The variegated form, 'Chameleon', has pink stripes mixed in with the greens and can look jolly. In a border, however, its spreading habit makes it a dangerous thug, as it gets into everything. Also it is apt to revert to plain green. I have been fighting a patch of it for years, planted when I was in ignorance of its habits.

The good news is that you can control and enjoy the plant if it is confined to a pot. It likes moisture and its colouring is best in sunshine, so you should plunge the pot into water at the edge of a pool.

Meantime, my original mistake of planting it into a mixed border continues to dog me. It is cheapest to learn from other people's mistakes.

Propagation

No self-respecting gardener should go anywhere without a sharp knife. Many cuttings can appropriately be taken now – especially of evergreen shrubs and of tender perennials that need overwintering under glass.

A useful point to remember with some of them, notably hydrangeas, fuchsias and bedding verbenas, is that they will root from internodal cuttings. These will give you twice the number of plants that could be obtained from the nodal equivalent. With the nodal cutting, there will (in the above examples) be a pair of leaves at the top, a stem shank beneath them and a node, with leaves removed, at the base. With the internodal cutting, you simply have the pair of leaves at the top and the shank. The pair of leaves below this will be the top of another cutting.

Correct choice of material for propagation makes a great difference and it is easy to go wrong. From a bush, for instance, and especially if it is growing in your own garden, you will be tempted to be discreet and to remove pieces from the side or bottom, where their absence won't be noticed. But these will be weak shoots. Generally it is the strongest, from the top of the bush, that will give best results. Strong plants are started from strong growth (though not, one has to add, exaggeratedly strong like the thick water shoot that might arise from a forsythia after it had been cut back).

Cuttings made from thin shoots on *Hydrangea aspera* Villosa Group or the oak-leaved *H. quercifolia*, for instance, will, if they root, give rise to plants that never seem to make any headway. Use strong shoots with large leaves. These can be reduced in size – both for convenience in their handling and to cut their loss of water through transpiration – by wrapping each lengthwise into four and then making a clean cross-cut halfway along their length. A vigorous young bush will be more successfully propagated from than an old bush whose growth has slowed down.

So, if your evergreen ceanothus is beginning to look somewhat long in the tooth and you are anxious to have a youngster from it to continue the line, it is unlikely to make a parent. You should have taken cuttings from it while it was young and lusty (and you didn't want any more of it, most likely). So there may well be a good case for buying your new plant when you need it, rather than wasting time and effort in attempting to propagate from an old lag.

Some shrubs can be rejuvenated, however, by a hard cut-back. These will respond by making strong, juvenile growth from old wood below where the cuts were made. This would not work, in most cases, with the aforementioned evergreen ceanothus, with cistuses, cytisus, lavender or many conifers. But it would work with camellias, many rhododendrons and azaleas and other shrubs known to respond rather well to hacking back. Nurserymen, who grow stock especially for propagation, will cut it back on a regular, annual basis, to give them suitably young and vigorous cuttings material.

Whenever possible, try to use non-flowering wood or shoots with which to make cuttings. If you can't avoid shoots with flowers, at least remove these. Or, if flower buds appear after the cuttings have been made and started – as with, for example, *Skimmia japonica, Osmanthus delavayi* or *Daphne odora* – remove them as they appear.

The propagation, as also the purchase, of variegated-leaved plants is often tricky. The more variegation there is in a leafy shoot, the weaker it will be, because there is less chlorophyll (the green part) there to give strength. In an extreme case, a shoot with no chlorophyll in it at all is being entirely supported by the rest of the plant that produced it, and will have to die before long for lack of what it takes.

On the other hand, if a variegated plant is what you want, you don't want too little of the white (or pale yellow or pink) that gives it its special attraction. The nurseryman who is looking for easily propagated plant material will find that those shoots with less variegation than some others will root and grow most easily. He'll be tempted to propagate from those. So, if we're talking about, for instance, the holly, *Ilex* x *altaclerensis* 'Golden King', a fair question is 'Which "Golden King"?', because you will get different results according to which shoots were chosen for propagation from the same bush. Some may have reverted to green all over, others yellow (no use at all) and there will be many intermediate states and degrees of variegation on our bush; some rooting easily, but poorly variegated, others heavily variegated, but poor doers.

I am besotted by the variegated form of the giant reed grass, *Arundo donax* – the strain that I grow has very wide, marginal white striping – but it grows to one-third the height of the unvariegated species and is far less hardy. It needs extra feeding and watering to give of its best and it is shy in producing suitable material for propagation. There are many clones of the same plant with far greener and less attractive leaves going around, but nurserymen have found them easier to propagate. *Caveat emptor.*

See your plant, in growth, before you make a purchase.

The border phlox, 'Norah Leigh', should have a quite tiny diamond of green in the centre of an otherwise white leaf. Very airy and pretty it is, but weak.

It needs the riches of a manure heap on which to grow if it is to be happy. In America, 'Norah Leigh' is much stronger-growing, but the variegation is greatly diminished.

Foliage as Foil

I was looking, with Rosemary Verey, at a dwarf bedding dahlia, 'Ellen Huston', and she remarked on the way that some flowers seem perfectly suited by their accompanying foliage, as this one; others, not. 'Ellen Huston' is red, semi-single with a bronze disc and its well-formed leaves are dark. All its parts seem well matched.

It seemed interesting to make further comparisons. Arum lilies (calla lilies as they are known in some countries, though the plant is neither a calla nor a lily), *Zantedeschia aethiopica*, have achieved a perfect foil to its white, painter's-palette blooms in the broad, spear-shaped, dark green leaves that enfold them. In a flower arrangement, you could hardly do better than to use 'own foliage', as they specify in the textbooks.

Daffodils, on the other hand, have stringy leaves with a strong tendency to flop. Although when you buy narcissi it is nice when they are sold with a few leaves of their own, it is better when arranging them to find added accompaniments. With yellow trumpet daffodils, Miss Jekyll liked to arrange wild arum – lords-and-ladies – leaves that you can pull from the hedgerows. They grow in clusters, which will break off intact if you grasp them at ground level and give a sharp tug. Another plant I find goes well with daffodils is *Danae racemosa*, a sub-shrubby evergreen, 60cm to 90cm tall, clothed in shiny lance leaves that are borne in sprays. It grows especially well in partial shade on chalky soils and 'February Gold' daffodils go well with it, when actually growing in the garden.

I like to pick long-stemmed snowdrops with smaller examples of the foliage, marbled in two shades of green, of *Arum italicum* 'Marmoratum'. Or with ivy leaves. Indeed, snowdrops look well when planted in a ground-covering mantle of a petite (not a bossy) strain of ivy. Snowdrop foliage is only occasionally significant in relation to the flower, as in hybrids of *Galanthus elwesii*, where the leaves can be broad and glaucous.

In the same family as ivy, *Fatsia japonica* is primarily a foliage shrub, with huge, fingered, evergreen and light-reflecting leaves. But when, in late autumn, it unexpectedly erupts with bullet-shaped buds which then explode into umbels of small white flowers, the addition, more endearing than spectacular, seems perfectly appropriate.

Yuccas, unless variegated, have rather severe foliage. In *Yucca gloriosa*, this is stiff, spine-tipped and very dark, being arranged in a large, globular rosette. What better plinth could be devised for the 1.5m-tall panicle of creamy bells which it will suddenly produce when conditions are right? Cannas are wonderfully served by the suitability of their leaves to the often gaudy bunch of satiny flowers that crown them. If they earn a bad name because of their mindless use as dot plants in public parks and garden bedding, that is no fault of theirs.

Cannas, well grown and used in mixed plantings, have retained their presence and dignity despite enlargement, which is so often the breeder's goal. Chrysanthemums and dahlias have not been so fortunate in those cases where a very large bloom has been the principal object. It has led to very large, coarse leaves as the accompaniment. The flower is then best cut and divorced from its foliage.

Many bulbs seem to think of leafing and flowering as two entirely separate operations. In autumn, such flowers as *Amaryllis belladonna*, *Nerine bowdenii*, the Scarborough lily, Vallota, several crocuses, such as *Crocus speciosus* and *C. nudiflorus*, colchicums and the chrome-yellow, crocus-like *Sternbergia lutea* – all of these start their growing season by flowering in bare soil, their foliage following later. In other cases, it is the other way round. The broad, chocolate and glaucous leaves of *Allium karataviense* are a feast in themselves in early spring, but have withered into a sordid mess by the time the flower globes are blooming. This is the case with many alliums. The tall *A. giganteum* is best sited behind a lowish shrub, so that its flowers can be enjoyed without the leaves spoiling the impression.

In the wild, this situation is generally catered for by the bulb in question being a part of the turf flora which engulfs it. In California, the glamorous Calochortus appear as gems in a lively sward. What their leaves are doing, you neither know nor care. The same flower, however, looks pathetic growing in a pot, its frail stalk accompanied by sere leaf remnants. Once you have seen this sort of flower in the wild, it should cure you of ever wanting to cultivate it at home in a cold frame or alpine house.

During our discussion, Rosemary talked about a plant that has only of recent years become popular, *Bidens ferulifolia*. Of a sprawling habit that suits it for use in tubs and ornamental pots or, indeed, as summer ground cover, it is thickly spangled all over with small, bright yellow, coreopsis-like flowers and the leaves, pinnate with narrow segments, are small and frothy. Its foliage suits it admirably. In a large old stone sink, I have this year combined it with the pink *Diascia* 'Ruby Field'. No diascia I have seen has leaves of any merit, but in this combination 'Ruby Field's' flowers are all that matter and it can borrow the bidens' foliage.

Both can do with a cut-back in mid-season, when their growth becomes overextended. Follow this by a feed (unless you have included a long-life fertiliser in the compost) and then a heavy watering.

Autumn Colour: Shrubs

While some shrubs, such as deutzias and philadelphus, look notably dreary after a season of flowering, others are as smart in autumn as at any time during the year. They may be evergreens, which have settled down and are lustrous with their summer's growth, but they are inclined to become rather battered by winter's end.

Choisya ternata, the Mexican orange, for instance, has bright, greeny, glossy leaves. In the south of the country, after a hot summer, it will often flower a second time, in October, with white-orange blossom that is markedly larger than May's main crop.

As this summer was relatively mild, however, we may miss out on that. Its yellow-leaved clone, Sundance, habitually looks a hospital case when grown in too much bright sun, but even that may be looking reasonably healthy at the moment.

Ivies do especially well in autumn, and most of them will be flowering until November. Their scent is sickly, but I like it, not least because it attracts wasps, hoverflies, bees and butterflies. Wild ivy, *Hedera helix*, is particularly handsome when it forms a dense column of greenery up an ash tree. Ash always has a thin crown of foliage, which lets through enough light to enable the ivy to thrive.

We have at last persuaded *Vitis coignetiae* to go a long way up an ivy-clad ash, and maybe it will go all the way before long. This is an exceptionally vigorous and large-leaved vine that colours spectacularly in autumn, and an ivy makes the ideal background for it. Though vigorous, the vitis needs good growing conditions to perform healthily. Ours sulked for years, because the ground at the foot of the tree was too rooty and dry. Now, after adding mulch and water, matters have improved.

One of the most luminous ivies is 'Buttercup', which is bright yellow during autumn, provided it receives enough light. Another fine ivy is the arborescent form of *H. canariensis* 'Gloire de Marengo', with green-and-white-variegated leaves.

Non-climbing, this eventually forms a rounded bush about 2m high. It flowers in November and is covered with globular umbels of flower buds for weeks beforehand – an unusual and arresting sight.

The hybrid between Hedera and Fatsia, x *Fatshedera lizei*, makes a rather lax shrub that benefits from quite heavy pruning each spring. This encourages it to produce large, bright green, glossy leaves, that are now looking their most glamorous.

Fatsia japonica, the largest-leaved hardy evergreen that grows in Britain, is now preparing for its annual autumn flowering. Huge, terminal shoot buds erupt into a branching inflorescence of globe-shaped, white-flowered umbels.

While bamboos tend to get battered during the winter, most of them are now at their smartest, and some varieties will have caught out their enthusiast owners by flowering. This virtually puts paid to the plant or colony, but you should certainly save any seed from it. A batch of bamboo seedlings is as rare as it is exciting, and they quickly develop into decently sized new specimens.

Hydrangea quercifolia is the king of its genus for foliage; large and with jagged indentations like an oak leaf, but with far greater substance. For quality of leaf, I prune a large part of mine every spring by cutting older branches back. Only a few are left to flower, since I consider the leaf of greater importance. Autumn colour is assumed gradually, often continuing into December. It is brownish-red and very handsome.

The true Virginia creeper, *Parthenocissus quinquefolia*, is my favourite of this tribe, because its palmate leaves have an interesting shape and its autumn colouring, assumed early, is warm red, not hectic magenta, like the Boston ivy, *P. tricuspidata*. This latter has one advantage, however: in certain circumstances, against a wall where there is little room for expansion, it keeps tight into the wall. *P. quinquefolia* is more relaxed, and tends to bulge outwards. Although self-clinging, trails of it explore spaces beyond its support.

Spindle-berries, *Euonymus europaeus*, make rough-and-ready bushes; they stand out in hedgerows when their leaves turn pink. The berries are pink, too, until they split open to reveal bright orange seeds. Whether or not you manage to plant a regularly fruiting form in your garden has an element of luck about it. Beth Chatto gave me a sucker from her plant, which she said was always spectacular, and so it is with me. My own attempts had been disappointing. Cross-pollination may be needed, and I have a wild one nearby. 'Red Cascade' is a well-known cultivar, but success with it is variable.

For autumn flowers, one of my greatest successes this year has been the Chilean myrtle, *Luma apiculata*, with its neat, evergreen leaves and terminal clusters of buds and white flowers that are followed by black berries. For most of us, this plant is not assuredly hardy, so give it a sheltered corner. Unless it is hit by a severe winter, it is a handsome shrub and flowers in both summer and autumn.

Autumn Scents

Damp, often muggy weather in autumn brings out the smells characteristic of the season. What exactly causes that sharp, nose-twitching aroma, savoured as you walk through a wood, I don't know. Fungi, very likely.

In the garden, it is easier to identify the aromatic plants. There is the gummy smell of cistuses, especially the sticky kinds such as *Cistus* x *cyprius*, the cedar-like smell of *Hebe cupressoides* and the heliotrope scent that waylays you as you pass *Olearia solandri* – not a spectacular shrub but pleasing year round, with its rufous stems and minute leaves. The flowers in August might pass unnoticed, except that they smell more strongly of heliotrope than the plant. The three are evergreen.

Sweet briar, *Rosa eglanteria*, will not be smelling much by now, unless you pruned some of it hard last winter or spring. That encourages the production of young shoots and foliage through to the late autumn, which in turn give off that stewed apple aroma.

The scent from late rose blooms is stronger during autumn than earlier in the year, particularly from the Hybrid Musks, 'Penelope' and 'Felicia'. Another rose generous in this way is the miniature-flowered 'Perle d'Or', sister to 'Cecile Brunner', but buff-coloured rather than pink.

Now is the time we most appreciate chrysanthemums and their unique 'chemist-shop' smell. Chrysanthemums, like Michaelmas daisies, move extremely well, just as they are coming into flower, from open ground where they have been growing through the summer to positions in main borders. We do this at Dixter into September, to keep the garden up to scratch. A heavy soaking before and after moving is important. You also quickly become aware of the need for careful handling because budded branches can easily snap. While moving the plants, you cannot help but become intensely aware of their smell.

Night scents continue to be the most prevalent, as in summer. Of honeysuckles, *Lonicera japonica* 'Halliana' is still productive, but a less coarse and equally generous species is *L. similis* var. *delavayi*. It flowers abundantly in early July; you then clip it and a generous autumn crop follows. It is an elegant plant, not hiding its white blossom among foliage. The white becomes buff yellow on the second day.

Verbenas smell strongest at night and on dewy mornings, particularly the bedding types, such as 'Loveliness', 'Lawrence Johnston' and 'La France'. The latter is quite vigorous and free with its dense heads of lavender blossom. Some of my plants have happily survived the last two winters outside. Cuttings taken now, in a cold frame, root quickly and should be kept in the same pots they were rooted in until next March, when they'll be treated individually. Verbenas, like fuchsias and the majority of hydrangeas, not to mention clematis, root well from internodal cuttings, which yield twice as many cuttings from the same material as nodals. All you need is a pair of leaves and a shank of stem of a length that would take it down to the next pair of leaves. Above these, you make your cut.

Hedychiums belong to the ginger family and many of them have a sweet, gingery night scent. Most notable just now is the yellow *Hedychium gardnerianum*, whose style and stamens are red. It makes a dense spike but, except in Cornwall, doesn't flower in time to beat the end of the growing season unless grown under glass.

So this is an excellent pot plant to bring into the house when flowering. Many of the other available species can be treated as hardy perennials. The white-flowered *H. forrestii* is a handsome 1.2m-foliage plant through the summer. *H. densiflorum* 'Stephen' is cream yellow, and that is strongly scented, but so late in the evening that it is more easily caught the next morning, if you are naturally an early riser.

Several well-known members of Solanaceae, the nightshade family, are night scented. The annual *Datura meteloides* is a handsome, structural plant, repeatedly branching in opposite directions, to make a symmetrical candelabrum. The white trumpets point upwards or outwards and are six inches across at the start of their season. It is fascinating, around sunset, to watch them open. The scent is not overtly strong but penetrating. The thorn apple, *D. stramonium*, is a weed of cultivation, vigorous in hot summers and has white, scented flowers. All these solanaceous plants are poisonous, including nicotianas. Best scented are *Nicotiana sylvestris*, which makes a stately 1.8m plant, white-flowered with a long tube and *N. alata*, listed by Suttons as *N. affinis*. This, again, is white, though much effort has been made to develop coloured (and dwarfened) seed strains. The white kind shows up best at night, which is when the flowers are fully expanded.

Finally, there is the shrubby *Cestrum parqui*, with panicles of pale green blossom from early July to late autumn. By day, any smell released is rather unpleasant, but at night it truly comes into its own with a heavy almond-like fragrance. Sprigs should be brought into the house to savour in comfort.

October

The Long View

To watch first-time visitors to my garden when they arrive is interesting. Some look around them to gain a general impression of the scene; others are immediately eyes-down, looking at details of the plants that interest them. Others still, filling in time between lunch and tea, are absorbed in continuing a conversation about their families, friends and their latest holiday abroad. They stride on pretty well regardless of their surroundings, or just head for the nearest seat. They are enjoying themselves in their own way.

Curiosity generally spurs me to take a good preliminary squint at my surroundings. Is the house visible and, if so, is it beautiful or hideous? If beautiful, do its surroundings set it off pleasantly? If hideous, how well have the owners managed to conceal the fact? Or perhaps they don't want to, and actually enjoy the very features that I find awful. That in itself can be fun. Especially if you're with a friend whom you can dig in the ribs and have a good laugh with.

Is the garden stuffed with features? Features, especially water features, are the in thing currently. My own garden's lack of piddling water spouts, of fountains or of rushing torrents seems to constitute a sad omission in the eyes of some, and they often comment on it. Personally, I hate to be fidgeted by features. The bones of a garden are quite another matter. Frills are easily overdone.

What part are trees playing in the garden you are in? Often they fail to be noticed, yet their role is vital. Also, they are not static but always changing, both with the seasons and with the years. They may develop in ways that the owners had not premeditated, and with so much of their own character that their individuality seems worth accommodating. Or they may simply become gaga and an eyesore, yet be hung on to out of familiarity or inertia, waiting for the next big storm to make a messy necessity of removal.

Often, you may, as a visitor, be close to, yet fail to notice, a fine specimen of a tree because it is way above your usual sight lines. The kind of tree that I greatly enjoy in an old, long-established garden is an ancient robinia – the false acacia. They become craggy, with deeply fissured trunks; the branches may be quite sparse and leaves scarcely yet apparent as late as early June. Then, giving themselves a shake, there they suddenly are, hung with tresses of white, dark-centred blossom, scenting the air around them. It is an extraordinary transformation and their leaves thereafter are of the airiest. Yet this may be decried as a tiresome tree, liable to sucker and with unpleasantly thorny branches that are prone to dropping off. For the care of anything alive, however, there are always penalties to pay. As visitors, we can applaud the owners' forbearance.

Small trees can develop as much personality as big. At Dixter we have consistently failed to please the walnut, *Juglans regia*. It is not really difficult; perhaps our soil is too clayey or insufficiently drained. The outstanding feature about a walnut, apart from its pleasing, rounded crown, is its pale bark, which stands out particularly in winter.

Fig trees, similarly, have very pale grey bark, which makes them a beautiful winter feature when trained into a wall. But a free-standing fig bush tree, with many stems, looks wonderful – witness the one standing at one end of the footbridge across the lake in St James's Park in London. That, after a big storm, was stooled to the ground, yet figs take to this treatment as though expecting it. They bounce back with amazing speed and vigour. Of course, a bushy tree of this sort does need a good deal of lateral space, a point that many gardeners fail to appreciate when first planting their gardens. They also fail to take the necessary steps when overcrowding obviously requires a few big decisions.

The other point about figs, of course, is the size and shape of their handsome leaves – some varieties, particularly the Brunswick fig, have notably more handsomely lobed foliage than others. A fig tree should immediately draw your attention when you catch sight of it in a garden. It is there to be noticed.

Tree ferns, notably *Dicksonia antarctica*, have become increasingly popular in south-of-England gardens since the onset of mild winters and the increased availability of imported material from Tasmania and south-east Australia (with what consequences to native populations, I wonder?). If they can retain their old fronds through the winter, they get off to a flying start the next year and nothing could look more handsome when viewed across a garden from the house's sitting-out terrace.

Another agreeably bold plant that has been advantaged by mild winters is *Astelia chathamica*, with soft, grey-green sword leaves having a bloom on them. They catch the light at varying angles and look strong without the stiffness or solemnity of, say, *Yucca gloriosa*.

We should ask ourselves, too, whether the garden's seats and benches contribute agreeably to its setting. Or do they look pinched and cramped, or clumsy, or stand out offensively because they are too brightly painted or heavily oiled? A seat at the far end of a pergola is a frequent solution for terminating a vista but, when sitting on it, what view have you? Often nothing better than the corner of the house and a couple of dustbins.

Canna and Dahlia

Keeping our cannas and dahlias from year to year must concern us now, because few are frost-hardy. If they are of several years' standing, they'll probably have good tubers, in which case you can wait to lift them until after the first frost. If they're young and you suspect they have no tuber, lift them, put them in a pot and keep them growing.

Otherwise, store them dormant in a cool, frost-free place – a cellar is ideal. A basement or a shed is OK, too, but must not be heated in winter. Tightly pack the tubers into a container – the tighter the better, as they won't be growing. A big pot, box or crate will be suitable. Don't split them now, while they are inactive.

Sawdust or wood chippings are fine for packing them into. Best of all, though, is old potting compost or peat; damp, but not wet. Too dry and the tubers will wither; too wet and they will rot. We give them a watering every so often. Have a look at not too distant intervals, to see what they need.

Some dahlias are very reluctant to make tubers. It is in their nature. The delectable pale mauve water lily dahlia, 'Porcelain', is one such. Commercial growers get over this by growing some in very small pots, which forces them to make tubers. When they sprout in spring, they take cuttings to increase stock.

Some people rather pride themselves on leaving their dahlias in the ground year after year and getting away with it. Good luck to them, but the quality goes off and they are at the mercy of those underground little slugs that feed all year round.

There is (or was) a bed of cannas at RHS Wisley that stayed untouched year after year. It was against the warm side of a greenhouse and terribly congested, but it survived. That's very gratifying when it works, though the results are second-rate.

It is not such a great effort to lift and store your stock. Just choose a dry day to do it. Get them out again next March, split the tubers if congested or you want to increase stock, repot in fresh compost and go on from there. Cold glass and sun heat may well be sufficient protection by then. We have an extra-deep frame for the cannas, which we store in crates. The cannas will already be growing when we bring them out of storage. They'll remain in the same deep frame until ready to plant out, hardening them off by eventually removing all protection.

Beyond the Rose Garden

An article in *Gardening Which?* tells us to shun the traditional rose garden. I agree – if you grow a lot of the same kind of plant together, it is an open invitation to all its pests and diseases to assemble there. As with children in a school, if one gets mumps, the rest all catch it. The *Which?* article tells us to mix our roses into a border with perennials 'for a more modern, naturalistic approach'. But there is nothing modern about it. It's just far more sensible and we have been doing it for many years.

The rose is many things. To those brought up on a diet of Hybrid Tea and Floribunda roses, many other kinds would not count as roses at all. I have a beautiful crop of long, red hips on my *Rosa setipoda*, which contrasts but gets on well with everything around it. Or take the sweet briar, *R. rubiginosa*, whose foliage smells of stewed apples on the air. It crops heavily with scarlet hips, though its flowers are nothing to shout about.

The Hybrid Tea types are not always easy to fit into a mixed border, but it is possible. I have a huge specimen of one given to me by

Linda McCartney which she named after Paul. It is bright pink and has an amazing fragrance. She planted a large area of it, intending to distil the flowers for attar of roses. But she died before fulfilling this intention.

My plant is more than 2m tall and, for added interest, I have underplanted it with a white-flowered everlasting pea, *Lathyrus latifolius* 'Albus', a herbaceous perennial that annually climbs into the rose. There is a purple clematis, 'Etoile Violette', on a pole behind it and a long-flowering blue cranesbill, Geranium Rozanne, underneath. A nice community.

Some roses I grow out of sentiment as much as for the rose itself. My plant of 'Mrs Oakley Fisher' came from a cutting given to me by Vita Sackville-West. Roses are often exceedingly long-lived and this one must be 50 years old. It has purple young foliage and single, apricot-coloured flowers.

The true Rugosa roses are a wonderful group, with healthy, rough-textured leaves and a great will to live. 'Fru Dagmar Hastrup' could be fitted in anywhere; I have even seen it as a hedge and I'm sure it gave no trouble. The flowers are single pink and the handsome, globular hips are bright orange. When you see both flowers and fruit together, it makes you pause. Nature can surely do no wrong, so who are we to say these colours can't go together? Of course they can.

Autumn-flowering Asters

The Michaelmas daisy season reaches its peak in the middle of this month and there are many delights to tempt us. Many, also, that we should be wiser to resist, although, having said that, I have a sneaking feeling that it is no bad thing to yield, savouring the moment uninhibited.

The largest-flowered and most glamorous of the Michaelmas belong to the *Aster novi-belgii* section. As garden plants, most of them look dull and heavy throughout the summer months, and that includes the dumpy little Dumosus types. Furthermore, they are particularly susceptible to verticillium wilt disease, to powdery mildew and to the attentions of a microscopic mite, which causes the inflorescence to form leafy rosettes instead of daisies. Poor flowering is the result.

Most of these troubles are absent from the other classes of Michaelmas. But when you see a lot of asters together, don't forget that they look their best in most gardens when integrated with other perennials, bedding plants or annuals.

In my garden I enjoy double hedges of A. *lateriflorus* 'Horizontalis' (replacing lavender, which loathes my heavy clay). This is sturdy, retaining its shape right into March, when we finally cut it down. Horizontally branching, it is a seething mass of tiny white, purple-centred daisies, above purplish-green foliage. The similar A. *l.* 'Prince' is darker in all its parts, but no improvement.

Some small-flowered asters have outstandingly bright, fresh green foliage in the long run-up to flowering. Both A. *ericoides* 'Esther' and A. *pringlei* 'Monte Cassino' belong here and both are excellent for cutting, their rays not rolling back after a day or two, as is the case with the *novi-belgii* types. 'Monte Cassino', 1m tall and less hardy than some, is purest white, at its best in the second half of October. 'Esther', only 0.7m at most, is self-supporting and starts flowering mid-September, being mauvy pink.

Another excellent spraying variety for picking is 'Little Carlow', which is as near to a blue shade of mauve as any aster. Other strikingly good A. *ericoides* hybrids include the late-flowering 'Brimstone'; 'Golden Spray', which has the most yellow in it; the well-named 'Pink Cloud', only 0.6m tall; and 'Ringdove'. 'Ochtendgloren' is 1.3m tall, pink-flowered and free, and obviously needs support (which should also not be grudged to many of the others, in exchange for grace of habit).

The A. *novae-angliae* Michaelmas are rough-textured, large-flowered plants, tall, yet self-supporting, with a great will for survival. The old 'Barr's Pink' (reddish-purple, really) can be seen from the railway in many a neglected back garden. Then came 'Harrington's Pink', which is a true, clear shade of pink but apt to be stemmy in its lower regions, so it needs to have a lower companion plant in front. Then 'Alma Pötschke' (short for 'Andenken an Alma Pötschke') which is brilliant rosy magenta. Not at all an autumnal colour, but nonetheless welcome. It goes well with the bulbous *Nerine bowdenii* and the rich, 0.4m *Aster amellus* 'Veilchenkönigin' – Violet Queen – by far the best of the

Amellus Group. These have large daisies, the best known being the lavender-blue 'King George', a bold flower, but whose stems, as with most Amellus asters, are too weak to support the flowers, even though the height is a mere 0.4m. Violet Queen is the sturdy exception.

The hybrid A. x *frikartii*, which has A. *amellus* as one parent and whose lavender daisies are quite large, is generally preferred when bought and sold as 'Mönch', though wrongly named as such. Never mind, so long as you get the best, which grows to rather less than a metre high and, once settled in, is pretty well self-supporting.

It has a fantastically long flowering season, from late July for a good two months. Its resting buds in winter are apt to be destroyed by small, black, underground slugs, particularly noxious on heavy soils. This and Amellus asters are best split or moved in spring, not autumn. The rest, which make fleshy rhizomes, can be moved at any time.

Indeed, asters, like chrysanthemums, can be grown in a reserve plot for the whole summer and only moved to their flowering sites when about to, or starting to, flower. Give them a heavy soak the day before this operation, and puddle them in on their replanting site; that is, tip a can-full of water into the hole, with one hand, while holding the plant steady with the other. As the water drains away, fill in quickly with the excavated soil.

This is an old device for prolonged flowering displays. Not in the least a cheat, as some would have it. Tying plastic roses on to shy-flowering bushes for the sake of TV filming, as was once performed in my rose garden, is a shameful cheat. Since then, I have got rid of the roses and am a happier man.

The Beauty of Fruit

There is great satisfaction in admiring bountiful crops of fruit, whether we want to eat it or whether it simply gives a sense of fulfilment to the close of the growing year. This has been a good one, largely, no doubt, as a consequence of the ripening effect of last year's hot summer on fruit-bearing wood.

For the first time in at least five years, I am looking forward to a heavy crop of quinces from my temperamental bush/tree down by the rubbish dump. Who planted it (before I was born) or what variety it is, I have no idea. Quinces, at least in my part of Sussex, were generally planted by ponds in the old days, and if there was sewage effluent enriching the water, so much the better.

The trouble with my tree is that its fruit and foliage are severely affected in more years than not with leaf blight, a fungal disease which appears as reddish-brown spots on both leaves and putative fruits when the weather is wet in May and June. The leaves often drop off and the fruitlets just disappear.

This year, we remembered to spray with a protective fungicide immediately after flowering. Whether for that reason or not, though probably because we had drought conditions through from April to August, a crop of near perfect fruits is developing. There are few more beautiful October sights than a tree laden with bright yellow, pear-shaped quinces. And there are so many things you can do with them. Jane Grigson's books are crammed with suggestions.

The rusty-brown fruits of medlars would not make the same impact but for their extraordinary shape, with a huge 'eye' framed by the whiskers of five persistent sepals. Medlars do not ripen until early November, but there is not a great deal you can do with them anyway, except to make jelly, and I find that hard to set. You should not wait till the fruits are bletted, which is to say soft and ripe, but take them at the end of this month while they are still firm.

Medlars make beautiful trees and are worth growing just for that reason, perhaps as a small specimen in a lawn. They are nearly always grafted on hawthorn, and grow much more freely if the graft is made close to ground level so that the trunk is of medlar, rather than running the thorn up as a trunk and grafting it at head height. The white flowers in late May are charming, the trunks become interestingly scaly with age and the foliage never fails to colour warmly in November.

Some apples are pretty when ripe, but they are not always the nicest to eat. 'Beauty of Bath', with its red-striped fruit as early as August, is a picture (wasps adore it) but the flavour is disgusting. Of crab apples, we have no expectations when raw, but they make the best jelly, ordinary apples being far too bland for the purpose. 'John Downie', with its glossy red, oval fruits, ripening in early September, is one of the best and makes a small, shapely tree, but is as subject to scab both on foliage and fruit in a wet season as any other apple.

'Golden Hornet' ripens about now, and its yellow colouring is wonderful in autumn sunlight. One of the best for ornament is 'Red Sentinel', whose fruits hang on long after the leaves have shed. In urban areas, where fruit-eating birds are scarce, the fruits may still be in condition at the time of the tree's next flowering, which is a bit creepy.

I don't really enjoy seeing the crimson berries of the fishbone *Cotoneaster horizontalis* still in position at winter's end, good value though that may be. We have a great crop. How long they will survive is anyone's guess. Some years the birds go for them immediately, and there is quite a range that may be interested – blackbirds and mistle thrushes for the pulp, greenfinches and bullfinches for the seeds.

But mysteriously, there are also years when they show complete indifference. The foliage changes colour to carmine quite late in November and you can then witness the intense and unusual combination of red and carmine together. One way or another, this shrub – which is underrated because it is so widely seen – is great value, with the fishbone structure of its branching and the way it can pile itself up the sides of a wall of any aspect without assistance by tying.

Rosehips are a great asset from midsummer on, starting with the ripening of the tomato-like ones of *Rosa rugosa*. 'Fru Dagmar Hastrup' is particularly generous, and its fruit colouring makes a strange contrast to its later pink flowers.

Rosa moyesii, of which the clone 'Geranium' is one of the brightest and most reliable in fruit, ripens in August as does *R. setipoda*, with long, whiskery fruits. Both are good mixed-border shrubs, with a double season of interest. Likewise *R. glauca*, sometimes still called *R. rubrifolia*, with its dusky, purplish foliage.

That fruits tellingly in September. However, you should always remove the fruited branches in the following winter, so as to encourage the production of strong young canes, and leave those of the previous summer's making entirely unpruned.

As good as any are the scarlet, shiny hips of the sweet briar, *R. eglanteria*, which combines magnificently right now with the cream-white plumes of pampas grass, *Cortaderia selloana* 'Pumila'.

Hawthorns

As small, ornamental trees there's a lot going for Crataegus, the hawthorn tribe. By and large they make shapely specimens, often with interesting foliage; they may specialise in spectacular flowers, or it may be their fruits that are the main attraction.

Just now, C. *persimilis* 'Prunifolia' is quite dramatic, with a heavy crop of deep red haws. If the crop is light, the leaves will be larger and they will have brilliant fall colour. If heavy, however, the effort of producing all that fruit much reduces leaf size and there'll be no colour to speak of. One way or the other, you'll get your money's worth. I must remind you, however, that hawthorns have thorns, quite long and sharp in this case. I scratched my scalp walking under a low branch of ours and had to have three stitches. My own silly fault.

Even more spectacular for its large, brilliant scarlet fruit is the North American C. *ellwangeriana*. But you'll have to excuse its plain, rounded leaves for being a bit dull. Hawthorns hailing from the New World, as do these two, have entire leaves; those from the Old World are deeply indented and much more interesting. The star, here, is C. *orientalis*, which I met in the wild in Turkey. It naturally makes a large shrub rather than a tree, though it can be trained as the latter. Its much indented leaves are silver-grey, right through the season. Following its white blossom in June, it sets a crop of magnificent orange (not red) haws, ripening in September, but lasting until blown off by autumn gales. I suggest growing it under meadow conditions and underplanting with blue autumn crocuses, *Crocus speciosus*.

May blossom arises from our native white C. *laevigata*, one of the most spectacular being the double red 'Paul's Scarlet'. I got mine by budding a scion from a friend's garden on to a bird-sown seedling that had turned up in my rose garden. After the bud had taken, I moved the whole plant into the old orchard, and it has made a specimen of which I'm proud. It is underplanted with 'S. Arnott' snowdrops (Galanthus). The scaly trunk of these hawthorns is a pleasure in itself.

When I was a teenage schoolboy at Rugby, in the Midlands, one of the mitigating features of being a boarder far from home was the avenue of double red (or were they pink? – just as good if they were) hawthorns along Moultree Road. That was in the 1930s. I hope they are still there.

Rejuvenating the Border

We never tear our borders to pieces and start all over again. Traditionally, this has been a widespread practice, repeated every three or four years. Unless your borders are in a terrible mess and riddled with some pernicious perennial weed, a piecemeal treatment is far to be preferred. One good reason for getting busy is if the ground is starved. This often shows up in the quality of your weeds. If they look pinched and unhappy, something must be wrong.

Plants or groups of plants will become congested, in time. Lift them and improve the ground. Take a good look at what you've lifted and break off the healthiest pieces for replanting. Say it's a border phlox (*Phlox paniculata*). It's better to deal with it now than to wait till spring, because it will start strongly into renewed growth in February. Don't replant single shoots in each planting position. You would have to endure a very thin display in the following season. As you don't want the border to look thin in any year, replant strong pieces with a number of buds.

You might want to adjust plantings because you don't like the present combinations. It may be a question of heights or colour, or perhaps you're just bored and want a change.

A third important reason for getting busy is when a rather aggressive border constituent is muscling out its neighbours. Persicarias are often like that. I have an autumn-flowering one, *Persicaria polystachya*, which seemed to be well behaved when I saw it in Beth Chatto's garden, but is anything but in mine. I like it, though. The October display of sweetly scented white blossom is very welcome. But it may need to be brought to heel as often as every other year.

Another favourite needs replanting every year without fail. This is the native blue lyme grass, *Leymus arenarius*. It has handsome blue leaves that arch over and catch the light. It is a splendid focus, right at the front of our principal mixed border, for annuals or biennials planted either side of it, varying their colours in different years. It shows up well against a background of purple canna leaves.

However, the grass is ferociously invasive, sending long runners horizontally underground, which emerge as new shoots a metre or more away. The whole lot needs digging up annually (you may prefer to do this in early spring), tracing every one of those rhizomes to its terminus. But Fergus is happy to do it, as the results are so satisfying.

The plants that never need disturbance compensate for the hard work that others demand. Never say die.

Alliums

It is possible to pack a mixed border with bulbs, without them getting in the way of your principal ingredients. Alliums are a good example of the flexible bulb. Between the different species they cover a long season, and the globe-shaped allium flower makes you sit up and take notice.

The most important kind of allium in parts of my garden is *Allium cristophii*. Given a start (and if you are not too busy a weeder), it will self-sow and take up residence in many places where it would have been difficult to establish anything deliberately. Its large globes are made up of stiff, star-shaped, pinky-mauve flowers, developing in early summer. But they retain their shape as they fade, and remain an asset. I like them especially among colonies of Japanese anemones, which they pep up during their dull period before flowering.

Taller, at 0.8m, and with smaller globes but a strong presence, is *A. hollandicum*, which is mauve and mixes nicely with 'Purple Sensation', of more intense colouring. These flower in May (but only for a couple of weeks) and we find many uses for them. They stand out well against the lime green of spurges, such as *Euphorbia palustris*, or hovering above pink campion, *Silene dioica* (I grow the double form that is so popular in Scottish gardens). An excellent setting for them, and of their own height, is the biennial sage, *Salvia sclarea* var. *sclarea*, with large, furry leaves. In that case, the bulbs will need to be dug up when clearing the sage away in late summer. However, in the company of the pinky-mauve, cow-parsley-like *Chaerophyllum hirsutum* 'Roseum', perhaps in a woodland setting, you can rely on their permanence and expect them to self-sow in due course.

The June-flowering *Allium* 'Globemaster' (1.2m) is an important-looking plant that will stand out in any mixed border, and holds its own with ease through the years. Mauve again, its leaves are coarse in the run-up to flowering and die as the flowers reach their peak. Ideally, you want to site this bulb in the middle of a border, so that its foliage is concealed when it needs to be.

Allium sphaerocephalon has dense, reddish-purple oval flower heads on rather flexible 0.6m stems, and I like them in the company of penstemon plantings. *A. carinatum* subsp. *pulchellum*, which flowers July–August at 0.3m, makes clumps of small, pinky-mauve flower heads with conspicuous, whisker-like bracts. There is also an albino form. This can self-sow rather too enthusiastically, but it is excellent in paving cracks, and I like it in a colony of the evergreen fern, *Blechnum tabulare*.

That only leaves me space for the August-flowering Chinese chives, *A. tuberosum*, again a clump-former, white and, with me, self-sowing along the front margin of my long border. It also interweaves there with *Rosa* 'The Fairy'. And that's just alliums. Species of bulbous irises could provide another mixed border theme, flowering from January through to July.

Garden Prejudices

Every gardener nurses prejudices against certain plants or flowers. It is not a bad idea to examine our own, from time to time, and to decide whether they have sufficient validity to be taken to our graves.

Take the aspidistra, for instance, which we associate with dark entrance halls of frowsty boarding houses. It has been there, taken for granted and unloved, for years. I think it deserves to be brought into the light, to be repotted into a strong John Innes compost and given a good wash. That way, it will regain its dignity and become a respectable house plant. You might give it an airing outside in the summer, too. Many house plants are overjoyed to receive this extra bit of loving care and will repay you amply.

If a plant bores you, something must be done about it. The simplest course, if it belongs to you, is to throw it out. If it is a good friend's, look the other way. If it belongs to someone you rather dislike anyway, don't be ashamed to let it confirm you in an inclusive repulsion. I believe that you owe it to yourself to react in some way. If you accept all your surroundings meekly, something in you will die. Thinking but keeping your mouth shut is acceptable, too, or you can confide in a like-minded friend. Going round someone's garden with a friend can be great fun, but do keep your voices low.

I have a slight dislike of camellias – all those smug little rosettes of colour, dotted over a bush. Heathers are apt to get me down. I realise they can do a splendid job in quite difficult situations, but there's nothing there to get your teeth into. Bold foliage to the rescue, please. You may be too exposed for that to flourish. In the end it may come to moving your home, as soon as you can afford to do so. At all costs refuse to accept that the meek shall inherit the earth.

There are many colour prejudices. I find salmon difficult. With others it may be red or white or muted pastel shades. Take a good look at yourself and decide whether your likes and dislikes are sensible. Lots of people have a thing about pink combined with yellow. 'I use pink and yellow all the time,' Beth Chatto once told me without a blush. Since then, I have become more sensible about the juxtaposition.

I love strong colour contrasts some, not all, of the time. They excite me. Save me from soft lights and sweet music. They will send me to sleep – and I'm no insomniac at the best of times.

Aralias

Big herbaceous perennials – and I don't mean necessarily tall – have certain distinct advantages. In an all-herbaceous border, where everything can be cleared at the end of the season, they are often a good substitute for shrubs, making bold features in a way that many perennials fail to do.

Aralias are imposing, with big, pinnate leaves. They take up a lot of space, but as you don't need to see them, once cut back (from now till a rather late reappearance in May), you can make use of the ground vacated. Plant it up with tulips, for instance, or with any other earlier-flowering spring bulb. Even the tiniest will show up, right at the back of a one-sided border, because there is nothing else, yet, to be seen between you and it.

Fergus and I are interested in the herbaceous aralias and are debating the merits of A. *cachemirica*, which I have owned for many years, and the similar A. *californica*, fairly new to us. It won't be worth keeping both. Above the foliage, they make a branching inflorescence, with globe-shaped flower heads resembling an ivy's, to which they are related. The flowers themselves are minute, but the stalks and stems behind them turn to purple, while the berries ripen black. I have quite often seen this used as a solo lawn feature, and it makes its mark.

Some aralias are shrubby, notably A. *elata* (long known as A. *chinensis*). Popularly called the devil's walking stick, it sends up thick, rod-like stems, armed with hard prickles. There is a handsome crown of pinnate leaves at the top and, in autumn, an eruption of white blossom, in a bouquet of panicles. This plant, which makes a colony of stems, looks even better from above than from below. The leaves often take on attractive autumn tints before shedding. The plant's obvious disadvantage is of suckering, especially if you dig around it, but I'm prepared to cope with that.

There are two much coveted varieties of A. *elata*: one, 'Aureovariegata', with its large leaves heavily margined in yellow; the other, 'Variegata' (which has the RHS Award of Garden Merit) similarly variegated white. They are expensive plants and one often hears of failures, when the roots of the stock take over and produce green foliage. Never dig around your variegated specimen, because that will also make it sucker green.

Ornamental Grasses in Autumn

There are two seasons when a gardening journalist is tempted to write about a plant: at the time that it should be planted, and at the time that it is looking its best. The first is the more useful to the reader, but the second is far more inspiring for the writer. There it is, in full panoply before him, and not merely in the mind's eye.

That's the way with the ornamental grasses that I am currently enjoying in my garden, where so many of them are in flower. Why they should have a preference for flowering in the autumn, I do not know, but some of them do it so late that in our climate, with its relatively cool summers, they fail to bring it off at all.

While we may admire these grasses now, it is not a good time for disturbing them. That should await spring. Even then, there are quite a lot that will take a couple of years to settle down fully, following a move.

Such are the molinias. Like many other grasses, they make wonderful solo specimens and are best seen rising head and shoulders above surrounding plants. Plant one on a bulge or promontory, in a mixed border setting. *Molinia* 'Transparent' keeps its foliage low but rises to 1.2m with a gauze of blossom which its name well describes. You can admire it but at the same time see what grows beyond. Self-supporting, the flowering stems are crowned by a dome of blossom. This begins to develop in early July, but reaches a peak in autumn. The similar 'Windspiel' has a little more substance, being rich fawn in colour, with a hint of purple. Both disintegrate completely under the stress of high winds in early winter.

Stipa splendens (1.2m) remains comely for much longer and is excellent in an open situation, which also encourages it to stand on its own legs. However, some support at a lowish level may still be advisable. I have sometimes successfully provided this by planting around it the stiffly branching *Lychnis coronaria*. Once the stipa is losing weight and becoming sere, it holds itself up much better.

Stipa splendens is all pale green and fluffiness when flowering (and its season is extensive, according to the age of the plants, which also self-sow), but then settles down for the winter with sheaves of beige plumes. One of the most rewarding.

Just about the longest-season grass is the low-growing *Hakonechloa macra* (0.3m), of which I grow the yellow-striped clone 'Aureola'. The leaf's the main attraction, but a modest haze of blossom is welcome in the autumn. The foliage is brilliant yellow with its first appearance, in April, remaining lively till after Christmas. On its own, this grass makes a superb tub or low, wide, pot specimen.

The Japanese *Miscanthus sinensis* is dominant in autumn, together with other Far Eastern species. They self-sow and can become quite a problem in some climates (like Georgia's in the USA), but where summer is cool, as in Britain, many clones fail to flower. This may not matter if the leaf is sufficiently good, and such is the case with M. *sinensis* 'Strictus', which grows to 2m when established (but gives an excellent account of itself at half that height, in its first year of planting).

Of notably upright habit, its leaves are prick-eared, like a terrier's. They are boldly cross-banded with yellow, which often takes as much space along each leaf as the intervening green. My colonies are making a half-hearted attempt to flower this month. This is often confused (both being known as zebra grass) with M. *s.* 'Zebrinus', but that has a far laxer habit. If your zebra grasses are weakly variegated early on, do not complain to or about the salesman; the variegation strengthens as the season progresses.

A large range of named miscanthus cultivars has been developed, in recent years, mainly in north Germany, that will reliably flower at full strength in high-latitude gardens before the growing season comes to an end. They have German names.

One of the first, and still one of the best, is 'Silberfeder' (Silver Feather) (2m). Starting purple in early September, it dies to palest grey and often remains in sound condition into December. You should really see a selection of named clones, when flowering in a nursery, before deciding which of them is for you.

Stipa arundinacea (1m) used to be one of my autumn favourites as a front-line specimen, beautiful both in flower and for the warm tints of its dying foliage. It self-sows, and seedlings make welcome presents. But in my garden it has lately been regularly disfigured by a rust disease. *Helictotrichon sempervirens* (which flowers in May) is another victim of the blue-leaved *Elymus magellanicus*.

Any of the forms of *Panicum virgatum* (1m) are a great joy in autumn, as their open-textured flowering panicles develop and the leaves gradually assume reddish autumn tins. 'Hänse Herms' and 'Rubrum' are the two I grow and there's nothing to choose between them.

A great favourite with me is *Chasmanthium latifolium* (1m). Its leaves are broad, arching at the top. The flowers are gathered into flattened, diamond-shaped units which put me in mind of a blood-sucking bug before it has had a meal. You'll love it.

Autumn Blooms

A recent visit to the West Country has brought a number of plants to my attention. Some were new to me, others grown in an unusual way that suited them.

Among the latter, at Kingston Maurward, near Dorchester, Dorset (a garden that should certainly be visited in summer or autumn) was *Ceratostigma plumbaginoides*, a late-flowering herbaceous perennial with deep blue flowers, which one normally sees (if one sees it at all) used as ground cover. It has a mildly running habit and grows little more than 0.3m tall. The foliage becomes rich crimson before dying. In winter, you can cut a whole colony back to the ground, making space for all sorts of small, early spring-flowering bulbs that will be out of the way by the time the ceratostigma has rubbed the sleep from its eyes.

Although this species will thrive in shade, its flowering then, in our climate, is too long delayed. It should be given a moderately sunny, open position for best results. What was unusual at Kingston Maurward (though I have seen it used this way, possibly accidentally, elsewhere) was its growth over a wide area on a vertical, east-facing retaining wall, where it vied with our old friend the Mexican daisy, *Erigeron karvinskianus*.

Planting into a ready-made wall is always tricky. The best way, in this case, would generally be to plant at the top and keep watering generously until the ceratostigma was well established and able to quest into the cool recesses behind the wall face.

Another plant that lends itself to this treatment is a bromeliad, *Fascicularia bicolor*, which has been flowering most freely during the past month. Bromeliads come from the tropics and subtropics of America, where they are epiphytic, gaining a foothold on the mossy or otherwise organic-rich surface of tree trunks and branches. *F. bicolor* is exceptional in being hardy through a large part of Britain. It makes hummocks of spiny, evergreen leaves, which are linear and arranged in rosettes. When a rosette is ready to flower, which happens in the autumn, its centre opens out to reveal a pad of baby-blue flowers, whose nectaries twinkle like tears. This is surrounded by a startling circle of deep red bracts, to which colour the 'leaves' have now changed.

In cultivation you normally see this plant making a mound on the level, but it is an ideal dry-wall feature if you can establish a single rosette in a crack, to get it started. Probably the best way to do this would be by first establishing a small rosette in a jiffy pot and then pushing that into a largish crack where several stones meet at a junction.

To my dahlia collection, I have added a plant of the dwarf, semi-double 'Bednall Beauty' (0.6m), which is an even richer, deeper red than 'Bishop of Llandaff'. The latter, at 1.5m, is currently looking smashing in my garden admixed with the light purple *Verbena bonariensis* (1.8m). 'Bednall Beauty', with similarly dark foliage, might mix well with *Verbena rigida* (0.4m). That is a super bedder with heads of small flowers in brightest purple.

I realise that diascias are extremely popular these days, but I have personal reservations. They are like perennial or semi-perennial nemesias, many of them pretty hardy and tremendously long-flowering. Two necessary points, with regard to their fully successful cultivation, are persistently overlooked. You must, even though they are flowering, cut them back midway through their flowering season. Otherwise they get hopelessly straggly and weedy-looking. Second: replace your stock with newly rooted cuttings on an annual basis. Young plants give by far the most satisfactory results. You could make your cuttings (of the Irish kind, with some ready-made roots already attached) now, overwintering them in pots under barely frost-free glass.

What I dislike about diascias is a kind of murkiness that overlies their colouring, whether pink, salmon, mauve, biscuit or red. They rarely come clean. I grow, or have grown, a number of them, but in the course of time they are apt to become, like certain marriages, a tedious habit rather than a renewable companionship. That said, I am taking a chance with Redstart, which seems a reasonably decent shade of red.

Vernonia crinita (2.5m), called ironweed in its native US, is one of those late-flowering hardy perennials that you might excusably be forgiven for dismissing as suitable only for large gardens, and barely there, considering its October season. But it has heads of fluffy, rich purple flowers, adored by butterflies (of which we have been enjoying a bountiful second hatch), and it stands on its legs without support – always a welcome attribute in tall perennials.

Furthermore, as it gets started late in spring, you can interplant or surround it with bulbs such as tulips (always visible at that early season, even at the back of a deep, one-sided border) and, later on, include a tall annual such as the pure white *Cosmos bipinnatus* 'Purity', whose flowering will continue so as, eventually, to coincide with the vernonia's. Even a single clump of ironweed could constitute a quorum.

Red

Suppose you liked the idea of a red border, how would you bring it into focus so that it didn't fall into the category of unplanned mess?

For one thing, I think you need a clear idea of season – early or late. A shrub like the rhododendron 'Elizabeth' or 'May Day' provides a blast of colour early on (difficult to match with any companion), but becomes a mere lump of dull green later.

The advantage of a season starting in early July is that you would be able to include many tender bedding perennials, and it is among these that much of your long-flowering material will be found. This could be alternated with red-flowered tulips and anemones, in spring.

Must the border be all red, or would you be prepared to be more flexible, and to back the red flowers up with flatteringly supportive neighbours? Remember that reds with a certain degree of blue in their make-up, such as *Monarda* 'Cambridge Scarlet' (which isn't scarlet), do not go well with pure orange reds – scarlet, in fact – such as *Lychnis chalcedonica*, or the original oriental poppy. A late border could include oriental poppies, because the clumps can be cut down to the ground in late June and interplanted with bedding.

The most useful shrubs to have in the border, as I would conceive it, would be for their purple foliage, acting as a foil. *Cotinus coggygria* 'Royal Purple', for instance; once established, it can be pruned hard back each winter, giving its best foliage on young growth. *Cercis canadensis* 'Forest Pansy' is similar, with more rounded heart leaves and it would not need much pruning.

As a flowering shrub, the Chilean fire bush, *Embothrium coccineum* 'Ñorquinco', with clusters of scarlet flowers in June, would be worth a try on acid soil. To liven it up, after flowering, I should plant *Tropaeolum speciosum*, the flame nasturtium, nearby to climb into it. The low-growing rhododendron 'Arthur Osborn' is a wonderful red and has the advantage of a July flowering season. As a companion on either side I might plant the lime-green-flowered *Euphorbia seguieriana* subsp. *niciciana*. Euphorbia yellow-green goes well with pure and orange reds.

Besides geums and potentillas, which flower their best early on and become rather weedy later, hardy perennials are not rich in long-flowering examples. There are the crocosmias, and I should include the late July-flowering 'Lucifer'. Though it is soon over, its foliage and seed heads remain good. One or other of the red hot pokers, Kniphofia, depending on whether I wanted orange red – 'Prince Igor', say, or slightly pink-tinted red, as in 'Lord Roberts'.

Thinking again of foliage to go with red flowers, a purple-leaved castor oil, *Ricinus communis* 'Gibsonii' or 'Carmencita', contributes handsomely palmate leaves.

Purple-leaved cannas will also contribute red flowers, as with the vigorous, though small-flowered *Canna indica* 'Purpurea' or the large-flowered 'General Eisenhower' with sculptural purple leaves. Neither would I hesitate to include 'Wyoming', although its flowers, above purple leaves, are orange.

Dahlias, of course, everyone's favourite being 'Bishop of Llandaff', with single red flowers and purple cut leaves. A small cactus dahlia, such as 'Alva's Doris', would be good, and, if a hint of purple at the centre of the bloom was no detriment, 'Wittemans Superba'.

Nasturtiums have a unifying way with them and any scarlet, trailing seedling would thread its way through other plants. The double red 'Hermine Grashoff' has to be overwintered, frost-free, from autumn-struck cuttings. The 'Empress of India' seed strain has dark leaves as well as red flowers.

Many tuberous-rooted begonias are suitable. An old single red one, 'Flamboyant', which I find a great stand-by, is not listed in the *RHS Plant Finder*. Hybrid bedding verbenas, kept going from cuttings taken now, include some good reds. Such is *Verbena phlogiflora*, and so is 'Huntsman'. They have such a long flowering season.

As an annual, *Amaranthus hypochondriacus*, with upstanding, purple-red plumes, has great presence and will reach 2m in a good season. 'Red Fox' is close to this; perhaps less tall.

Roses can be included, hiding their stemmy habit with leafier neighbours. Singleton specimens or small groups will help to achieve this. Think carefully about the quality of red that you want in them, whether pure, orange red or red with a trace of purple, sometimes only showing up as the blooms fade. You could also include a shrub rose such as *Rosa moyesii*, grown principally for its hips. By the same token, *Viburnum opulus* 'Compactum' would be an excellent candidate, its clusters of shining red berries ripening in August and lasting particularly well.

Glaucous foliage should not be overlooked, since it highlights red so well. The large, jagged-margined pinnate leaves of *Melianthus major* (hardy once established) are supreme. But a grass such as *Elymus arenarius* would also be effective, provided you realise that its spreading habit must be controlled.

Black

Black exerts a curious fascination among gardeners: black flowers, black foliage, black flower centres, as in 'Black-eyed Susan', a name applied to more than one flower. Anything in a Latinised name with the stem or adjective being '*niger*' or '*atro*' tells of blackness.

Helleborus niger, the Christmas rose, has white flowers, but the blackness referred to in its title is in the roots. However, there are a number of strains of Lenten roses, generally referred to as *H. orientalis*, whose flowers are very dark indeed. As these hellebores are dreadfully slow to propagate by division, they are generally offered as seedlings, featuring, in this case in the *RHS Plant Finder*, as 'black seedlings'.

But what is the point? I am inclined to ask. After all, you have to be very close to the flower to be able to see it properly. Perhaps this element of mystery and surprise is a part of the appeal. It's certainly not for any contribution the flowers can make to the garden scene. Yet the owner of a black hellebore is apt to be inordinately proud of it, much in the same way as was the case with Dumas's *The Black Tulip*, set in the period of Dutch tulipomania.

There is great pride attached to possession and success with *Cosmos atrosanguineus*, which became widely available when it turned out to be easily increased by micropropagation. This tuberous-rooted perennial has always seemed to me to be more like a dahlia than a cosmos. The plant is stringy but the flowers, which smell of cocoa, are certainly very dark. How to keep the plant from one year to the next has been my unsolved problem, but, in some gardens, once established, it behaves like any normal hardy perennial. As it doesn't like me, I have ceased to like it, much.

The true dahlia, 'Dark Stranger', grown in the dahlia trial held at Wisley this year, is a semi-cactus and certainly a very deep red purple in colour, but as near to black as you will find is a single called 'Dark Secret', shown by Avon Bulbs at the Great Autumn Show in Westminster. The leaves are dark and ferny, but what I particularly liked about this plant was the contrast between its black petals and the rich yellow of the stamens forming the central disc.

I suppose 'Royal Velours' is as near to black as a clematis has yet reached, and that is certainly a seller. It is a viticella hybrid, easily grown and prolific, and very dark purple. When mine is flowering, someone usually points it out to me before I have noticed it for myself. With these dark flowers, presentation needs to be at close range; your plant should be near a path along which you often walk and positioned where the sun strikes it. Otherwise, it is a real waste of effort.

Black hollyhocks are rather good, and close to the real thing. A whitewashed wall would make a good background. *Alcea rosea* 'Nigra' is the proper name, and it is quite widely on offer. You can keep your black pansies and violas, so far as I am concerned. They need a mini-setting. If you grow them at ground level, make sure that your knees are still supple enough for close examination.

The hardy cranesbill, *Geranium phaeum*, has many friends, but I am not one of them – a 1m plant, generally grown in shade, its small, beaky flowers are unquestionably near to black, but they make no sort of impression, except on the drooling owner and his or her cronies. The white variant shows up better, but it is still a miserable thing. When there are so many good cranesbills, why bother with such as these? The annual climber, *Rhodochiton atrosanguineus*, on the other hand, is a wonderfully rewarding plant – there are always 50 places where it can easily be fitted in, lightly draping any other plant that will offer it support. It makes garlands of blossom, which are comely at every stage from bud to seed. The persistent calyx is like a purple lampshade, but the tubular corolla, which spreads out into five limbs at the mouth, is short-lived. It is pitch black, but the stamens have pure white anthers. Such a contrast; it is hard to tear your eyes away.

Of black-centred flowers, yellow rudbeckias of the 'Black-eyed Susan' persuasion are supremely effective. The bedding variety that I grow as an annual is 'Indian Summer'. Of yellow perennial sunflowers, *Helianthus* 'Monarch' is the most striking, though up to 3m tall.

Black foliage, too, has its place. The great thrill as a novelty in my garden this year has been *Colocasia* 'Black Magic', which came to me from America. This is as happy in shallow water as in a well-nourished border. The elongated heart leaves are truly amazing. I have set them among white-variegated foliage, to highlight them – *Plectranthus madagascariensis* (syn. *coleoides*) 'Variegated Mintleaf' beneath, and the white-striped *Arundo donax* var. *versicolor* behind. The three of them have to be housed frost-free for the winter, but the colocasia goes dormant with a tuber, which should be easy to manage.

The black strap leaves of *Ophiopogon planiscapus* 'Nigrescens' are rather fascinating, evergreen on an almost prostrate plant, but it is not easy to use effectively.

An interplanting of snowdrops is sometimes recommended, but that will contribute for only a short time early in the year, after which the dying snowdrop leaves are something of a liability.

The creeping New Zealand fern, *Blechnum penna-marina*, which is rich green for much of the year, can be a suitable partner.

Weeding

'I think I'll do a little gentle weeding,' did you say? Well, let me tell you that, except on the scale of a window box or two, weeding is never gentle.

It started that way with me. Our gardens are full of self-sowns that are not exactly weeds, but we get too many of them. I decided to get rid of an excess of *Strobilanthes atropurpurea*. This is a tough-rooted perennial carrying light purple flowers, tubular, but with a kink in the middle, as though doubled up with indigestion.

I welcome a bit of this sown where I shouldn't be able to plant anything deliberately, but I don't want it all over the place. On the way to it, teasel seedlings need removing. At this time of the year, I begin to decide which to keep for flowering next year. In their first season, they make a large rosette of ground-hugging leaves. The healthiest plants are those that received plenty of light, and I try to keep some of them. They are often close to a path, but that is nice.

Of course, I was down on my knees, close enough to the ground to see exactly what was where. This was on the edge of a large planting of long-established hydrangeas. When these are still naked, in the spring, I like to enjoy the bonus; first of snowdrops, then, in April–May, of yellow and orange Welsh poppies, which are great colonisers. But I hadn't been among these hydrangeas for a couple of years, and there were several hundred each of young or well-established ash and ivy seedlings. When they get into the crutch of a many-stemmed hydrangea, they are a problem, first to see and then to extract (I have a narrow, sharp-pointed trowel).

The ash seeds blow in on the prevailing wind from a plantation on our south-west boundary. I could cut them down, but I love them. They never look heavy in summer and they make wonderful silhouettes against the sunset sky. I had contemplated cutting out all the female, seed-bearing trees and merely retaining the males, but some of the best specimens happen to be females. Your problem may well be sycamores, which are even more prolific. Sometimes, in a town garden, a self-sown sycamore will be overlooked, and before long it has become a tree and a very great nuisance, but expensive to remove, and very possibly with a tree preservation order protecting it.

Ivy has plenty of human enemies. Many hate it, while never stopping to consider its merits. It grows well up ash trees, since the crown of an ash will always admit plenty of light. This suits ivy which, albeit shade-tolerant, grows more strongly with light reaching it. The leaves are glossy, cheerful in winter and often take on purplish tints in cold weather. When the adult stage is reached and climbing has ceased, ivies branch out and flower, abundantly, in early autumn, scented and alive with a range of pollinating insects. The deep, purplish-blue berries ripen in February and are great food for the birds, while the branches offer ideal nesting sites. All well and good, but the bird-distributed seeds become a problem.

It is no use getting someone else to do this sort of weeding for you. Their approach is sure to include an element of the cosmetic. If a seedling is broken off, it will temporarily become invisible, but next year will grow again with increased strength and toughened rootstock. 'We have scotched the snake, not killed it,' said Macbeth, when his hired assassins reported that, while Banquo had been murdered, his small son, Fleance, had escaped. I often think of that line when weeding.

So I am thorough, if slow, short of breath and sweaty. But there are rewards. Those interesting seedlings that crop up unexpectedly. Two or three were of yew. We always save these, potting them up and growing them on. They will come in handy, for instance, to replace one or more of our topiary specimens.

There are quite a lot of self-sown *Daphniphyllum* subsp. *macropodum* from a big old specimen nearby. This is one of my favourite evergreens: about 4m high, with large, ovate-lanceolate leaves, not unlike a rhododendron's, but glaucous underneath and with leaf stalks and main veins that turn pinky-red in winter. It always looks smart, even at winter's end, which is the hardest test for an evergreen.

The variegated *Arum italicum* 'Marmoratum', has fresh foliage all winter. Its self-sowns can be a problem, but hardly so in the crutch of a deciduous shrub. It is the same with the *Iris foetidissima*. Its evergreen foliage gets in the way, but it is shade-tolerant and perfect where taking up no space of importance. Hawthorn seedlings can be a liability. Most were of the American *Crataegus prunifolia*. I sometimes find a use for them. There were other excitements. A satisfying afternoon.

Bed and Border Changes

First, forget about categorising borders. This is old hat, though still taught in many institutions. The annual border, herbaceous border, shrub border, cottage border, rose border – categorising in this way is simply lazy-minded. Plants, whether categorised or not, will help each other and it is silly not to allow them to do so. Assuming, then, that you are open-minded about the kind of plants you are prepared to put together, what about colour schemes? These are fun to work out and help to train your eye in deciding just why some colours work well together in certain circumstances but not in others. Be adventurous. There is too much safe gardening being practised: white borders, silver and grey borders, gardens in which all the colours are in soft, pastel shades.

Strong colours are a challenge. You could juxtapose magenta and bright yellow, say *Geranium psilostemon* and *Achillea* 'Coronation Gold', perfectly successfully if the neighbouring flowers were rich indigo aconitums, soft mauve *Campanula lactiflora* and grey-leaved santolina. Scarlet oriental poppies are thrillingly electrifying among the greens of a border where, at the turn of May and June, all is still green, for green is a very positive colour.

To limit your palette makes life simpler, though more restrictive. 'I like red but I can't take orange,' many people tell me. This is a pity as there is so much vitality in orange flowers, especially at sunset. The orange of *Tithonia rotundifolia* 'Torch' in the evening is so exciting; Mexican hats spangled over a 1.5–1.8m annual of amazingly rapid growth. Or, at the other end of the scale, there is the single 'Disco Orange' marigold, no more than 23cm tall but the flowers are in scale with the size of the plant (often not the case with marigolds), which can form an apron to ferns, perhaps, or to the brilliant green of the annual *Kochia* 'Evergreen', which is a perfect complement to orange or yellow flowers.

But you may home in on purple and yellow (too much of this can become rather obvious), or purple, mauve and pink, or on yellow and white – a sure success, some of the yellow contributed by foliage.

There should be substance and structure in your border. Too many flimsy flowers or plants will lack cohesion and focus. Find bold contrasts to plants such as *Gypsophila paniculata*, *Gaura lindheimeri* and *Origanum laevigatum* 'Hopleys'. They tend to create an undifferentiated haze, whereas fennel, *Foeniculum vulgare*, although its leaves are filigree and its flowers minute, is a strongly structured plant.

With their big expanse of leaf, hostas and bergenias are used over and over again as focal points, and that is fine, so long as you realise there are alternatives. Bergenias, being usually evergreen, can look heavy, like tough old leather, and they generally need replanting more often than you thought (or the pundits told you) they would. Hostas are bewilderingly numerous, many of them scintillating in spring, but too early becoming tired and riddled with obtrusive slug and snail channels. Try rodgersias for a change.

If a leaf is not only bold but shiny also, reflecting light from the sky, it has added value. *Fatsia japonica* is incomparable, with its huge, fingered, evergreen leaves. If it is taking up too much space, it doesn't mind being cut hard back, though the job is best done in stages, not all at once. Or you could, on a somewhat smaller scale, use its hybrid with ivy, x *Fatshedera lizei*, which makes a floppy, spreading bush, but is easily shaped and controlled by annual shortening of last year's growth.

Then you want to give thought to your border's season. Let it have a high spot so that plants flowering earlier or later do not spoil the climax. Successions can be arranged, one flower following another in the same area, this being greatly facilitated if you set aside a reserve plot or standing ground, from which plants can be drawn on or to which they can be returned, as the need arises. Greenhouse and cold frames will play their part here too.

Draw up a list of the plants you would like to include. Then, to scale, outline your border on paper and make a plan. When you put your plan into action, it may turn out slightly differently. You may find that your groups were too small or too tight or that you left insufficient space between them. And almost certainly it will not contain all the plants that you originally listed and will include others that you thought of subsequently.

The way I start a plan is to choose and mark in an important-looking plant that will occupy a salient bulge or corner at the border's margin; something that will be agreeable to look at for much of the year. It might be a yucca, if sharp leaf points were not a danger, or the glaucous, rosette-forming *Kniphofia caulescens*, or one of the bergenias that I do like. Then, sighing deeply, I turn to my list and think which plants would make pleasing neighbours to my first choice; then which plants would look good next to my second selection, and so on.

This exercise needs considerable concentration. At the end of it, I have earned a nap because it has been an exciting act of (as yet unrealised) creation. The knowledge that you won't have to be a slave to your plan and that it can be flexible is also reassuring. There will be mistakes, of course, but also triumphs, and the triumphs will be your own.

When to Cut Back

There are various schools of thought about whether we should cut down the perennials in our borders at the end of the season. Generally, in my garden, we don't cut until we are working on that bit of border, for several reasons.

For a start, old top growth protects the soil. We've found from experience that the soil under a border with all the skeletons left until the last minute is in a more workable condition. The skeletons are also a useful reminder of where plants are. If everything is cut down in the autumn, you are left scratching your head in the spring as to what's there at all.

The skeletons also tell us how plants are doing. Masses of thin phlox stems, for example, immediately say the plant is congested and needs rejuvenating. You will be told that phloxes need dividing every three or four years, but you should judge this from the state of the plant, rather than from any rule.

Another reason to let things be is so the birds can enjoy the remains. It seems crazy to ply our birds with food at a table throughout the year and then discourage the natural sources that may already be present.

Some remains make pretty skeletons: the golden seedheads contrasting with the dark stems of *Telekia speciosa*, *Serratula seoanei* (just as pretty when dried out in March as when flowering in the autumn) and certain asters. The giant yellow daisy, *Inula magnifica*, looks rather a fright until its old leaves drop off, but stately after that.

Many tidy-minded gardeners consider seed heads and skeletons messy (and in some cases they have a point). So they would rather make a clean sweep than be bothered to differentiate. If there are early bulbs around, such as snowdrops, miniature daffodils or *Scilla siberica*, you'll not want to mask them with old debris.

Another point to consider is that certain plants remain green at the base throughout the winter and could suffer beneath the debris of their own old stems. The cushion of young green shoots kept by the invaluable *Helenium* 'Moerheim Beauty', for example – this must not be overshadowed, otherwise it will quickly perish. Slugs are also encouraged by old vegetation.

Be practical. If the plant looks a mess, tidy it up and take away all the dead matter. If you want to work on a bit of border to replant, go ahead and cut down. But if there is no reason to do so, leave well alone.

November

Knowing Your Garden's Conditions

There are many ways in which we can improve our gardening, if we learn to understand how our plants are likely to behave in varying circumstances.

Not many of us, I suppose, have the space or, indeed, the yearning for double borders, with a path running through the centre. But those who have, often seem to be striving for a perfect balance, groups of the same plant nodding to one another from either side.

Plants, however, have a way of turning towards the sun. If the path runs east–west, flowers in the border on its north side will turn towards you, as desired, because you are on their sunny side, but those in the south border will turn resolutely with their backs to you. Too bad. You should have grown non-orientating plants in that border. With a north–south alignment of path and borders, everything will look towards you if you walk the path from south to north, but away from you if you return from the opposite direction.

Box hedging will grow more strongly on the south-facing vertical side, but will be more thinly furnished on its north face. You will notice the difference if it is flanking an east–west path.

Then there is the wind factor. The strongest winds in Britain come from the south-west so that, other things being equal, plants will develop a south-west to north-east lean. However, if there is a wall on the north-east side of a border running parallel to it, the plants will be blown forward, because the wind, after hitting the obstacle, will bounce off at increased speed. That is an advantage if you are looking at the plants from a path running along the front of the border, but it does mean that you should plant anything of a sideways-blowable nature well back from the path's margin; otherwise it will soon be growing or flopping over half the path.

Planting symmetrically with feature plants, as on four corners or in an evenly spaced row, is always risky, because at least one of those plants is likely to let down the side by behaving differently from the rest. This is often on account of a difference in the soil depth where each plant is growing, or in its drainage. If you can make your points with groups, rather than individual accents, then differences in behaviour won't matter; they may be an asset.

Remember that various seedlings will always behave differently from one another because of genetic variation. So, a lavender hedge composed of seedlings will cause more headaches than one raised all from the same clone. However, if the cuttings from which the hedge components originated were taken from different clones, there'll be trouble again. I rarely see a large planting of box in which there are not obvious differences in colour, leaf size or vigour between some of the units used. This will ruin any formal application of box, as for a knot garden.

Soft, fast-growing shrubs, which it is tempting to grow for quick results, are far likelier to let you down after a few years than those of slower, tougher growth. The juniper called 'Skyrocket' has been a terrible let-down in many examples I have seen and, of course, being opened apart by heavy snowfall is an added risk where growth is soft. I am impressed by the performance of a small-leaved holly, *Ilex aquifolium* 'Hascombensis'. If a fastigiate habit is not entirely natural to it, it can quite easily be imposed by a few annual snips with the secateurs.

Sun versus shade for your plants is another question that needs understanding. Many plants that are merely tolerant of shade are dubbed as shade-lovers, though in fact they will perform a lot better in sun or, at most, in dappled shade. Such are periwinkles, or the majority of spring-flowering anemones. Periwinkles will certainly cover the ground in deep shade, but they will be mighty dull cover. In sun, and especially if mown to ground level every other year or so, their flowering will be abundant. The same is true of the much-abused snowberry, Symphoricarpos. It will make a suckering thicket in difficult shade, but only when brought into sunlight will you be able to enjoy its bountiful swags of white berries at this time of the year.

By the same token, we are often told that certain wall shrubs are for certain aspects. It may be good to be able to make use of morello cherries, say, or of *Cotoneaster horizontalis*, or of many camellias, against a north wall, but they will do just as well on any aspect or, indeed, out in the open and away from any fence or wall. The self-clinging climber, *Hydrangea anomala* subsp. *petiolaris* is usually recommended for a north wall and is fine there. But where it can catch the autumn sunlight, it will give far more pleasure and excitement when its foliage changes to yellow before being shed.

We all know that there are late years for flowering and early, according to air and, consequently, soil temperature. Flowering this year remained late throughout the growing season because it was cool. However, when autumn-flowering bulbous plants start their new season, soil moisture makes a notable difference. The hardy *Cyclamen hederifolium*, grown at the foot of a rooty shrub like a lilac, may still be flowering just before Christmas, instead of its more normal time in September. If you want the flowering of *Nerine bowdenii* to coincide with that of the rich purple Michaelmas daisy, *Aster amellus* 'Violet Queen', give the nerine bulbs a heavy soaking late in August to get them moving, otherwise they may flower too late.

Organic Feeding

'Feed the brute' has traditionally been the recommendation to a bride from an older, experienced matron in respect of the husband. That may or may not be out of date with people, but it is still broadly applicable to plants. In general, undernourishment is still the norm. Plants cannot cry out or go on strike in protest. They simply do not fulfil their potential. In our ignorance, we fail to recognise the evidence.

Currently, I am looking anxiously at my self-sown forget-me-nots, which are a great spring feature in most of my borders. True, they sow themselves much too thickly, which needs to be sorted out, but in some areas they have a deprived look about them, a brownish tinge on the margins of their leaves with the centre a reluctant shade of green. Even discounting overcrowding, they are not as healthy as they should be.

Probably the best way to have malnourishment brought home is to visit a garden where the plants are quite evidently enjoying themselves. But even then, we are apt to remain blind, in self-protection. After all, it's none too flattering to have to admit the inadequacies of our role as guardian and protector. 'You're so lucky with your soil,' we reassure ourselves, complacently.

Of course, there are good soils and bad. The one that everyone hopes to retire to in their latter days is greensand. I'm not quite sure what greensand is, but it certainly stands for all that is most fertile, combined with excellent but not excessive drainage.

I am on clay – Wadhurst clay. Unimproved, it makes an excellent basis for meadow gardening, although drains may be needed to prevent the incursion of bog-loving rushes. The poorer your soil, the easier it will be to have a meadow that sustains a wide range of species, both native and introduced.

For other kinds of gardening, fertility is the watchword. Even shrubs noted for thriving on hungry soils – brooms and cistuses, for example – seem to revel in fertility, when given the option. You can spot, immediately, when the soil is lacking in the nutrients and the physical well-being that will promote joyous plant growth: the weeds will look peeky. If your sow thistles and fat hen are of giant physique, you may congratulate yourself on having got the balance right for many plants.

At this time of year, the ground needs improving with bulky organic matter. That will introduce physical reserves – an open texture in which plants will love to explore. It will also provide reserves of many trace elements, which are beneficial to plant growth. When you are digging a piece of ground over, work in your bulky organics to as great a depth as possible. If this is not on because of the presence of plants that cannot be moved or whose roots you don't want to upset (particularly important with fleshy-rooted plants such as magnolias), lay on a generous surface dressing, fork it in a little, where no damage will result, then lay on some more as a mulch. Earthworms will thrive on this diet and will drag much of your mulch down, along their aerating channels, to a lower level. The rest will act as a buffer against water shortages, next spring and summer.

What you use for your bulky organic material will depend on availability. Use your own garden compost, of course, though this is rarely sufficient by itself. The grass mowings from a meadow will rot down into excellent compost. As the heap is built up, we apply dressings, every 15cm or so, alternately of sulphate of ammonia and of garden lime – calcium carbonate.

The heap should be as open-textured as possible, allowing air and moisture to do their work in combination with nitrogen and lime. We water the heap as it is being built.

You may be able to get cheap organic material from other sources.

Spent mushroom compost, turned out of mushroom sheds after the crop has been taken, is one that we use extensively. One has to remember that there is lime in it, which will be beneficial to most vegetable crops and many plants, but harmful to those that are calcifuge, such as many heathers, rhododendrons and other ericaceous shrubs, camellias, Himalayan poppies and some others. Mushroom compost should be weed-free; if it has been hanging around for a while before you receive it, it is liable to have been seeded into by neighbouring nettles, thistles and other undesirable weeds which you won't want to pay for. Spent hops are a possibility, after they have been used by the brewers.

It is in the spring, when rapid plant growth needs fostering, that quick-acting fertilisers come into their own. We use Growmore, which offers the plants their three main nutrients in quickly available form. Being concentrated, the pellets need to be applied keeping your hand low among the plants, so that they do not lodge on or in foliage (tulip leaves seem expressly made to collect fertiliser pellets). If you can do the job so that it is followed by a shower, that is ideal. The fertiliser will be quickly dissolved.

Long-lasting fertiliser pellets are valuable in releasing their nutrients over a period of months. Osmocote is one of these and we feed our yew hedges with it. There are different grades which last for different lengths of time and operate at different temperatures. If applied in April, say, the grade that operates freely at 16°C will provide feed for four to five months, which is just about right for many plants.

Begonias

Begonia is an amazing genus. There are well over 1,000 species and, between the tropics of Capricorn and Cancer, they extend right round the world. *B. rex* has a lot going for it. Each leaf is more than 30cm across and the texture is puckered, making it satisfying to handle. Dark on the outside, then light green, then dark again at the centre.

One of the distinguishing features of begonias is that they are always lopsided – enlarged on one side, flattened on the other. And only *B. grandis* subsp. *evansiana* has any pretensions to hardiness, but it is popular for summer bedding and thoroughly enjoys being outside from June to October.

There are various methods of storage, depending on the type of rootstock. Those with tuberous roots can often be dried off and overwintered somewhere cool and frost-free, and completely dark. In spring, they can be started off again in damp peat, either under heated glass or, if it's late in the season, in a cold frame.

Begonias like some shade in the summer, so they're a good understorey for taller plants. If you are growing, say, B. *rex* indoors, never stand the pot in water – try it on wet pebbles. Aim at a minimum 10°C.

One of the most useful begonias is B. *scharffii*, with its pale pink flowers that are seldom out of bloom and dark green foliage that is purplish-red on the underside. It's good on a windowsill in winter. But our favourite is the handsome B. *luxurians*, whose leaves are divided to the centre into 11 fingers. In its second year, a plant will be up to 1.8m tall.

B. *metallica* is an old favourite, with a metallic sheen over the whole upper surface of the leaf. In 'Little Brother Montgomery', the leaf, which is divided into long, sharp points, is dark at the centre and margins, while the band in between is a mosaic of dark and pale, the main veins being dark. You never get bored with a leaf like this.

We recently acquired 'Bonfire', which is low-growing. The smallish, spiky flowers are dazzling scarlet. How we shall get on with it remains to be seen, but it certainly keeps the old arteries alive. With begonias, you are experimenting all the time.

Tulips: Companion Planting

It is depressing to see tulips or other bulbs sparsely scattered in untenanted border soil. They should be provided with backgrounds or companion planting of their own height. If you must plant tulips on their own, at least do so thickly, with the bulbs not more than 10cm apart. Then their foliage will do the ground-covering.

Traditional carpeters beneath tulips (which can then be spaced further apart, at 15cm intervals) are myosotis, bellis, pansies and polyanthus. Keep to single-colour strains. Mixtures are fussy and the bulbs will not be revealed effectively above them. Some strains of pansies flower as early as March and can suitably partner early tulips or maincrop hyacinths. That there should be coincidence of the flowering partners is important, and needs planning ahead.

The 'Crescendo Red' strain of polianthes is also early and makes a good carpet for the large, white fosteriana tulip 'Purissima', or the pale yellow fosteriana 'Yellow Empress'. Daisies and forget-me-nots are generally at their best from mid-April. The most useful type of daisy, in my experience, is the quilled, pomponette type, also known as buttons. They are neat, prolific and showy red, pink, white or (to be avoided) a mixture. Pink pomponettes go remarkably well with the lily-flowered tulips, 'China Pink'.

You may be too late to try out some of these ideas for next spring, but plants or seeds can be ordered now and raised for bedding out next autumn. Bellis, for instance, can be sown in early July and will make fine plants by the autumn. I generally sow the normal run of wallflowers (again in separate colours, or in two separate colours combined) late in May, though you can delay a month. That is *Erysimum* (better known as Cheiranthus) *cheiri*.

The so-called Siberian wallflowers make a low cushion of growth and are coloured dazzling orange. Of similar habit, though lower growing, is the mauve-flowered *Erysimum linifolium*. Both these flower from mid-May and combine well with a late tulip such as the orange 'Dillenburg'.

The orange Siberian wallflower also looks nice with pure white *Allium neapolitanum*. Late June is early enough to be sowing this type of wallflower; any earlier and the plants tend to weaken themselves by flowering at half-cock the first year.

Many perennials go well with bulbs. Lupins, for instance, have beautiful young foliage to make a background for tallish tulips. Carnations make pale silvery-grey hummocks of linear leaves and I like them as a background for the red tulip species, *Tulipa eichleri*, which is black at the centre. The best carnations for this purpose are raised from seed (sow February to April) and treated as biennials. The Floristan mixture or Floristan Red are ideal, and wonderfully scented.

The metre-tall *Allium aflatunense* (*A. hollandicum*) 'Purple Sensation' is effective rising above the double pink campion, *Silene dioica* 'Flore Pleno'. But in a friend's Scottish garden in early June, I also liked it among the rosy-mauve cow-parsley-like *Chaerophyllum hirsutum* 'Roseum'. Both are self-seeders and of about the same height.

Arabis alpina 'Snowpeak' makes dazzling white cushions. Sow it in spring and line out the seedlings to grow on. It flowers through March and I grow it with the cyclamineus Narcissus hybrid, 'Jetfire', which is deep yellow with an orange trumpet.

Another early, and somewhat unlikely, combination that I go in for is an interplanting of the low, abundantly free-flowering *Bergenia stracheyi*, which is mauve-pink, interplanted with blue *Scilla siberica*. The slightly earlier *S. bifolia* is intense blue, and I combine that with the bright yellow-green young foliage of *Valeriana phu* 'Aurea', which later has white flowers at one metre.

Primula 'Wanda' is an early, low-growing primrose in brilliant magenta. For those with strong nerves, I recommend growing it beneath the no less brilliant scarlet, multi-headed *Tulipa praestans* 'Fusilier'. No one will miss noticing them.

I was not the first to discover that the bronzy purple young fennel foliage of *Foeniculum vulgare* 'Giant Bronze' makes an unusual, light and feathery accompaniment to pale yellow, May-flowering tulips. Use seedlings raised the previous year. If you grow the plant at all, there will be masses of these that you'll be glad to transfer from where they self-sowed with embarrassing freedom.

The Cold Frame

Most gardeners only feel the need for cold frames in the spring, when hardening off seedlings and cuttings or starting cucumbers, but a good reason for writing about them now is that one might make a good Christmas present for a loved one.

In fact we at Great Dixter have made great year-round use of cold frames for the past half-century. Certainly they are in great demand in spring for both raising and hardening off seedlings. Also, they will be useful for establishing newly potted, rooted cuttings taken off soft perennials in the autumn – verbenas, fuchsias, felicias, diascias, 'geraniums', gazanias and many more. These will have been overwintered under just frost-free glass, but from March onwards should be treated individually in a potting compost. The cold frame gets them started until they can be stood outside.

In May, we shall still be sowing tender annuals such as ipomoeas, zinnias and cucumbers (for growing on the compost heap). But we also make late sowings of quite ordinary annuals such as cosmos and marigolds, annual rudbeckias and dahlia seed strains, so as to have a follow on in the borders to plants that fizzle out after the end of June. This keeps things looking fresh right into October. We also make late dahlia cuttings for the same purpose.

Before this, cold frames are useful for starting dahlia and canna tubers into new growth when they come out of winter storage. They are bedded into moist peat and the frame is at first kept closed but able to be shaded if the sun is hot. We sow our pansies and violas in July, but they need to be kept cool in order to get a good, even germination, so no frame for them. A pane of glass over the pot or seed tray and a position under a tree will suit them, but the frames are still useful at this time of year as a standing area for young plants that were raised from cuttings – hydrangeas, for instance. The frames' sides are a protection against wind.

In autumn, nearly all my display pots containing tulip, narcissus, hyacinth and other bulbs are placed in a cold frame, where the amount of rain they receive can be controlled and they will often remain there until just bursting into flower, the protection having advanced their flowering dates by a week or two ahead of those that were planted in the garden, so you get a nice succession.

The frames offer protection to many potted plants in winter – most of it young stock later destined for the garden. It is not just a question of a higher temperature; it may be little warmer inside than outside, but the frame also keeps out desiccating winds. In my opinion, it is essential that a frame should have solid walls. These give you far greater protection and control over temperature fluctuations. An all-glass or poly-carbonate version heats up famously – probably too much – during the day, but temperatures plummet as soon as the sun is gone. Residual warmth is all-important. This is ensured partly by solid wooden or concrete walls and partly by mats (any old matting or piece of carpet, hessian or blanket, supposing it hasn't already been destroyed by your dogs) put over the frame in the evening and removed the next morning.

Probably the most satisfactory example will be the one you have made yourself. Use treated (what is known as 'tanalised') pine, which will last for 10 years. You want a double layer of boards for height, each 14–15cm across. Then a third layer of board sawn at an angle so that they are three boards high at the back and two at the front. This will give you the sloping lid that throws off rain. The whole frame should be roughly facing the sun. The boards are screwed at the frame's corners into uprights of what you order as lengths of, say, 5cm x 5cm tanalised pine (the sides may also need strengthening with uprights). Poly-carbonate sheeting is ideal for the lids, being lighter than glass and less easily broken. This is nailed or screwed to a wooden frame.

It is usually a good idea to build a central partition into the frame, with a light over each section. This will allow you to treat the two halves separately, the one kept closed, most probably, till seeds have germinated or cuttings rooted, the other ventilated for hardening off.

Be very careful to avoid sun-scorch by day. Clear glass will give some protection. So will ventilation. Damp the foliage down in the morning with a fine spray from a can. The ideal to aim for is moisture by day but dry foliage by night. Under close conditions when you don't want to admit air, a weekly spray with a fungicide (varying the active ingredient so as not to allow resistant strains of fungi to develop) is important. The grey mould botrytis fungus can do so much damage so quickly.

Melianthus major

To be asked what is my favourite this or that always throws me. Among my favourite replies is, 'The plant I'm looking at.' Otherwise why grow it? If I am in the mood to pin myself down, however, high on my list will be *Melianthus major*. It is a shrub but looks best grown as a herbaceous perennial. I should add that in New Zealand's north island, to which it was introduced, it has run riot and is classed as a noxious weed. This is so often the way with introduced species.

'Is it hardy?' will be one of the first questions at this time of year. Well, it is, once established. The roots will go quite deep, thereby protecting themselves from penetrating frosts, though I help them with a winter blanket of fern fronds.

The leaves are pinnate, glaucous and with heavily toothed margins. In winter sunlight, they cast shadows on one another with a three-dimensional effect. That is why it looks so good in early winter sunshine, when shadows are long. You want to site it accordingly.

This melianthus makes a slow start in spring but keeps on getting better, until it makes an impression from a considerable distance. However, it combines well with other plants and is easily adaptable to any small garden. Mine is close to the autumn-flowering orange *Kniphofia rooperi*. And it is in strong contrast with the annual mallow, *Malope trifida* 'Vulcan'. It is native to South Africa and, according to the *RHS Dictionary*, India. When bruised, the plant smells of rancid peanut butter – but why bruise it in the first place?

The flowers, in terminal spikes, are borne on second-year wood. The only time I have seen them looking good was in California, when a large bush of them was in bloom.

This species comes from the south of Cape Province. *Melianthus villosus* comes from the Drakensburg, Natal, and should have hairy leaves. By October, they appear to be notably bright green for the time of year, because their colouring does not change with the season, though a hard frost will put paid to them. In both species the pinnate leaves are some 30cm long and both are worth having, though M. *major* is the more glamorous.

Cistuses

Someone politely asked if they could quote me as saying that I liked the sun rose, *Cistus* x *pulverulentus* 'Sunset', because of its bright colouring. I certainly do like it, partly on that account. The flowers are on the small side but brilliant magenta. However, there are additional and equally important assets: it has a dwarf and comparatively compact habit, the leaves are on the grey side of green and it flowers over a long period – not just out and over, like most.

Out in a big flush and then finish is, admittedly, the most dramatic way that a plant can present itself. But we are naturally greedy and prefer them to go for a long season. The price is that the display is never with all the stops pulled out, but always rationed. So I want the wow! as well. My favourite is C. x *cyprius*. For at least a month in early summer, it opens a huge array of its large, fragile white blossoms (with a maroon blotch at the base of each petal) every morning. If the day is hot, they will shatter at midday, but never mind that. You'll have had your fix and there'll be another one the next morning. C. x *cyprius* makes a big, rather loose bush up to 2m high with a considerable spread. In winter, the leaves turn to the colour of oxidised lead. It gives off the typically spicy cistus aroma that we associate with Mediterranean hillsides.

I find it long-lived, which most sun roses are not, and it is a lot hardier than many, but by no means fully so. Still, there'd be little fun in gardening if we didn't take risks. The cistus likes a hot, dry bank with fairly poor soil and this promotes added hardiness. But when these plants get long in the tooth, chuck them out without compunction and start again. Being fast growers, they are easy-come, easy-go shrubs, like brooms, tree mallows and tree lupins.

There are lots of different kinds to choose and as they give such quick results, you can run through quite a selection of them in the course of your gardening life. Always plant in spring and always buy young plants that haven't become pot-bound. Once the roots have curled up within their container, they'll have lost the capacity to explore new territory, which means that they'll never become wind-firm, but will be blown out of the ground. Quite unnecessary, once you are aware of the danger.

There is a range of colour and sizes, variations on pink, magenta and white. One I repeatedly come back to is C. x *corbariensis*, now C. x *hybridus*. It has neat, wavy-edged leaves which turn bronze in winter and a big flush of small, white flowers from pink buds, in June. The bush, though fast-growing, is compact, 1m high by 2m across.

November Jobs

Gardening when the days close in almost as soon as they have started, when your tools are permanently slimy and rain arrives just as you have settled into a job, is not the greatest fun. But it isn't winter yet, and there is a lot more useful work to do than cutting things down or back that will either not get done otherwise, or else will be unnecessarily delayed until spring, when we so often run into drought.

If you move plants around now, you can still see, or remember, where and what they are. Some are inclined to be aggressive and to muscle out their neighbours. If I like the plant, I don't resent its colonial inclinations at all, but I check them.

I love *Inula hookeri*, for instance, with its finely spun yellow daisies, but it puts out investigatory rhizomes beyond its allotted area. The perimeter of its colony needs to be chopped around and the straying bits removed. You might decide to replant the core area, while you are about it, as that will become congested within a few years, starving itself. If you improve the soil with some nice organic stuff and replace a few healthy lumps, they will respond with larger flowers and a more extended season.

Sinacalia tangutica (*Senecio tanguticus*, 2m) is a handsome, late-summer-flowering perennial, for foliage, flowers and seed heads but, by dint of its Jerusalem-artichoke-like tubers, it is a great spreader. That must be brought to book, pretty well every year.

As you do it, you might plant some *Aconitum carmichaelii* 'Kelmscott' in the vacated space, so as to have contrasting yellow with deep blue. Aconites make tubers that can do with frequent splitting and replanting. The creamy 'Ivorine' is an exaggerated case in point; it ceases to flower altogether if not split and thinned. As most of these monkshoods start into new growth as early as January, now is the moment to get busy.

I had better mention a perennial that I don't like, because it is more than likely that you do. *Persicaria amplexicaulis* 'Atrosanguinea' (1m), with its deep red pokers, flowers non-stop for several months in summer, steadily muscling out its neighbours while you croon over its persistent contribution. As a plant, it has little personality. Still, there we go. *Persicaria polystachya* (2m), by contrast, is underrated, being dismissed as an aggressive monster, which it is not. It only spreads at a very decent rate and is easily controlled (now). It makes a stately presentation of its sweetly scented, white panicles from mid-August, for a good two months.

Another plant that stops flowering if you don't frequently divide it is the early summer-flowering cranesbill, *Geranium clarkei* 'Kashmir White' (0.4m), with deeply incised foliage. I intend to move from elsewhere, some of the loosely doubled, light mauve-blue meadow cranesbill, G. *pratense* 'Plenum Caeruleum' (1m). It will replace a colony of *Morina longifolia*, a perennial that grows well for me but flowers too spasmodically and in a wan, indeterminate shade of pink. The glossy leaves are prickly edged and smell citrous, when crushed. The flowers are borne along a broad spike (0.8m), tubular, open at the mouth.

Behind the cranesbill replacement is the magenta *Cistus x purpureus* (1.5m) and in front, the dense, reddish-purple spikes of *Francoa sonchifolia* Rogerson's form. So this is a colour harmony, but the geranium also contrasts well with yellow, especially with the free-flowering *Hemerocallis* 'Corky' (0.8m).

Day lilies love to be split, now. Many of them become active with young shoots quite early in the year. Crocosmias, too. Their young shoots, even while still underground, become terribly brittle if allowed to grow too long before handling the corms.

We are doing newly conceived plantings, now. For instance, in a rather shady, north-west-facing border corner, I have the South American evergreen fern, *Blechnum chilense* (1m) happily established. As a partner for that we shall move in already well-established stock of the aroid, *Arisaema consanguineum* (0.8m), with tuberous roots now dormant. The narrow, radiating leaflets of its compound palmate foliage are most beautifully mottled, while the arum-like flowers are sinister, with purple and green streaking, the spathe extended into a longish tail.

We grow the dragon arum, *Dracunculus vulgaris* (1m), well, since Fergus got the length of its foot, lifting and dividing its dormant tubers in winter and heavily manuring the site with mushroom compost. After producing its wicked purple flower in June–July (they smell of carrion), the plant rapidly dies off. We intend masking with some pink Japanese anemones in front, which will perform late in the season.

Currently, we have a blazing display of scarlet berries on our hermaphrodite form of butcher's broom, *Ruscus aculeatus*, seen against its own dark, evergreen background and set alight by low winter's sunshine. But I should like a bright evergreen foreground and have decided on that excellent form of polypody fern, *Polypodium* 'Cornubiense' (0.3m). Its leaves are quite heavily dissected and it grows into a mat. The ruscus will hold on to its fruit until well into next summer.

Taking Cuttings

The precautions that we take against a hard winter depend on how fatalistic we are by temperament. 'If I lose it, I lose it,' is an attitude easy enough to adopt about a plant we are not over-fond of but don't like to give the coup de grace ourselves. Somehow it seems to have official sanction if the winter gods do it for us.

But there are many friends in my own garden I should hate to lose, and it isn't much trouble to take cuttings from them. Neither, so long as their top growth hasn't been frosted, is it too late. The cuttings, overwintered in a barely frost-free frame or greenhouse, may not root until next year (or they may), but there is no hurry. In fact, the less growth they make, the less space they'll require and space under glass is at a premium just now.

I have a Hebe called 'Jewel', currently smothered in spikes of sweetly scented lavender blossom – its second flowering of the year. It isn't reliably hardy and its predecessor was clobbered three years ago in a moderate winter, so I know what to expect. Stock is worth saving because young bushes quickly make sizeable plants. Cuttings couldn't be easier to root.

Penstemons for bedding have masses of young tip growth just asking to be struck. The nearly related Phygelius are just as easy from cuttings. Half-hardy perennials often give much better value than annuals, though their flowering tends to occur in spates. Their foliage will stand a few degrees of frost, so it is probably not too late to be propagating the majority. Your favourite gazania plants will be worth preserving through cuttings. It is true you can start again with a seed strain, but some of the seedlings, even in F1 hybrids, will be greatly inferior to others.

Many of the bushy daisy argyranthemums have been selected and given names like 'Vancouver' (deep pink and anemone-centred) and 'Jamaica Primrose'. *Argyranthemum foeniculaceum* is the species they grow as standards at Sissinghurst; those are old plants, but cuttings taken now will make large, bushy specimens next summer.

Like many South African daisies (osteospermums are another example), they have a way of flowering freely in spring, before you really want them to, then not again until the shorter days of autumn. *Euryops chrysanthemoides* makes a bush with bright green leaves and its daisies, well displayed on longish stalks, are a richer shade of yellow than in any argyranthemum, but they are at their most prolific from September to October.

Salvias, whether shrubby or herbaceous, vary greatly in hardiness. One of the most persistent in flower, from May to October, is *Salvia microphylla* var. *neurepia*, a Mexican shrub with bright (but not harsh) pink flowers borne in pairs. In a warm corner, that will make a 90cm bush (best pruned back by half in spring), but you could lose it altogether, and cuttings are easily struck.

Quite different is the 1.8m tall herbaceous *S. uliginosa*, with pure sky-blue flowers, each having a white fleck in the centre. This flowers in late summer and autumn, and it is a see-through plant which you can place at a border's margin without blocking the plants behind. The root stock runs a little, but the plant's hardiness is not certain. Either take cuttings of young side shoots or dig up and pot a piece of root and overwinter under glass. I shall dig up some of my stock of the South African *Tulbaghia violacea*, even though it hasn't flinched through the past two winters. It looks and smells like an allium, with loose heads of lilac-mauve flowers borne over a long summer-autumn season. The root stock isn't bulbous, but can be cut into pieces before planting out again in spring.

Tigridias will often survive the winter near to a warm wall, but it is safer to lift their corms because they are caviare to mice. Hang them in a net bag from a hook in the ceiling of a cool cellar or shed.

Magnolias

From where I am sitting, I am looking out on the sunlit branches of *Magnolia* x *soulangeana* 'Lennei'. They are presently adorned with scarlet seeds, revealed when the grotesque, puce-pink seed pods (always a cause of interest to the public) split open.

This is the magnolia's last flourish of the year, but when its leaves fall and perish, they retain their venation in a beautiful filigree. As is the way with magnolias, the furry flower buds that will be next spring's blossom give us pleasing anticipation, throughout winter, of good times to come.

In April, and for a long succession of six weeks or more, it opens large pink goblets that are white within. The shrub/tree has flexible branches, the lowest coming down to the ground so you can admire the blooms at close range. It has a pleasing scent, too.

As this magnolia's branches are so flexible, the best way to grow it is against a high wall – some branches can be tied in while the rest loll forwards. A good deal of space is needed. As it leafs out fairly late, it is nice to underplant with early-flowering bulbs – I have a carpet of self-sowing, light blue *Scilla bithynica*. As that returns to dormancy, complete darkness envelops the ground where there is now a canopy of magnolia leaves.

It is a feature in early-flowering magnolias to bloom on naked branches, so you can appreciate their blossom to the full. But not everyone approves of this and I have heard visitors to our garden tut-tutting and commenting, 'No leaves', as though there were something indecent about this. You find the same reaction to autumn-flowering colchicums, which pop up without foliage and have been given the vernacular names of 'naked ladies' and 'naked boys'. There is clearly a pejorative innuendo.

Magnolias are among the most glamorous trees or shrubs we can grow, but you do need to anticipate the space they will occupy. Another important consideration is colour. Ordinary M. x *soulangeana*, as you see it in many front gardens, is rather a muddy pink, and muddiness is a tendency in quite a number, but there are plenty of selections for bold colouring. If you like white, that is well catered for. My own favourite, M. *denudata*, has a long history. It develops into a round-topped canopy of waxy, white, lemon-scented blossom. Perhaps it is less robust than some gardeners might wish, but I shouldn't let that put you off.

Autumn Perennial Planting and Moving

Many perennials are best established in their permanent homes in the autumn. Often, they are spring-flowering and need to settle down some months ahead if they are to flower in a worthwhile manner. Others are not dormant for long, if at all, so the less we check their growth, the better for them.

A few, however – delphiniums, for instance, and pyrethrums – tend to rot if disturbed when dormant, and so these should be left alone until they can be seen to be on the move next year. As soon as you see them shooting, which is often as early as February, you can, weather permitting, move them around. It is hard actually to kill a bearded iris, but if you didn't get them settled by July, it's better now to wait until they show signs of shooting next spring.

Of those perennials that should be dealt with now, oriental poppies are among them. These poppies will have lain almost dormant in summer, after they have flowered, but they will already be active by this time of year and will have a much better chance of performing next May and June if settled in soon.

Which colours to go for depends on your preferences. If you like a strong crimson red, say, I think Goliath (in a good strain) is unbeatable, and better than 'Beauty of Livermere'. Tall, at 1.3m, and strong in the stem, it is an imposing plant. On the scarlet front, straight *P. orientale* takes a lot of beating, in my opinion. Many soft shades have also been developed.

Of the whiter poppies, 'Black and White' makes the strongest impression, having a large, black, central blotch. 'Cedric Morris' has appeal, with frilly petals, the colour greyish with a hint of pink and a good basal blotch. 'Patty's Plum' sells largely on its name (so important in any flower). It is a dirty, purplish-plum colour, and I can't help rather liking it. As for salmon pink, 'Karine' is now one of the prettiest: neat, upright, fairly short (0.8m) and with an abundance of smallish, cupped flowers. 'Khedive' is semi-double, with crumpled petals, freely flowering and deep salmon in colour.

Lupins are very early on the move in the new year and should be established now. Although your own seedlings raised from one or more of the better seed strains will give you a lot of pleasure, there is no question that selected, named cultivars are superior. 'Troop the Colour', for instance, is an amazing red.

Dianthus are evergreen and do not take kindly to disturbance after the new year. Tall anchusas of the *Anchusa azurea* type, are flowering before the end of May and need to be established in good time. There is some pretty ropy stuff around, and we really need some improved seed strains. But of the named kinds, if true to name, 'Opal' is one of the most satisfactory. If you buy plants with good roots, take a few 7cm pieces off the bottom, plunge them upright in grit outside for the winter, their tops just covered, and they'll be making new plants by the spring.

I love the freshness of doronicums in spring, with their cheerful, yellow daisies, usually 0.8m tall, and with white or mauve tulips. To be well established, these tufted perennials should be given homes now, though not in a position too exposed to sunshine, as the flowers bleach.

Of the genus dicentra, *D. spectabilis* (0.6m) is much the showiest in spring. Called lyre plant or lady's lockets, it carries arching racemes of dangling, clear pink rockets that are white in the centre. Plant it now, and it will start sprouting in March. Its roots are fleshy, so it needs good drainage, but moisture, too. 'Alba' is pure white, with bright green leaves, while 'Gold Heart' combines pink flowers with yellow leaves in an extraordinary, yet successful way. It might even start you off on a pink-and-yellow colour scheme.

Many monkshoods do not flower until autumn and yet are already leafing in January, notably the varieties of *Aconitum carmichaelii* among them. When their nut-like tubers become congested, which happens quite quickly, they flower less well, so need fairly frequent replanting in improved soil. Do it now, before they're on the move.

Aquilegias belong to the same family, and are best established in autumn, in the expectation that they will make a good display in May–June. I am thinking especially of the long-spurred hybrids, which can, when mature, reach a height of a metre or more and look charming among Rugosa roses, pruned so that they do not grow too tall.

Trollius, the globeflower, in shades of yellow or orange, flowers quite early and needs settling now. It likes a moist position and, in hotter areas, some shade. You can split up old clumps, now.

I don't think it matters leaving crocosmias untouched until spring – except that they make new shoots from their corms so early and these are easily broken off when handling – bang goes your flowering spike for next summer, though the corm will sprout again, less strongly. Take into account that some crocosmias are not of the hardiest.

The November Garden

Quiet November days are highly conducive, I find, to browsing through the garden. I should, of course, be hard at it – bedding out, especially. We have just moved a batch of 200–300 auriculas from their summer quarters in a nourishing vegetable plot. Originally raised from seed five or six years ago, they have increased prodigiously. A bed of them (well, two, actually) scents the air all around for a long, late-spring spell – much longer than related primroses or polyanthus.

But there are lots of good things to enjoy in the garden right now. We have not yet had a frost, so dahlias have run on – a star among them for a long while past has been the collerette 'Chimborazo'. Basically single, it is deep, ruby red, with a collar around the disc in primrose yellow. This makes a striking contrast, and no one misses it, like it or not.

A rose that gives great pleasure and that is not in the least pinched by the lateness of the season is Bonica, mysteriously classified as ground cover. It is a self-respecting shrub that blends admirably with mixed border fellows, and the colour is the kindest shade of pink (similar to that of 'The Fairy').

Another left-over from summer that is still in mint condition is the cranesbill, *Geranium* 'Dilys', which starts late, but then runs on with a rambling habit. Just the one plant is now covering an area of some 2m across, spangled all over with flowers coloured a light, rosy purple. This kind of geranium can be planted around with small, early-flowering bulbs, as it dies back to a central crown and leaves plenty of tempting space for use in the early part of the year.

The last of the year's crocuses to be in bloom is *Crocus ochroleucus* – a frail-looking little thing, white shading to yellow at the base. Actually, it is not frail at all and spreads to make a good patch. I have it at the edge of a border and am rather astonished to see that it is actually spreading into the lawn turf in front.

Another flower of the season is *Buddleja auriculata*, which is particularly free this year, with drooping panicles of off-white flowers that are yellowish at the centre. The flowers are tiny but abundant, and they waft great bouquets of the true buddleia fragrance. The lance leaves are elegant and glossy – not what you really expect of a buddleia – the habit is lax, and it will scramble to the top of a two-storey building, given the chance. It needs a sheltered position. You might say it was tender but, once truly established, it will never be killed, and will always come back from its mildly suckering roots. I have grown this shrub for 40 years and it has amply rewarded me.

Coronilla valentina (0.4m) is just starting to flower now and will run on, taking advantage of every mild spell, right through the winter, winding up in March–April with such a burst of its yellow, generously scented pea flowers that hardly a leaf will show. In some winters, it hardly flowers at all and concentrates all its efforts to spring, so it keeps you guessing. This is clearly an 'on-year' for my colony, and it is an incredibly lively little shrub for the season when it chooses to get going. Give it a sunny, sheltered position.

A rather amazing biennial yet woody mallow that splits the gardening community down the centre – some are painfully repelled by it, others revel in its jazzy variegation – is *Lavatera arborea* 'Variegata'. My tallest specimen is now 2.7m high. Through the summer, its soft, rounded foliage is plain green with only a hint of variegation. But, as growth slows down, the variegation intensifies with more and more white splashing until, by early spring, the plant presents an extraordinary appearance. Then it flowers, which is no event for celebration, before finally running to seed and dying. It leaves masses of seed, however, some of which will self-sow. One of my plants is coming out of the centre of a yew hedge. There is a place for curiosities of this kind and, in its way and at its best, some of us think it rather beautiful.

Another crazily variegated variegation, this time in summer, is that of *Ampelopsis glandulosa* var. *brevipedunculata* 'Elegans'. It is a Virginia creeper, but one that is so inhibited in vigour by its pink-and-white variegation (the stems are deep carmine) that I find it best grown as ground cover. Feed it well, and trim it over lightly in spring. The point of my mentioning it now is that, after a warm summer like the last, it sets some of its brilliant blue, grape-like berries. These can be a lot more prolific on the far more vigorous plant, A.g. var. *brevipedunculata*, with green leaves. This is vigorous enough to be treated as a normal climber and makes an interesting feature on a pergola.

The last words go to butcher's broom, *Ruscus aculeatus* (0.5m), a stiff and spiny evergreen shrub. You must insist on getting the hermaphrodite form, as this freely sets and ripens a glamorous array of crimson berries, three times the size of a holly's. They ripen in early autumn and stay until the next summer. Great value, but it is a plant that gets going slowly.

Pollination

Most plants manage their sex affairs without bothering us. They flower, fruit, set seed, and we can remain uncaring as to pollination.

But then, sometimes, if it doesn't happen, that may affect us and we'll feel frustrated. With fruit trees such as the Victoria plum, for instance, self-pollination may work in some cases, but cross-pollination is necessary in others, as with the old English greengage. Coincidence of flowering will also be necessary, so we'll not only need another plum at hand, but it will need to flower at the same time as our gage. Many pollination rules and tables have been devised, though, on the whole, unless we are commercial growers, we take the availability of pollinating insects for granted, even in London, where there are more bee-keepers around than you might suspect. In other cases, such as sweet corn, the wind blows male pollen on to receptive female ovaries.

Sex has serious consequences. Many plants, particularly woody ones, are either male or female – that is, dioecious (Greek for two houses). If you bought a female *Garrya elliptica* – which we grow for the sake of its long, grey-green catkins that flower in January – you would be disappointed to find its flowers quite stumpy. It is the male that produces the goods, and it can generally be assumed that if you ask the salesman for a garrya, it is a male that you will get.

In other cases, you will want a female, generally because it is this sex that bears the desirable fruits. Females of *Skimmia japonica*, for example, cover themselves with clusters of bright red fruits that are half as large again as a holly's. But this will be possible only if a male and bees are at hand for pollination. If you have a skimmia that you had hoped would bear fruit but doesn't, there are two possible explanations: it may be a male, or it may be an unpollinated female. But given a rudimentarily trained botanical eye, you can sex your plant at its time of flowering. Males will show a ring of stamens with pollen-bearing antlers, but no central ovary; females will, at best, have rudimentary stamens, though probably none, and no anthers, but will have the central blob, which is the ovary that could, if pollinated, become a fruit.

There is a pleasing complication in this skimmia's case, inasmuch as the males bear conspicuous and very sweetly scented panicles of blossom in quite early spring. 'Kew Green' is one such that is worth growing simply as a flowering shrub. 'Rubella' is another, with flower clusters that are in place throughout winter as comely, reddish buds surrounded by leaves that are themselves of a reddish colour. Females also bear scented flowers, but the clusters are small and nothing much to look at. The berries, however, are often disregarded by birds and will hang on all winter and even into early summer.

Viburnum davidii is another interesting case. It is a lowish, evergreen shrub whose tough leaves are deeply grooved. It is often grown simply for its ground-covering greenery. If it becomes too tall, it can be cut back into old wood, from which it will break again and be rejuvenated. Its flowers are unremarkable, but females, if pollinated, will bear flattened clusters of bright blue fruits. Plants are not quite as easily sexed as in other cases of dioecious species. But many suppliers in the *RHS Plant Finder* now differentiate between male and female. If you are planting a colony, one male plant will suffice to pollinate quite a harem of females.

With *Hippophae rhamnoides*, the sea buckthorn, sex is rarely stated at point of sale for two reasons: first, the shrub is beautiful as a grey-leaved, foliage plant and its suckering habit suits it, particularly as a barrier against wind – especially sea breezes – on a garden boundary, and especially on poor, sandy soils; and second, the plants are most easily raised from seed, and are sold as seedlings that have not yet flowered and shown which sex they are. But one of the sea buckthorn's greatest assets is its garlanding with sizable, luminous orange berries on female plants. Still, a few nurseries listed in the *RHS Plant Finder* do offer named, sexed clones, such as 'Leikora' female and 'Pollmix' male.

The butcher's broom, *Ruscus aculeatus*, is a native sub-shrub, sombre, evergreen and prickly – its spines, in awkward, often shaded places, are a convenient defence against delivery men and students taking unwanted short cuts (encouraged by the bad planning of your garden or forecourt). In this role, it is a depressing feature, but it is dioecious and, in the wild, you will often see it carrying large red berries. In the gardener's case, the situation is transformed if you acquire the hermaphrodite form, which also comes true from seed. A colony will be well worth its position, if you choose a site where the fruit will catch the rays of low winter sunlight, and this condition will persist for half the year as the berries are long-lasting. Your only duty will be to remove any tired old shoots and cut them back to ground level after they have done their duty for two or three years.

The Privet Hedge

Among the most used and most abused of shrubs in our gardens is privet. It deserves better. The hedging privet, *Ligustrum ovalifolium*, grows fast, but its roots are excessively greedy and it loses enough leaves in autumn to look scanty and dejected in winter.

Golden privet, *L. o.* 'Aureum', has often been thought of as the answer to this problem, and it is certainly a cheerful colour. But as a hedge, it is rather too assertive, while as a rounded, regularly clipped specimen it tends to look lumpy and smug. But if you treat it as a self-respecting shrub – pruning it selectively so that some older branches are removed while others are allowed to grow unpruned, it becomes a luminous feature – particularly handsome against a dark background, such as a conifer.

Gertrude Jekyll grew it at the back of her famous colour-graded flower border – one of the twentieth century's most influential garden designs – allowing some trails of white everlasting pea to thread over it. And she liked a tall clump of stripy miscanthus (called Eulalia, in her day) to act as a graceful contrast in front. 'The Golden Privet,' she writes, 'is one of the few shrubs that has a place in the flower border. Its clean, cheerful, bright yellow gives a note of just the right colour all through the summer.' Even better, in my opinion, is the hybrid 'Vicaryi', which appeared on the scene in 1922. Its leaves are about twice the size of 'Aureum' and greeny-gold all over. It has been good all summer, and is still at its best now. I have this at the back of my mixed border, about 2.5m high, set against a yew hedge. This year's long young shoots will be covered with white blossom next June, which looks fine, but something then has to be done about the hangover that follows. You can simply prune out all the flowered wood, preferably to different levels, so that the shrub retains an informal appearance. It won't look much for the rest of that summer, but the next year it will be at the top of its form as a foliage specimen, though without flowering.

The following year, you'll be back where you started.

Ideally, it is better to prune selectively at the end of the year (or, better, at the beginning of the next) in which it made quantities of new growth. Remove about half of this. New shoots will be made in the next growing season from the point you cut back to, while the unpruned growth will flower. When you prune the flowered shoots the following summer, there will be a furnishing of vegetative growth that can be left. In this way, half the shrub will flower each year, while the other half will be making new shoots, which are the ones that carry the best foliage.

I have gone into this in some detail, as it applies to many shrubs with an inclination to flower either a lot or not at all – in alternate years. The smoke bush, *Cotinus coggygria*, is another example.

Probably my favourite privet is *L. quihoui* (named in honour of a Paris park superintendent, Monsieur Quihou), which benefits from exactly the same treatment as 'Vicaryi'. It is grown principally as a large, late-flowering shrub, and is usually at its best in September, when it is bowed down with swags of white blossom – a wonderful sight at that time of the year. The scent, as with all privets, is heavy, but you can get used to it if you make up your mind that you will. Its foliage is small and neat, almost deciduous, and though slow-growing in its early years, it catches up and eventually reaches 4m at least.

Another species with a welcome autumn-flowering habit is *L. lucidum*. Its large, glossy leaves are like a camellia's – they are very dark, but the gloss gives them light and life. That can make a tree, growing to 10m, but is better kept lower, by pruning as described above, otherwise it can become scrawny, with an accumulation of spent, flowered wood.

Make sure you get the right species and not *L. japonicum*, which is often confused with it in commerce. It is a decent shrub, but smaller in all its parts and it flowers in summer, not autumn.

L. lucidum has a strikingly bold white-variegated form, 'Tricolor', but it is often weak-growing and, when grafted, may easily revert. However, as a half-standard, it makes a strong feature in opposite pairs along double herbaceous borders at The Old Vicarage, East Ruston (near Cromer) in Norfolk. And not one specimen in this formal feature has let the others down.

Our native species, nearly always found wild on limy soils, is *L. vulgare*. It makes a rangy shrub, wider than it is high, and loses most of its foliage in winter, so has been superseded by *L. ovalifolium* for hedging. When used at all, it is given the worst possible conditions, often in heavy shade, which it hates but (unfortunately) survives. Out in the open, it flowers freely at midsummer. I found it a delightful feature on Braunton Burrows, in North Devon, where it makes widespread scrub among the sand dunes.

In autumn, it (and *L. ovalifolium* also, if left unpruned) is loaded with panicles of black berries, which makes a striking contrast, in a cut arrangement, with pink and orange spindle berries.

Underplanting Hedges

There is often a boring gap between a hedge bottom and the lawn in front of it. Obviously the lawn cannot be allowed to reach right up to the hedge, but the width of the gap is unnecessarily increased through the use of that iniquitous tool, the half-moon edge cutter. No garden task makes a man feel prouder of himself than setting out a line and chopping away a sliver of turf (which can never be replaced) to make the edge neat. Thus, the gap becomes ever wider and weeds in it have to be dealt with, using a hoe. It is not a winning situation.

However, if yours is not too rigid a disposition, the gap can be turned to ornamental account by allowing nice-looking plants to grow in it. In fact, the plants will often put themselves there, anyway, and it will then only be a question of not weeding them out with the weeds. Just a small shift in attitude. Hedges are pretty sombre and so are lawns, so a ribbon of colour, seen from across the green blank, makes a welcome break (to borrow a motorway phrase).

My favourite gap, in front of the house where there isn't much going on (we have ferns against the house itself), is really lively in spring. All the plants were self-appointed – they arrived as seeds – and my role is simply that of referee.

There are wallflowers, which go on from year to year in a situation where no one is busy replacing them with summer bedding. They exhaust themselves or succumb to viruses (which make their flowers stripy) after three years or so, but their own seedlings provide replacements.

Then, there is honesty, the biennial *Lunaria annua* (who was the idiot who named that, I wonder?). In this case, it is the bright purple strain that Miss Jekyll grew. But you also have the choice of a pure white and of two variegated strains, one with mauve flowers, the other with white. I think the purple honesty goes well with the brown wallflower.

Originally a seedling, there is now a strong colony of *Euphorbia amygdaloides* var. *robbiae*, whose dark evergreen rosettes of foliage look smart throughout the winter. They remain quite low, so there is no question of competition with the bottom of the hedge itself – a point one has to bear in mind. The elegant flowering columns, in bright, pale green, expand in April and are very long-lasting.

There are dog violets – the non-scented kind that grow wild in the woods around us. They flower in April–May, a bit later than the scented *Viola odorata*, which would be another suitable candidate.

Sometimes there is mullein, which makes a low rosette of furry leaves, but eventually soars to two metres or more, but it leans away from the hedge, where it can get more light, so no harm done. The same goes for biennial foxgloves. And I allow the odd teasle, *Dipsacus fullonum*. It makes a big, branching structure but casts little shade.

Nasturtiums look wonderful climbing up a dark hedge, especially if they are on its shady side. 'Surely they would damage the hedge?!' you might exclaim, but that has never been my experience. After all, they are not there for very long. They do rather hate being in powder-dry soil, however.

The peach-leaved *Campanula persicifolia*, with 0.8m stems of blue or white bells in June–July, loves a bit of shade and is happiest on heavy soils. That makes mats of shiny green rosettes in winter, and is a true perennial. It will often poke its head out of the cracks in a hedge, some way up from the bottom. Being a native of woodland margins and glades, it will be happy on a hedge's shady side.

So will Cyclamen – C. *hederifolium* (C. *neapolitanum*) being the easiest species and having the liveliest marbling on its foliage. This varies from plant to plant and some nursery specialists make a point of breeding well-marked strains. The foliage on C. *hederfolium* is at its smartest from now till next spring, but some of my plants still have flowers – white, or in shades of pink. Those growing in the driest positions flower the latest. The earliest are already in bloom by late July.

Another good plant for a shady hedge bottom is the lungwort, Pulmonaria, whose leaves are often as interesting as its flowers. Much breeding work has lately been carried out on this genus, and there is currently a pulmonaria trial at Wisley, which will come into its own next spring and should certainly be visited.

Small bulbs are a great asset, in our context. If there becomes a danger of exposing them through weeding or hoeing in their vicinity, you should top up, from time to time, with old potting soil. *Allium moly* is our longest-standing success, the colony dating back undisturbed to the thirties. This opens heads of bright yellow flowers in early June.

Snowdrops are admirable – the common snowdrop, *Galanthus nivalis*, is as good as any. Dig up a congested clump after it has flowered, pull it apart and replant singleton bulbs in any of those bare spots that are so obvious in winter and early spring. Crocuses, likewise.

Give the mauve, February-flowering *Crocus tommasinianus* a start, and it will do the rest for you, not only clumping up, but self-sowing, too.

December

Great Dixter: The Future

Does a garden die with its owner? It's a question that is often asked. Don't worry, I'm not thinking of dying, and it's not necessarily a gloomy question at all.

A garden is bound to change when its creator is no longer there. If they are simply moving house, they may want to take plants with them, perhaps in the knowledge that their successor isn't in the least interested, anyway. Or maybe they want to make a new start.

I, of course, wonder what is likely to happen at Dixter. I want it to continue to be dynamic, and most certainly not to be set in aspic, as can all too easily happen. I want it to be, 'That's the way he always liked to have it' – that sort of thing.

Fergus Garrett, my head gardener and closest friend, wants the same dynamism. All being well, he will remain here, and there will be no fossilisation with him around. He is a brilliant teacher, for one thing, and people long for the opportunity to learn from him. He knows how to get the best out of people, which is where I sometimes fail. If he is to be interviewed, for example, he asks the interviewer about themself and how they came to be interviewing in the first place. This breaks the ice and a relationship is established. When I was once interviewed at the same time, I terrified my interviewers by pointing out when they said something stupid or repeated a question.

Between the two of us, we're a pretty dynamic couple. Gardening should be a partnership, and we are both interested in how to keep ours dynamic. Sometimes we like things to stay as they are, while at others change seems to beckon. I don't much care for the question, 'What changes are you planning for this year?' because it pins me down, but changes there will be, you may be sure. Dynamism is in our bloodstream.

We want this spirit to carry on, and have set up a trust to work with our management team to run the place. The people who are involved are well aware of what Dixter represents and what its aims should be. The trust is appealing for financial help to secure its future. Its members understand what it's all about, so the future is bright – insofar as we can look into it at all. We have always been optimists.

Spring Bedding

As soon as we had closed the house and gardens to the public at the end of October, we were in a great tizz to catch up on a mountain of autumn work. First, the frost-tender stuff had to be housed – begonias, succulents and much else. Then the meadow areas were given a last, close cut, so that they would be all spruce and ready when the bulbs pushed through; some have already started to do so. Most testing and complex (because we have such a lot of it), we have been bedding out in readiness for spring.

For this, we used a lot of perennials, as well as obvious biennials such as forget-me-nots, pansies and wallflowers. You may care to try some of them next year; start gathering ideas when you go through the seed catalogues.

Carnations are excellent, particularly the Florestan strain. Sow in early spring (they germinate at quite low temperatures), line out for the summer and bed out next autumn for the following summer, interplanting with tulips. Carnation foliage makes a good background for red tulips. Dianthus, sweet-smelling pinks, are also good treated this way; I like Thompson & Morgan's Sonata strain. Or there's *Dianthus* 'Rainbow Loveliness', with shaggy single flowers and a scent on the air you wouldn't have believed possible. Sow July–August, overwinter in pots under cold glass and plant out in spring to flower May–June.

Doronicums (leopard's bane), with their cheerful yellow daisies in April–May, are good in partial shade. Sow in April, grow the plants on during the summer and bed them in autumn, interplanting with white tulips or, perhaps, 'Shirley', white with a mauve rim.

We use aquilegias year after year, cutting them back when they have flowered, removing them to purdah, where they can spend the summer unseen and bringing them back in autumn. You could interplant with Dutch bulbous irises.

We are currently using the Gallery seed strain of lupins. Sown in summer, we bedded them out last month, interplanted with tall, late red tulips. Lupin foliage makes an admirable background for them. Come July, lupins are thrown out and dahlias or cannas replace them.

Silene dioica 'Flore Pleno' is the double version of our wild pinky-red campion. We keep that from year to year, dividing it when necessary and transferring it to a shady spot for the summer. It flowers in May and we interplant with *Allium hollandicum* 'Purple Sensation', whose flowering coincides at the metre-high level.

Much earlier is *Bergenia stracheyi*, a low, neat-leaved species with brightest pink flowers in April. It does not at all object to being moved to and fro and looks lovely with aubrieta, although I find the timing of that a bit tricky, from seed. A yellow jonquil, not too overpowering and muscular, goes well with the bergenia, too. The key is never to think of plants in isolation, but always in some combination. That's where the art of gardening comes in.

Favourite Trees

If you intend to buy an unusual tree, or one likely to sell out before you have made a move, act quickly. Even if the ground is not currently suitable for planting, you can easily keep your purchase happy until it is.

A bare-root tree can be kept wrapped and damp in a cold shed until things improve. But if you are planting in turf, the soil beneath is usually friable and in reasonable condition, so long as you complete both the preparation and planting all in one go. Don't let the site become soaked between exposing the soil and putting in your tree. To find the tree you want, turn for sources to the *RHS Plant Finder*. Here are some of my favourites . . .

A black mulberry, *Morus nigra*. Fruit is produced from quite an early age and ripens in August–September. Don't make the mistake of buying the useless white mulberry, and do remember that the berries make a terrible stain – no matter if it's lawn beneath them, still it's a nuisance if you wanted to sit there.

The false acacia, *Robinia pseudoacacia*, is grumbled at for dropping

351

spiny branches. Also, if its roots are damaged, for suckering. But it becomes a lovely, light-textured tree with a beautifully fissured trunk, while its pendant racemes of white blossom, late May or early June, are most deliciously fragrant on the air. Particularly beautiful is the variety 'Rozynskiana', its pinnate leaves long and drooping. In early June, that flowers as well as any.

With so great a preponderance of blossom in the spring, late-flowerers are especially valuable. The Indian horse chestnut, *Aesculus indica*, flowers in late June or July. Its growth is similar to the ordinary chestnut's, so it'll need space, but its blush white flowering candles make a great display.

Koelreuteria paniculata, sometimes called Golden Rain, carries its panicles of small, yellow flowers late in July. It makes a charming small tree and is at its best in London, appreciating the extra summer heat. Its elegant pinnate leaves are shrimp pink in spring and change to apricot orange before falling.

A tree doesn't have to flower to be good company. With so many flowering cherries, crabs and prunuses all around us, we might do well to try something different. Years ago, I fell in love with an oak, *Quercus pyrenaica* 'Pendula', which was growing in Holland Park, and I'm very glad I planted one soon after. It makes a beautifully shaped tree, upright in habit but with drooping branches. The long, deckle-edged leaves are quite pale on their undersides. Late in spring, it is briefly covered with long catkins among the unfolding leaves.

A not over-large but spreading tree is made by the deciduous conifer, *Pseudolarix amabilis*. In spring, its young foliage is the freshest green, long retained, but warm yellow in autumn. Cones, exactly the shape of tiny globe artichokes, are borne on the upper sides of some branches, not on others. It keeps you guessing. I killed my young one, I think, by planting it in dense turf where it was starved. But a weeping silver lime, *Tilia* 'Petiolaris', has done extremely well in such a position.

Next to my lime, I have an Italian alder, *Alnus cordata* (nowadays often planted as a windbreak along the boundaries of commercial fruit orchards). It has very large, handsome catkins in March, being one of the latest alders in flower. The foliage is healthy, glossy deep green.

Certain evergreen conifers are tempting – *Sciadopitys verticillata*, for instance, sometimes called umbrella pine because its leaves radiate from a central axis like the spokes of an umbrella. It does not usually make a big tree but is one of the freshest, and at its best if allowed to carry its branches right down to ground level throughout its life.

That goes for many conifers, too, and it is not an unpractical treatment in many private gardens. The Korean silver fir, for example, *Abies koreana*. If it does its stuff as expected, it carries upright cones like short purplish candles on the top of its horizontal branches. I use it as a mixed border plant. When it grows too large for its position, I start again with another youngster, but first use the top of my old one as a Christmas tree.

Fastigiate trees are often useful for taking up little lateral space, but many of them have a stiff and gawky branch system. One of the worst, in this respect, is the far too popular semi-double pink cherry, *Prunus* 'Amanogawa'. It is only tolerable as a baby, becoming increasingly ugly year by year from then on. In a key position, I was recommended to plant the fastigiate version of the white pine, *Pinus strobus* 'Fastigiata', and I have not regretted it. Its fine needles, five to a cluster, are glaucous blue. The tree has remained well furnished right to its base, and when it shows a slight inclination to obesity around its waist, we lightly prune the young terminal shoots with secateurs.

Winter Pruning

Cutting back overlarge or scruffy shrubs and small trees is mainly performed in winter when, in the case of deciduous kinds, you can see the structure better; also when the plant is relatively dormant, the shock is less. If there's a hardiness question, however, operations are better deferred until March or April.

One reason for its popularity is that it provides energetic exercise and a compensation for being shut indoors; it warms you through at a time when the weather is apt to perform a numbing exercise on thought as well as limbs.

But are we doing more harm than good? Harm to whom or what, you then have to ask. I sometimes wish my onslaughts would kill the victim but fear that they may not. Family feeling can run strong on matters of this kind; iconoclast versus conservationist. Tender-heartedness is more often than not a mistake in gardening, but I do like to retain control of the decisions.

It is often far from clear how a hard cut back will affect the patient (or victim). It's nice to have a feeling of certainty before you start, but general rules are never certainties.

If you cut a yew hedge or tree hard back, it will usually react splendidly, breaking into new growth from the centre rather than from shortened branches. So this can be the best policy; not merely when a hedge has become over-bulky and is bulging over a path, but also when it has become senile. The cause of senility may have been starvation at some stage or poor drainage. Typical symptoms would be extremely slow, patchy growth and the appearance of lichens on the wood behind the foliage. The lichens are not themselves doing harm; they are merely the symptom that your yew or other shrub has become senescent.

Unlike us, plants can often be rejuvenated by correcting the drainage and feeding with slow-acting organic fertiliser. On our yews we use fish, blood and bone. You'll need to cut back all that lichened, senile growth – and to cut hard. No use going halfway back towards the centre, leaving a lot of dead branch ends. Go right back to the centre. Minimise the shock by doing half the hedge or bush one year, the other half a couple of winters later.

It is with the greatest difficulty that I can convince any tender-hearted amateur that this drastic treatment is for the best; the sight of what appears a maimed bush, improving little in appearance for months afterwards, fills him or her with horror. This is a pity, especially as I have to add that very occasionally the treatment doesn't work. But nearly always it does.

We have a tall hedge of holm oak, *Quercus ilex*, which is evergreen. That responds, like yew, from the centre but not from shortened branch ends. Lawson cypress is noted for failure to respond to severe treatment and Leyland cypress is not much better. You can reduce its circumference moderately but not into completely bare wood. *Thuja plicata*, on the other hand, breaks well from hard cutting.

We had an old juniper, *Juniperus communis*, that looked thoroughly ga-ga. I thought that was worth experimenting on, rather than grubbing it forthwith. But it didn't respond and had to be grubbed anyway.

We're used to giving the commonest willows cavalier treatment by regularly pollarding them – *Salix alba* and *S. fragilis*, for instance, and the red-stemmed willows, which are reddest on young wood. But not all of them, by any means, enjoy a severe cut back. Take *S. sachalinensis* 'Sekka', a large shrub with twisted and flattened scroll-like growth that appeals to some of us, not to others. If never pruned, it ceases to make the scrolls. But if cut hard back on a regular basis it is apt to die – the silver leaf fungus gets in and kills it. I think one should be severe on it every four years or so, but take a few hardwood cuttings, in case you lose the parent.

Lilacs are exceedingly tough and respond wonderfully to being cut back into quite old wood. As they become gawky with age and overlarge, I should do something about it now.

Elders, varieties of *Sambucus nigra* and *S. racemosa*, can be kept young by annual pruning. Thin out old, flowered wood on those you're growing for their flowers (excellent for elderflower cordial and to add a muscat flavour to gooseberry recipes); those growing for their purple, yellow, or variegated foliage, you can prune hard back all over and every year. If eventually weakened, start again with a hardwood cutting made from a strong young shoot (now is a good moment). But if you have a large, unruly elder tree that has been left unattended, cut that hard back, say to within four or five foot of the ground, now. You'll lose a season's blossom but that's all.

A large, unpruned philadelphus or deutzia, weigela, or kerria, may need drastic reduction. Cut it flush with the ground. It won't like you, but you won't kill it. If you're anxious to remain in its good books, cut one half of the thicket back to the ground this winter and the other half next. Subsequently, prune selectively by leaving straight, young unflowered rods untouched but cutting out the flowered growth.

Viburnums, evergreen or deciduous, respond well to severe cutting and so, surprisingly, do camellias. Forsythias less. Better to remove a proportion of the old branches and thus to rejuvenate over a period of several years.

I should cut that hopelessly dense and tangled bamboo to the ground. If it subsequently dies, the fault will not be yours but the fact that it has taken to flowering. This is bad news in any bamboo.

With regard to exposed wounds, my advice, based on experiments made in the US, is to leave them open, not to dress them. Wound dressings are at best cosmetic.

Planning Ahead

Gardeners look fore and aft at the turn of the year. We learn from past mistakes – or think we shall – and we plan that this time it will all be different. I wrote to a friend in Australia on 16 August that Fergus and I (and we are self-critical) felt that the garden at Great Dixter had never looked better. The summer had been cloudy and cool, which had suited most plants admirably; nothing had scorched and the dry spells had not been exacerbated by heat.

We had had an early spring again – our daffodil orchard was already looking its best by 23 March, I noted – and were lucky to escape an April frost. Magnolias were especially magnificent. But then, in April and May, it was wet; the daffodil foliage succumbed to fungal disease and I know perfectly well that, as a consequence, next spring's display will, on the whole, be very weak. Nothing I can do about that.

Fergus and I were far too late in planting up our Exotic Garden with all the really tender stuff that we'd grown under glass and that was kept waiting for too long. It caught up in the end, but we'd wasted a whole month. I had taken a couple of weeks off in Scotland, in the middle of June, and what with catching up with all the arrears of work on my return, this was fairly disastrous.

So, we have made a resolution. I shall not go north until October next year (it's lovely to see the birches changing colour). Both Fergus and I will keep our diaries free of engagements for one whole week in the middle of June and really get to grips with that subtropical planting. We shall be out there at 6.30 each morning (he would have liked it to be earlier still) and can get in a couple of hours' work before the day's inevitable interruptions begin – telephone, mail, staff requiring attention, visitors and all that. At this distance in time, it looks a wonderful plan; perhaps some of it will work out.

Then we had that fantastically wet tail end to the year. If October hadn't been by far the wettest month we (in East Sussex) have endured since we started keeping records in 1913, then November would have been. The ground is one big squelch. Thank goodness that way back in the 1460s we were sited on a hill. We look down on a lake, which is the Rother valley, and are at a safe distance. Yet I have no doubt there will be periods of drought in 2001, as in every other year.

Really, your garden needs to be prepared for all sorts of weathers. In some departments, it will fail; in others, it will turn up trumps. In general, I am a gardening optimist. This means, inevitably, that there will be disappointments, but I also have the useful fall-back of forgetting failures extremely quickly.

I get fed up with the killjoys who, if a fine, warm spell turns up early in the year, shake their heads and say, 'We shall pay for it later; you just see.' They cannot enjoy the present because of their wretched hypothetical future. However, I do admit that, if a fine sunny day arrives in February, it is unwise to sow masses of seeds whose progeny you will be quite unable to keep happy during the weeks and months that must elapse before it is safe, or you have the space ready, to plant them out.

On the whole, I don't think we do a lot of planning ahead, or, if we do, we find in the end that half our schemes go by the board. Either something fails, or another plan overtakes the first one. It is no bad thing to be pragmatic and to await developments before making decisions. That said, we shall definitely make plans when deciding which seeds to order – something you may well have done already, but which we not infrequently leave until as late as February. Not on principle, certainly, but because there seem to be so many other demands on our time. Who said that winter was a slack season?

Though I sometimes find myself giving in to a deep-seated urge to plan something different, I do not believe in change for the sake of change. I speak of a garden – mine, and very likely yours, too – that already has a good bone structure and, therefore, doesn't need to be changed. Before developing a new area, consider first whether you are making the best use of the old. It may be better to renovate than to yield to the lure of greener grass on the other side of the fence.

I have so often seen gardens in which areas, even quite close to the house, have ceased to be thought about creatively, and all the effort has been concentrated on some new area that seems to represent a new life. Personally, I can always find satisfaction in adjustments. Most established gardeners could make a useful start by clearing away or cutting back old hulks of overgrown and no longer contributive trees and shrubs. Then you can admire the cleared area and go from there. Most

357

shrubs deserve only a limited amount of space. When they become really bulky, they are covering a greater area than their value warrants.

The seed catalogues make us plan on a smaller scale. 'Wouldn't it be nice to grow such-and-such again next year?' we think. And that is quickly followed by, 'Where shall we plant it, and what will go well with it?' Planning has many aspects and ramifications.

Hands-on Gardening

It is a grey morning, as I write, the sky above us like a dustbin lid, to borrow Beth Chatto's apt simile, with a threat of rain. It is always a 'threat' in the weather forecasts, never a 'chance', which the anxious gardener or farmer might well think more appropriate when we are desperate for it. Just now, I am wholeheartedly with the forecasters: rain, currently, is a bore – though Fergus and his team always work doggedly through it. (I do not, seeing as I am getting on.)

No passionate gardener, even though distracted by the prospect of Christmas family gatherings, will have their minds totally divorced from what's going on out there. Where shall they get their inspiration? Of course, we rely on the successes of others – I do that myself – yet what we are offered of a practical nature is minimal. So, the actual practice of gardening (taking cuttings, how to dig, how to prune, and suchlike) becomes increasingly neglected. If teachers themselves are uninterested in practice, there will soon be no one to teach the skills required for good hands-on gardening, and they will atrophy and be lost.

There is, thank goodness, a public demand for these skills, yet the actual demonstration of them (in contrast to books about them, which are never so immediate), and the opportunity to try them out for oneself, is increasingly rare. The horticultural colleges impose an increasing squeeze on any time allocated to, say, looking after the college gardens.

Lloyd seems to be getting a bit gloomy. But when meeting examples of the new generation, I am sometimes enormously encouraged. Genius and inspiration are inevitably in short supply, but those who have it keep coming along. Some are passionate about plants from the start. Our gardens at Dixter are open to the public from April to October, so

I see a good sample of them. Or Fergus does and calls me over to meet, perhaps, a child brought by its mother, but already fantastically clued up.

These will become intelligent gardeners from an early age. But there are others, scarcely less valuable, who, having started off in the wrong direction and decided that the rat race is not for them, switch careers (at considerable material deprivation to themselves) and become passionate gardeners and careerists in gardening, when verging on middle age. They bring to gardening an unstoppable sense of direction, intelligently applied. And they keep coming along.

But the hands-on skills still need cherishing, their value recognised and rewarded as they deserve.

A note about seed and bulb catalogues and suppliers

Christopher Lloyd always mentioned specific suppliers in his columns in the *Guardian*. His favoured sources included Chiltern Seeds, Parkers and Thompson & Morgan. For the purposes of the selection in this book, names and addresses of catalogues and suppliers have been deleted from the main body of the text, in favour of listing them here. However, where strains of seeds are mentioned as being available only from a specific supplier, the name of the supplier has been retained in the text.

Chiltern Seeds, Bortree Stile, Ulverston, Cumbria LA12 7PB.
Tel: 01229 581137. Email: info@chilternseeds.co.uk
Website: www.chilternseeds.co.uk

J. Parker Dutch Bulbs Ltd, 452 Chester Road, Old Trafford,
Manchester M16 9HL. Tel: 0161 8481100.
Email: enquire@jparkers.co.uk. Website: www.jparkers.co.uk

Moles Seeds Ltd, Turkey Cock Lane, Stanway, Colchester,
Essex CO3 8PD. Tel: 01206 213213.
Email: sales@molesseeds.co.uk. Website: www.molesseeds.co.uk

Peter Nyssen Ltd, 124 Flixton Road, Urmston, Manchester M41 5BG.
Tel: 0161 7474000. Email: peternyssenltd@btinternet.com
Website: www.peternyssen.com

Thompson & Morgan Ltd, Poplar Lane, Ipswich, Suffolk, IP8 3BU.
Tel: 01473 688821. Email: ccare@thompson-morgan.com
Website: http://seeds.thompson-morgan.com/uk

Appendix

The artiles collected in this book appeared in the *Guardian* on the following dates:

Great Dixter, 16 October 1999

JANUARY
New Year's Resolutions, 3 January 2004
The Winter Garden, 23 January 1999
Conifers, 28 January 2006
Planning for Late Summer, 4 January 1997
Winter Scent, 29 January 2005
Witch Hazels, 7 January 2006
Winter Stems and Bark, 19 January 1991

FEBRUARY
Combining Colour, 4 February 2006
Pears: Fruit and Tree, 11 February 2006
Ordering Seed, 8 February 1997
The February Workload, 5 February 2005
Early Bulbs, 3 February 2001
The First Snowdrops, 10 February 2001
Pruning Clematis and Roses, 14 February 1998
Consistently Good Performers, 10 February 1996
How to Space Plants, 2 February 2002
Wisteria, 14 February 2004
When to Cut Back, 17 February 2001
Ferns, 22 February 1997
Garden Worries, 15 February 1997

MARCH
An Early Spring, 7 March 1998
The Importance of Feeding, 1 March 2003

Crocuses, 10 March 2001
Pruning: When and Why, 16 March 1991
Sowing Annuals, 11 March 2000
Splitting and Replanting, 21 March 1992
The Perfect Tulip: Queen of Sheba, 23 March 2002
Spiky Plants, 31 March 2001
Soil Sickness, 14 March 1998
Bamboo, 21 March 1998
Choosing a Tree, 17 March 1990
The Exotic Garden, 23 March 1996
Succession Planting: The Theory, 13 March 2004
Succession Planting: Bulbs, 20 March 2004
Succession Planting: Self-Sowers, 27 March 2004

APRIL
Taking Risks, 13 April 2002
Sowing Seed, 4 April 1998
Plants in Unusual Places, 1 April 2000
Greeny-Yellow Foliage in Spring, 9 April 2005
Planting in Pots, 12 April 1997
Tulips, 15 April 2000
Succession Planting: Bedding Plants, 10 April 2004
Succession Planting: Climbing Plants, 3 April 2004
Clematis, 8 April 2000
Perennial Favourites, 20 April 1996
Perennials as Bedding Plants, 21 April 2001
Planting between the Roots of Trees, 16 April 2005
Sunflowers, 18 April 1998
Spring Scent, 19 April 1997
Fast-growing Shrubs, 13 April 1996
Dahlias, 6 April 1996
Grey Foliage, 26 April 1997
Meadow Planting, 22 April 1995

MAY
May Borders, 13 May 2000
Birds in the Garden, 5 May 2001
May Sowing, 1 May 1999

Young Foliage, 3 May 1997
Plants for Paving Cracks, 8 May 2004
Pruning Spring-flowering Shrubs, 16 May 1998
Experimenting with Colour, 27 May 2000
Mulching, 17 May 2003
Planting Garden Steps, 10 May 1997
Vegetables in a Small Garden, 19 May 2001
Planting Partners, 30 May 1998
Staking Tall Plants, 27 May 1995
Cottage Gardens, 28 May 2005
May Bulbs, 29 May 1999
Canna, 22 May 1999

JUNE
June Gardens, 1 June 2002
Poppies, 5 June 1999
Pondside Planting, 29 June 2002
Small Trees, 14 June 2003
Dianthus, 19 June 1999
More Colour Combinations, 26 June 2004
Muted Colours, 28 June 1997
Garden Scent, 28 June 2003
Euphorbias, 16 June 1990
Philadelphus, 17 June 1989
June Jobs, 20 June 1998
Serial Planting, 24 June 2000
Sowing Biennials, 26 June 1999

JULY
The Garden at its Peak, 6 July 1996
Dry Conditions, 2 July 2005
Choosing the Right Rose, 7 July 2001
Collecting Seed, 10 July 1999
Fuchsias, 12 July 1997
Climbers for Trees, 5 July 1997
Perennial Planning, 8 July 2000
Coarse Plants, 4 July 1998
Ornamental Grasses, 13 July 2002

Plants for Ponds, 9 July 2005
July Jobs, 18 July 1998
An Early Morning Walk, 21 July 2001
Summer Climbers, 23 July 2005
Positioning Plants, 26 July 1997
Summer Pruning, 18 July 1992
Looking After a Meadow, 28 July 2001

AUGUST
The August Garden, 7 August 1999
Blue, 9 August 2003
Cranesbills, 8 August 1998
Drought-Tolerant Plants, 19 August 1989
Red Hot Pokers, 4 August 2001
Summer Evening Scent, 15 August 1998
Summer Bedding, 18 August 2001
Attracting Butterflies, 24 August 1996
Dahlias Revisited, 17 August 2002
Combining Plants, 17 August 1991
August Shrubs, 11 August 2001
Phlox, 23 August 2003
Evergreens, 15 August 1992
Late-flowering Perennials, 23 August 1997
A Visit to the Exotic Garden, 25 August 2001
Dogwood, 30 August 2003
Late Summer Plants, 21 August 1993
Planting Autumn Bulbs, 21 August 1999
Ordering Next Year's Bulbs, 12 August 2000

SEPTEMBER
Gardening in Your Own Way, 24 September 1994
Continuous Planting, 6 September 1997
Eupatorium, 3 September 2005
Serial Planting for Autumn, 16 September 2000
Late-flowering Shrubs, 7 September 1996
Pots for Porches, 14 September 1996
Autumn Planting of Shrubs, 11 September 1999
Marigolds, 17 September 2005

Ground Cover, 25 September 1999
Teasels, 24 September 2005
Propagation, 27 September 1997
Foliage as Foil, 23 September 1995
Autumn Colour: Shrubs, 26 September 1998
Autumn Scents, 30 September 1995

OCTOBER
The Long View, 28 October 2000
Canna and Dahlia, 8 October 2005
Beyond the Rose Garden, 2 October 2004
Autumn-flowering Asters, 12 October 1996
The Beauty of Fruit, 5 October 1996
Hawthorns, 16 October 2004
Rejuvenating the Border, 18 October 2003
Alliums, 20 October 2001
Garden Prejudices, 1 October 2005
Aralias, 26 October 2002
Ornamental Grasses in Autumn, 25 October 1997
Autumn Blooms, 18 October 1997
Red, 19 October 1996
Black, 31 October 1998
Weeding, 30 October 1999
Bed and Border Changes, 14 October 1995
When to Cut Back, 29 October 2005

NOVEMBER
Knowing Your Garden's Conditions, 9 November 1996
Organic Feeding, 2 November 1996
Begonias, 5 November 2005
Tulips: Companion Planting, 8 November 1997
The Cold Frame, 4 November 2000
Melianthus major, 12 November 2005
Cistuses, 10 November 2001
November Jobs, 21 November 1998
Taking Cuttings, 21 November 1992
Magnolias, 20 November 2004
Autumn Perennial Planting and Moving, 13 November 1999

The November Garden, 27 November 1999
Pollination, 22 November 1997
The Privet Hedge, 30 November 1996
Underplanting Hedges, 23 November 1996

DECEMBER
Great Dixter: The Future, 17 December 2005
Spring Bedding, 1 December 2001
Favourite Trees, 2 December 2000
Winter Pruning, 15 December 1990
Planning Ahead, 30 December 2000
Hands-on Gardening, 21 December 2002

Index

Pruning 60.